Talking to Our Selves

Talking to Our Selves

Reflection, Ignorance, and Agency

John M. Doris

OXFORD
UNIVERSITY PRESS

OXFORD

UNIVERSITY PRESS

Great Clarendon Street, Oxford, OX2 6DP,
United Kingdom

Oxford University Press is a department of the University of Oxford.
It furthers the University's objective of excellence in research, scholarship,
and education by publishing worldwide. Oxford is a registered trade mark of
Oxford University Press in the UK and in certain other countries

First Edition published in 2015

Impression: 1

Published in the United States of America by Oxford University Press
198 Madison Avenue, New York, NY 10016, United States of America

British Library Cataloguing in Publication Data

Data available

Library of Congress Control Number: 2014948349

ISBN 978–0–19–957039–3

Printed and bound by
CPI Group (UK) Ltd, Croydon, CR0 4YY

For Stephen Stich

Contents

Advertisement

In 1957, a marketing consultant named James Vicary reported huge sales increases at a New Jersey theater concession. All one need do, Vicary said, was intermittently flash *Eat Popcorn* and *Drink Coca Cola* on screen for 1/3000th of a second, and unsuspecting moviegoers ate more popcorn and drank more Coke. Before long, subliminal advertising was a staple of Cold War paranoia. Exposés like Vance Packard's *The Hidden Persuaders* and Wilson Brian Key's *Subliminal Seduction* glutted bookstores, while *The New Yorker* pronounced Packard's opus an "authoritative and frightening report on how manufacturers, fundraisers and politicians are attempting to turn the American mind into a kind of catatonic dough that will buy, give or vote at their command." Pretty creepy stuff, this catatonic dough: movie night as *Night of the Living Noshers*, with film buffs cast as junk food zombies.

The hysteria hadn't to do with over-indulgence in sugar, salt, and grease, about which Americans have little compunction. What was sinister, according to alarmists, was that victims of subliminal sales techniques were *made* to do things; people's desires were manipulated without their knowledge or consent. Clearly, something sneaky was going on: in 1974, federal regulators stepped in, ruling subliminal advertising deceptive, and "inconsistent with the obligations" of licensed broadcasters.

Turns out the alarmists were unduly alarmed: after decades of research, scientific evidence for the effectiveness of subliminal advertising remains in short supply (Pratkanis and Greenwald 1988; Dijksterhuis *et al.* 2005). By 1962, Vicary had recanted, admitting that the Coke and popcorn "study" was a publicity ploy for his marketing business. Near enough, he was never heard from again.

Not everyone thinks it's safe to go back in the theater. Surveys indicate that a majority of Americans have heard of subliminal advertising, and a majority of these believe it works (Rogers and Smith 1993). Books like *The Secret Sales Pitch* (Bullock 2004) and *Subliminal Persuasion* (Lakhani 2009) are still getting written; a celebratory 50th anniversary edition of *The Hidden Persuaders* appeared in 2007.

Perhaps this persistence is due, as with other urban legends, to a kernel of truth: neighboring paranoid fantasy is a large body of psychological fact. Since we're talking seduction, you'll be interested to learn that anxiety can increase attraction (Dutton and Aron 1974); maybe your seat-mate on that turbulent flight was drawn to your winning smile and artful patter, or maybe he's just a phobic flyer. Turning from the romantic to the pragmatic, naming your child Denise could make her more likely to become a dentist (Pelham *et al.* 2002): maybe he's a neurologist because he's named Russell Brain, she's a tennis pro because she's named Margaret Court, and he's a urologist because he's named— I'm not making this up—Dick Finder.

Major life choices, like location and vocation, can be corrupted by factors that the choosers themselves would regard as irrelevant, or worse, were they made aware of them. In brief: you may not know what you're doing, or why you're doing it, and if you did know, you might not like it. Evidently, the subversive unconscious is everywhere at work (though these workings may be more absurd than Oedipal). Should you take this prospect seriously, you ought begin to wonder about who—or what—is running your show.

You'd then be wondering about what philosophers call *agency*, the ability of human beings to direct their own lives. Famously, these queries lack easy answers, partly because they're ensnared in the most Gordian of philosophical tangles, free will and determinism. Such conundrums often evaporate into thin metaphysical air, but nearby is trouble of concrete practical significance, that of determining when people are morally responsible for their conduct: when is someone appropriately lauded for her good deeds, or excoriated for her bad? The difficulty is complicated, perhaps fatally so, by the sort of psychological phenomena I've just recounted. Should he be admired for a life aiding the neurologically afflicted, if that life was shaped by the surname "Brain"? Should she celebrate your love, if that love is a symptom of anxiety?

This might sound like panicking over "catatonic dough." Folks aren't completely reasonable, but they often enough seem to have their reasons, and they often enough seem to act on them. Every day, people deliberate, decide and, so far as anyone can tell, end up doing what they've decided. After all the philosophizing and psychologizing is done, we're left to make our worlds, much as we did before all the philosophizing and psychologizing.

Unfortunately, when such reassuring good sense is scrutinized, it is difficult to sustain: what's now known about the mind presses hard questions about agency and moral responsibility. This book is in the business of asking these questions, and attempting to answer them. I'll trace prominent themes in the philosophy and psychology of the past hundred years or so, and argue that if the psychology is taken seriously, some of the philosophy must be taken less seriously.

The philosophy at issue subscribes to *reflectivism*, a doctrine according to which *the exercise of human agency consists in judgment and behavior ordered by self-conscious reflection about what to think and do*. Typically, this doctrine is associated with a corollary: *the exercise of human agency requires accurate reflection*. In an exercise of agency, as construed by reflectivism, a person correctly divines the beliefs, desires, and other psychological states relevant to her decision, makes her decision in light of these states (sometimes called her reasons), and acts accordingly. There's difficulty in the details, but at the outset it's enough to recognize a pervasive and plausible assumption: when human beings are able to direct their lives in a manner approximating that philosophers dignify with the honorific "agency," it's because they know what they're doing, and why they're doing it.

However attractive, this assumption is compromised by decades of research in the social, cognitive, and behavioral sciences. Empirical research suggests that reflection appears in a limited portion of human conduct; very often, behavior is altogether thoughtless, and quite unconstrained by the deliverances of reflection. And on those instances when people do reflect, there is little warrant for confidence that these reflections are informed by accurate self-awareness. If so, there's something seriously wrong with both reflectivism and its corollary.

Maybe what's wrong is that people don't often function as agents; maybe reflectivism has the standards for agency right, and human beings routinely fail to meet them. There's precedent for pessimism; many a philosopher has rued, as Plato did, flesh and blood failing philosophical ideals. Provenance notwithstanding, this is gloominess I'll resist. At least in the cultures that are home to the Western philosophical tradition, there is an entrenched practice of people treating one another as morally responsible agents, and although this practice is sometimes egregiously infelicitous in its particulars, I'm convinced it is tolerably functional—in any event, considerably more functional than going without it. On my view, the trouble is not so much with the practice, but with extant attempts to provide theoretical support for the practice: reflectivist understandings of agency have prevented philosophers from understanding the ways in which human beings do, in fact, function as agents.

I envisage an alternative theory. The theory is *anti-reflectivist*: it does not require reflection and accurate self-awareness for the exercise of agency. The theory is *valuational*: it locates the exercise of agency in the expression of a person's values. The theory is *collaborativist*: it understands individual exercises of agency as products of social interaction. The theory is *pluralist*: it allows that a diversity of processes may effect the exercise of agency.

Working all this out makes an intricate undertaking, as my stated aspiration to "theory" warns. In the first half of the book, I'll develop the problem, first tracing the outlines of reflectivism, and then canvassing the psychological evidence that threatens reflectivism with skepticism about agency. In the second half, I'll try to ameliorate the problem I developed in the first, by articulating my alternative to reflectivism. If I succeed, I'll have a theory of agency sensitive both to what human beings are like—creatures with disorderly psychologies, and what human beings need—an ethical ordering of the lives they live together.

I

I

1

Staging

The history of ideas in the twentieth century was a history of disintegration: physics rendered nature into infinitesimal particles, anthropology sundered humanity into incommensurable cultures, politics divided nations into irreconcilable factions, and literary theorists deconstructed what little remained. Being a philosopher of mind and morality (as is sometimes said, with pleasing ambiguity, a "moral psychologist") I've taken my turn at stirring this watery broth, for nowhere has disintegration been more evident than in the various fields investigating human mentation.

Minds, we're told, are uncertain conglomerations of systems and subsystems—"modules" on one influential family of theories—cobbled together by natural selection with little regard for the people toting them about. These systems are supposed to toil in mutual indifference, rather like laborers who don't much care for their co-workers, and less for the designs of management. More than occasionally, the systems are not indifferent, but hostile: sometimes the right hand doesn't know what the left hand is doing, and other times the right hand opposes what the left hand is doing. So understood, cognition appears disconcertingly chaotic; the history of mind in modernity (and post-modernity) is the history of a fragmented psyche (e.g. Stich 1990).

As a philosopher of mind, I reckon this history sounds about right: the mental is rather a mess. As a philosopher of morals, I don't think it sufficiently enriching; with human beings, I want to find a there there—a person, rather than a haphazard muddle of cognitive systems. In this, I'm not alone. People see much that is true and important in traditional beliefs about such reassuringly sturdy entities as Reason and Virtue, despite threats posed by the new sciences of mind. But unlike some traditionalists, I don't suppose the threats are easily forestalled: if the old wisdoms are to survive, they require revision.

To choose a history's beginning is to make an arbitrary choosing, but if forced to say where the bother began, I'd start with Thorndike's (1906: 248) declaration, at the twentieth century's inception, that "training the mind means the development of thousands of particular independent capacities." One thing that impresses those following Thorndike is the difficulty with which facility at one task transfers even to related tasks, even closely related tasks (Ceci 1996; Detterman 1993): for example, workers frequently have trouble deploying skills learned in job training when actually on the job (Baldwin and Ford 1988; Gist *et al.* 1990). Overall, cognitive performance is remarkably—not to say ridiculously—context-specific (Olin and Doris 2014): to mention a couple of representative findings, people may be good at estimating distances on lawns but not in hallways (Lappin *et al.* 2006), and better able to detect erroneous statements written in difficult fonts than in fonts that are easily read (Song and Schwarz 2008).

Despite abundant evidence for the specificity of intellection, the dominant understanding of cognitive ability has for generations followed Spearman's (1904; 1927: 161–98) theory of "General Intelligence," or *g*, which Spearman believed to be measurable by the Binet-Simon *IQ* ("Intelligence Quotient") scale. A person's level of general intelligence, quantified as *IQ*, is supposed to explain their cognitive acuity (or its lack) across every domain: allegedly, "tests of mental skills invariably point to the existence of a global factor that permeates all aspects of cognition" (Gottfredson 1998: 24). Although I view both *IQ* and *g* with a jaundiced eye, I'll not take sides in the ongoing, and often unpleasant, intelligence debates (for guidance, see Nisbett 2009). Here, it's the history that wants remarking on. When the twentieth century began, the unity of mind was in doubt; as the twenty-first century gets under way, doubt persists.

Another manifestation of disintegration concerns not the smart, but the good. Or rather, the opposite of good: the carnage of the First and Second World Wars, together with the atrocities that have since continued without pause, from Rwanda to Abu Ghraib. Just as success at one cognitive endeavor does not guarantee success in another, the attainment of ordinary (or even extraordinary) decency in one regard does not guarantee decency in others. People exhibit astonishing susceptibility to social and material influence, even when that influence is employed in the service of flagrant inhumanity, and the perpetrators of atrocity, more often than not, are disquietingly like the rest of us (Doris 2002: 53–8; Doris and Murphy 2007). As Solzhenitsyn learned in the Gulag, the line dividing good and evil crosses every human heart.

Then the current epoch is inhospitable to both the Classical notion of "rational animals" and the Enlightenment notion of "sovereign artificers"; from the prison camps to the parade grounds, *Homo sapiens* has been incessantly revealed to be badly less than rational, and badly less than sovereign. In fact, the edifice of Enlightenment was fissuring hard and fast before the twentieth century began. Particularly destabilizing was the discovery of the unconscious, which perturbed psychiatric medicine well prior to emerging, under the midwifery of Freud, as a psychological commonplace (Altschule 1977; 199: Ellenberger 1970). My angst about the disintegration of the mind is loosely Freudian in spirit, since it is unease instigated by the observation that human minds contain unaccessed and unruly depths. While it's possible that neither the depths nor the methods best suited to plumbing them exhibit Freudian drama, the existence of an unconscious at odds with deliberate intention presents recalcitrant challenges to the philosophies of mind and morals. Customarily, these challenges are formulated in terms of the self.

Self

Talk of the self appears across a miscellany of disciplines, in a multitude of theoretical contexts, and there's no hope of accounting for it all. I'll therefore proceed by fiat, and take up three problems of self—*continuity*, *identity*, and *agency*—that have preoccupied philosophers. It's likely these preoccupations afflict people (at least some of the people, some of the time) who are not philosophers, so while I'll be indulging in philosophical rumination, I suppose that such musings can both inform and be informed by less academicized thinking.

Perhaps most philosophically conspicuous among the many problems of self is the problem of personal identity (Johnston 1987; Parfit 1984; Shoemaker 1985; Sosa 1990; Williams 1976). What makes me tomorrow, or me in twenty years, the same person as me today? This discussion has tended to inhospitable regions of metaphysics, replete with Byzantine thought experiments, and there are those who doubt its fecundity (Velleman 2006: 172). But as with other philosophical puzzles, the fantastically abstruse is the child of the painfully familiar, and the obscuranta have general resonance.

"I'm not the man I was," I lament, pondering a lifetime of compromise and disappointment; "You're not the person we used to know," complains a friend, as she watches the bohemian give way to the bourgeois. I can contest such charges, of course; maybe what really matters to me, deep down, hasn't really changed, despite all the superficial flux. Even so, there had better be movement, and lots of it, on pain of necrotic adolescence: "If I still cared about all the stuff I used to care about," I might remark, while culling my collection of appallingly low-fidelity Grateful Dead recordings, "I'd be really pathetic." Yet if someone underwent change substantial enough to warrant saying they'd *literally* become a different person—if there were a failure of numerical identity, so the change involved not one person, but two—this would be seriously disturbing. Are there such catastrophic disruptions of identity? Can a *somebody* become a *somebody else*?

It's not easy to articulate the sort of identity these questions presuppose. Never mind the incessantly changing entities that are persons: metaphysicians face considerable difficulty in specifying identity conditions for humdrum material objects like doorstops and dishrags (Hawthorne 2003: Lowe 2002; 23–76). One strategy takes the metaphysics head-on, and forwards a general account of identity applicable to material objects and persons alike (Sattig 2012, 2015). Another shirks the metaphysics of identity, and seeks an alternative notion to make sense of how human beings understand themselves and each other as persisting creatures with a past (to be proud or ashamed of) and a future (to anticipate or dread).

A familiar option is psychological continuity—continuity for short—and that's the option I'll pursue (cf. Parfit 1995). I'm not sure continuity portends easier going than identity, but it makes a serviceable entree. Sometimes, psychological pathologies—late-stage Alzheimer's type dementias, perhaps—disrupt the continuity of persons, and it seems right to say that while the body goes on, the person does not; irrevocable loss precedes the loss of life (cf. Craver 2012). But ordinary human lives are also filled with perturbations—finding religion, say, or disowning political convictions—that result in dramatic discontinuities. In this regard, the normal has more in common with the pathological than one might expect. Continuity is fragile, and the first problem of the self concerns what sustains and subverts it.

The second problem has to do with identity at a time rather than continuity over time: how are individual people individuated? Once again, psychopathology makes a provocation, in the form of disorders where individuation fails. With Folie à Deux (less charmingly, "shared psychotic disorder") two people share fantastic beliefs, such as paranoid delusions; the interpersonal checks and balances that help to regulate cognition break down, and selves become inappropriately intermingled (Enoch and Ball 2001: 179–208). Speaking figuratively, there are too many bodies for the selves, or not enough selves for the bodies. The opposite also occurs: too many selves for not enough bodies. In dissociative identity ("multiple personality") disorder there appear to be numerous people, or perhaps parts of people, living in the same body (controversy acknowledged; Humphrey and Dennett 1998). Most folks escape such unlikely fates, and there usually seems to hold something like the expected one body/one self correspondence. Yet the exotic anxieties resemble more ordinary wonderings: "Who am I, really?" and "Could I be losing myself in this relationship?"

This uncertainty emerges in the second person as well as the first. At the limit, one might wonder about which identity one was dealing with, when encountering someone with dissociative identity disorder. One might also experience a related, if less ostentatious, trepidation when navigating relations with the constitutionally insincere, or the social chameleon: "What is she all about?" and "Does he stand for anything?" The second problem of self concerns what it is to have a (more or less) definite, sharply delineated, identity, and what factors facilitate success in developing and maintaining it.

I've already fretted the third problem of self: agency, or self-direction. On my understanding this problem is closely related to the problem of moral responsibility; it's tempting to think that for someone to be appropriately held morally responsible, her behavior must be an exercise of agency (entities that are poor candidates for agency, like hiking boots and spaghetti squash, are generally poor candidates for responsibility). Famously, the philosophical intricacies are legion, but questions about responsibility are plenty prominent outside the lecture hall. Recall the younger George Bush scolding Americans, after his administration's inept response to Hurricane Katrina, for playing "the blame game." That people readily play the blame game is not in question; post-Katrina, even television news people expressed outrage at the Bush administration's fecklessness. What *is* in question is whether attitudes and practices associated with the blame game withstand theoretical scrutiny. More than a few philosophers have voiced skepticism about responsibility (e.g. Rosen 2004; Smart 1961; Strawson 1994), and if nobody's responsible, it's unclear why anyone's to blame.

In fact, difficulty is apparent before philosophical behemoths like freedom and determinism blot the horizon. Is the person who kills their family during a psychotic episode morally responsible for their abhorrent deed? The problem is not limited to the psychological fringes, but pervades the routine: perhaps I'm the victim of circumstances, like a troubled childhood, that obviate my responsibility for my many blunders and shortcomings (cf. Buss 1997). How to decide such questions—under what circumstances, if any, are human beings able to function as morally responsible agents?—is the problem of self animating this book.

It may be unclear how agency is related to my official preoccupation with the disintegration of mind. Well, the term "unified agency" makes frequent appearances in moral philosophy—especially in moral philosophy associated with Kant—and it is not uncommonly supposed that personal unity is necessary for agency (Darwall 1983: 101–13; Korsgaard 1996: 229–33; 2009: xii). I won't rest on Kantian precedent, but will instead develop an observation that seems to me fairly plain: where there's trouble about continuity and identity, there's trouble about agency.

Start with continuity, which might be cast as diachronic unity. Suppose someone's preferences exhibit wild temporal fluctuation: Monday she loves beans and hates steak, Tuesday it's the other way around, and on Wednesday beans once again taste fine. She'd have a hard time buying groceries—or she'd be condemned to buying groceries all the time. If she was similarly unsettled about major commitments like work and love, it's hard to see how she could organize her life—in any event, she'd have difficulty with the kind of temporally extended planning that seems to be characteristic of human agency (Bratman 2007).

Related remarks apply to identity, which might be cast as synchronic unity. Suppose someone is prone to strong and simultaneous conflicting preferences: he's often in positions like desperately wanting to go out for steak and desperately wanting to stay in for beans—at the same moment. If these conflicts were extensive enough, the victim might experience a sort of practical paralysis—an inability to settle on the kinds of plans and policies needed to direct his life as an agent. (With sufficiently severe conflicts, he might be unable to form and execute intentions.)

Were it not for people's abiding preoccupation with practices and attitudes associated with morally responsible agency, questions of continuity and identity would seem a deal less interesting: why care who inhabits what body, unless you're wondering where your enmities and affections should lie? Indeed, on one way of thinking about it, the three problems of self grow from a single root: if a "warring states" model of mind is correct, and human psychology is radically disunified, continuity, identity, and agency are all jeopardized, in so far as all three seem to require a more or less integrated self. I'll proceed as though the problems are thus intertwined, and I'll eventually apply lessons learned about agency to continuity and identity. This may seem an imprudent aspiration: a comprehensive theory promising to simultaneously fell three notoriously difficult problems. Yet in as much as the difficulties are co-joined, vaulting ambition is the spawn of sober exigency.

Vaulting ambition notwithstanding, there may be no single notion of the self fit for all the work that might be asked of it across the full diversity of theoretical and practical contexts; the best hope may be multiple theories rather than a unified theory (Velleman 2006: 2). Certainly, my framework neglects any number of historically important issues associated with the self, such as the question of what it is to be a subject of experience or a locus of consciousness (Strawson 2009).[1] Here again, I suspect the issues intermingle, since the problem of agency

---

[1] There are perspectives according to which *no* problems of the self are important, such as "experientialist" utilitarianisms where only enjoyment and suffering are ethically fundamental (Bernstein 1998: 35). This approach to normative and applied ethics is disputed; even Singer (2011: 78–81), a utilitarian with strong experientialist leanings, rejects it. In any event, experientialism elides, rather than addresses, central problems in moral psychology.

has much to do with the experience of agency. But if the problems diverge, no matter. That's the joy of stipulation: to each their own, and let's see where each ends up. No reason we can't share terminology, so long as we're clear on the use we're making.

This isn't to say that terminological questions are always innocent questions; for instance, the question of who gets termed a person is anything but. The exclusion of peoples from the community of persons has long been associated with ethical calamity; the case of chattel slavery is but one egregious example. Similarly, issues concerning who gets labeled an agent may be ethically substantial; for example, it's because children are not yet agents that states are justified in denying them full political rights. Theorizing about moral matters may have moral implications, and if the theorizing is done badly, these implications may be morally reprehensible, as in the case of racial pseudoscience. But this isn't reason to eschew such theorizing; it's reason to theorize better. That's what I'll be trying to do.

Freedom

It may be surprising to find that I'll say little about freedom, a notion philosophers commonly associate (if not equate) with morally responsible agency (e.g. Campbell 1957: 159; Fischer 2005: xxiii; Levy 2011: 1; Nichols 2008: 10; O'Connor 2008; Strawson 1994: 8; Vargas 2007b: 128–9). When freedom is understood as the absence of causal determination, the association is easily made. It's readily supposed that if someone's behavior is causally determined by factors "external" to them, they did not act freely: when a very large man shoves me into a display of Steuben crystal, I don't decimate the Steuben "of my own free will," and neither am I responsible for the resulting damage.

Extend this thought with a deterministic understanding of the cosmos, where all events are linked to antecedent events by causal laws. Add the following assumptions: human behaviors are events governed by the laws, and human beings are powerless to change either the past or the laws. Assumptions granted, it's hard to avoid concluding that all behavior is causally constrained by the laws and the past, and is therefore not "up to us," and not free (cf. Kane 2002: 11–12; van Inwagen 1983: 16). If you also buy the association of freedom and responsibility, you're bound to think people aren't responsible, either. Like any formulation, this formulation of the problem is contestable (Dennett 1984: 1–19). Nevertheless, the traditional avenues of response are well established; while they are (painfully) familiar to those versed in the literature, a brief re-walking will help illuminate my chosen route.

Two stripes of incompatibilists accept some version of the conditional: if determinism obtains, human freedom doesn't. Stripe one, the hard determinists, embrace determinism and conclude, with either horror or delight, that people aren't free (e.g. Smart 1961: 303–36).[2] Stripe two, the libertarians (e.g. Kane 1996), posit exceptions to determinism in the form of human decisions that are exempt from causal determination, and locate freedom in these exceptions. Seizing a *tertium quid*, compatibilists deny there is a tension (e.g. Ayer 1980); people may be free even in a deterministic world. While the incompatibilists dispute amongst themselves about the conditional's antecedent, the compatibilist rejects the conditional.

Few philosophers are especially pleased about any of this: the literature is mired in a "dialectical stalemate," where everybody has damning complaints about everybody else, and nobody has fully satisfying rejoinders (cf. Doris *et al.* 2007; Fischer 1994: 83–5; Nagel 1986: 112–13, 117–18; Vargas 2004: 218). By many lights, hard determinism is unpalatably skeptical, while libertarianism escapes the skeptical at the risk of the fantastical: how could human beings (if human beings are part or product of nature) be exempt from natural laws, and how is this wondrous undetermined agency to be understood? Compatibilism, for its part, looks like small beer: freedom compatible with one's behavior being determined doesn't look like the sort of thing those associating freedom and responsibility are looking for—even if (in the perhaps unlikely event) all parties agree to call it freedom.

My approach to the stalemate involves distinguishing two questions: Is *freedom* compatible with determinism? Is *responsibility* compatible with determinism? I contend these queries can be treated independently: questions of responsibility can be asked, and answered, without questions of freedom being answered. Thus, I'm a compatibilist about responsibility and determinism, and take no position as regards freedom and determinism (following Fischer's (2006: 76–8) "semicompatibilism"). In effect, the many philosophers who associate freedom and responsibility see one question instead of two: if you deny unfree beings responsibility, the freedom and responsibility questions come to much the same thing. If, on the other hand, you disassociate the two questions, you can allow that there may be responsible beings in a world without freedom.

---

[2] Kane (2002: 27–32) observes that while few contemporary philosophers are unqualifiedly committed to hard determinism, numerous theories, such as Strawson's (1986, 2002) and Pereboom's (2001, 2002), reside in the vicinity, rejecting the possibility of moral responsibility (but without requiring determinism). For variations on the traditional problematic, see Watson (2004: 197–215).

To see why the disassociation makes sense, consider libertarianism, which secures freedom by rejecting determinism. This might be accomplished *via* indeterministic interpretations of physics; if the best science shows that not everything in the world is determined, maybe there's wiggle room for human freedom (Bishop 2011; Bishop and Atmanspacher 2011; Hodgson 2011). Yet it's not obvious this good news for freedom is also good news for responsibility. Perhaps we should say that a behavior with its origins in a chance event is not determined, and therefore free, but that's not the same thing as saying the agent herself determined it (Loewer 1996: e.g. 105–6). If agency has to do with self-determination, not-other-determined won't get us all the way there, and indeterminacy is not enough for responsible agency.

Now consider a scenario where determinism is true, and incompatible with freedom, so nobody's free. It doesn't easily follow that nobody's responsible. For often, in thinking about responsibility, the concern is not *that* decisions and actions are caused, but *how* they are caused. "He did it because he was forced to" and "she did it because it mattered to her" are both causal stories, but they are very different causal stories, and it's sorely tempting to suppose the difference might be cut along a dimension of responsible agency. Viewed this way, the big question concerns whether human behavior is ever caused *in the right way* to count as an instance of responsible agency. (A question about which psychology might have much to say, except for the regrettable fact that many psychologists seem to have embraced incompatibilism without exploring compatibilist alternatives.[3]) If the question about responsibility is how-caused rather than that-caused, it's not clear freedom is required for responsibility.

To state the conclusion of some decidedly less than rigorous argumentation with old-fashioned rigor, freedom is neither necessary nor sufficient for responsibility. If that's right, compatibilism about freedom doesn't secure responsibility, and if the compatibilist about freedom also wants to be a compatibilist about responsibility, she'll need to put more work in. The compatibilist about responsibility who isn't a compatibilist about freedom has rather less to do: she doesn't have to fight for freedom to win responsible agency.

As I've said, a lot of people treat the two questions together, and I don't expect the one question crowd to be convinced by the foregoing gestures (gestures, they'll say, of a familiarly unsatisfying sort). Here, it's enough if they can exercise patience. The disassociation of responsibility and freedom is not a conclusion of

---

[3] In the collection *Are We Free? Psychology and Free Will* (Baer *et al.* 2008), I count five mentions of compatibilism by psychologists, none of which are particularly detailed or sympathetic (e.g. Schooler in Shariff *et al.* 2008: 195–7).

my argument, but a supposition. I'm attempting to develop an account of morally responsible agency that does not require freedom from causal constraint; indeed, as we'll see in due course, my approach positively *celebrates* constraint. If I succeed in this development, I will have provided an "existence proof" for the wisdom of disassociating freedom and responsibility, by identifying a legitimate form of morally responsible agency that does not require freedom.

I'll generally be operating as a compatibilist about responsibility. But in the end, I'll be parting company with compatibilists, since I think that they and their incompatibilist adversaries are often united in favoring monistic theories, where the same set of considerations is always and everywhere relevant to agency and responsibility. Instead, I'll forward a pluralistic approach, one where agency takes a variety of diverging forms, and the attribution of responsibility across different circumstances is governed by markedly dissimilar considerations. At day's end, there's considerable benefit in this messy and ecumenical pluralism. Not only will it account for the multifaceted psychology of agency, it will circumnavigate the entrenchments of dialectical stalemate.

Method

It should already be evident that my methodological proclivities are "naturalistic": I believe philosophical questions, ethical questions included, should be considered in light of the best going scientific picture of humans and their world (Brink 1989; Gibbard 1990; Harman 2012; Railton 1995, 2003; Sturgeon 1988). Accordingly, I won't address the problems of self by plumbing the mysteries of soul. Like many contemporary philosophers, I tend towards materialism, but even some materialists (Lycan 2009) admit that the arguments for materialism are not decisive, and I'm not going to presume anything's been decided. I want to understand the appearance of disintegration in human cognition and behavior, and the explanatory strategy I think most promising doesn't make reference to souls. Others may take a different course. As ever, theory choice is comparative: you go your way, and I'll go mine, and after the theories are in, let the devil—be he material or immaterial—take the hindmost.

That much naturalism appears to come pretty cheap: many contemporary philosophers get on without souls (and decisive arguments for materialism), while philosophers manifesting a diverse range of methodological predilection and substantive conviction seek to situate their philosophical tectonics in the world as revealed by science (e.g. McDowell 1998: 165-6). My execution of naturalism—call it bare-knuckle naturalism—presses a bit harder, since I'm of the opinion that very often, philosophical progress will be made—if it be made at all—through sustained and intimate interaction with empirical science.

This is debatable: many distinguished philosophers, such as the holders of Oxford's venerable Wykeham Chair in Logic, have treated many philosophical problems, such as the nature and possibility of knowledge, by means that are *a priori* and conceptual rather than *a posteriori* and empirical (Williamson 2007). I won't debate it: the empirically oriented philosopher can hardly dispute the historical prominence of *a priorism*, nor should she disparage philosophers working this tradition. Philosophical problems are numerous and various, so one should expect that the means of addressing them will likewise be numerous and various. If any observation can safely be made about "the philosophical method" it's that in practice this method is, and always has been, vibrantly eclectic (imagine a methodological debate between Plato and Hume). Determining what works where, it seems to me, is a determination that will be made on substantially *a posteriori* grounds, by evaluating the progress shown by the different approaches (in as much as the decision to wait and see proceeds the actual seeing, this *a posteriori* approach itself manifests *a priori* commitment).

As to the prospects of bare-knuckle naturalism, it is obscure how the philosophical relevance of science could be decided without detailed inquiry concerning what the science actually shows, and how it manages to show it. This realization prompts a general point of philosophical order: methodological questions are illuminated not by general edict, but by close examination of the fruits borne by particular approaches to particular problems. When a method is vindicated, it is vindicated in relation to some matter of substance, with the vindication consisting in the method revealing something interesting about the substance (i.e. the best way to do "metaphilosophy" is to do philosophy). My method—if a method it be—is Napoleonic: "One jumps into the fray, then figures out what to do next!" (*"On s'engage et puis on voit!"*).

In the case of ethical theory, moral philosophers have, as a matter of fact, long been in the habit of making empirical assertions (Doris and Stich 2005: 115). Hardly surprising that this should be so: if one is wondering about what a good life for human beings requires, or what is right for human beings to do—wonderings that have long been at the heart of ethical enquiry—it seems altogether appropriate for this wondering to involve questions concerning what human beings are actually like. Furthermore, it is at least prima facie plausible to suppose that these questions can be helpfully addressed with the help of the human sciences. This supposition is nowadays well subscribed: empirically oriented approaches to ethical theory are increasingly favored by researchers in both philosophy and psychology departments (Andreou 2007; Doris and Stich

2005, 2006; Doris *et al.* 2010; Knobe and Nichols 2008; Nadelhoffer *et al.* 2010; Sinnott-Armstrong 2007a, b, c; Tiberius 2014).

Empirical orientation needn't slight the "normativity" of ethics; no credible naturalist supposes that normative questions are decided by scientific enquiry alone. With respect to the matter at hand, attributions of agency are "thick" (Williams 1985: 16–17, 128–9, 140–1, 148). They are simultaneously descriptive, appealing to various facts about their subjects, and normative, assessing their subjects relative to some standard, which underscores the difficulty of solidifying the vaunted "fact/value distinction." A theory of agency that aspires to be both empirically adequate and ethically defensible—as the theory presented here aspires—will advert to considerations from both sides of that craggy divide.

Whatever one thinks of my particular product, this strategy has benefits for a variety of interested parties. The human sciences have produced innumerable results illuminating cognition, emotion, and motivation, with the potential to enrich theorizing on philosophically central topics surrounding rationality, agency, and the self. At the same time, theoretical structures derived from philosophy have the potential to impose order on the large and disorderly mass of empirical findings. Integrating these resources in an interdisciplinary moral psychology can facilitate increased discussion across boundaries demarcating the philosophy of action, the philosophy of mind, ethics, psychology, and the cognitive sciences. That's conversation worth having more of, whether or not one agrees with everything that get's said.

Character

One place bare-knuckle naturalism has been deployed with discernible effect is the moral psychology of character. The effect in question exemplifies the decompositional zeitgeist framing the present discussion: numerous psychologists and empirically oriented philosophers, myself included, have voiced skepticism about familiar understandings of character as a unified psychological structure issuing in behavior that is consistent across diverse circumstances.[4] The motivating observation for character skepticism is drawn from decades of experimentation in "situationist" social psychology: unobtrusive features of situations, such as the presence of a pleasant ambient odor (Baron 1997; Lilenquist *et al.* 2010), have

---

[4] See Doris (1998, 2002, 2005, 2006, 2010, forthcoming) and Doris and Stich (2005, 2006). For related positions, see Alfano (2013), Harman (1999, 2000b), Machery (2010), Merritt (2000, 2009; Merritt, Doris, and Harman 2010), and Vranas (2005). The classics in psychology are Mischel (1968) and Ross and Nisbett (1991); a variety of later perspectives are collected in Donnellan *et al.* (2009).

repeatedly been shown to impact behavior in seemingly arbitrary, and sometimes alarming, ways. If the sound of a lawnmower makes the difference between helping an injured person or not (Matthews and Canon 1975), what other bits of situational detritus are crudding up the ethical works? If the works are so easily crudded, why suppose that people are possessed of sturdy characters? And if people are not possessed of sturdy characters, whither the virtues, which are supposed to be the sturdiest character attributes of all?

Skepticism about character has not been greeted with unmixed enthusiasm, and the ensuing scuffles have been, to judge by the numbers showing up at the schoolyard, of considerable interest.[5] But I'm not here to declare a winner. On the contrary, I'm wondering about how to go on without a clear resolution—that is, in just the sort of ambiguous rhetorical circumstances that mark nearly every philosophical debate. There's one part of these circumstances I'm particularly keen to get past; the charge that character skeptics have had much to say about situational variation in behavior and little to say about the psychological processes underlying it, with the result that they overlook the rational order in people's lives (Adams 2006: 115–232; Annas 2005).

That behavior matters for morality is not easily denied, yet it's also true that "what's inside" is of abiding interest for both psychology and ethics. Moreover, behavioral variation alone does not entail disintegration. The virtuous person, such as Aristotle's exemplary *phronimos*, may sometimes tell it straight and sometimes shade the truth, or sometimes stand his ground and sometimes run like a thief, but this considerable variety is structured by orderly patterns of cognition and motivation—say by an abiding conception of what makes a life good. Perhaps the *phronimos* makes his end a life rich in emotionally intimate relationships: sometimes such a life is facilitated by being bluntly honest, and other times not. And so for other goods: a life of martial valor sometimes requires the ultimate sacrifice, and other times requires fighting another day.

This picture is appealing, but encounters awkward questions about the nature of cognition. As I've already said, human mentation is a shaky business, and if anything, there is *more* empirical work making trouble for familiar conceptions of rationality than there is work making trouble for familiar conceptions of

---

[5] Philosophical responses to situationist skepticism are found in Adams (2006), Annas (2005), Appiah (2008: 33–72), Arpaly (2005), Badhwar (2009), Besser-Jones (2008), Flanagan (2009: 54–6), Kamtekar (2004), Knobe and Leiter (2007), Kupperman (2001), Miller (2003, 2013a, b), Montmarquet (2003), Prinz (2009); Russell (2009), Samuels and Casebeer (2005), Sarkissian (2010), Solomon (2003, 2005), Snow (2010), Sreenivasan (2002), Swanton (2003: 30–1), Upton (2009), and Webber (2006a, b, 2007a, b). For an extensive bibliography, see *Skepticism about Character*, edited by Mark Alfano, at: http://philpapers.org/browse/skepticism-about-character

character: psychologists and cognitive scientists have endlessly documented a dispiriting range of reasoning errors (Baron 1994, 2001; Gilovich *et al.* 2002; Kahneman *et al.* 1982; Kahneman and Tversky 1982; Kruger and Dunning 1999; Nisbett and Borgida 1975; Nisbett and Ross 1980; Stich 1990; Tversky and Kahneman 1981). One can therefore be forgiven for supposing that when the champion of character turns from behavior to cognition he tumbles, hand in hand with the *phronimos*, from frying pan to fire. However, research supporting this discouraging assessment of human rationality is controversial (Samuels *et al.* 2002), and not all psychologists think things are so bleak (Gigerenzer 2000; Gigerenzer *et al.* 1999). I'll duck the controversy; I contend not that human beings are rationally *deficient*, but that the ways they order their lives are *different* from those envisaged by traditional conceptions of practical rationality.

Although these issues are related to the character controversy, I will make little reference to character in my discussion of agency. This omission might be thought mistaken: perhaps it is only the virtuous who can properly direct their own lives, meaning virtuous character is necessary for agency, and character skepticism entails agency skepticism. We'll eventually see that this contention is multiply unappetizing; there's considerable warrant for distinguishing virtue and agency, as the practice of holding people responsible for vicious deeds apparently attests. It is true that if a theory of virtue presupposes the conception of agency I criticize, it will implicitly be subject to criticism, but I won't make the criticism explicit.

Signpost

Contemporary developments in the psychological and cognitive sciences intimate the disintegration of mind, which further problematizes three enduring problems in moral psychology: continuity, identity, and agency. I aim to articulate a theory with the resources to ameliorate these difficulties, most especially, the difficulty of skepticism about agency. Before responding to this skepticism, I'll first make clear what is, starting with an explication of a philosophical doctrine on which the difficulty is particularly acute, a doctrine I'll call reflectivism.

2

Reflection

People do a lot of thinking about what to do, and all this thinking is supposed to have much to do with what they do eventually do, and how well they do it. In American vernacular, the inconsiderate are *thoughtless*, the impulsive are urged to *stop and think*, while the regretful wonder, *what was I thinking*? Likewise in philosophical vernacular. Throughout philosophy, human beings are thinking things who think a lot about themselves: it's widely assumed that self-conscious mentation differentiates human beings from other species, and further differentiates those human beings who flourish from those who falter. Such assumptions, I'll say, manifest the doctrine of reflectivism.

Reflectivism

I'm ascribing reflectivism to lots of philosophers. I'll document my ascription, but I won't discuss any philosopher in full detail. Rather, I mean to discuss general themes that are implicit, and often enough explicit, in quantities of writing on topics like agency, responsibility, and the self. This procedure is not without risk, rather like drawing a composite face that looks a little like many faces, but not a lot like any particular face. Those possessed of the particular faces—that is, the particular philosophical positions—may say that the homeliness I remark on does not afflict their countenance. Of course, they might well say the same thing if I *did* discuss particular positions in detail—the charge that a critic has misconstrued their target likely being the modal philosophical reaction to criticism.[1] Nevertheless, I'm betting that the face I depict is easily recognizable: the commitments here depicted in composite strongly resemble commitments actually held.

This wager is not a reckless gamble. A preoccupation with reflection is, arguably, the Western philosophical tradition's most distinctive feature, in both

---

[1] In responding to a collection of essays on his work, McDowell (2002) apparently argues that all thirteen contributors have misread his positions (see Genova 2003).

historical and contemporary contexts (Kornblith 2010: 2; 2012: 1). Not only because philosophical inquiry might itself be construed as reflective activity, but also because philosophers frequently articulate key notions by reference to reflection.

In ethics, Aristotelians have implicated reflection in virtue (Annas 1993: 67–8), Humeans have associated reflection with practical reasoning (Tiberius 2002: 13), and Millians have made reflection a condition of happiness (Brink 1992: 79; Mill 2002: 60–1). In political philosophy, the autonomous person is widely understood as someone who "conducts himself according to principles that he has himself ratified through critical reflection" (Appiah 2005: 38; cf. Dworkin 1988: 15–20), and one needn't squint to see reflectivism in Rawls' (1971: 408, 417) hugely influential method of reflective equilibrium. In epistemology, Shoemaker (1996: 32–3) asserts that reflection is required for rational belief change, and Sosa (1991: 240) distinguishes animal knowledge, which has "little or no benefit of reflection and understanding," from the reflective knowledge characteristic of humans, which manifests understanding of how that knowledge comes about.[2]

The idea that reflection separates human from non-human animals is an enduring theme. Among canonical philosophers, we find Locke's (1975/1700: sec. 2.27.9) account of a person as "a thinking intelligent Being, that has reason and reflection, and can consider it self as it self," while in the twentieth-century Anglophone tradition, McDowell (1994: 114–15), distinguishes human beings from "mere animals" by reference to humans' capacity for self-critical reflection. The exception supposedly proving the reflectivist rule is Frankfurt's (1988: 18–19; cf. 1999: 105–6) celebrated human non-person, the *Wanton*, who, by virtue of his inability or disinclination to engage in reflection, is "no different from an animal."

If philosophers are mistaken about reflection, they're mistaken about a lot of things. But my concern is with mistakes in moral psychology, where reflectivism appears to be pervasive (Arpaly 2002: 20; Smith 2005 is an instructive exception). More precisely, my concern is with reflectivism about agency, where the most obvious—but by no means the only (e.g. Ekstrom 2005: 57; 2011: 371)—examples are theories in the tradition of Kant. According to Korsgaard (2003: 60), Kantians "typically place a high value on reflection"; in Korsgaard's Kantianism, the human mind is "essentially reflective" (Korsgaard 1996: 92–3), and reason is "a power we have in virtue of a certain type of self-consciousness – consciousness

---

[2] For a critique of reflection in epistemology, to which my critique of reflectivism about agency bears affinities, see Kornblith (2012).

of the grounds of our own beliefs and actions" (Korsgaard 2009: xi; cf. Moran 2001: 127). It's a short step from rationality to agency, and Kantians frequently assert that reflection is necessary for agency, resulting in a literature rich with terminology like "reflective agent" and "reflective agency" (Kennett and Fine 2009: 84; Velleman 1989: 5; 2000: 12, 26–9, 124, 191–6; Wallace 2003: 437; 2006: 150–1).

Reflection can be understood as "[t]hinking about one's own mental processes from a first-person point of view" (Kornblith 2012: 28), which looks a lot like what often gets called introspection. My arguments are partly directed at introspection, since I'll argue that people frequently err in the detection of their own psychological states, including beliefs, desires, emotions, and motives. But introspection might be interpreted capaciously, to include first personal thinking on things not readily described as mental states, such as habits and dispositions (Robbins 2006). Whether or not this should be counted introspection, it ought be counted as reflection: I might reflect that I habitually study at Kaldi's coffee shop, or that I'm disposed to curt responses when conversing with Edgar. Reflection may also be directed more outwardly than inwardly. If you like, call this extrospection: I might reflect that Nedra is often at Kaldi's when I'm there, or that Edgar is insufferable because he's insecure. Where I claim there's difficulty about reflection, I'll be using "reflection" quite broadly, to cover a range of introspective and extrospective processes.

Just as there's a diversity of thinking that might be called reflection, there is, as we've just seen, a diversity of philosophical positions that might be called reflectivist. A tractable exposition therefore requires distillation, and I'll continue schematizing reflectivist doctrine as I did at the outset: *the exercise of human agency consists in judgment and behavior ordered by self-conscious reflection about what to think and do.* I'll also continue discussion with my statement of reflectivism's corollary: *the exercise of human agency requires accurate reflection.*

In Plato's (1997: *Phaedrus* 229e) telling, Socrates was much taken with the Delphic maxim, "Know Thyself," and contemporary writers on agency are no less impressed. (Characteristically, Nietzsche (1974/1882: 263) makes a dark exception: "'know thyself!' addressed to human beings by a god, is almost malicious.") On reflectivism, agency requires that the actor detect salient facts about herself, like the motives of her behavior (Velleman 2000: 12); as Tiberius (2002: 13) puts it, a "person who does not know her deepest motivations because she is very psychologically complicated, or because she has formed impenetrable layers of self-deception, is missing something she would need to deliberate well." If deliberation—which might be thought of as practical reflection—is predicated on erroneous self-understandings, agency is supposedly imperiled.

Instead of Wanton, imagine Clueless, who incessantly and earnestly reflects, but always gets it wrong. No matter how he tries, he's in the dark about his actual motives (and the motives he actually desires to have). Clueless is not Wanton; on the contrary, he's a pathetically thoughtful sort of creature. But he's a creature who appears to be an inobvious candidate for agency: how can one effectively direct the course of one's life, if one is always wrong about the contours of one's self?

Luckily for Clueless, he's only a thought experiment, but actual cases present kindred distress. Successful practical reasoning seemingly requires at least the rudiments of self-awareness: knowing that one is not dead, which apparently escapes victims of Cotard's syndrome, and knowing that one is not grossly infested with parasites, which apparently escapes victims of Ekbom's syndrome (Enoch and Ball 2001: 155–78, 209–23). (If one *is* dead or grossly infested, the situation is different.) There also appear to be many subclinical cases where failures of self-awareness, though falling short of delusional, have disastrous practical implications: you thinking your unvarnished lust is something finer may result in painfully misguided romantic choices, and me thinking my meager talent is something finer may result in painfully misguided vocational choices.

If the accuracy corollary required comprehensive self-awareness, it would be a non-starter; instead, the standard should be something like "moderate" self-awareness (Tiberius 2008: 115). People are typically unaware of countless facts about their bodies and their circumstances, such as the precise number of hairs on their head, or the exact number of seconds it would take them to travel from their present location to the highest point in Chugwater, Wyoming. There's also substantial ignorance of cognitive processes: when I ask you to recall your mother's birth name, you may remember it without having a clue as to how you did so (Nisbett and Wilson 1977: 232). Similarly for neural processes: most people I know can't accurately report on the individual brain events implicated in their behavior. Plenty of ignorance about, but plenty of it does little to imperil agency.

Moreover, there are areas where self-awareness is pretty good. There's a venerable tradition in philosophy maintaining that self-knowledge is especially "epistemically secure" in that people have "privileged access" to their mental states (Gertler 2011: 59–86). I won't be directly engaging this tradition, but if I'm right about the empirical evidence, there's good reason to doubt the extent of this privilege (cf. McGeer 1996). All the same, I won't be broaching skepticism about "phenomenal" experiences of things like pain and colors; while some philosophers have doubted the veracity of phenomenal reports, few have argued that people often get their "current conscious experiences" seriously wrong

(Schwitzgebel, in Hurlburt and Schwitzgebel 2007: 44, 53). Nor will I contest findings to the effect that people can in some conditions accurately report on the processes involved in problem-solving (e.g. Ericsson and Simon 1980).

Finally, I'll remain agnostic on the exact mechanisms underlying self-awareness. I'm neutral between "theory-theory" accounts, where self-awareness is based on theoretically mediated inferences from behavior, similar to the inferences people make about others (Carruthers 1996; Gopnik 1993; Gopnik and Meltzoff 1994: 168), and "monitoring" accounts, which posit direct first-personal access to mental states (Nichols and Stich 2003: Ch. 4). I find theory-theory surprising (must I see myself pull the lever to know whom I'm voting for?), but my concerns about the accuracy of self-awareness are "process neutral," and obtain whether people have direct introspective access, or only indirect inferential access, to their mental states.

While the contemplated skepticism is qualified, none of the qualifications do much to dampen skepticism about trickier subjects of self-awareness, such as "I'm not angry with her," and "I have a real gift for conversation," or "I'd be happier living in the country" (cf. Gertler 2011: 70–80). Indeed, it often seems that the more interesting self-awareness is from the perspective of practical reasoning, the more cause there is to distrust it. I'll call failures of self-awareness *self-ignorance*, and I'll say self-ignorance is *practically relevant* if, should the actor become aware of what she is ignorant of, she would behave—or argue, judge, feel, etc.—differently: when I notice that I'm nibbling out of anxiety rather than hunger, I may return the almonds to their rightful place in the pantry, and when I realize that my refusal to negotiate is due not to conviction but vanity, I may rethink my intransigence. Even where the amelioration of self-ignorance does change behavior, it may influence emotions or attitudes: pride may turn to shame, if I come to view my obstinacy as petty rather than principled.

There's loads of difficulty here. It's easy, as it always is, to make trouble for a counterfactual fix, because it's easy to concoct unlikely counterfactuals, where the irrelevant is made relevant: when a thug with a philosophical agenda threatens violence if I cannot accurately report the number of hairs on my head, my ignorance takes on pungent practical interest. (I refute you thus, the thug might gloat.) In the absence of principles for deciding the relevance of counterfactual circumstances—and there is such an absence—there's not going to be anything tidy to say (Doris 2002: 117–18). Fortunately, serviceable examples of practically relevant self-ignorance abound, and we'll encounter enough of these along the way to enable forward movement, even as we sidestep deep-rooted philosophical difficulties.

To say that people suffer practically relevant self-ignorance is not quite to say they reason fallaciously. There's a difference between detecting mental states and reasoning about mental states: one might make valid inferences from delusional beliefs about oneself, and one might make invalid inferences from true beliefs about oneself (Nichols and Stich 2003: 151–2). For all I'll say here, people may quite often reason validly in conditions of self-ignorance. But they won't be reasoning soundly, and this sort of failing, as we'll see, has skeptical implications for the exercise of agency—skeptical implications reflectivism is poorly equipped to ameliorate.

Like any philosophical doctrine, reflectivism might be interpreted more than one way. First, reflectivism could involve an empirical generalization to the effect that reflective self-direction is the *most commonly observed* form of agency. A second reflectivist claim with empirical aspect asserts that reflective self-direction is somehow *practically dominant*, meaning that on occasions of importance, such as career choices and mate choices, reflective self-direction is the most frequently observed form of agency. This interpretation, unlike the first, does not require that reflective self-direction occur with relative frequency, but it involves a strong empirical claim, to the effect that reflective self-direction often occurs at critical junctures, meaning it has much to do with how people's lives go. Finally, reflectivism might involve a contention of the sort philosophers sometimes call conceptual: reflection is *necessary* for the exercise of agency. This is not a straightforwardly empirical assertion, since it entails no predictions as to whether agency is ever exercised.

My assessment is that the published record contains material—sometimes explicit, perhaps more often implicit—indicative of all three renderings. There's no shortage of claims that look empirical: from reading the literature, one certainly gets the impression that reflection is thought to be a characteristic human activity, an activity actual people actually engage in as they figure out what to think and do. At the same time, conceptual inquiry might be more typical in the philosophy of the past century or so than is empirical inquiry (despite the frequent appearance of undeniably empirical claims). Moreover, in recent years, as empirical arguments have proliferated in philosophy, defenders of threatened positions have sometimes distanced themselves from empirically assessable assertions, as they have in debates about character skepticism (Alfano 2013: 63–4; Doris 2005: 661–6). Perhaps the presumption should be that reflectivism is a conceptual thesis, contrary evidence in the literature notwithstanding.

Here, there's no need to decide: I contend *all three* renderings of reflectivism are false, or at least dangerously overstated. I'll develop an empirical argument to the effect that people relatively seldom function as depicted by reflectivism: human organisms reflect less, and less accurately, than reflectivist theories usually suppose. This means trouble for the first rendering. Additionally, I'll fashion an epistemological argument to the effect that there is usually insufficient warrant for attributing the exercise of reflective agency, including on occasions of practical importance. This means trouble for the second rendering. I'll also forward argument against the conceptual claim that reflection is necessary for the exercise of agency, by developing an account where exercising agency does not require reflection. This means trouble for the third rendering. If I'm right, reflectivism is seriously problematic, *whichever* of the three interpretations one favors.

Agency

I'll make a start on agency by way of responsibility, and presume that attributions of responsibility affix to exercises of agency. An oft-used beginning is P. F. Strawson's account of the "reactive attitudes,"—resentment, indignation, anger, gratitude, forgiveness, and the like—the guiding presumption being that when someone is appropriately subject to these attitudes they are appropriately attributed moral responsibility (Strawson 1962; Vargas 2004, 2008, 2013b; Watson 1993).[3] On my way of working things, thinking about what (if any) reactive attitudes are apt helps to establish whether someone is responsible (or not): I shouldn't be angry at the puppy that chews up my slippers, but it's perfectly reasonable for me to be angry if my regrettable acquaintance Smitty, whose sense of humor was nurtured in fraternity houses, does the same thing. The reason for the differing reactions, as the story goes, is that Smitty was responsible for his behavior, and the puppy not. The difference in responsibility, as it goes on, is explained by the observation that Smitty was exercising agency, and the puppy not.

Of course, I'm causally responsible for all manner of happenings, like the shadows I cast when standing in sunlight, that don't look like exercises of agency (regards the shadows, not the standing).[4] So too, there are exercises of agency that don't invite attributions of moral responsibility. Many of life's little doings look this way: when you find me carefully straightening the papers on my desk, you'd

---

[3] I adopt the fairly conventional assumption that responsibility is "symmetrical" across good and bad behavior. This may be mistaken; perhaps the conditions of responsibility for wrongdoing and rightdoing differ (Nelkin 2011: Ch. 2). If so, the pluralism I will defend can accommodate the asymmetry.

[4] Psychologists often use "agent" for something like "entity capable of initiating its own movement" (e.g. Arico *et al.* 2011; Johnson 2005), which sets the bar for agency considerably lower than my use of the term; to keep the books straight, we might say that the psychologists' notion is of *causal* agency, while mine is of *morally responsible* agency.

probably not hesitate to count my behavior as an exercise of agency (supposing you're moved to think in such terms), but I doubt you'd thereby be inclined to the attitudes associated with moral responsibility. On the other hand, if you discovered that this ostensibly unexceptional occasion was more interesting than you originally thought—perhaps I'm pointedly straightening papers to annoy my sloppy office mate—you might think the attribution of moral responsibility appropriate. We should adopt a restriction: attributions of moral responsibility attach to exercises of agency only where the behavior in question is of moral interest (departing Fischer 2006: 67–8; Fischer and Ravizza 1998: 8 n11).

Then an exercise of agency is insufficient for attribution of moral responsibility. Neither, perhaps, is it necessary. For example, the chaotic horror of combat may impair cognitive functioning to the point where the exercise of agency is impaired, yet one might still insist on holding the perpetrators of combat atrocities morally responsible. Alternatively, it may sometimes be appropriate to hold someone liable to punishment, without judging him morally responsible. This would be a sort of "strict liability," where someone can be punished without being subject to reactive attitudes like anger: perhaps those who have lost their souls in war should be pitied rather than blamed, even if there are compelling reasons to punish them, such as the maintenance of military discipline and communication of moral outrage (Doris and Murphy 2007).

Strict liability has been sharply criticized by legal theorists (Wasserstrom 1974: 70), and to be sure, there's something unfair about punishing those who are not morally responsible for their deeds. Yet making no response to heinous wrongdoing is hardly better. This problem, though, is not mine to solve: I assume that moral responsibility and criminal liability are dissociable, and I'll be focusing on moral responsibility at the expense of criminal liability, and associated issues of punishment, throughout. If it is characteristic of negative reactive attitudes to urge punishment (Boxer 2013: 91), then my view has implications for punishment, but this is not an association I insist on. The connection I will maintain—and later argue for—is between agency and moral responsibility: the aptness of moral responsibility attributions and the associated reactive attitudes are, for behaviors of moral concern, characteristic symptoms of agency.

What are these symptoms symptomatic of? I'll say a behavior is an exercise of agency when the actor is *self-directed* while performing it. Next, I'll say that self-directed behaviors are sourced in features of the self, such as desires or beliefs, as opposed to features of the environment that are "external" to the self, such as political regimes or natural disasters. Deciding what is internal and external to the self is, notoriously, a passel of grief. But one has to start somewhere, and I'm going to blunder ahead with the notion of value, and say that behavior is self-directed when it expresses the actor's values (after Watson 1975, 1996; cf. Bratman 2007: 48; Smith 2005; Sripada in prep. a, b).

This enables some pretty plausible observations: I'm not tempted to see my rowdy puppy as self-directed because I'm not tempted to see his behavior as an expression of his values (I don't think he *has* values), but I am tempted to see the deplorable Smitty's similarly destructive behavior as self-directed, since I suspect it expresses the value that Smitty places on a life of boisterous immaturity. The same expedient might be thought to distinguish different behaviors by the same actor: when the nicotine addict guiltily succumbs to craving and lights up, his behavior is not self-directed, but when he manages to resist a craving because he values his health, his behavior is self-directed.

Another way to appreciate the allure of this account is to consider life in the *absence* of valuing. Meet the unfortunate Milksop: none of his inclinations are very strong, and none of them are very enduring; they simply fade away, or are displaced by other (equally infirm) inclinations. Milksop doesn't fail to reflect, like Wanton, or reflect ineptly, like Clueless; it's just that he doesn't come out anywhere. In short, he's unable to much care about anything. My instinct is that the appropriate attitude towards Milksop would be indifference or pity (assuming his soppiness was no fault of his own), rather than responses like anger or outrage that track morally responsible agency. If you share this instinct, you may think agency has something to do with valuing.

There's a bit of nuisance about the fortuitous realization of values. Imagine that as I reach for a smoke, a premonition of premature disability and death sends me into a faint, and when I awake the craving has passed, and I go on my increasingly healthy way without lighting up. One way to describe this is to say my valuing health helped cause the faint, which in turn helped me forgo the smoke. But it seems objectionable to conclude that this happy accident is an expression of my values. One wants to build something into "expression" that excludes the fluky, but it had better be something more than an ad hoc "no fortuitous realizations" rider.

The obvious something is intentional action. Note that the (blurry) line between exercises of agency and behaviors that aren't such exercises is not collocated with the (blurry) line between intentional and unintentional actions; there are many breakdowns of agency, like succumbing to coercion or addiction, that are perfectly good candidates for intentional action. It's not as though the robbery victim surrenders his wallet or the nicotine addict lights up her smoke by accident; these are things the actors mean to do, but they're not the kind of things that make promising candidates for exercises of agency. The question of whether a performance is an exercise of agency seems to be a question we ask *about* intentional actions; that the action was intentional is apparently presumed.

This presumption may be treacherous, since the notion of intention is itself a minefield (e.g. Mele 1992, 2009b; Pacherie and Haggard 2010). Fortunately, there's a reasonably innocuous instrument at hand: some behaviors, like lighting a smoke, are "goal-directed," and some, like fainting at the thought of death, are not. It is these goal-directed behaviors—roughly, those guided by a representation of a desired future state—that are candidates for agency. This seems a reasonable way of thinking about intentions. But for present purposes, it's enough if it allows us to tighten up the notion of expression to exclude behaviors that fortuitously conform to a value. A behavior expresses a value, we can say, when that behavior is guided by a value-relevant goal.

I've now a sort of blueprint: agency gets understood in terms of self-direction, and self-direction gets understood in terms of expressing values. Then typically, behaviors are exercises of agency when they are expressions of the actor's values. So how do values get understood? Or perhaps more perspicuously for present purposes: how does valuing get understood? (Here, the relevant notion is subjective: chic and chastity may be values, but I don't value them.) Starting with desires looks unavoidable: where there are values there are also desires (Bratman 2007: 47–67; Harman 2000a: 135). However, not all desires involve values. Some desires, like my vague fancy to ask my neighbor what she paid for her new car, seem too faint to fund values, while others, like my momentary urge to call an old friend, seem too fleeting. The desires associated with value should be desires of some strength and duration. While one should probably concede the possibility of "just-this-once" valuings (Bratman 2007: 258)—Gradgrind might value looking up from his grindstone on a uniquely special occasion—this will not be the usual case.

To say that a desire endures is not to say that one is continuously experiencing the desire; better to say that many enduring desires, like a desire for regular dental check-ups, are "standing" desires that are (at most) occasionally present to consciousness (Stich *et al.* 2010: 195). The desire for regular dental check-ups may be a (standing) desire of long standing, and it may be a desire of considerable strength—one often has to go to heroic lengths in scheduling an appointment. Yet it seems strange to count such an uninspiring experience as involving a value. That's because the desire for regular check-ups is an instrumental rather an ultimate desire. I desire dental check-ups for the sake of vibrant health and a radiant smile rather, than as is said for the objects of ultimate desires, "for their own sake." If my desire for good health is an ultimate desire, my desire for health is at least partly independent of any beneficial consequences health brings (Stich *et al.* 2010: 150–1).

Then why not understand value in terms of ultimate desires with a certain strength and duration? That's a pretty good start, but even simple animals with simple desires, like a dog and his bone, may meet this standard. You might, like me, doubt that animals go in for valuing, but more important is that in humans, addictive and compulsive desires are characterized by strength, duration, and ultimacy. Strength and duration are obviously present; that's part of what makes compulsive desires so problematic. One can always quibble about ultimacy—do I desire pleasure for it's own sake or the sake of relaxation?—but it looks like compulsive desires are in the hunt. If anything, the objects of compulsive desire are desired not *for* their consequences, but *in spite of* their consequences; yet it's often wrong to say that people value the objects of their compulsive desires. Self-loathing is a familiar companion of addiction (Flanagan 2011: 282); while there may be "willing addicts" who value their fix, people often struggle against their compulsions. (Ultimacy can also depart from valuing in less sinister cases, with trivial ultimate desires.)

Another piece is needed. Perhaps it's something like endorsement, and only desires the desirer endorses are associated with value. We might try explicating this hierarchically, and say that my values are the desires I desire to have (Frankfurt 1988): it's because I desire to desire a healthy life that I value a disciplined and temperate lifestyle. But what's so special about these "second-order" desires, and what reason is there to favor the first-order desires that my second-order desires favor? And what about "third-order desires" for favored second-order desires? Where, in this thicket of desires and meta-desires, are we supposed to find the materials for agency (Bratman 1996; Ekstrom 2005: 49–51; Velleman 1992: 470–6; Watson 1975: 218)?

To go further, I'll appropriate a suggestion from Bratman (2007: 64–6): the desires properly associated with value are those desires the actor accepts in a determinative role for her practical planning. This acceptance is often manifested in behavior; when a desire is awarded a determinative role it typically will, all things equal, structure conduct. But this won't be enough, since the unwilling addict's unwelcome craving can also do so, and there's good reason to suppose she doesn't value drug use. For a desire to be associated with a value, it must also have a justificatory role: it must be something that the planner is amenable to employing in justification or defense of her plan, which the unwilling addict presumably would decline to do with her drug use.

The planner need not be aware of her willingness to assign this justificatory role; people may have desires, values, and plans that they are quite unaware of, and their behavior may express their values without their knowing that it does so.[5] This is a crucial feature of my account, since it makes room for agency in the absence of reflection. But now the pesky counterfactual fix has resurfaced: so understood, the justificatory requirement maintains that the actor would avow a justificational role for the desire in question, if he were subjected to the appropriate examination. As we'll see, the depths of the unconscious are muddy enough that the investigative process may be rather arduous; oftentimes, it isn't easy to determine whether someone holds a value, even when the someone is oneself. The attribution of value will often present epistemological difficulty; this, in turn, presents epistemological difficulty for the attribution of agency.

I'll return to the epistemological issue, but for now, note one further marker of value, non-fungibility: if the object of desiring can be replaced without loss—if life can go on pretty much as it did—then that object is not an object of value. In the event you're worrying about animal valuing, you might find this reassuring, since fungibility seems characteristic of animal desires. Much as it pains me to say it, I'm readily replaceable in my kitties' affections; for them, one warm lap is as good as another. Significant human relationships, on the other hand, aren't supposed to be so easily interchangeable: the jilted and bereaved may learn to love again, but some of what they lose may seem quite irreplaceable.

The non-fungibility requirement could also be erected as a bulwark against the somewhat unattractive thought that "mere needs" are values. If alternate modes of nutrition were readily available to humans, it might be that people could forgo eating with no loss; eating is the object of desire, yet doesn't have the "special-ness" associated with value. (That gourmets, gourmands, and other foodies could not switch without loss makes the point; they *do* value eating.) In the end, a mere needs exclusion might not be mandatory; in conditions of scarcity, the objects associated with mere needs can start to seem pretty special.

I suspect that non-fungibility is an imperfectly reliable marker of value, and the same may be said for other markers I've suggested. But I've now an adequate rubric: values are associated with desires that exhibit some degree of strength, duration, ultimacy, and non-fungibility, while playing a determinative-justificatory role in planning. It's likely that each of these markers may be present to varying degrees, or perhaps even absent, in the many and varying samples of valuing. Doubtless, there are better and worse samples, and there's plenty of room for

---

[5] Bratman (2007: 28, 67, 91, 165, 192) might demur; he apparently thinks of valuing and the exercise of agency as more reflective processes than do I. As would Levy (2011: 188–94), who holds that to pervasively influence behaviors, values must be consciously entertained; I take the evidence on unconscious determinants of behavior I present here to suggest otherwise.

contention around the margins. But we can now see enough of what value might look like to begin to see what agency might look like.

Before getting to the particular skeptical challenge at issue here, I should linger momentarily on a cluster of more established difficulties. Familiar theories of agency, it is sometimes argued, are afflicted with vicious regress (Arpaly and Schroeder 2014: 29–33; Buss 2012: 656). Consider accounts requiring some operation of mind, such as an instance of deliberation, for an exercise of agency. Since the required deliberation is itself an action, there ought be an operation of mind that confers agency on it, or else the eventuating action is not agential, because the originating deliberation is not agential. If, on the other hand, the deliberation *is* agential, a deliberative account seemingly requires a second deliberation conferring agential properties on the first. But now, we must ask whether the second deliberation is agential, and we're off on a regress.

The regress is generated by the assumption that exercises of agency must have antecedents that are themselves agential; accordingly, the most expedient way of evading the regress is by dispensing with this assumption, and declining to require a prior agency-conferring action for an exercise of agency (cf. Arpaly and Schroeder 2014: 42; Buss 2012). I'm neutral as to whether deliberative accounts can be formulated to take advantage of this expedient (for doubts, see Arpaly and Schroeder 2014: 33); where deliberative accounts are reflectivist accounts, as they often enough seem to be, I've got other concerns. What matters here is that valuational accounts like the one I'm defending make good this escape, for they locate agency not in an originating action, but in a valuational state of the agent, for which there is no further action required.

The regress of action is thereby avoided, but inconvenience remains, for we'll want to know something about the etiology of the relevant valuational states. Depraved upbringings or totalitarian cultures may coercively instill in their victims despicable values, and there's discomfort in claiming that the victims are responsible for behaviors governed by these values (Wolf 2003: 379–80): should those reared in the Hitler Youth to be blamed for their racism?

It's not clear that such people are possessed of—or rather, stuck with—values that are genuinely "unsheddable" (Mele 2009a: 470). There frequently appears "a not too onerous inferential route" from worse values to better (Maibom 2013: 276). For example, Greek slaveholders presumably regarded slavery as a terrible fate; they might reasonably be expected to have discovered that inflicting this misfortune on people much like themselves was deplorable (they might also have noticed that these people were in fact people much like themselves), and reasonably be held responsible for not reforming their values and behavior.

But suppose these inferential routes are generally impassable, and the despicable values of despicable people are typically unsheddable. Pursuing this thought, one fears, leads inexorably to skepticism, since the same might be said for *all* people, and *all* values; familial origins and cultural locations, whether malignant or benign, have profound influence on their subjects, and it is far from obvious this influence can be evaded. The formative influence of these circumstances looks to be a matter of luck—"constitutive luck" as it's called (Levy 2011: 29–35)—about which the individuals so constituted had little to do. (However lamentable the consequences of me not being born richer, smarter, and better looking, these aren't failings for which I ought be blamed.) The general point is that one is not responsible for much of who one is, and if who one is accounts for what one does, responsibility is jeopardized (Strawson 1994).

The constitution problem recalls the consternation dogging "historicist" accounts of responsibility, which require that morally responsible agents have appropriate causal histories. The trouble is that every behavior somewhere has decidedly non-agential origins. If responsible agency requires an unbroken history of responsible antecedents, we are, inevitably, dragged backwards to a place where agency fizzles out: your conceptus is causally implicated in your current condition, but it is surely not agentially implicated (cf. Mele 2006: 188–9).

To avoid this sort of skepticism, one might adopt a libertarian incompatibilism, and attempt to identify an event in an action's past that is undetermined by antecedent events (Kane 2000; cf. Fischer 2000). There's an end to history, on this approach, when we get to the libertarian's undetermined (or self-determined) event. On the other hand, if one wants to go compatibilist, the easiest way to avoid the journey is to refuse the first step, and source responsible agency in the current state of the agent as she acts (Frankfurt 1988: 54; 2002: 27). Formed this way, the valuational account says that if your action properly expresses your values, it's an exercise of agency, regardless of whence your values came.

This "currentism" doesn't deny that history is relevant: history is epistemologically relevant to the extent that one references a person's history in establishing whether her current state can support exercises of agency (Vargas 2013b: 269). So too, history is causally relevant: a person's past has much to do with whether or not she has the psychological capacities needed for the exercise of agency. But currentism does deny that responsibility is, as sometimes said (Fischer 2006: 236–9), "essentially" or "deeply" historical. For on this approach, once we have established that the agent was, at the time of action, in the appropriate condition, we know all that's needed to be known for the attribution of responsibility.

Currentism avoids skeptical regress, but avoiding skepticism better not be its only attraction. If the sole rationale for a theory is its avoidance of skepticism, that's not rationale enough (many anti-skeptical theories are dumb theories). I'll argue that, in addition, my theory has a further rationale: current valuational states make a compelling target for the reactive attitudes, which means the theory can provide an appropriate undergirding for responsibility relevant practices (cf. McKenna 2004: 182–3, 187–9).

No doubt, currentism requires some biting of bullets, arguably bullets of jaw-breaking dimensions (McKenna 2004: 171). I'm bound, for example, to maintain that the driver who hits a pedestrian while seriously impaired by alcohol is not responsible ("directly" or "non-derivatively" responsible, anyway) for the accident itself, but for his reckless drinking in a situation where he could reasonably expect to operate a motor vehicle. Personally, I don't find this too much of a mouthful, especially as the impaired driver getting in an accident (when he does) is accidental, in a way that injudicious drinking presumably is not. One implication of this is that liability to punishment for things like inebriated accidents may have to be justified on teleological grounds, like deterrence or communication of outrage. But teleological justifications of punishment, while not universally endorsed, are not manifestly implausible, so this admission needn't be a deal breaker.

Currentism also seems to go a little sour in cases involving strongly coercive indoctrination, such as that which Patty Hearst suffered when kidnapped by the Symbionese Liberation Army (SLA) in 1974. It strikes me as outrageous that Hearst was sentenced to 35 years for crimes she participated in while held by the SLA, and indeed, she was eventually pardoned. But to some eyes, Hearst became committed to the SLA; if her behavior at the time was an expression of her current values, my currentism seems to—wrongly—attribute her responsibility.

Maybe not. Either the cognitive and other capacities requisite for agency were substantially impaired by Hearst's treatment, or they were not substantially impaired. On the first reading, Hearst lacked the capacities associated with morally responsible agency, and currentism gets the intuitively plausible verdict. In the terms of a valuational account, one may fairly doubt whether it was Hearst's values finding expression in her behavior—or whether she was expressing values at all. If, on the other hand, there was no substantial impairment, and Hearst's values were being expressed, it looks like I'm bound to say she was responsible, but I think this a tolerable result (with Arpaly 2002: 162–68).

As a theoretical matter, I'm not sure that personal continuity is maintained through radical evaluative transformation (see Chapter 8), a realization which might help quell anxieties that in cases like Hearst's, read the second way, blaming the miscreant would be blaming the victim. For in such cases, it may be that the victim no longer exists, but has in effect been replaced by the miscreant, which, while a tragedy, is not a case of unwarranted blame. As an empirical matter, I expect the first reading represents the more usual case; indoctrination (that is, torture) like that suffered by Hearst, I'd speculate, frequently results in substantial impairment.

For the empirically less likely case of coercive indoctrination without impairment, there is some embarrassment for currentism, as can be seen when we contrast Two Jerks with identically unsavory values, and identically unimpaired psychologies, one the victim of coercive indoctrination, and the other with an ordinarily tolerable upbringing. Currentism has to bite the bullet here, and say both are equally responsible, which looks to violate considerations of fairness; it seems iniquitous to totally discount the past victimization, and treat both actors the same (cf. Levy 2011: 195–200). But again, this circumstance seems empirically unlikely; coercive indoctrination, I conjecture, will very often have responsibility-relevant effects on the current states, in which case the past victimization is not discounted (but indirectly counted).

If one must bite bullets, one's detention will fare better if the biting is fewer and farther between, so I'd rather have to say the awkward thing for unusual cases like the Two Jerks (and ditto for science fiction-y cases of "globally manipulated agents" (McKenna 2004; Mele 2009a). The historicist, it seems to me, scrambles to avoid awkwardness for the quite usual cases of agents with a past, and this is hardly a more enviable position. To be sure, others may count the costs differently, as historicists do, and the method of cases may very well end in "intuition stand-off" between historicists and currentists (Vargas 2006: 371). All the contestants can do, it seems to me, is attempt to optimize the balance of costs and benefits in their overall theories. And that is what I'm attempting.

My overall theory forms a nest (or mare's nest) of notions—agency/responsibility/reactive attitudes/self-direction/value—into a valuational account of agency. I've so far only a sketch, but there's enough in place to grapple with the skeptical difficulty. Skepticism in epistemology can be appreciated (as in fact it is) without there being an uncontroversial account of knowledge (as in fact there isn't), so long as there's reasonable conjecture about the epistemic conditions incompatible with knowledge, and reasonable concern that such conditions obtain. Similarly, I can vivify skepticism about agency without a fully realized theory of agency, by adducing relatively clear departures from agency.

I'm going to identify a class of phenomena that can undermine the exercise of agency, and ask how their presence may be ruled out when assessing people's behavior. Since the answer to this question is obscure, I'll argue, there is reason for skeptical anxiety. While the phenomena in question should be thought troubling on a wide range of anti-skeptical thinking about agency and moral responsibility, some approaches may be better suited to ameliorating skepticism than others. When it becomes clearer what this amelioration requires, we'll find what is needed is substantial departures from reflectivism. The theory I have just sketched will facilitate the required departures, because the expression of values associated with the exercise of agency need not be a reflective process.

Skepticism

The skeptical difficulty derives from taking *empirical adequacy* as a constraint on theory construction in moral psychology. Questions of empirical adequacy raise delicate issues in the philosophy of science, but I intend something fairly plain: theorizing about agency is constrained by systematic observation. Here, the paradigm of "systematic observation" is the contemporary human sciences; if this seems wrongheaded, I can do little more than refer you back to my remarks on method, and forward to what the method reveals. In present application, a commitment to empirical adequacy comes to the following: if systematic observation does not reveal that "normal, healthy, human adults" function, with some regularity, according to the criteria outlined by a theory of agency, so much the worse for the theory (difficulty demarcating "normal" and "healthy" noted; see also Chapter 4).

This rough thought carries an anti-skeptical conviction that people often act as agents. If you share this anti-skeptical conviction, and you take empirical adequacy seriously, you should find reflectivism, understood as the "conceptual" claim that reflection is necessary for the exercise of agency, unpalatable, for if the exercise of agency must be the exercise of reflective agency, we're unlikely to find many exercises of agency about.

For illustration, here's a simple *modus ponens*:

1. If reflectivism is true, it is not often warranted to attribute human beings the exercise of agency.
2. Reflectivism is true.

It is not often warranted to attribute human beings the exercise of agency.

This simple form elides a crucial assumption: the first premise gets its bite from a family of empirical observations indicating that reflection does not play the sort of role in self-direction that reflectivism supposes. Making things explicit, the first premise gets amended to:

Given a family of empirical observations, if reflectivism is true, it is not often warranted to attribute human beings the exercise of agency.

Now, the argument is not so simple, since developing the empirical observations is anything but. I defer that development to Chapter 3. For now, if the empirical observations are defensible, and reflectivism is true, we are left with the possibility that human beings pervasively fail to exercise agency.

Since I find skepticism unappealing, I'd rather reflectivism be false than the exercise of agency be uncommon: I want it to be the case that people pretty often function as agents. At the same time, I accept the empirical observations. I therefore favor morphing the skeptical *modus ponens* into an anti-reflectivist *modus tollens*:

1. If reflectivism is true, it is not often warranted to attribute human beings the exercise of agency.
2. It is often warranted to attribute human beings the exercise of agency.

Reflectivism is not true.

The first premise is the same as in the *ponens*, so this argument also requires the empirical backing I've deferred to Chapter 3. But what, aside from anti-skeptical faith, motivates the second premise? Adopting the contrary sensibility is certainly a defensible option: skepticism about agency appears in the philosophical canon, and the empirical literature I'll canvass is plausibly thought to lend it further plausibility. So maybe it's "so much the worse for people" and not "so much the worse for reflectivism."

Maybe not. Consider a preliminary remark: many psychopathologies are "disorders of volition" (Sebanz and Prinz 2006) that appear to involve breakdowns of self-direction. The rare case of "criminal insanity," where diminished responsibility eliminates or mitigates criminal liability, makes a flamboyant example (Neu 2012: 129–58; Robinson 1996), but more common afflictions also manifest impairments of agency. Most obvious are addictive and obsessive-compulsive disorders: some addicts very much want to quit, but aren't able to (Ainslie 2001; Elster 2000: 71–2), and some obsessives are repulsed by their obsessive thoughts, but can't escape them (Abramowitz and Houts 2002; Simpson and Fallon 2000). Uncertainties of psychiatry notwithstanding, there are frequently obvious differences between clinical and healthy populations, and some of the most important differences, it seems to me, are appropriately marked as differences in self-direction: healthy people control their behavior and order their lives in ways that many suffers of mental illness cannot. If that's right, normal and pathological psychologies can sometimes be distinguished along dimensions of agency (Buss 2012: 667–78), and it becomes tempting to suppose that the many people fortunate enough to enjoy some measure of mental health also enjoy, in some measure, the exercise of agency.

Not everyone thinks this contrast bears the weight I think it does. Wegner (2002: e.g. 88, 143–4) claimed that pathological failures of self-direction are closer to normal than you might have thought; on fuller examination, the exception turns out to be the rule. I'd be the first to admit that Wegner's concern with (or delight in) the outlandish phenomena was well placed: when one considers the evidence, it's harder than one thought to distinguish normal and pathological agency (and failures thereof). Nonetheless, I'm convinced the distinction is genuine, and points in the direction of agency. Substantiating this gesture is the task of my positive theory; why the task wants doing will become evident with Chapter 3's survey of the empirical literatures. But before getting there, we should consider two ways the skeptical problem might be nipped in the bud.

Scarcity

It's easy to envisage a tough-minded philosopher wondering what my fuss is about: "It's no surprise that agency is hard to come by," she might say. "That's a staple of the philosophical tradition. Morally responsible agency is not birthright, but an achievement, and it may be a scarce achievement. But scarcity does not entail skepticism, it simply manifests appropriately demanding standards for the exercise of agency."

This recalls a familiar response to empirically motivated skepticisms about character, a response suggesting that empirical questions concerning the psychological realizability of virtue are otiose, because virtue reflects a demanding normative standard, the realization of which is quite correctly expected to be rare (Kupperman 2001: 242–3). The same thing might be said for skepticism about agency: evidence suggesting that exercises of agency are scarce presents little difficulty, because exercising agency is an infrequent best case.

I'm unpersuaded by such defenses of virtue (Doris 2002: 110–12; 2010; Doris and Stich 2005: 120–2), but the thing to see here is that this expedient is quite uninviting when applied to agency. Dispiriting observations about the rarity of virtue boast a provenance going back at least to Plato, and have the advantage of conforming to what one sees on television. The allied claim for agency is less expected. If exercises of agency are rare, and the exercise of agency is usually a requirement of morally responsible behavior, it appears to follow that morally responsible behavior is similarly rare, which entails that much moral practice (at least in some cultural locales) is predicated on error. As I've said, numerous philosophers have asserted that no one is ever morally responsible. But this is a skeptical view, and views that closely approach it, as does the scarcity response, are themselves closely approaching skepticism. The scarcity response is not a *rejection* of skepticism, but a *capitulation* to skepticism—at best, a near capitulation.

Suppose, reasonably enough, that agency "comes in degrees," and some behaviors are more exercises of agency than others: it's an exercise of agency when you're holding up your end of a desultory conversation about the weather, although less so than when you're actively defending your pet theory against a determined interlocutor. With this in mind, it's not entirely surprising to say that agency par excellence is rare; for example, there may be highly demanding standards of agency associated with virtue—where the exercise of virtuous agency is maximally self directed, optimally rational, and consistently good—that are seldom met. The reflectivist might suggest something similar: fully responsible agency must be "fully reflective," but less reflective activity may also count as an exercise of agency, albeit to a lesser extent. Precifying this graded standard is a delicate operation: if too little reflection is required (at the limit, no reflection) the standard is no longer distinctively reflectivist, but if too much reflection is required, countless minimally reflective and unreflective activities that are putative exercises of morally responsible agency, such as goal-directed habits, are not in fact such exercises. Where these activities are excluded, one is saddled with a view so revisionary as to closely approach skepticism; for anti-skeptical triumph to be more than a pyrrhic victory, it should make ample room for the many activities that, while falling far short of agency par excellence, or fully reflective agency, are customarily treated as exercises of morally responsible agency.

Still, there's a tempting strategy for bulking up scarcity. Perhaps reflective agency is rare, but what of it there is tends to obtain on practically significant occasions; maybe it's quality rather than quantity that matters. Eventually, I'll develop some reservations about this approach, but at present, note that it continues in a strongly revisionist vein, since people are apparently held morally responsible for their conduct in a wide range of occasions, not just important ones. When you think about it, most days, and most lives, are pretty thin on Big Events: the quality of a life can often be found in little things, and it's sensible to think I'm no less responsible for my frequent lapses into minor inconsiderateness than I am for my infrequent eruptions of major rudeness. Of course, if this turns out to be misguided, the charge of revisionism turns out to be a recommendation. But it's not obviously misguided, and for those whose anti-skeptical predilections have them wanting more instances of agency instead of fewer, the scarcity response is unlikely to satisfy.

Capacity

I've been presuming: for someone to be counted as an agent, she should do what agents do. Possibly, this is contestable. Perhaps the heart of the matter is not the *exercise* of agency, but the *capacity* for agency (see Herman 2007: 11). Someone who so locates the issue might say: "The question of whether people are agents is not a question of what they're *doing*, but what they *are*. For surely I'm an agent when asleep, daydreaming, or absently scratching my ear. If an organism has the capacity for agency, they are an agent, whether they are exercising their agency or not."

Doubts about agency are supposed to follow from doubts about the exercise of agency, but the contemplated response rejects this inference, insisting that lack of capacity cannot be inferred from lack of exercise. Even if I never count backwards from 1264 while listening to *A Wunnerful, Wunnerful Christmas with Lawrence Welk* and eating a peanut butter and caper sandwich on rye, there's little reason to doubt I have the capacity to do so; I would perform such a feat in appropriate circumstances, like those with impressive financial inducements. Similarly, attributing agency to someone (tacitly) affirms a range of counterfactuals regarding the conditions in which they will exercise agency: when in circumstances appropriate to the exercise of agency, their behavior will be self-directed, and when not, it won't.

Setting the counterfactual range makes a tricky business, and missteps will result in an unseemly proliferation of agents: the brain dead, for example, who may function as agents when medicine is adequately advanced, and the dead, who may function as agents at whatever time the prophecies come to pass. Yet again, we've got the trouble of tightening up the counterfactuals, such that the dead don't get to be agents but the daydreamers do, much as we do for the equally troubled counterfactual analysis of dispositions (Bird 1998; Lewis 1973, 1997; Martin 1994). But however that trouble be solved, settling questions about the capacity for agency wouldn't settle questions about the exercise of agency, nor would it give us reason to think that the latter sort of questions are unimportant.

Suppose that future neurologists develop brain-imaging technology into an Agent Scanner, a technology that definitively identifies the agency capacity, and therefore allows the confident attribution of capacity without observation of the corresponding activity. Suppose further that under the auspices of a program designed to reform the practice of criminal law, a Universal Agent Scanning

Program is instituted, and the results are as expected: healthy human adults scan positive for the agency capacity, while "lower" non-human animals, human children (and the dead and brain dead!) test negative. Suppose now that the Agent Scanner turns out to have an alarming side effect: for the duration of every full moon, all scanned individuals, although continuing to "scan positive" and remaining capable of reflexive bodily movement, are unable to initiate coherent purposive activity. Until each full moon wanes, everyone has the capacity for agency, but nobody is exercising it. (The limited temporal duration of the affliction makes continued attribution of the capacity seem especially plausible, just as for sleep.)

The moral of this unlikely story: during the full moon, one may adopt a kind of skepticism about agency. Minimally, one should abjure attributions of moral responsibility for behaviors performed during this period, and it is the vitiating of responsibility that might be thought the sharp edge of agency skepticism. Suppose, finally, that the alarming side effect becomes permanent. Would "there are lots of agents, they just don't exercise agency" count as a compelling response to the skeptic? In fact, where the infirmity is permanent, there would seem to be rather little gained by continuing to attribute the agent capacity, Agent Scanner positives notwithstanding.

The important point is evident enough without pondering silly fictions. To focus solely on capacity provides limited traction on some of the most pressing questions associated with agency: when someone or other does something or other, are they justifiably attributed responsibility for what they did? These questions, it seems to me, are inescapably questions about whether that someone or other was *exercising* agency. Of course, if the question of whether someone has the capacity for agency is answered negatively, the question as to whether that someone is engaging in the activity of agency is also, and straightaway, answered negatively. But not so, in reverse: a positive answer regards capacity does not entail a positive answer regards activity.

It's true—on some readings trivially true—that the capacity for agency is necessary for the activity of agency. It's also true—on some readings trivially true—that the capacity for agency is insufficient for the activity of agency. What's importantly true is that discussion of agency doesn't end with capacity, because someone having the capacity for agency is quite compatible with her being in excusing conditions, such as those involving ignorance or coercion, that are incompatible with the exercise of agency and block the attribution of responsibility. I'll have plenty to say about the sorts of capacities associated with agency, but acknowledging the importance of capacities does not make questions about activity idle. Indeed, it's hard to see why questions of capacity should be so interesting, if not for their connection to activity. Failing to find exercises of agency does not entail skepticism about the capacity for agency, but neither does establishing the presence of the capacity answer skeptical questions about its exercise.

I'll therefore frame my questions in terms of whether or not someone is exercising agency, instead of whether or not someone is an agent. I suspect that often enough (in some cultures), thinking of one another as (more or less like) morally responsible agents is the default assumption in adult social interactions. Adults may encounter one another with the expectation that their opposite number is an agent, in contrast to their expectations for the rosebushes they prune, the dogs they walk, or the children they scold. Of course, the default can be destabilized, as when someone's behaviors or circumstances are deranged or disordered. Occasionally, it may be determined that an individual lacks the capacity for morally responsible agency; these individuals, like the seriously mentally ill, may be judged generally exempt from attributions of responsibility and the corresponding reactive attitudes (Doris 2002: 129–30; Watson 2004: 223–25). In other cases—very likely, the more usual cases—people are not exempted, but excused: there's no reason to suppose they lack the capacities requisite for agency, but they are subject to pressures, like duress, that make the exercise of such capacities impossible. Accordingly, the practice of attributing responsibility (or withholding responsibility) commonly appears concerned with the exercise of agency, even if it typically assumes the capacity for agency.

Articulating this assumption by means of contrast with other organisms, as is frequently done, need not be thought an arbitrary speciesism. Normal human adults have cognitive and psychological capacities that are necessary for the exercise of agency, which other critters lack, and normal healthy children will eventually have such capacities, while other critters never will. However, if this isn't speciesism, it may be a pernicious intellectualism, since it endorses differential treatment according to cognitive endowments, which might be thought to imply abhorrent conclusions, such as discrimination against the cognitively disabled. Not so: the issue here concerns conditions for agency, not entitlements to moral protections. The claim that certain cognitive endowments are required for agency and its exercise is, as we shall see, altogether plausible; it does not commit one to the deeply suspect assertion that agents are the only entities due moral regard.

Furthermore, nothing about assuming that adult humans are the paradigmatic agents rules out discovering non-human agents, be they artificial or extraterrestrial. Neither does it entail denying that some of the known non-human organisms—smart animals such as dolphins, apes, and elephants—may, sometimes, to some extent, exercise agency. Nor does it entail denying that human organisms with a range of cognitive attainments may exercise agency. In the known world, it can fairly be supposed that it's adult *Homo sapiens* who are most frequently found exercising agency; nevertheless, agency admits of degrees, and some degree of agency might be exercised by organisms with lesser cognitive attainments.

Signpost

If reflectivism is true, and a certain empirical picture of human cognition and behavior is also true, skepticism threatens: for if the exercise of agency requires the exercise of reflective agency, human beings don't exercise agency very often. Two initially appealing responses to this skepticism, one adverting to scarcity and the other to capacity, are less than fully satisfying. I therefore favor a different scheme: resist skepticism by jettisoning reflectivism. To make the need for such a scheme apparent, I need to show that the "certain empirical picture" is true. It's time, then, to consider the facts.

3

Skepticism

If you've worked in an office, you're probably familiar with "honor box" coffee service. Everyone helps themselves to stewed coffee, adds to the lounge's growing filth, and deposits a nominal sum in the honor box, with the accumulated proceeds being used to replenish supplies. Notoriously, this system often devolves into a tragedy of the commons, where too many people drink without paying. Unless some philanthropic soul goes out of pocket to cover free-riders, the enterprise ends in the red, and everyone's back to extortionate prices at the cafe.

Fortunately, the tragedy of the honor box may be readily ameliorated; if images of eyes are placed prominently near the coffee service, deposits increase. Or so Bateson and her colleagues (2006) found: the take in a Psychology Department's honor box (computed by amount contributed per liter of milk consumed) was nearly three times as large when the posted payment instructions were augmented with an image of eyes as when they were augmented with an image of flowers (Figure 3.1).

In other studies, displaying eye images has been associated with:

- increased generosity in a "dictator game," where people decide how much of a windfall they will share with another person (Haley and Fessler 2005; cf. Rigdon *et al.* 2009);
- increased donations to a communal pot in a "public goods game," where people decide how much of a windfall to keep and how much to contribute to a shared resource (Burnham and Hare 2007);
- decreased littering in a self-service cafeteria, where patrons bus their own tables (Ernest-Jones *et al.* 2011).

The eyes don't have to be especially realistic; stylized "eyespots" can do the trick (Figure 3.2).

On the standard interpretation, the eyes remind people that they may be seen—not so easy to stiff the honor box in front of a disapproving colleague— and pay a reputational cost for freeriding (Bateson *et al.* 2006: 412; Haley and

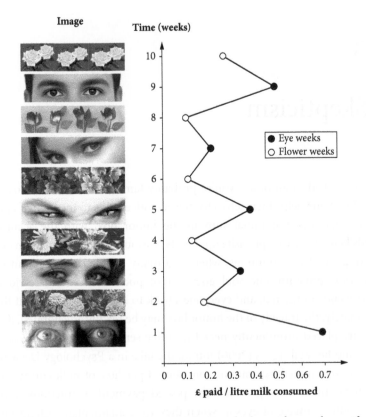

Figure 3.1 The Eyes Have It: honor box contributions higher with eyes than with flowers (Pounds paid per liter of milk consumed as a function of week and image type; from Bateson *et al.* 2006: 413)

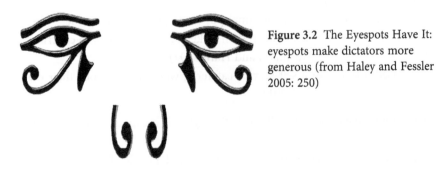

Figure 3.2 The Eyespots Have It: eyespots make dictators more generous (from Haley and Fessler 2005: 250)

Fessler 2005: 254). Since human beings are social organisms who are sensitive to reputational considerations, they may thereby be moved to donate.[1]

Participants in these studies are not typically debriefed, so we don't know for sure what they were thinking. But the most likely reading is that people were, in a sense, not thinking much of anything. That is, the Watching Eyes Effect is supposed to involve unconscious, effortless, processing, rather than conscious, concerted calculation; the eyes are hypothesized to influence behavior without those influenced being aware (Bateson *et al.* 2006: 413; Haley and Fessler 2005: 254; Rigdon *et al.* 2009: 359; Tane and Takezawa 2011: 24). Given how much social perception human beings have to do, and how quickly they have to do it, it wouldn't be surprising if they were able to do it without exerting conscious effort. Conversely, it's unlikely that people explicitly reason, "Ah, a picture of eyes. That reminds me! I'm a social organism, and mindful of my reputation. Free-riders may pay a reputational cost. I had better behave pro-socially."

If people aren't typically aware of the Watching Eyes Effect when they're being affected by it, what might they think, if they found out afterwards? A cheapskate with a policy of free-riding might feel a little resentful; he's been made to do something he doesn't judge sensible. A more upright sort might think she's done the right thing, but not for the right reasons; doing it because you're watched is not the same thing as doing it because it's decent, honest, or fair. Those who favor fair play only when it burnishes their reputation might also have qualms, since Watching Eyes may influence people in conditions conducive to anonymity (e.g. Haley and Fessler 2005: 250). In none of these cases does "I did it because of the eye spots," sound like a compelling rationale.

The Watching Eyes Effect is part of a large family of studies identifying influences on behavior that are both unconscious and unexpected. From the perspective of agency, the unconscious part is interesting, since it can be hard to control what one is unaware of. But more interesting is the unexpected part— unexpected from the perspective of practical reasoning. Like Watching Eyes, many studies identify causes of behavior that are not plausibly taken as reasons for behavior. Talk of reasons is philosophically dangerous talk, but one doesn't need a fancy theory to appreciate the difficulty. A simple, broadly subjective, account here serves: when someone treats a consideration as a reason, they

---

[1] As usual, results are mixed across different experimental conditions (Ernest-Jones *et al.* 2011: 176–7). For instance, Tane and Takezawa (2011) failed to find the effect when participants were in a dark soundproof room, where the salience of reputation may be muted. A meta-analysis of seven dictator game studies by Nettle *et al.* (2013) found that Watching Eyes did not "robustly" increase the mean donation, but did robustly increase the odds of people donating something rather than nothing.

should be willing to treat that consideration as a justification for their judgment or behavior. The notion of justification has its own difficulties, but once again, an elaborate theory isn't needed (and still less, need one be attributed to the reasoner). People commend and defend what they think and do, both to themselves and others, everyday, and when they do, they are engaged in a reason-giving, justificatory practice. For my purposes, the relevant divergence of reasons and causes obtains when they would decline to reference the causes of their behavior and judgment in this practice. Unrefined as this characterization may be, it will be sufficient to articulate the skeptical challenge.

Disturbances

Ideally, a philosopher exploiting empirical materials would advert only to observations of "the textbook variety" (Becker 1998: 76, 123): those supported by robust experimental literatures, and uncontroversial enough to appear as accepted generalizations in standard texts. Findings of the sort I'll describe have appeared and reappeared in a mass of articles, monographs, and anthologies,[2] so I won't be making radical departures from the textbook standard.

Nevertheless, some controversy is unavoidable. At this writing, social psychology is being shaken by charges that many published findings, including numerous iconic findings, do not replicate when tested by independent investigators. Cyberspace is thick with skirmishes between Replicators, who broadcast the failed replications, and Finders, who insist that their findings are real. Viewed from a safe distance, it's all good fun, the sort of academic kerfuffle that makes for diverting reads in those corners of the media where academic kerfuffles get covered. Unfortunately, I'm not at safe distance. Here, as elsewhere, I've repurposed psychological findings in philosophical argumentation. Awkward for me, if the findings are false.

Popular reports on RepliGate link the controversy to notorious cases of scientific misconduct (Bartlett 2013; Yong 2012). But the big problem's not a few cheaters, or even a few more than a few cheaters; if the Replicators are right, the infirmity results from *standard practice* in experimental psychology. Consider the disciplinary norm for "statistical significance," a "*p*-value" of 0.05 or less. When a finding is reported with this value, it means that if the experiment were

---

[2] The mass is substantial. *Monographs:* Greene 2013; Haidt 2006; Haybron 2008; Kahneman 2011; Mlodinow 2013; Stanovich 2004, 2011; Wegner 2002; Wilson 2002. *Anthologies:* Bargh and Uleman 1989; Bornstein and Pittman 1992; Chaiken and Trope 1999; Evans and Frankish 2009; Hassin *et al.* 2005; Vazire and Wilson 2012; Wyer 1997.

run 100 times, and the phenomenon is not real, that is, if the null hypothesis is true, the finding would appear "by chance" five times or fewer. The 0.05 is supposed to warrant confidence that the effect in question is real, but it also entails that "about 5% of the time when researchers test a null hypothesis that is true (i.e. when they look for a difference that does not exist) they will end up with a statistically significance difference" (Pashler and Harris 2012: 531).

This depiction perhaps underestimates the appearance of false positives in the published literature. Some grounds for suspecting this are dauntingly technical, and involve complex models requiring contestable assumptions (Pashler and Harris 2012: 531–2; cf. Ioannidis 2005). Others—the most prominent being the Publication Bias and File Drawer Effect—are more easily grasped. The Publication Bias is a pervasive tendency for psychology journals to publish only effects that are novel and statistically significant, with the result that most investigators, unless they strike gold every time, are likely to have a File Drawer full of failures to find significant effects, very often in the immediate vicinity of those effects their publications indicate exist. In the worst case, assuming a significance threshold of 0.05, a researcher who only investigated phenomena that did not exist could have 95 failed experiments for each 5 successful ones they publish. If all researchers were worst case, *every* published finding could be a false positive capitalizing on chance, an alarming circumstance concealed in vast File Drawers of failure (Simonsohn 2012: 597).

It's probably not exactly like this, but neither is it completely unlike this. Experimenters start with a protocol, and if it doesn't produce the hoped for result, they tweak, and re-tweak, the protocol in order to find their finding. Along the way, some failed experiments that ought be treated as non-occurrences of an effect are instead treated as imperfectly designed pilot studies and interred in File Drawers. No surprise then, if there are considerable numbers of unpublished failures haunting many published successes.

That much might be good faith science; there's a thin line between refining a protocol and the not-quite-kosher-not-quite-misconduct "questionable research practice" of "selectively reporting" only findings congenial to one's research program in the papers one submits for publication. But other tricks of the trade, informally known as "*p*-hacking," are rather shadier. For example, there's "optional stopping," the practice of continually checking results and halting an experiment as soon as $p < 0.05$ is reached, which substantially increases the probability that significant findings are a function of chance; during data collection, the *p*-value fluctuates, and even where there is no effect it will sometimes reach 0.05. Such practices are likely to be common: in an anonymous survey of some 2,000 psychologists, over 50 percent admitted selective reporting, and over 20 percent admitted optional stopping (John *et al.* 2012: Figure 1).

All this considered, one might predict that many published findings will fail to replicate (capitalizing on chance is a chancy business). Unfortunately, it's hard to know exactly what's going on: the Publication Bias militates against the appearance of failed replications, but it also militates against the appearance of *successful* replications, because journals typically require novel findings (though failed replications may now be getting published more frequently; e.g. Pashler *et al.* 2013). The 64,000-dollar question concerns what molders in all those File Drawers: how many interesting but non-significant failed replications, and how many significant but boring successful replications?

The Replicators suspect there's a lot of failure moldering, and if that's right, tribulation is inevitable, when the published work gets checked. In fact, on a website serving as a repository for replication attempts, psychfiledrawer.org, there seems to be a fair bit of just that. Among the hardest hit are some studies most congenial to the arguments I'm making here, those involving subliminal "priming" of behavior.[3] The classic is an experiment by Bargh and colleagues (1996: 236–7) that found exposure to words invoking elderly stereotypes (e.g. *grey, wrinkle, Florida*) resulted in healthy young people walking more slowly, without being able to attribute their performance to the "semantic prime."

The Infirm Words Effect was much celebrated; I celebrated it myself (Doris 2009: 57; Merritt *et al.* 2010: 374), since I thought the existence of such quirky influences on behavior undermined philosophically standard accounts of agency. My merrymaking was truncated, however, for along came a failed replication by Doyen and associates (2012), joining another failure to replicate by Pashler and colleagues (2011) that appeared on psychfiledrawer.org. In response, Bargh (2012) noted two replications of Infirm Words appearing in a top journal (Cesario *et al.* 2006; Hull *et al.* 2002), together with two replications on science television (!). Moreover, the effect has appeared in a range of domains: exposure to material associated with stereotypes of the elderly may also slow decision-making (Dijksterhuis *et al.* 2001; Kawakami *et al.* 2002) and weaken memory performance (Dijksterhuis *et al.* 2000; Levy 1996).

My hunch is that the priming studies have themselves been victims of a prejudice, the Incredulity Bias, which presumes that if a study reports a surprising

---

[3] According to Cameron *et al.* (2012), "[p]riming involves presenting some stimulus with the aim of activating a particular idea, category, or feeling and then measuring the effects of the prime on performance in some other task." Not much in a name, methinks: this description looks to hold for a variety of experimental manipulations.

finding, there must be something fishy. On the other hand, there's also a Surprising Effect Bias, where editors favor incredible findings, in hopes of garnering attention for their journal. (Less cynically: if scientific findings weren't surprising, why would we need experiments and publications?) In a perfect world, unlikely findings would be both published and scrutinized—and maybe that world's not so far from the world we have. Still, the evidence appears to be badly mixed; can any conclusion—save that we've got a mess on our hands—be safely drawn?

Hard to say, partly because the feuding parties feud about what should be counted as successful replication. In a *direct* replication, the new investigator tries to exactly copy what the original investigator did. Variation in time, place, and resources means the copies won't be identical (the Pashler *et al.* attempted replication of Infirm Words is listed as "fairly exact" on psychfiledrawer.org), but if they're close enough, they may bear quite closely on the question of whether the original finding can be trusted. *Conceptual* replications, on the other hand, don't exactly follow the original; they aim to extend the effect, by testing whether the process at issue obtains in other domains. Thus, the extension of Infirm Words from walking to memory might be counted as a conceptual replication, suggesting not only that the original finding was tracking something real, but also that the finding may generalize beyond the original domain.

For the academic psychologist, conceptual replications are more professionally advantageous, since they, unlike direct replications, meet the novelty standard for publication. The problem with conceptual replication is that it ain't replication; if a study's different enough from the original to count as novel, its finding could be real while the original finding is not (or vice versa). Moreover, failed conceptual replications may be even more likely to end in File Drawers than failed direct replications. If an investigator fails to conceptually replicate a study with which he is sympathetic, he may be tempted to treat the failure as an injudiciously large deviation from the original study instead of failure to replicate, meaning a (non-) finding that ought to raise questions about the original study doesn't get treated as doing so. At the same time, successful conceptual replications will frequently be deemed publication worthy, so the practice of conceptual replication may be biased in favor of validating previously published effects (Pashler and Harris 2012: 533).

This doesn't mean conceptual replications say nothing about the reality and generality of an effect; when a cluster of conceptual replications accrues around a finding, it should increase confidence that there's something real around which the cluster is accruing. Of course, if you're in sympathy with the Replicators, you might have doubts about many studies comprising the cluster. But something like the Publication Bias is arguably present in all scientific journals, so to require dismissing all published research where the bias is present "leads," as one psychologist (himself a Replicator) put it, "to the absurd conclusion that all published scientific knowledge should be ignored" (Simonsohn 2012: 598).

Maybe the absurd conclusion isn't so absurd. In a paper entitled "Why Most Published Research Findings Are False," Ioannidis (2005) deployed statistical techniques to argue just that: the majority of science is not to be believed. Certainly, the *tsuris* goes beyond psychology. Scientific medicine and genetics have both been unsettled by controversies akin to RepliGate (e.g. Begley and Ellis 2012), with the debate in genetics involving strikingly similar concerns about direct versus conceptual replication (e.g. Karg *et al.* 2011; Munafò *et al.* 2009; Risch *et al.* 2009). Does this mean the findings of these fields should be ignored? Absolutely—the minute we have something better. No doubt there's some trouble in genetics. But this doesn't mean we're better off consulting soothsayers about heredity than we are consulting geneticists. Likewise, there's some trouble in medical research (which has been in a bit of a rut since identifying the importance of good hygiene in controlling infectious disease). But that doesn't mean we're better off consulting crystal healers about cancer than we are consulting oncologists.

And so too, there's some trouble in psychology. But that doesn't mean we're better off trusting "common sense" than we are trusting the best available systematic study. There's good, bad, and indifferent in psychology, just as in all of science, and the existence of the bad and indifferent shouldn't dissuade us from figuring out what the good is. Doubtless, numbers of scientific findings should be discarded, but if *all* scientific findings were cast aside, we'd have a lot bigger problems than working out the right account of agency.

When the dust of RepliGate has settled, some currently venerated findings may be less venerated, and some currently commonplace research practices may be less commonplace. But we're talking about an extensive and variegated field, and it's not easy to predict what the casualties will be, and what forms retrenchment will take. (Norms requiring larger sample sizes would make a good start; larger samples reduce random error, because more observations decrease the influence of random fluctuation, thus reducing the margin of error (Fraley and Vazire 2014)). Priming effects range over perception, behavior, and motivation, and in each domain, effects vary with both individual differences and situational variation (Loersch and Payne 2011). With this much diversity, indiscriminate statements like "priming studies have been challenged" don't mean very much. Difficulty with one priming study does not entail difficulty for all studies in its domain, and difficulty with priming studies in one domain does not entail difficulty for all priming studies. Still less does difficulty with priming studies entail that all experimental psychology is in the soup.

When facing conditions of scientific uncertainty, caution is in order. This is nothing new: scientific conditions are *always* conditions of uncertainty, and caution is *always* in order. (Where certainty obtains, what call is there for science?) There's no science without a story, and if a large body of perplexing fact is to have theoretical utility, the theorist is forced to make editorial decisions that may require taking sides in scientific controversy. Conscientiously assuming this risk requires identifying the *drift* of a literature, or better yet, a range of literatures, where we find the strongest trends in results, even as we acknowledge the existence of results, and the possibility of future results, that don't conform to these trends.

Reservations about the Publication Bias notwithstanding, patterns of conceptual replication are one important way to get the drift. Also important are meta-analyses, which average the results of a large number of studies, and allow more confident assessment of effects than is possible with a single study. For example, a meta-analysis of 167 priming studies (Cameron *et al.* 2012) found moderate relationships between priming manipulations and both behavioral measures and explicit attitude measures, while a meta-analysis of 65 priming effects in social cognition found effect sizes ranging from "small to medium" to "medium to large" (DeCoster and Claypool 2004: 9). These meta-analyses give reason to think priming effects are real, even as individual priming studies receive unflattering scrutiny.

In any event, the broader lesson remains: don't lean too heavily on any one study, or one series of studies, in theory construction. All the more so, where there have been difficulties with replication. With this caution in mind, I'll resist my impulse to make hay with the Infirm Words Effect, as delightful as I find it. But even if numerous celebrated priming studies turned out to be problematic, the philosophical position I advance would still enjoy abundant support.

The support is derived from a wealth of research on "dual process" theories of cognition. I'll get to the substance of this research momentarily, but the present point is that these theories are founded on quantities of convergent evidence drawn from across the human sciences (e.g. Evans and Frankish 2009; Stanovich 2004). Accordingly, patches of unrest such as RepliGate are insufficient to repudiate the psychological theory that serves, broadly speaking, as the inspiration for my approach. If a wide range of evidence from a wide range of research programs were *all* discredited, I'd experience serious discomfort. I'm wagering this won't happen. It might: such are the hazards of empirically motivated theorizing. But in current epistemic conditions, I'm making a sensible wager.

Divisions

Dual process theory partitions human cognition in two general types: *automatic* ("Type I") processing is supposed to be fast, effortless, unconscious, and uncontrolled, while *analytic* ("Type II") processing is supposed to be conscious, effortful mentation effecting "executive control" over thought and behavior (Stanovich 2004: 37–47; cf. Wilson 2002: 52–3). Evidently, analytic processing supports practical reasoning of the sort discussed in philosophy: reflection about what to do and think, and why to do and think it (cf. Frankish and Evans 2009: 15). Automatic processing, on the other hand, appears "deeply unintelligent," and unworthy of the title *reasoning* (Stanovich 2004: 37–9); it is implicated in humble behaviors like wrinkling your nose at a noxious smell, fiddling with your pen during a boring meeting, or smiling back at a stranger who smiles at you.

There's considerable difficulty about how dual process theory should be interpreted, and how best to understand the cognitive structures and neural anatomy implicated in the different sorts of processing (Moors and De Houwer 2006; Samuels 2009; Stanovich 2004). It's doubtful that all psychological phenomena can be bunched in only two baskets (Stanovich 2011), and it's likely that much human behavior is simultaneously supported by both analytic and automatic processing (Merritt *et al.* 2010: 372–3; Railton 2009). Nevertheless, approaches that can be characterized as dual process have been proposed for almost everything psychologists study: attention (Schneider and Shiffrin 1977), learning (Reber 1993), memory (Roediger 1990), perception (Norman 2002) reasoning (Evans and Over 1996), decision-making (Kahneman and Frederick 2002), person interpretation (Gilbert *et al.* 1988) delay of gratification (Metcalfe and Mischel 1999), psychopathology (Beevers 2005), and moral judgment (Cushman *et al.* 2010).

Doubtless, this diversity of work reflects a diversity of methodological and theoretical perspectives. But for my purposes, what's crucial is an observation that's very widely endorsed: different kinds of cognitive processing can proceed independently of one another. A study of anterograde amnesiacs—patients for whom brain injury has impaired their ability to retain new experiences, while sparing many other cognitive functions—makes a good illustration (Warrington and Weiskrantz 1970: Experiment 2). When asked to recall words from a previously encountered list, or asked to identify previously encountered words on a new list, amnesiacs performed worse than healthy controls. But when given word fragment identification and stem completion tests where performance was helped by previous exposure to the words, amnesiacs performed about as well as controls; the improved performance on these tasks over the explicit recall tasks suggests that these patients are able to make use make use of information they cannot recall.

Similar patterns have been repeatedly demonstrated in healthy populations. Among the many "varieties of memory" identified by psychologists (Tulving 2007) are two (more or less) distinct memory processes: an explicit process involving the conscious, effortful, recall of information, and an implicit process that retains information which is exploited in cognition without conscious effort, and may remain hidden from consciousness even when effort is made (Roediger 1990; Schacter 1987; cf. Roediger 2003).

This isn't an obviously unintelligent arrangement: if you had to engage in constant efforts of recall to perform every task, even simple things, like knotting neck ties or tying shoes, would be onerously cumbersome. At the same time, conscious efforts have their place, as when explaining to beginners how to do things, like tie knotting and shoe tying, you usually accomplish without thought. The two memory processes serve the organism in different ways: in some circumstances, slow and thoughtful is what's wanted, while in others, quick and thoughtless does the trick.

Unfortunately, things aren't always so tidy. The messy cases are those where the two processes are not independent, but opposed: the outputs of automatic processing can conflict with the outputs of simultaneously executed analytic processing, and vice versa. For an informal demonstration, consider the Müller-Lyer illusion (Figure 3.3), where two equal lines look unequal in length, because one line has outward pointing tails making it look longer, and the other has inward pointing tails, making it look shorter (Stanovich 2004: 41–3). Most everybody's seen this (or almost everybody who's read a little psychology), and most everybody who's seen it knows it is an illusion (cultural differences in susceptibility noted: McCauley and Henrich 2006). But in this case, believing isn't seeing: perception doesn't listen to reason, and the lines continue to look different in length. (When I teach Müller-Lyer, I terminate the lines at the same blackboard seams to demonstrate their actual length.) At the same time, reason is happy to return the favor; the illusion does not cause you to question your judgment, once you've recognized the illusion for what it is. I'll call this circumstance, where different psychological processes issue divergent outputs with regard to the same object, *incongruence* (cf. Merritt *et al.* 2010: 371–7).

Figure 3.3 Your Eyes Deceive You: The Müller-Lyer Illusion

Incongruence takes various forms. There's *akrasia*, which can be understood as desire moving someone to act against their better judgment (Holton 2009: 72). This sort of practical infirmity often comes with an experience of conflict, as when one succumbs to an unwelcome temptation. In the cases of incongruence that interest me most—and, I think, the cases that press the hardest questions about agency—there's frequently no experience of conflict; it's not as though reason is somehow overwhelmed, and people knowingly (if reluctantly) act against it, as happens with temptation. Instead, the behavior is influenced by a process that the actor is unaware of, and would not recognize as a reason justifying the behavior, were she so aware, as is apparently the case in the Watching Eyes Effect. Here, reason is not overwhelmed, but somehow "bypassed" (cf. Nahmias 2011: 560–3). Rather than joining battle and losing, reason doesn't take the field.

In many such cases, one doesn't suspect reason would work up much of a sweat, if it did enter the fray: I'd guess it's not unduly difficult to disregard the Watching Eyes, when made aware of them. That's part of what makes the phenomena so disturbing: hardly surprising that people can be moved by strong desires, rather more so, that they can be moved by factors that are scarcely intelligible as the objects of desire.

Not every case of bypassing is a case of incongruence; when one reflexively pulls one's hand from a hot stove, reason is not engaged, but avoiding pain and tissue damage is something reason can respect. Conversely, not every case of incongruence is a case of bypassing in the sense I'm after here; my desire for a second slice of pâté runs counter to my considered judgments about what I ought do for my health, but this is a conflict of which I'm painfully aware, and when better judgment loses out, it's not because it was given no opportunity to compete. The examples I'll draw from the empirical literature will tend to involve incongruence with bypassing; these cases are different from philosophical stand-ards like *akrasia*, and they pose different challenges to agency.

Since I've just been reporting on scientific controversy, in what I hope was a fair-minded way, I should take a moment to thump the table. On just about any reading of the psychology literature, it is apparent that the existence of incon-gruent processing is *not* in doubt—any contention afflicting particular studies notwithstanding. It is this *un*controversial empirical observation on which my argument and theory centrally relies. To be sure, I'm putting this observation, which I'm confident large numbers of psychologists regard as uncontentious, to work in service of conclusions that I'm confident large numbers of philosophers will regard as contentious. That's why I'm resorting to argument and theory. But to say my position is philosophically controversial is not to say it is founded in equally controversial psychology. I've taken care to acknowledge the existence of scientific debate, and the inescapable truth that progress sometimes requires partisanship, but it is no less important to acknowledge that my central empirical observation approaches a commonplace.[4] Now, the evidence for it.

Incongruence

I'll start with an amusing demonstration of the Pronoun Effect (Gardner *et al.* 1999: Experiment 1; cf. Brewer and Gardner 1996: 89–90; Gardner *et al.* 2002). There, participants were asked to circle the pronouns in a written paragraph about a visit to the city. One group was given a version featuring first personal plural pronouns (*we, ours*), while the other group was given identical text, except that first personal singular pronouns (*I, mine*) were substituted for plurals, so that some people read about a social trip, and others read about a solo excursion. When completing a values questionnaire, those who had read the social text were more likely to identify "collectivist" values (e.g. belongingness, friendship, family safety) as a "guiding principle in their lives," while those who read the solo text were more likely to so identify "individualist" values (e.g. freedom, independence, choosing one's own goals). The effect is not limited to values: in laboratory studies, the plural prime increased the "field" sensitivity of visual perception (Kühnen *et al.* 2001: 405–6), and the likelihood of offering a bribe, both tendencies associated with "collectivist" cultural perspectives (for a supportive meta-analysis, see Oyserman and Lee 2008).

Pronouns? In different times and places, different things matter differently: the temple and the tavern, like the boardroom and the bedroom, don't celebrate the same things, and quite properly so. But should conviction vary according to the grammar of one's reading material? It would make an unconventional justification, when forsaking friendship for independence, to observe that you'd just read an autobiography loaded with singulars (in what I suspect is the unlikely event you were aware of the influence). What counts as reasonable justification is, of course, debatable; for one of countless examples, think of controversy about whether partiality based on family, friendship, or nationality is ethically

---

[4] To re-emphasize: the conclusions I draw from the commonplace are contestable. Nahmias (2007), Railton (2009), Suhler and Churchland (2009), Vargas (2013a), Wigley (2007), and Wu (2013) are philosophers who apparently favor more sanguine readings of the literature on automatic processing, while Levy and Bayne (2004) seem to share a bit more of my skeptical anxiety. In psychology, Kihlstrom (2008) has energetically critiqued "the doctrine of automaticity," but the claims he associates with it, such as that "consciousness plays little or no functional role in thought and action," are stronger than anything I defend.

appropriate (Jollimore 2008; Keller 2007, 2013). But there are plenty of cases where ethical judgments are influenced by factors that *obviously* lack justificatory force, and it seems surpassingly unlikely that people would regard such factors as reasons. For instance, those faced with Tversky and Kahneman's (1981) famous "Asian Disease Problem," favored different responses to a hypothetical epidemic depending on whether the intervention was described in terms of the number who would be *saved* or the number who would *die*, despite the fact that the expected mortality was identical under both descriptions. This study exemplifies an extensive research tradition on "heuristics and biases" in cognition, which indicates that ethically arbitrary factors—for the Asian Disease Problem, how the problem was verbally "framed"—can strongly influence moral judgment (Doris and Stich 2005; Horowitz 1998; Sinnott-Armstrong 2006, 2007d; Sunstein 2005). A similar lesson derives from work on emotion and moral cognition (Cameron *et al.* 2013; Eskine *et al.* 2011; Kelly 2011: 101–52), which indicates that emotions (such as disgust at a gross picture) can influence moral judgments (such as by making them more punitive) to which they bear no justificatory relation.

This divergence exemplifies what I'm calling incongruence, which is manifest not only in cognition, but also in behavior. Consider "implicit egotism," where folks (frequently unconsciously) prefer things associated with them, no matter how inconsequential the associations. In the Name Letter Effect, people favor letters that appear in their own names (Kitayama and Karasawa 1997; Nuttin 1985, 1987), while in the Birth Date Effect, people favor things associated with their birthdays (Kitayama and Karasawa 1997; cf. Finch and Cialdini: 1989: 224–6). Implicit egotism may influence moral behavior: Miller and colleagues (1998) found that people were more likely to cooperate in a prisoner's dilemma game when they believed their opposite number shared their birthday, while Burger and colleagues (2004: Study 2) found that women donated twice as much to charity when the solicitor wore a name tag indicating that she shared the prospective donor's first name. Few ethical theories, I presume, would find the materials for justification here.

So far, we've a suggestive run of laboratory studies, but we'll want to know how lab relates to life. Implicit egotism seems a likely thing to look for "in the wild," since it might be thought to fund real world phenomena like sports fandom, where fanaticism is fired by the flimsiest of associations. In fact, Pelham and colleagues (2002) discovered evidence for implicit egotism in public information such as Social Security records, census data, and the membership rolls of professional organizations: across ten studies, the results uniformly indicated that implicit egotism influences major life decisions. For example, "women were about 18% more likely to move to states with names resembling their first names than they should have been based on chance"—36 percent more likely for the perfect matches, Virginia and Georgia (Pelham *et al.* 2002: 474).

The effect also appears in career choices: Pelham's group (2002: 480) found that men named *Geo*ffrey or *Geo*rge were 42 percent more likely than expected to be *geo*scientists, compared to the frequency of names used as controls, such as Daniel, Kenneth, and Bennie. It's not just geoscientists: you might think that your *den*tist is in it for the money (if you don't much like him), or to help others (if you do), but would you have thought that the decision to spend his professional life poking about in the fetid maws of an ungrateful public had something to do with the fact that his name is *Den*nis (Pelham *et al.* 2002: 479–80)? Where you live and work matter: too much, one might think, to let the decision be influenced by the letters of your name.

Names might sometimes be tie-breakers, I guess: all things equal, why shouldn't Georgia have a slight preference for living in Georgia instead of Carolina, and Dennis for dentistry over the law? At least, they'd have material for conversation starters. But I suspect the percentage of races running *that* close will be rather small; for name similarity to fund a rational preference, it seems to me, one would need to be running near a dead heat.

Not everyone is convinced about the potency of names; Simonsohn (2011a, b) argues that the findings of Pelham and colleagues are "spurious" and admit of alternate explanations. For example, the Dennis the Dentist Effect might be a cohort-confound stemming from changes in a population's distribution of names, rather than implicit egotism (Simonsohn 2011a: Study 6). Name popularity fluctuates over time: just as the mob of little Jennifers and Jessicas in daycare gives way to a mob of little Isabellas and Sophias, the distribution of names in the working age population varies temporally. For example, if Walter is an "older" name than Dennis, the Dr. Walters will retire before the Dr. Dennises, resulting in a disproportionate number of Dr. Dennises in the dentist population. If there is a cohort effect, we should expect to find a disproportion of Dennises relative to Walters in the *lawyer* population similar to that in the dentist population, which is exactly what Simonsohn found.

Still, it would be a little surprising if a laboratory phenomenon supported by evidence Simonsohn (2011a: 1) himself calls "abundant and convincing," completely dissipated in the field. With regard to the Georgia Effect, Pelham and Carvallo (2011: 29) are inclined to be concessive, on the grounds that the data is drawn from an era when women may have had little discretion about where they lived. I wonder if this understates the number of independent decisions made by these women, and their influence on family decisions, but no matter. Pelham and Carvallo (under review: Study 3) also identified the phenomena with men named

"Cal" and "Tex," who are—you guessed it—more prone to relocation in California and Texas, respectively. With career choices, even if the effect is debunked for imperfect first name matches such as Dennis the Dentist and George the Geoscientist, the phenomena may be more robust for tighter matches, as when Mr. Farmer and Carpenter set to work in their aptronymic fields (Pelham and Carvallo, under review: Study 1).

Personally, I can't get myself to believe it's coincidence that the congressman forced to resign for sending women images of his privates was named Weiner. Pending a decisive resolution of all controversy in the delicate science of *onomastics* (who knew?), I'd advise prospective parents to take no chances, and choose names like "First Round Draft Pick," "Rock Star," and "Nobel Laureate." But whatever names one favors, the existence of ongoing scientific controversy makes a teachable moment. At the risk of repeating myself: little gets decided by a study or few. What's needed are generalizations based on a range of convergent evidence. No matter how it turns out for any individual study, I've plenty of evidence to choose from.

At stake is not only the fate of people, but also the fate of polities. Some elections display a Ballot Order Effect, where candidates at the top of the ballot enjoy an advantage in their share of the vote that can amount to several percentage points (Krosnick *et al.* 2004: 61–8; cf. Lutz 2010; Marcinkiewicz 2014; Meredith and Salant 2013; Webber *et al.* 2014). In close races, that's enough to matter. Whether or not it matters electorally, what does it say for the affected members of the electorate? The relevant studies tend not to directly address voters' reasoning, and it's possible that some citizens consciously decide their vote by ballot order. Possible, but not probable: far more likely is that the effect is an unconscious influence on cognition and behavior, an influence that voters would be unlikely to cite as justifying their vote. Even in an American polity where some regard *Drill Baby, Drill!* as the formulation of serious energy policy, *Vote for the Guy at the Top of the Ballot!* is an insubstantial electoral sentiment.

There appear to be suspicious influences on money as well as power: the early performance of initial offerings on the stock market is better when the stock's name is easier to pronounce (Alter and Oppenheimer 2006). For wealth, so too for health. Drug names are a critical aspect of pharmaceutical marketing (Robins 2001): the identical chemical compound used to treat hypertension sold five times as well when branded Dyazide as when branded Moduretic, despite being supported by sales staffs of similar size. Doesn't much increase your faith in modern medicine, but it does make you wonder why onomastics isn't a more celebrated field.

For a final illustration, consider the many studies on implicit bias. In one experiment, Bargh and colleagues (1996: 238–9) set non-African American participants to work at a computer monitor; the task, which was designed to be tedious, involved sorting groups of geometric figures according to whether their number was even or odd. As participants looked at the images on the monitor, they were primed with photographs depicting either a young African American male or young Caucasian male, which flashed on the screen too quickly for (95 percent of) participants to consciously process. On the 130th trial of this exercise, the computer "crashed," and participants were told they would have to repeat their work. The dependent variable was, near enough, how crabby they would be on hearing this unfortunate news: those in the African American condition manifested more hostility than did those in the Caucasian condition. While the process is incompletely understood, exposure to the picture of a young African American male apparently "activated" in cognition a stereotype that includes the representation of hostility, which somehow made hostile behavior more likely.

Whatever the process, most pertinent for my purposes is that self-report questionnaire measures of participants' racial attitudes were not strongly associated with hostile behavior; participants with low scores for racist attitudes were about as likely to display hostility when exposed to the African American prime as were participants with high scores (Bargh *et al.* 1996: 239). Conscious, explicit processing and unconscious, implicit processing of racial stimuli may disassociate; although early work suggesting complete independence between implicit and explicit bias (Greenwald *et al.* 1998) has been supplanted by studies suggesting complex associations (Nosek *et al.* 2005), that the two processes often are substantially disassociated is not in doubt. To judge from an extensive literature, implicit bias is pervasive; it has been repeatedly demonstrated with a range of methodologies, not only for race, but also for age, gender, sexuality, weight, religion, and disability.[5]

Implicit bias may help explain the persistence of discrimination where egalitarian ideology is widely (if not always sincerely) accepted. In a disturbing study, Bertrand and Mullainathan (2003) responded to employment advertisements in Boston and Chicago papers with fabricated résumés, using both "very African American sounding" names, like Lakisha and Jamal, and "very white sounding"

---

[5] On race, see Amadio *et al.* (2003); Banaji (2001); Dasgupta and Greenwald (2001); Devine (1989); Devine et al. (2002); Fazio *et al.* (1995); Greenwald and Banaji (1995); Greenwald *et al.* (1998); Lane *et al.* (2007); Nosek *et al.* (2005); Phelps *et al.* (2000); Vanman *et al.* (1997). On age biases, see Levy and Banaji (2002); on gender biases, see Lemm and Banaji (1999); on sexuality biases, see Banse *et al.* (2001); on weight biases, see Schwartz *et al.* (2006); on religious and disability biases, see Lane *et al.* (2007). For valuable discussion, see Kelly *et al.* (2010).

names, like Emily and Greg. When topped with white sounding names, résumés elicited 50 percent more interview callbacks; Bertrand and Mullainathan (2003: 10) estimate that the competitive advantage of a white name over an African American name was equivalent to that conferred by *eight additional years* of employment experience. Explicit racism probably had a role here: some managers may have had conscious thoughts to the effect of "I don't want to hire an African American," or "I don't want to hire someone with a name that's too African American." But in major urban areas like Chicago (home base for America's first African American president) and Boston around the turn of the twenty-first century, it's probable that many managers engaging in discrimination were not consciously entertaining racist thoughts as they skimmed piles of resumes.

Employment is not the only affected domain. Payne (2001: 188–90) discovered that non-African American participants forced to quickly identify artifacts were more likely to misidentify pictures of tools as pictures of guns when primed with the picture of an African American male face; apparently, stereotypes of African American males make representations of guns more accessible. Payne's effect grimly recalls the 1999 killing of Guinean immigrant Amidou Diallo, when four white New York City police officers mistook Diallo's reaching for his wallet as reaching for a weapon, and shot him dead. Some cops are racist, just as are some people in other walks of life, but the experimental literature suggests that *explicitly* racist thoughts are not necessary to explain the shooting, which took place in a matter of seconds.

Obviously, racism remains a pervasive problem. Nevertheless, "I did it because I'm a racist," and "I believe that because I'm prejudiced" are not widely accepted justifications. One might hear such things (or things rather like them), from some people in some places, and other people might think them, even if they are unwilling to flout social norms by saying so. However, in many cases, people probably manifest implicit bias while explicitly, and sincerely, disavowing that bias. As Kelly and colleagues (2010: 456) summarize the literature on racial cognition, many Americans are "explicitly racially unbiased while being implicitly racially biased." Once again, we've got incongruence.

Perhaps the disconcerting empirical record can be put off to the Surprising Effect Bias: counter-intuitive results are the ones that get published, a circumstance favoring publication of findings that undermine, rather than confirm, familiar notions of agency. On this view, perusing the journals for failures of reflective self-direction is rather like perusing the "true crime" literature for grisly homicides. In both cases, market pressures result in frequent depictions of phenomena that are in fact rather infrequent, and the unexceptional rule is buried under the newsworthy exceptions. There's perhaps some reason to be concerned about the Surprising Effect Bias, but for the present topic, there are lots of surprising effects, enough to strongly suggest that the world, not just the lab, contains its share of surprises.

Although the effects are surprising from the perspective of practical rationality and ethical theory, they are quite unsurprising when one considers the prominence of the emotions, as they "play on a central stage in our lives" (Prinz 2004: vii). Emotions have a role in most everything we do, but emotions are not always our doing. Many affective processes, particularly those involving the "basic" emotions such as anger, fear, and disgust, are "mandatory," "irruptive," or "ballistic," meaning they are difficult to "rationally terminate" once initiated (Griffiths 1997).

Imagine I give you a piece of artisanal fudge, which you happily gobble down. Now imagine that I offer you a second piece of the same fudge, cunningly shaped like a dog turd. Still tempted? Why not? After all, you know it's not actually shit. Maybe you think you're a coolly rational type, and would happily snarf the fudge, despite the scatological associations of its form. Well, this might make you rather unusual: Rozin and colleagues (1986: 704–7) found that participants who had eaten a piece of "high quality" fudge were subsequently much less keen for a second piece shaped like a "surprisingly realistic piece of dog feces," than they were for an innocuously disc-shaped piece. Similarly, Rozin's group (1986: 704–7) reports that liking for a sample of fruit juice plummeted when participants were told it had been in contact with a dead cockroach, even though the roach was described by the experimenter as "sterilized, dead, [and] ... perfectly safe." Perhaps this is nothing to get excited about. It's not easy to turn off disgust, maybe, but why should it be? As any chef knows, presentation matters, and many fine restaurants avoid dishes that formally invoke fecal matter.

The argument is not about the niceties of cookery, but the unruliness of emotions—whether they serve good taste or bad. In his work on "moral dumbfounding," Haidt (2001: 814) presented participants with a case of sibling incest, written so that the obvious negative consequences do not obtain: "Julie" and "Mark" use contraception, their relationship is not harmed, and so on. According to Haidt (2001: 814), people "immediately" condemn the incest, and then begin "searching for reasons." As the story is told, however, readers are deprived of familiar justifications, like the potential for an impaired infant, so the search tends to end in failure. Nevertheless, people are not usually moved to revise their initial condemnation. A plausible explanation invokes dual processes: the initial condemnation results from an emotional aversion to sibling incest, and once this response is in place it is very difficult to reflectively dislodge with the thought that one doesn't have good reasons for one's response (Cushman et al. 2010: 57–8).

You may think it right to condemn sibling incest, no matter the circumstances. Maybe it's not resulting harms that make incest wrong; maybe incest is contrary to reason, or a violation of natural law. Moreover, there's no call to suppose the moral output of automatic processes should in every instance be discounted (Pizarro and Bloom 2003); perhaps gut reactions to incest apprehend the moral truth. Perhaps. But the present question concerns not whether the condemnation of incest is wrong, but the extent to which this condemnation is amenable to reflective control. Apparently, not so much.

This is not to say that people never successfully manage their emotions; sometimes folks "get a grip" on themselves, and bite back anger or tamp down fear. But this kind of thing is likely to require substantial effort, which limits the occasions on which it can occur. In a demonstration of "ego depletion," Baumeister and colleagues (1998: 1258-9) asked people to suppress emotional reaction to comic and tragic video clips. Those in this suppress-emotion condition were subsequently less persistent in solving anagrams than participants in a no-regulation condition, who were instructed to "let their emotions flow" during the video. Emotion suppression apparently carries a "psychic cost," which left people with fewer of whatever volitional resources—"will-power," as Baumeister and Tierney (2011: 22-3) have it—are required for perseverance with difficult problems.

At the same time, affect comes easy. Marshaling emotional resources usually doesn't take a lot of effort; one usually doesn't have to work at being angry or scared. In fact, these efforts are frequently futile; think of trying to talk yourself into being angry with your irresponsible-but-charming friend, or trying to talk yourself into regarding the seductive-but-deadly sugar or tobacco with appropriate aversion. Still, that emotions are headstrong and heedless is often a blessing. Stopping to deliberate in the thick of action is a good way to find oneself under a bus; in the day, it was a good way to become supper for a Short Faced Bear (Peacock 2013). While irruptive emotions may often be implicated in judgment and behavior that fails plausible standards of rationality and morality, the liability to such responses is a felicitous frailty. Felicity, however, is not the same thing as agency. And where emotions are infelicitous, there may be little one's better judgment can do.

For some incongruence associated with emotion, the subject may be very aware of the perturbation, as when anger forces words one knows they will regret. Other emotional incongruences have the character of bypassing. Although emotions are naturally thought of as having an experiential component, there's evidence that emotional processes may in some conditions be unconscious, and people may be subject to an emotional influence without being aware of it

(Winkielman and Berridge 2004). It's worth taking a bit of care over the referent of "unconscious," since people may be conscious or not of a mental state itself, its origins, or its influence; I might know I'm feeling disgust without being aware of how my disgust affects my other cognitive and emotional states (cf. Gawronski *et al.* 2006). It sounds rather more probable that people are unaware of disgust's effects than that they are unaware of being disgusted, but this raises complex (and substantially empirical) questions I don't need to sort out. It's clear that there's incongruence involving emotion, and very likely that some of this incongruence has the character of bypassing. Given the ubiquity of the emotions, incongruence ought be expected.

In sum, the empirical literature indicates that evidence of incongruence is readily obtained across a wide variety of experimental protocols. This circumstance, while surprising from the perspective of practical reasoning, is quite unsurprising when one considers the pervasiveness and potency of emotional processing. Taken together, these observations make plausible the supposition that incongruence is widespread in everyday life.

Sizes

Many of the discomfiting experimental effects may be comparatively small. That would help explain the unevenness that concerns the Replicators; the weaker the signal, the more it will get drowned in the noise. Really potent phenomena, like gunshots to the knee, don't drown; they have dramatic behavioral effects near very time. The great majority of effects published in psychology journals are rather less impressive. But small isn't the same as unreal, and neither does small entail a lack of practical and theoretical import.

To be sure, if we're faced with an isolated finding with a small effect size, we should hesitate to conclude the effect is real. But that's not the situation at hand; we're considering a range of effects, some of which may be quite small, that point in the same direction: towards the existence of incongruence. The question is not whether the effects are real, but what to make of small effects.

To begin thinking about this, let's briefly return to Georgia. (To allay suspicions that I'm violating my own rule against overweighting individual bits of evidence: Georgia's role at this point is illustrative, not evidential.) If all states are equal, and there are 50 American states, the chance that a mover will select any given state is 2 percent. In fact, number 9 Georgia has something like 20 times the population of number 50 Wyoming, but that's beside the point. On our simplifying assumption, the "base rate" chance that Georgia will move to any state is roughly 2 percent, and if her name makes her 36 percent more likely to move to

Georgia, that bumps the likelihood up to 2.72 percent. That is, the difference is a bit more than 0.7 percent. Stated differently, the difference is more than a third. Is it a big difference, or a small one?

Judgments of effect size are complicated—enormously complicated—by the fact that there are numerous pertinent notions of size, which don't always go together. When psychologists talk about effect size, they are frequently interested in issues of *statistical* size, descriptive issues concerning the magnitude of relationships between variables. This discussion is often couched in terms of correlation coefficients, which quantify the strength of the relationship between two variables; at one pole, a coefficient of 0.00 represents no relationship, at the other, a coefficient of 1.0 represents a perfect relationship. A standard convention for assessing correlations is due to Cohen (1988: 77–81), who suggested that a correlation coefficient of around 0.10 should be regarded as "small," around 0.30 as "moderate," and around 0.50 as "large."

The problem is that for much psychological research, correlations rating a Cohen large, or even a moderate, occur relatively infrequently (Hemphill 2003). Moreover, this observation is not limited to the "soft" science of psychology; consider a rendering of effects in biomedical research as correlation coefficients (Meyer *et al.* 2001: 130):

Regular aspirin consumption and reduced risk of heart attack: 0.02
Chemotherapy and surviving breast cancer: 0.03
Ever smoking and lung cancer within 25 years: 0.08

The medical details (and how they may change with future research) are inconsequential here; what matters is that the reported relationships provide concrete objects for thinking about effect size. On their face, these numbers are tiny; pennies on the dollar, if you will. The relationships they represent are not relationships, like the correlation between being human and being mortal, strong enough to be detected by "the naked eye" without the aid of statistical magnification (Jennings *et al.* 1982: 216–22). Additionally, they are clearly small by the lights of Cohen's convention.

It's not obvious that either of these comparisons is the right one. Hardly shocking that many of the relationships uncovered in biomedical research are not evident without statistical intervention; that's one reason we need biomedical research. Neither is it clear that a convention like Cohen's is the appropriate standard of comparison. The "small" relationship between aspirin use and reduced coronary risk might be thought pretty large, compared to something that (presumably) has no relation, like owning a grey coat, or something that has a negative relationship, like obesity. Furthermore, taking aspirin together with other interventions, like losing weight and exercising properly, might have a considerable cumulative effect.

Whatever gets decided about statistical size, questions of *practical* size are importantly different. For expository purposes, let's grant that the relationships we've been considering are not statistically large, or even moderate. It remains likely these small correlations have practical implications: take the aspirin, endure the chemo, and don't light up. In the case of aspirin, for example, the health benefit may be comparatively minor: if your habits or genes are bad enough, aspirin ain't gonna save you. Yet the costs associated with taking an aspirin every day or two are pretty minimal, so if you're at risk for a heart attack, why not? For some people, like those with ulcers, the potential negative effects of taking aspirin might outweigh the potential positive effects; in each case, what makes sense for a given patient to do is decided by considering the balance of costs and benefits. Seen this way, the problem is not a descriptive problem in statistics but a normative problem in practical reasoning, and it can't be solved by reference to statistical size alone.

The third relevant kind of effect size is *theoretical* size. Here's an example. Many people appear to think that intercessory prayer, or praying on behalf of others, has clinical value; praying for the sick, these people believe, can help the sick get better. The actual evidence is underwhelming; studies have found that intercessory prayer is not of clinical benefit (e.g. Benson *et al.* 2006). But let's stipulate the studies are wrong, and there is clinical advantage. Additionally, let's say this effect is statistically small, like other effects in medicine. The effect might yet be theoretically large. For if the best explanation of the (stipulated) positive effect of intercessory prayer adverted to supernatural phenomena (as I believe the believers believe) that might very well demand sizable changes in the theoretical picture of the world commended by natural science. And this would be true even if the implications were of negligible practical size; say, if the clinical benefits of intercessory prayer were judged too small to justify diverting resources from other interventions, like buying the patient flowers, or visiting her at the hospital.

In general, judgments of effect size will very often be comparative, and relative to a particular interest or context (Northcott 2005, 2012). For the particular psychological effects I'm discussing, while some may be statistically small, they may yet be practically and theoretically large. Workplace discrimination, for example, is of practical import, and if accounting for some of the psychological processes involved requires revision in thinking about agency, the effects are theoretically large. To be sure, identifying statistically small effects does not allow confident conclusions about particular outcomes for particular individuals. But the effects must be making a difference in *some* individual cases, or there would not be an effect. Given the multitude of influences likely operative in any instance, one cannot confidently say where the difference was made, but this sort of uncertainty is actually part of the problem: *what's* making *which* difference for *whom*? If eyespots and pronouns are in the mix, what other non-reasons might infect deliberation?

It's a bit like the camel and the tent, where innocuous entrance of a nose enables intrusion of the whole hulking beast. Once we see that there are some arbitrary influences on cognition and behavior, we are bound to admit there may be others; if something like *that* can make a difference, there could be *many* goofy influences in any particular instance. While the impact of each individual goofy influence may be statistically small, just as with medical interventions, the aggregate effect may be quite potent; for all one knows, any decision may be infested by any number of rationally and ethically arbitrary influences. Now, there's a large, odorous, and ill-tempered animal under the awning of agency.

One might doubt that these modest effects can impact lives in an ongoing way. But rapid temporal decay does not imply a lack of consequence. If the Watching Eyes Effect induces donations to the honor box, that's practically and theoretically interesting, whether or not those influenced are thereby moved to behave better for the rest of their days. The claim is not that any one of the influences in question is momentous in the way illness, bereavement, and unemployment can be. Rather, the thought is that statistically small effects can sometimes be practically consequential—and an aggregation of such influences even more so. And this, I'll argue, is of very considerable theoretical importance.

Hackles may now be raised: in espousing character skepticism, I've groused about small effect sizes in personality psychology, and it's arguable that some effects in personality are larger, perhaps considerably larger, than the kinds of effects I'm now relying on. Fair enough, but attending to rhetorical context should be soothing. For character skepticism, my concern was not that the personality effects are small, but that they are likely to be *smaller than should be expected* on many theories of character and personality (Doris 2002: 68, 71–5). For agency, my position is the converse: the effects in question, small though they may sometimes be, are *larger than should be expected* on many theories of agency and responsibility. It is this misproportion that makes the trouble, and forces rethinking approaches to agency.

Defeaters

I'm now in position to schematize the skeptical challenge. Where the causes of her cognition or behavior would not be recognized by the actor as reasons for that cognition or behavior, were she aware of these causes at the time of performance, these causes are *defeaters*. Where defeaters obtain, the exercise of agency does not obtain. If the presence of defeaters cannot be confidently ruled out for a particular behavior, it is not justified to attribute the actor an exercise of agency. If there is general difficulty in ruling out defeaters, skepticism about agency ensues.

The reason for thinking general difficulty about defeaters obtains is the large empirical literature demonstrating the existence of incongruence, where different psychological processes issue divergent outputs with regard to the same object (cf. Davies 2009: 149–50). I don't suppose that all incongruences are defeaters, first because I don't suppose all incongruence involves causes of behavior that are not appropriately treated as reasons, and second because not all behaviors are ones where demands for reasons are appropriate (more on the second point in a moment). But a subclass of incongruences is aptly described as defeaters, and as survey of the empirical literature suggests, this subclass is substantial. Substantial enough, anyway, to motivate the skeptical argument.

The argument takes a familiar form. A skeptical hypothesis is one that cannot be ruled out, and would falsify some belief, or category of beliefs, if true: if I cannot rule out the existence of an epistemically malicious Demon, or that I'm frolicking in a Matrix, or that I'm an envatted brain (insert whatever skeptical scenario moves you), I haven't knowledge of the external world (Chalmers 2003). The present skeptical hypothesis maintains that for any putative instance of agency, one cannot rule out a defeater (or defeaters) in the explanation of that behavior. Where one cannot rule out this alternative, one cannot justifiably posit an instance of morally responsible agency. Therefore, one is never justified in positing an instance of morally responsible agency. Like other skeptical arguments, the contention is not that the phenomenon in question does not exist, but that there are not sufficient grounds for believing it does.

This skeptical argument might be thought to have something else in common with other skeptical arguments: rigging the game by setting overly stringent requirements for anti-skeptical victory. One such rigging requires epistemic certainty, or conclusive justification, for a belief to count as knowledge; since it would be vanity to insist that humans are possessed of *conclusive* justification regards many paradigmatic candidates for knowledge—who can say what our epistemic future holds?—skepticism quickly follows (Stanley 2008). In response, many philosophers endorse fallibilism, according to which knowledge has its basis in *defeasible* justification (Pryor 2000: 518). I'll follow the many. Like attributions of knowledge, attributions of responsible agency do not require conclusive justification.

The manifest question concerns how much defeasible justification is enough. I've not much to offer, but it's instructive to notice that for attributions of morally responsible agency, the relevant standard is at least partly ethical, because such attributions are associated with the distributions of burdens (like punishment and blame), and benefits (like reward and praise). The requirement that defeaters be "confidently"—not conclusively—eliminated can be understood as a demand for a kind of *moral* confidence: the conviction that, were one's initial judgment that an exercise of morally responsible agency obtained (and defeaters did not) overturned in light of new evidence, one would not be guilty of wrongdoing for having apportioned burdens and benefits according to this judgment. Accordingly, the skeptical thought is that the requisite moral confidence is never justified. So understood, the skeptic is not making an unreasonable demand for epistemic certainty, but an eminently reasonable request that moral judgments be morally defensible.

There's also potential for excessive skeptical exuberance in promulgating hypotheses. Demons, Matricies, and envatted brains are pretty loopy stuff, and while it may be unclear what could rule them out, it's also unclear why sensible folks should want to rule them in. These sensible anti-skeptics may claim the loopy skeptical hypotheses aren't "relevant" in most epistemic circumstances, and thereby reject the skeptic's demand for a ruling out.

Articulating standards of relevance makes consternation for epistemologists (Shaffer 2001; Sosa 2004), but there's not insurmountable difficulty in this case. An obvious gloss is probabilistic: to be relevant, a skeptical hypothesis must have some non-trivial probability of being true. Even on a demanding precisification of "non-trivial," there's little cause to think that the present skeptical hypothesis, concerning the availability of behavioral explanations referencing defeaters, fails this standard. This hypothesis is not a loopy (and perhaps massively unlikely) proposition like skeptical propositions involving Demons, Matrices, or envatted brains. Rather, it is a "live" hypothesis (Frances 2005: 560–1): it has been vetted by the relevant experts, and judged by a substantial number of them, on the basis of good evidence, to be about as likely as competing hypotheses (cf. Davies 2009: 169). Never mind whether Demons and their ilk meet a probabilistic standard of relevance; it's credibly maintained that the skeptical hypothesis in question does so.

Relevance might instead be understood pragmatically: if whether a skeptical hypothesis is true or false has no effect on the conduct of a practice, the skeptical hypothesis is not relevant to that practice. However, theoretically interesting skepticism about the external world might be, for example, one can't straight away conclude that it bears practical import. When the treacherous

Cypher contends, in *The Matrix*, that he doesn't care whether his steak really exists, so long as it's juicy, we might judge him (among other things) an epistemological philistine, but we shouldn't doubt he's enjoying his meal. Cypher, perhaps, dines in the spirit of Hume (1978/1740: I.iv.7): why should the rules of backgammon, or the pleasure derived from playing it, be any different in a Matrix?

Something similar might be said for responsibility, as when Strawson (1962) dismissed worries about determinism and responsibility as philosophers' "panicky metaphysics." The everyday practice of responsibility, for Strawson, is structured by human beings' natural tendency to regard one another with the reactive attitudes; given that this propensity cannot be expurgated, the metaphysical issues are otiose, with respect to the practice. Even in the unlikely event these propensities were eliminable, the Strawsonian argument continues, such a reformation would deprive human beings of much they find valuable in their interpersonal relationships (McKenna 2005: 166–8).

Strawson's arguments on these points have been, in my view, persuasively disputed (Pereboom 2001, 2011), but here, this is neither here nor there. For the present skeptical hypothesis is not concerned with metaphysics, panicky or otherwise. It's a psychological hypothesis, and matters of psychology are relevant to the practice of responsibility, not least to the practice as understood by Strawson himself, which is centrally concerned with actors' "quality of will" (McKenna 2005: 170–3). While "quality of will," isn't a transparent notion, it's clearly enough a psychological notion; Strawson (1962: sec. III) insists that people's reactive attitudes depend upon their beliefs about the "attitudes and intentions" others direct towards them.

The point applies widely. In many places, at least in the places at home to the tradition at issue here, the practice of morality in general, and responsibility in particular, involves *psychological assessment*—as indeed the many locutions of an ilk with "he meant well" testify (Gray *et al.* 2012; Young and Tsoi 2013). If so, the skeptical hypothesis at issue here looks to be of inescapable practical relevance. For it is a psychological hypothesis, which asserts that people cannot confidently assess others' psychologies, particularly with respect to whether her motives are ones she would consider reasons, an assessment which bears on the question of whether their conduct was an exercise of morally responsible agency. The hypothesis might, of course, be dismissed on probabilistic grounds, practical relevance notwithstanding. But as I've just said, the case for probabilistic relevance looks sturdy enough. Then the skeptical hypothesis appears both probabilistically and pragmatically relevant; it remains appropriate to demand a ruling out.

Perhaps some defeaters are best thought of as partial rather than total defeaters—impediments to agency rather than eliminations of agency. But now the skeptic can amend her demand for a ruling out of defeaters with a demand to distinguish cases of partial defeaters from cases of total defeaters. Why suppose meeting the amended demand makes an easier job? The skeptic needn't deny the existence of partial defeaters having only limited impact on agency, she need only to insist on the difficulty of establishing, in any particular case, that it is only such comparatively benign influences which obtain. The ruling out problem remains.

Notice that this skeptical challenge is not exactly an empirical generalization to the effect that defeaters are widespread. The empirical evidence indicates that defeaters occur quite frequently in everyday life, frequently enough, anyway, that the skeptical hypothesis is "live," and has some non-trivial chance of being true. But so far as I can see, nobody has any very exact idea what the frequencies are. It's obvious why; comparatively little behavior is closely observed, still less behavior is observed in controlled conditions, and for the behavior that is observed, there's often little assurance about psychological antecedents. If the skeptical challenge traded in frequencies, it would begin, and end, at impasse. However, the challenge can be put without committing to estimations of frequencies, for the critical question concerns not how often defeaters should be thought to obtain, but how their presence can be ruled out.

It may not be immediately evident that acknowledging the empirical evidence changes things. We don't need a bunch of psychology experiments, it might be said, to know we should be on the lookout for defeaters: disruptions of agency are routine occurrences. People have always gotten tired, angry, confused, and inebriated, and none of this should incline us, unless we suffer from philosophical paranoia, to skepticism about agency.

This response understates the difficulty. Familiar disruptions of agency are often readily ruled out (or in): whether someone is seriously inebriated, for example, isn't usually a mystery. Not so for the kind of influences we've been considering: the range of potential defeaters is large, diverse, and often quite unexpected. Tough to know where to look, when looking to rule them out. One might be tempted to shift the argumentative burden, and insist it falls to the skeptic who's attacking common sense, rather than the anti-skeptic who's defending it. But there's little pressure for the skeptic to acquiesce in shifting: if what's at issue is whether to take common sense seriously, there's little rhetorical advantage in observing that common sense takes itself seriously. The difficulties instigated by the empirical literature aren't negated by gesturing at a common sense that hasn't yet accounted for the literature.

The operative notion of defeaters requires some restriction. Behaviors and cognitions are typically complex, and include numerous components. Planning a trip, for example, is a multifaceted activity: cognitive processes support my searching the internet for bargain hotels, while physiological processes support my respiration as I search, and so on. Physiological processes are not properly cited as justificatory reasons for my breathing, but it seems histrionical to call these processes defeaters, and conclude that my respiration is not an exercise of agency. It's not wrong, exactly: respiration, like much (or most) of human functioning, doesn't usually involve the exercise of agency. It's that we didn't need to go hunting defeaters to see this.

Questions about defeaters are usually appropriate only in circumstances where questions about reasons for (or justifications of) behavior are apposite. In ordinary contexts, *Why are you breathing?* is malformed; it borders on unintelligible (except where insulting!) to demand from someone a justification for their respiration. The diagnosis of this appearance is evident enough. Attributions of agency target the intentional components of behavior, so questions about defeaters do not arise for non-intentional components. Sometimes respiration involves intentional components, as when I attempt to slow my breathing when I'm angry, scared, or stressed. But here, questions about agency *are* appropriate; one wants to know if they can be expected to do the things their martial arts teacher tells them to do. Among intentional components, some may be afflicted by defeaters, and some not, and some may be associated with exercises of agency, and some not: perhaps, as I planned my vacation, my choice of hotels was swamped by defeaters, but my decision to sojourn in Poughkeepsie rather than Paris wasn't. Much human behavior, then, may be a composite of agential and non-agential components, and questions about defeaters are asked with reference to particular agential components.

The paradigmatic instances of defeaters are incongruences where automatic processing swamps analytic processing. This is not to say that exercises of agency require the actor be consciously aware of her reasons when she acts, which would exclude many habitual behaviors that make plausible candidates for attributions of agency. That's why I've explicated the notion of defeaters counterfactually, in terms of what the actor *would* recognize as reasons, if she were aware of them at the time of performance.

Notice the appearance of a certain asymmetry: while it's easy to imagine defeaters where the automatic subverts the analytic, it's less easy to concoct examples where things go the other way around. This appearance might be thought misleading. Many emotional processes are automatic, and many philosophers, such as those in the long-running sentimentalist ethical tradition, have celebrated the role of emotion in judgment and action (D'Arms and Jacobson 2000b; Gibbard 1990; Nichols 2004; Prinz 2007). This celebration of sentiment will seem altogether sensible to anyone who's ever "trusted their feelings," and indeed, it's easy to concoct cases where passion ought trump prudence: when the ambitious young man forsakes true love for a strategic marriage, he trades authentic happiness for hollow success. Can workings of the analytic system be defeaters?

Perhaps, but such cases seem atypical. Let's say our young man would have been better off following his heart rather than his head; if you like, his strategic ratiocination resulted in an irrational outcome. He's guilty, let's therefore say, of flawed practical reasoning. But if we further stipulate that he knowingly chose his strategic union, it seems perfectly appropriate to count his conduct an exercise of agency. He might come to regret his decision, with fuller information in the fullness of time, but that doesn't affect the question of whether he exercised agency at the time of his decision.

Conversely, when a rationally arbitrary influence has you doing what's best for you, that doesn't mean it has you doing so as an agent: agency isn't about happy endings. Defeaters may facilitate outcomes that are good for the actor, as well as outcomes that are bad for her, and these serendipitous defeaters may also subvert agency; to put the point in terms of my favored theory, although the outcome *conforms* to the actor's values, the outcome is not an *expression* of those values, and is therefore not an instance of agency. Whether they serve the fair or the foul, defeaters do not serve agency.

One might wonder if my account of defeaters makes agency too hard, or—to look from the other end—makes getting out of trouble too easy. Saying that a person fails to exercise agency every time their behavior is sourced in psychological processes they would not reference as a justifying reason sounds like saying that people fail to exercise agency every time they do something they feel badly about, which leaves a *lot* of defeaters lying around. And on the sensible supposition (explicitly defended below) that the exercise of agency is a standard condition of responsibility, this seems to excuse many inexcusable behaviors, such as the betrayals of the *akratic* philanderer, who cheats against his better judgment.

I'm not sure I get the wrong result in such cases, as can be seen by contrasting two readings. In the first reading, the *akratic* cheat in fact treats his illicit lust as a justification. While he'd likely hesitate to invoke it as an excuse when confronted by his aggrieved spouse, he behaves as though it counts as a reason, as witnessed by the complex and costly campaigns many adulterers wage for their assignations. Under this description, the psychological states implicated in the infidelity don't get counted defeaters, and we're able to go sternly forward with our attribution of responsibility.

But suppose this reading is wrong, and the cheater regards his illicit lust as no reason at all; it connects up with absolutely nothing he regards as a legitimate justifying consideration, even at the very moment he acts on it. I'm not convinced this represents the typical case—do fingers move to zippers as if possessed by some foreign intelligence? The "alien hand" syndrome that sometimes afflicts victims of neurological insult might plausibly be so described, but these movements do not meet minimal standards for intentional action, while much garden variety practical weakness surely does (Buss 2013: 24; Doody and Jankovic 1992). Somewhat more likely is that some cheaters suffer an overwhelming desire or compulsion of the sort that might be said to afflict those characterized with "sex addiction" or "hypersexual disorder" (Kor *et al.* 2013). On this reading, I'd allow that the desires and compulsions are of a piece with what I'm calling defeaters. And in these (perhaps rather unusual) cases, it doesn't seem crazy to suppose the miscreant was not exercising agency, and not responsible for what he did, if addictions are sometimes appropriately invoked as excuses.

No doubt, there's much between the extremes just sketched: not compulsion, but not an unconflicted embracing of reasons, either. I'll need to say more about this in developing my own account of agency, but for now it's enough to see that my understanding of defeaters doesn't necessarily make agency too hard. It does suggest that agency ain't easy. But this implication isn't the makings of an objection. Agency is an achievement; if it weren't, we'd not have to worry about skepticism.

Mediation

A possible strategy for blunting the skeptical challenge proceeds by distinguishing mediated and unmediated influences. Once again, Georgia makes a convenient illustration (and once again, *only* an illustration). In a case of unmediated influence, the fact that someone is named Georgia causes, more or less directly, an increased preference for Georgia. This is supposed to be disconcerting; the mere fact of one's name is not usually a good reason to move somewhere. In a mediated case, the name Georgia might result in the singular attractions of Georgia having increased salience for those Georgias who are attracted to the singular attractions, with the result that those Georgias—but not the Georgias who aren't so attracted—move to Georgia. If not for the Name Letter Effect, the Georgia-suited Georgias wouldn't have noticed how well Georgia suits them, and had they not noticed, they wouldn't have made the move. These Georgias decamped for Georgia on the basis of good reasons, even if a non-rational factor was causally implicated in them appreciating those reasons. And likewise: eye-spots might remind you how much you care for your reputation, and plural pronouns might remind you how much you care for your family.

I'm still worried. As I've already implied (Chapter 1, pp. 3–4) there's abundant evidence that cognition is highly sensitive to epistemologically arbitrary inputs; human judgment is routinely influenced by factors without evidential value. If so, the cognitions that pattern motivation may be no less subject to capricious variation than the motivations themselves.

Imagine a circumstance with no rational basis for preference; there's an approximately equal weight of reason-apt considerations on each side of the question. Imagine further that a non-reason-apt factor tips the balanced scales: with the attractions of the Peach State made salient over the equally attractive attractions of the Tar Heel State, Georgia is off to Georgia rather than Carolina, despite the fact that there was (*ex hypothesi*) no rational basis for this geographic preference. There are certainly cases where it's better to make some choice rather than no choice; remember the unhappy fate of Buridan's ass—or Al-Ghazali's camel (Kane 2005: 37)—forever stalled between two equally appealing incentives. (My apologies for invoking two proverbial camels in a single chapter.) For the present instance, however, choice is determined not by the reason-apt factor of needing to make some choice, but by the salience of incentives. It looks as though difficulty has recurred, at one remove; now, the problem concerns rationally arbitrary influences on the saliences that help structure preference.

Maybe this argument overreaches. Practical reasoning frequently takes inputs that are rationally arbitrary (cf. Buss 2013: 27): I flip to this page in a cookbook rather than that, and it's risotto rather than ratatouille for dinner, or a search engine turns up this webpage rather than that, and it's a visit to Dr. Nocera instead of Dr. Nijhawan. That a bit of practical reasoning is shaped by happenstance does not necessarily render this reasoning irrational: if risotto would make a fine dinner, no matter if its appearance at the table was facilitated by a flip of the page, and if Nocera is a competent clinician, this circumstance is unchanged by the fact that Google slighted Nijhawan. Inasmuch as there's a measure of happenstance in everything people do, to require its complete absence for agency is to set a standard that can't be met—and as the above examples tell, needn't be.

Best to distinguish cases where happenstance engages rational capacities from cases where happenstance bypasses rational capacities. I've been worrying about cases of bypassing: influences that are not vetted by rational capacities. The mediating saliences we're now considering may be cast as cases where rational capacities are engaged: when I flip to the risotto recipe, I recognize it's decadent creamy-starchiness I crave, and not the brooding stew of tomato and eggplant I'd previously contemplated. (The recognition may be conscious or not; but there better be something like recognition, or it's hard to see how reason gets engaged.) I've no stake in denying the existence of such cases, even many such cases. But this does not rule out the existence of bypassings, where reason does not get engaged, and the causal story does not have the makings of a justificatory story. It is these that must be ruled out, if the skeptical challenge is to be disarmed. We do well to acknowledge that that the origins of behavior are complex, and will often include any number of mediating factors. But this complexity does not resolve the problem of incongruence.

Triage

The reflectivist, together with anyone else not impressed by the empirical evidence, may continue to insist that reflective control worthy of the title agency obtains—when judiciously applied at appropriate junctures. Nobody thinks it possible, or desirable, to incessantly reflect. On the one hand, there's limited capacity for reflection ("I can't think about that right now!"), on the other, reflection can be counter-productive ("Don't just stand there, do something!"). Then the exercise of reflective agency is supposed to involve a kind of meta-rationality: the ability to discern when it is most possible, and most productive, to reflect. In other words, reflective agency requires reflective triage.

Archetypal examples of predicaments where reflective control appears to get the call involve delayed gratification, which people are able to do from an early age. In a classic series of studies on "self-imposed delay," Mischel and colleagues gave children, aged around four, a choice between more and less preferable rewards, such as one marshmallow vs two marshmallows (Shoda *et al.* 1990: 980; cf. Metcalfe and Mischel 1999; Mischel *et al.* 1972, 1988). After choosing, the children were left alone in a room with both rewards. They could ring a bell to recall the experimenter and claim their reward at any time, but there was a catch: recalling the experimenter meant a child earned only the less preferable reward, whereas waiting for the experimenter to return would earn the more preferable one.

Children who were able to employ strategies of self-distraction did much better: in one version, those encouraged to "think about fun things" lasted around 12 minutes, those allowed to play with a slinky lasted around 9 minutes, while those who were not provided a distraction held out less then a minute (Mischel *et al.* 1972: 207). Metcalfe and Mischel (1999: 4) explain this via dual process theory: the interplay of a "hot emotional system" which is fast, automatic, and controlled by external stimuli, and a "cool cognitive system" which is slow, reflective, and the source of self-control. With the right sort of help, such as distractions directing attention away from the urgings of the hot system, the cool cognitive system may prevail. This looks like what the reflectivist is looking for: the rudiments, at least, of something like reflective self-direction.

Related models have been proposed for instances where adults encounter sticky predicaments involving not marshmallows, but morality. In Greene and colleagues' (Greene 2007, 2013; Greene *et al.* 2004) remarkable neuroscientific research, when people are confronted with particularly challenging moral dilemmas, their judgment sometimes seems to be influenced by reflective effort. For the Crying Baby dilemma, participants are asked to imagine themselves in the position of a villager who must smother her own baby so its cries will not alert pillaging enemy soldiers to where parent, child, and other villagers are hiding; if the parent fails to do so, the soldiers, drawn by the noise, will find and kill all of the hidden villagers, including parent and child (Greene *et al.* 2004: 390). The utilitarian counsel seems clear: sacrifice one to save many. But this is to counsel something emotionally repugnant: a parent smothering their own child.

There's something to be said on both sides. Better that the villagers survive, and better that a parent not kill their child. Experimental participants did not exhibit a clear consensus, with some judging it permissible to smother the baby, and others not. Apparently, the decision is not an easy one: response times were longer for Crying Baby than for a case of more obviously impermissible infanticide, and brain imaging (fMRI) indicated increased activity in the anterior cingulate cortex, a region believed to function as a "conflict monitor" in cases of competing cognitive demands (Greene *et al.* 2004: 392; cf. Botvinick *et al.* 2001). For those participants that favored smothering the baby, there was greater activation of the dorsolateral prefrontal cortex, a region believed to be associated with abstract reasoning and cognitive control (Greene *et al.* 2004: 392-3; cf. Miller and Cohen 2001). It appears that people who made the utilitarian judgment had to somehow "override" the emotional response prohibiting infanticide; whether you think them right or wrong, they looked to exercise something like reflective control. In moral judgment, it seems as though the cool analytic system can sometimes dominate the hot automatic system (cf. Cushman *et al.* 2010); evidently, these are instances of reflective self-direction.

If we want to rule out the possibility of defeaters, the reflectivist might now say, the answer is easy: look to instances where people engage in concerted reflection. Unfortunately, there are grounds to mistrust the deliverances of such cognitive activity, as an impressive run of experiments led by Wilson (2002: Ch. 8) has shown. In one, Wilson and his colleagues (1993: 333-7) presented participants with a group of posters, including both art prints (e.g. Van Gogh's *Irises*), and "humorous" posters like those of the ghastly "captioned kitty" genre (e.g. cat at fence, titled *One Step at a Time*). Participants in the "reasons condition" were given a questionnaire instructing them to describe why they liked or disliked each poster, while controls were asked for background information regarding educational and career decisions. Subsequently, all participants were allowed to take a poster of their choice home. After a few weeks, experimenters interviewed participants by phone, and participants in the reasons condition were found to be *less* satisfied with their choice. (Amusingly, reflectors were more likely than controls to choose the captioned kitty abominations over the art prints (Wilson *et al.* 1993: 334).)

Why does reflection falter? For one thing, folks aren't especially good at assessing their inner states (Wilson 2002: Chs 5–6). Consider a diabolical study by Dutton and Aron (1974) on "source misattribution" (a supportive meta-analysis in Foster *et al.* 1998: esp. 99). There, an "attractive" woman approached men in a park and asked them to fill out a questionnaire; afterwards, she provided her phone number and offered to discuss the study further. The dependent variable was whether the men would call and ask her out. The independent variable concerned where the contact took place: some men were approached on a scary footbridge over a deep gorge, while others were approached after they had crossed the bridge and were relaxing on a park bench. The result: 65 percent of men in the bridge condition asked the pollster for a date, compared to 30 percent in the bench condition. Dutton and Aron's (1974) hypothesis is that men in the bridge condition misattributed arousal due to fear—they were often perspiring, short of breath, with a rapidly beating heart—to sexual interest: apparently, the cold predations of fear were mistaken for the warm enticements of lust.

According to lore, crushes cause anxiety, but it may be as near the truth to say that anxiety causes crushes. How many relationships, I wonder, are originated in source misattribution, where the fabled spark is struck by social anxiety rather than sexual chemistry? If we don't know what we are feeling, or why we are feeling that way, how may we reflect effectively?

The triage response allows that reflective self-direction may be comparatively infrequent, while insisting that people reflect, and reflect effectively, when the chips are down. Yet chips-down situations are likely to be situations of considerable stress: *How can we keep this marriage together? How can I avoid foreclosure? How can we pay for mother's long-term care?* When important decisions are not so grim, they can still be emotionally charged: *Should I move to California? Should we get a puppy? Should I ask him to marry me?* Here's a reasonable speculation: the situations in which reflectivists suppose people most need to reflect (and, perhaps, the situations in which people are most likely to do so) are exactly the situations in which unruly automatic processes, such as emotional perturbations, are most likely to be running amuck. The probability of difficulties in reflection may well increase with the situation's practical import; the more chips on the table, the greater the risks of misplaying a card.

This observation is important in its own right, but it also helps explain why a familiar response to philosophical exploitations of psychology is at present inapplicable. Experimental situations are trivial, it is said, and seldom involve situations of much practical interest, so their relevance to real life situations is supposed to be quite limited (Solomon 2005). Shortcomings in the lab, the story goes, don't tell us much about shortcomings in life.

But if people blow it in trivial situations, why suppose they will get it right in serious situations? This sounds like saying my ineptness in practice is unrelated to my performance in The Big Game. Perhaps there are clutch players, like baseball's legendary Mr. October, Reggie Jackson, who perform their best when the pressure is worst. The empirical evidence for this phenomenon is uncertain in both professional baseball (Birnbaum 2005) and professional basketball, where players' reputations for hitting the big shot in "crunch time" seem quite tenuously related to their actual shooting percentage late in close games (Siegel 2010). What would a clutch reflector look like? Someone who would be less susceptible to temptation when tempted, or less susceptible to anger when being provoked, or less susceptible to favoritism when considering their favorite? Could be, I guess. But it also could be that, as with sport, people are prone to performing *worse* when the pressure is on.

In some circumstances, reflection may help secure agency. At the same time, there are grounds to mistrust the deliverances of reflection, which leaves us with the problem of when to trust reflection and when not. If this is the situation, it's hard to see how appealing to concerted reflection enables the confident ruling out of defeaters, since there's reason to withhold confidence in the process which is supposed to enable the confident ruling out. There's much more to be said on this point, and I'll have a go at saying it in Chapter 4. For now, it is not obvious that triage can center a successful response to the skeptical challenge.

Signpost

I've identified a psychological phenomenon I call incongruence, where the causes of, and reasons for, cognition and behavior diverge. I argued that this phenomenon intimates the existence of defeaters, which undermine the exercise of agency. I followed this with a challenge taking a familiar skeptical form: how can the presence of defeaters be ruled out? I now turn to the most obvious material with which one—especially one with reflectivist predilections—might attempt to construct a ruling out: the experience of agency.

4

Experience

Confabulations, the extravagant fabrications produced by patients suffering neurological trauma or psychiatric illness, have long been a staple in the clinical literature:

[T]he certainty and decisiveness, as well as the liveliness and apparently plastic, deeply felt conviction, with which he produces his weird confabulations, are remarkable. He loves to broadly expose his stories, to recount many names and details...and always wants to prove the veracity of his point by seeking his papers. If one were not perplexed by the many temporal contradictions, one would easily take his stories for true. (Kalberlah 1904, quoted in Schnider 2008: 24)

As psychologists have continuously documented failures of self-awareness in healthy people, it's become customary to suggest that the unafflicted confabulate, much as the afflicted do. Proffered incautiously, these comparisons threaten to mislead. But considering the juxtaposition will help answer the question with which Chapter 3 left off: does the experience of agency disarm skepticism about agency?

Error

Whether you're skeptic or anti-skeptic, not everything feels like a train wreck; people experience some events in which they figure as involving things they *do*, and not just as things that happen to them. There's likely more than one way to experience a doing, but my concern is with doings as depicted by the reflectivist: an individual's experience of her conscious and self-conscious thought shaping what she does. If such *agent experiences* are characteristic of human life, it appears that skepticism dissipates in face of the obvious.

It's not just that agent experiences are common, but that their contraries are uncommon. Think of "waking up" during a long drive, with no idea what (or who!) you've been driving over (Armstrong 1968: 93). Or suddenly finding yourself in a little used room of your house, clueless as to how you got there

(Albritton 2003: 412). Such occurrences are arresting, I suspect, partly because they are rare: it seems that when people think about it, they usually think they know what they are doing. Yet if I'm right about the evidence, these unsettling lacunae may better represent the psychological reality than the reassuringly mundane agent experiences with which they contrast. There apparently obtains a phenomenal inversion: the atypical experiences actually present a circumstance that is altogether typical—an absence of reflective agency.

Then why are agent experiences so prominent? Indeed, why are people subject to such experiences at all? As I've said, people do lots of things *better* while unencumbered by reflection: while the exact nature of expert attention is incompletely understood (Montero 2010), the difference between the Big Leagues and sand lots is not, I'm pretty sure, that Big Leaguers deliberate more about each play. Easy enough to imagine critters that are not prone to agent experiences— Agential Zombies, if you like—who muddle along rather well.

The Agential Zombie, though he may have many and various experiences (unlike the philosophically iconic Zombie of Chalmers 1993), never has experiences of agency. Residing at the other end of the experiential spectrum is the agent of philosophical lore, who routinely experiences her behavior as structured by her reflective deliberation. There's lots of space between the extremes; maybe some non-human animals enjoy experiential states typical of agents, like those involving (rudimentary?) desires and (rudimentary?) intentions, without having experiences of reflective agency. A Wanton looks to be one intermediate manner of beast: all sorts of inner states associated with agency, but no ability or inclination to reflect on them. This needn't be a misery: the suspicion is that Wantons fail to exercise agency, not that they fail to have a good time.

Could the propensity for agent experiences be a historical contingency rather than an inescapable feature of human life? Jaynes (1976: 69, 75) asserted that there "is in general no consciousness" in the *Iliad*: "Iliadic man did not have subjectivity as do we; he had no awareness of his awareness of the world, no internal mind-space to introspect upon." The evidence for this provocation is, inevitably, rather spotty; the problem of inferring inner states is harder when the bearers of those states are dead. All the same, Odysseus makes a rather different hero than J. Alfred Prufrock, and Odysseus, if I rightly recollect, makes out all right in the end.

Whatever one thinks about the psychohistory—and Jaynes' analysis doesn't want for detractors (e.g. Block 1981)—there's likely cultural variation in the proclivity for self-awareness in general, and agent experiences in particular (a question to which I'll return). Yet in some cultures, like the culture we are sharing with this book, agent experiences appear ubiquitous, and this is something, given the uncertain utility of such experiences, that wants sorting out.

To persuasively contend that the experience of reflective agency is frequently misleading, as I'll attempt to do, one must dispense with two burdens: the descriptive burden of establishing the existence of a mistake, and the explanatory burden of showing how the mistake comes about. If the explanatory burden is unsupportable, the descriptive burden grows heavy, for without an explanation of how people came to be so sadly misguided, it will seem incredible that they occupy such an unhappy state. The descriptive burden is itself two burdens, the first being to establish what it is people experience, and the second being to show that what people experience is misleading. If there's reason to believe an experience is misleading, but no reason to believe that people have this experience, there's no reason to believe people are mislead.

Characterizing folk belief is risky, even when there's an abundance of systematic study. And save for a single experiment indicating that people think they can usually see what leads them to make decisions when they "pay attention" (Kozuch and Nichols 2011: Experiment 2), I know of little direct evidence regarding the prevalence of agency experiences. But notice how readily recognizable philosophical reflectivism is; it doesn't have the feel of inaccessible abstraction, or radical innovation. The cause of this familiarity, it seems to me, is that there exist strong affinities between folk belief and philosophical theory when it comes to reflectivism (cf. Carruthers 2008).

I suspect many philosophers agree, and the experience of reflective agency likely figures in the diagnosis of anti-skepticism's appeal. Indeed, some philosophers seem to take experiences of this sort—consciously deciding to do something in light of the reasons that favor it—as evidence against skepticism (e.g. O'Conner 1995: 196–7). And certainly, philosophers (e.g. Jack and Robbins 2004; Mele 2009b: 91–115; Nahmias 2010) have resisted claims by psychologists such as Wegner (2002) to the effect that the experience of consciously willing one's action is an illusion; if the experience is not a prominent feature of human life, why commit to the resistance?

Furthermore, denying that the experience of reflective agency figures prominently in everyday life would undo the response to skepticism now under consideration, which suggests that skepticism about reflective agency is undermined by the prominence of agent experiences. If experiences of reflective agency are not prominent in ordinary experience, I can't establish that ordinary experience is widely mistaken, but neither can an experiential argument be deployed against skepticism about reflective agency.

Of course, if you already doubt that agent experiences are accurate, or are disinclined to feature them in a response to skepticism, I'm about to take more pains than you require. Nevertheless, these pains still have an important role in the dialectic, for agent experiences have a place in my positive theory.

In Chapter 3, I discussed surprising causal influences on behavior that are not plausibly forwarded as reasons for behavior. In this chapter, I'll argue that people do not typically reference such influences in explaining their behavior, and suggest that these omissions manifest self-ignorance. I'll go on to explain why these omissions may be expected to occur; if the error admits of plausible explanations, its existence is less incredible. My exposition will consider phenomena in the vicinity of confabulation—people's extraordinary facility in explaining themselves and their behavior, despite limited self-awareness. The upshot of this consideration will be that appeal to agent experiences makes an inadequate response to skepticism. I won't, however, leave the argument in a skeptical place. In later chapters, I'll argue that while agent experiences are epistemically infirm, they are not, in many cases, practically infirm: they are the materials from which a large measure of human agency is wrought.

Analogy

"Confabulation," seems first to have appeared as a clinical term of art in the early twentieth century, particularly with reference to the Russian neurologist Korsakoff and the alcoholic psychosis that bears his name (Berrios 1998). Confabulatory patients present with impaired self-awareness, while fluently reporting, and sometimes acting on, their inaccurate understandings of self. I'm convinced these phenomena provide materials needed to help unravel the problem(s) of agency, but my conviction provokes immediate suspicion regarding the relevance of the "pathological" to the "healthy"—the lives of the sick may make poor guides to the lives of the well. (With the difficulty of such determinations flagged, I'll henceforth omit scare quotes around *pathological, healthy* and allied terms.)

Suspicions notwithstanding, the philosophical exploitation of pathology enjoys ample precedent: moral philosophers (Maibom 2005; Nichols 2004: 65–82; Roskies 2003) have supposed that psychopathy illuminates normal moral motivation, philosophers of mind (Noë 2004: 3–7) have supposed that sensory pathologies illuminate normal perception, and so on. To say it's been done is not to say it should have been done, but the general idea seems solid enough. For instance, one might learn something about the functional significance of a neurological system through consideration of the deficits emerging when that system has been damaged or disrupted (e.g. Ellis and Young 1988, 1990; Shallice

1988): if you don't know what that widget does, see what happens when you run the machine without it. In laboratory animals, this can be accomplished by "selective lesioning" of the brain, but such study is—the intermittently horrific history of psychosurgery noted (Slater 2005: 223–47)—prohibited in humans. And even the brains of cognitively fancy animals like monkeys are missing some of what makes human brains human. So neurologists look to brain injuries and pathologies as a proxy for selective lesioning, and philosophers look to neurologists.

It's not entirely clear how this should get done. As I've said, the affinities between normal and clinical populations are often noted, where it's repeatedly asserted that confabulation is common in healthy people (Berrios 2000: 362; Carruthers 2009b: 126–7, 130–3; Gazzaniga 2000: 1316–21; Hirstein 2005: 13–14; Nisbett and Wilson 1977: 233; Wilson 2002: 97). But these suggestions are not often enough systematically explored, and the clinical and non-clinical literatures make substantial reference to one another with insufficient regularity (Schnider 2008: 193). I propose to draw the literatures closer together, operating on the supposition that the sick and well share many of the same motives and needs. (You don't want love the less for having a cold.) Cognitive and behavioral processes in psychiatric and neurological patients, while generated and experienced in abnormal ways, may have a functional significance closely related to the functional significance of related processes in normal subjects. If so, pathological confabulation can provide important clues about normal behaviors related to confabulation (Johnson *et al.* 2000: 384).

Unfortunately, the clinical literature on confabulation is, however rich, a rich source of confusion. Since clinicians tend to describe—and journals publish—the more spectacular cases, readers may get a skewed impression of confabulatory syndromes. Philosophers are no less inclined to remark on the exceptional, so this selection effect may be redoubled at philosophical remove. Furthermore, clinical observation is often reported in the form of case studies, which sometimes drift uncomfortably close to anecdote. And where more systematic study is possible, the conditions of interest are comparatively rare, meaning that samples are likely to be rather small (Schnider 2008: 75).

Yet as one canvasses the clinical literatures, one finds repeated observations of certain flavors, repeated often enough to give a sense of things. We ought remember the revealing vivacity of the best psychological studies prior to the fetishization of control in contemporary experimental work; while anecdotes are not data, it is equally true that quantitative data can't substitute for textured clinical narratives. The indispensability of narrative texture is especially obvious where one desires to understand the phenomenology. In trying to understand agent experiences, that's exactly what I desire.

Illness

If there's good reason to engage the clinical literature, there's good reason to do so with trepidation. Confabulatory syndromes have been associated not only with Korsakoff's, but also with aneurysm of the anterior communicating artery (ACoA), brain injury, split brain syndrome, anosognosia (denial of illness), delusions of misidentification, dementias, and schizophrenia (Hirstein 2005: 8; cf. Johnson et al. 2000: 387–90; Schnider 2008: 51–2, Ch. 5). "Clinically pertinent" confabulation is not common, and is not uniformly present even in the conditions classically associated with it, such as ACoA aneurysm and Korsakoff's (Gilboa et al. 2006: 1400; Talland 1961: 361; Victor et al. 1989: 43, 50). Confabulation is standardly thought of as co-occurring with amnesia, but not all patients with memory loss confabulate, and confabulation occurs in conditions that do not obviously involve memory problems (Gainotti 1975: 104–5; Hirstein 2005: 3, 65–6; pace Mercer et al. 1977: 433). Anatomically, the sites of damage in confabulating patients are widely dispersed, and there is no type of brain injury or lesion area that invariably causes clinically pertinent confabulation (Schnider 2008: 142). Finally, researchers recognize various forms of confabulation, and a range of forms may be associated with a single clinical condition, and co-occur in individual patients (Schnider 2008: 57–9). Given this variegated pattern of etiology and symptom, there is little reason to think confabulation can be explained by reference to a single underlying mechanism (Gilboa et al. 2006: 1411), nor are there accepted necessary and sufficient conditions—whether functional or anatomical (Fotopoulou et al. 2004: 727). It is therefore unsurprising that attempts to "define" confabulation have been inconclusive (Hirstein 2005: 7, 187–203; Whitlock 1981).

While nature may not be kind, neither is it completely chaotic. There are iterated themes in the clinical literature, and these themes ground some fairly sturdy generalizations about pathological confabulation. Confabulating patients often present with (1) deficient self-awareness and (2) impaired control of thought and behavior, and their confabulations often (3) involve a motivational component and (4) violate conversational and other social norms.

Confabulations are associated with erroneous cognitions, sometimes involving "matters of fact," such as those associated with semantic memory, but perhaps more typically, and also more interestingly, involving "matters of self," such as those associated with episodic or autobiographical memory (Dalla Barba et al. 1990; Dalla Barba 1993; Talland 1961: 365; on types of memory, see Baddeley 2002; Craver 2012; Eichenbaum and Cohen 2001). Confabulations of self are most central to agency, and it is to these my proffered generalizations most readily apply.

Although non-verbal behaviors may also be considered confabulatory (Lu *et al.* 1997: 1318), confabulation is typically understood as verbal expression of deficient self-awareness; within the general category, *provoked* and *spontaneous* variants are commonly distinguished (Kopelman 1987; cf. Berrios 2000: 351; Fischer *et al.* 1995). Provoked confabulations, such as inaccurate responses on a test of recall, are reactions to external stimuli, resembling the relatively innocuous memory lapses displayed by healthy people (Kopelman 1987: 1486; cf. Fischer *et al.* 1995). Spontaneous confabulations, such as a retired patient insisting he is needed at work, may be associated with more severe disability, and more pervasively implicated in behavior (Kopelman 1987: 1482; Schnider 2008: 59–62).

I should emphasize the possibly obvious point that confabulating patients are not liars. Although the degree of conviction manifested in confabulation varies (DeLuca 2001: 121; Schnider 2008: 70–1), many observers have concluded that patients are typically sincere in their confabulations, and are, unlike prevaricators, unaware of their inaccuracies (Johnson *et al.* 2000: 383; Moscovitch 1995: 226; Ramachandran 1995: 28–32; Talland 1961: 362–3). It is frequently observed that confabulators uphold their stories with "rock-like" certitude; in one dramatic case, a head injured soldier with anosognosia refused to accept a Purple Heart for his wound (Weinstein and Kahn 1955: 16; cf. Talland 1961: 366). In fact, confabulations may carry more conviction than accurate statements: an ACoA patient accepted her confabulations as veridical twice as often (86 percent v. 43 percent) as she did descriptions of events she had actually experienced (Dalla Barba *et al.* 1997: 430). Such misplaced confidence may confound caregivers, and ward staff may be forced to adopt expedients like playing "office personnel" to manage a patient who believes he is at work (Schnider 2008: 120).

Yet confabulations are not always—or even often—*completely* false. For instance, those having to do with episodic or autobiographical memory may reference actual states of affairs, but miscontextualize them in time (Dalla Barba *et al.* 1990; Talland 1965: 56); a mother may rightly recollect that she has children, but not recall that they've grown up and left home. Nor are typical confabulations mere ravings, and some clinicians exclude patients in delirious or hallucinatory states from the diagnosis of confabulation (Berlyne 1972: 38; Talland 1961: 366; but see Schnider 2008: 82–4). Furthermore, although cognitive difficulty may be associated with confabulatory syndromes, confabulation may occur with negligible cognitive impairment (Feinberg and Roane 2003: 349).

Nevertheless, for confabulation to occur, something, or several somethings, must go wrong. First, there is an inaccurate representation, such as a temporal miscontextualization. Additionally, although details vary, it is widely posited that there is a failure to suppress representations—*needed at work*—inappropriate to the patient's circumstances—*retired for years* (Mercer *et al.* 1977: 433; Moscovitch and Melo 1997: 1029; Shapiro *et al.* 1981: 1074–5). Finally, there may be a failure effectively to process external cues –*doctors, hospital*—indicating that a representation is inappropriate.

Thus, confabulation may be understood as involving deficiency at any (or all) of three stages: formation, adoption, and correction (cf. Johnson, Hayes, *et al.* 2000: esp. 385–6). I presume that control of thought and behavior in healthy people involves all three: people form representations, accept or reject representations for the selection of behavior, and alter or maintain representations and behaviors in response to environmental contingencies. Of course, folks form all sorts of representations and intentions that are inaccurate or inapt: they fantasize, misremember, and miscalculate. But these productions are subject, in healthy people, to heavy editorial oversight: inappropriate representations may be discarded, and inappropriate intentions may be aborted.

Ordinarily, the internal censor has powerful external allies: environmental cues, like burned fingers and withering looks, which militate against inappropriate actions and utterances (Rolls and Grabenhorst 1998: 238–40; Zald and Kim 2001: 53). Such editorial work may proceed effortlessly and unconsciously; one of the miraculous things about human beings is their capacity to calibrate and recalibrate their behavior in response to rapidly and radically shifting environmental cues, even cues that are not consciously accessible. But for many confabulating patients, this capacity is compromised, despite the presence of decidedly unsubtle signals, like the evident incredulity of their caregivers.

In fact, confabulators are often quite unconcerned when confronted (Whitlock 1981: 216; cf. Weinstein 1971: 442). Weinstein and Kahn (1955: 17–18) describe patients with anosognosia as possessed of "serene faith" that they are well, while Fulton and Bailey (1929: 264), rather unkindly, remark on the "fatuous serenity" of such patients (cf. Stuss and Benson 1986: 109–12). Although some sufferers become violent (Förstl *et al.* 1991), many individuals with Capgras' delusion, the belief that an intimate has been replaced by a replica, seem not much troubled by this disconcerting circumstance, as in the case of patient who "showed no anger or distress about his first wife's desertion, and specifically expressed thankfulness that she had located a substitute" (Alexander *et al.* 1979: 335; cf. Breen *et al.* 2000: 81–82; Hirstein and Ramachandran 1997: 438; Young 2000: 53).

When patients are able to correct confabulations, they often lapse back into their confabulatory state (e.g. Zangwill 1953: 700), as did a patient who misidentified his wife of some 20 years as a stranger: "when confronted with reality, he would reluctantly admit to it for a moment without any sign of surprise or insight, but soon would go back to his former interpretation" (Mattioli *et al.* 1999: 417–18). Relatedly, confabulators sometimes seem curiously unconcerned by contradiction (Mercer *et al.* 1977: 431). One was convinced he had met an old friend with whom he had lived abroad; when reminded that the friend was deceased, he replied, "Yes, that must cause some interesting legal problems – being dead in one country and alive in another" (Kaplan-Solms and Solms 2000; in Turnbull *et al.* 2004b: 6; cf. Breen *et al.* 2000: 92–93).

This equanimity undermines the notion that many confabulations are "confabulations of embarrassment" meant to cover a "gap" in memory (Bonhoeffer 1901; quoted in Schnider 2008: 22). In fact, confabulatory patients may be little more prone to gap filling than healthy people experiencing memory lapses, and seem able to respond with "I don't know" when that answer is appropriate (Dalla Barba *et al.* 1990; Mercer *et al.* 1977: 431).

Although confabulation is not primarily due to embarrassment, it is very often a social phenomenon. (So the roots suggest: the *Oxford Latin Dictionary* has *confabulor* as "[t]o talk together, converse; (tr.) to talk about.") Confabulation typically involves conversation, but conversation gone wrong; the confabulatory patient is unable to appropriately engage a healthy interlocutor. Matters are intriguingly different when the interlocutor is also confabulatory; Talland and associates (1967: 181) describe a case where two young patients, "E.R." and "G.O.", were placed in the same room after surgery for ACoA aneurysm, and confabulated happily together for some weeks:

E.R. told of his going to various places the day or night before, places he had been in the habit of frequenting but could not have revisited without leaving the hospital. He regularly referred to G.O. as an old friend from the army, and related things they had done together, his roommate cheerfully agreeing although he had never been in the army. [G.O.] ... in turn later reminisced about meeting E.R. in the navy.

Babblers and bores excepted, healthy people are extraordinarily sensitive to social cues. Incredulous stares, raised eyebrows, and long-suffering sighs may not force philosophers to change their minds, but they surely change the course of conversations. It is just this sort of stimulus that is lost on confabulatory patients (cf. Hirstein 2005: e.g. 101–6). In a sense, confabulation is facilitated by *failures* of embarrassment.

Where there's sociality, there's status, and the content of confabulations reflects this fact. Since Korsakoff's (1889) early description of patients with his "peculiar form of amnesia" recounting "unusual voyages" (Victor and Yakovlev 1955: 397), it has repeatedly been observed that confabulation, particularly in more severe spontaneous forms, exhibits *grandiosity* (Berlyne 1972: 32–3; Fischer *et al.* 1995: 22).[1] For instance, there's the stroke patient who claimed to own eight homes, speak many languages, and serve as a General in the Air Force (Gentilini *et al.* 1987: 901), and the ACoA patient who was, during post-operative recovery, intermittently convinced he was a "space pirate" (Damasio *et al.* 1985: 263–5).

Such excess may be comparatively rare (Schnider 2008: 87), but where there are not delusions of grandeur, there are frequently illusions of normalcy. Confabulations often reference a pre-trauma reality where the patient, if not a space pirate or Air Force general, was at least a valued participant in the world: a parent, a lawyer, or a diplomat (Schnider 2008: 1–2, 116, 118–24, 188, 234). Such cases abound: a vascular dementia patient attempted to leave his hospital room and go shopping for new clothes (Dalla Barba 1993: 4), while another patient, recovering from subarachnoid hemorrhage, claimed to have business meetings scheduled, and often dressed for dinner parties, when in fact he was disabled, and attending a day care center (Kapur and Coughlan 1980: 461).

Anosognosia is the most incredible illusion of normalcy. Patients with Anton's syndrome, the denial of blindness, may attribute their visual impairment to dim lighting, a headache, or wearing the wrong eyeglasses (McDaniel and McDaniel 1991: 102; Stuss and Benson 1986: 111). Similar misattributions occur in denial of paralysis, as for this patient with hemiplegiac anosognosia: "I have never been very ambidextrous"; "I've got severe arthritis in my shoulder"; "Doctor, these medical students have been prodding me all day and I'm sick of it. I don't want to use my left arm" (Ramachandran 1996: 125). The last is especially suggestive, as it substitutes agency for infirmity: for those relegated to the passivity of the patient-role, confabulation may be an avenue, albeit a tragically ineffectual one, for the assertion of self.

More generally, there appears to be a tendency for confabulations to present things in a favorable light. In a survey of the literature, Turnbull and colleagues (2004a: 492) identified 16 confabulations of place, all of which substituted more pleasant places, such as university or home, for medical facilities. When they analyzed the confabulations of three patients with lesions to the ventromedial frontal lobes, Turnbull's group (2004b: 12) discovered that while patient reports of mood during the confabulatory episodes were overwhelmingly (78 of 87)

---

[1] Schnider recounts numerous descriptions of confabulatory grandiosity in languages other than English: Amarenco *et al.* (1988; in Schnider 2008: 98); Benon and LeHuché (1920: 318; in Schnider 2008: 25); Bleuler (1923: 191; in Schnider 2008: 112); Bonhoeffer (1901; in Schnider 2008: 22); Flament (1957: 144–5; in Schnider 2008: 33); Kraepelin (1886: 834; in Schnider 2008: 16–17).

negative, the content of their confabulations was overwhelmingly (73 of 87) positive. Similarly, Fotopoulou and colleagues (2004) found that the confabulatory statements of a man suffering complications from the removal of a brain tumor were more congenial than the "confabulations" of healthy controls asked to compose fictitious statements about themselves; the frequency of pleasant fabrications was 79 percent for the patient, versus 46 percent for controls.

What might explain this positivity? Conway and Tacci (1996: 337) understand "motivated" confabulations as "attempts to escape an unbearable reality" which may serve a self-protective function (cf. Conway and Fthenaki 2000: 300–1; Zangwill 1953: 700–1). Similarly, Gainotti (1975: 100) argues that "confabulations of denial" may forestall "catastrophic reaction" to disability (cf. Feinberg and Roane 2003: 255–7; Sandifer 1946: 128). Confabulation tends to ameliorate during recovery from illness or injury, often in a relatively short period (Hirstein 2005: 135; Schnider 2008: 142; Weinstein 1996), which makes it tempting to suggest that confabulation may serve as a temporary "coping mechanism" allowing patients to gradually "come to terms" with their disability (*pace* Bisiach and Geminiani 1991: 24–6).

This is not to say that all confabulation admits of motivational interpretations. Critics argue that these approaches poorly fit important neurological observations (Schnider 2008: 207–8), such as the apathy exhibited by many brain injured patients (Moscovitch 1995: 232), the higher incidence of hemiplegiac anosognosia after right hemisphere damage (Bisiach and Geminiani 1991: 24–6), and the peculiar fact that irrigating the outer left ear canals with cold water can temporarily ameliorate this condition (apparently by stimulating the vestibular system; Cappa *et al.* 1987).

To say that psychological explanations aren't always appropriate is not, of course, to say they never are. Moreover, failures in psychological explanation, and successes in physiological explanation, should not drive us to neuroanatomical imperialism. Identifying a regularity at the physical level—*Jones punches Smith in the nose every time Smith douses Jones with a bucket of steaming sheep entrails*—does not render an explanation at the psychological level—*Jones punches Smith in the nose when he is angry at Smith*—otiose. Explanations of psychopathology, and cognitive and behavioral phenomena more generally, are likely to be richest when they proceed on a variety of dimensions, including the anatomical, psychological, and social (Craver 2007; Doris and Robins 2007; Murphy 2006; Young 2000: 58). For example, the perception of unfamiliarity implicated in Capgras delusion may have an organic cause, but the reasoning leading to *she's an imposter* rather than *she seems a bit off today* might be affected by psychological factors such as mood and propensity to biases (Breen *et al.* 2000: 778–9;

Davies and Coltheart 2000: 12–16). Furthermore, if one wanted to explain why the patient identifies the imposter as a "clone," one will be at a loss if one refuses, in the interests of hard-headed brain science, to reference culture: misidentification of intimates as clones can only occur where human cloning is part of the cultural data base (cf. Davies and Coltheart 2000: 10).

While I mostly engage psychological and social explanations, I would be troubled if there were well-established findings in brain science that clearly conflicted with my account—for example, if it turned out that some function I posit cannot be realized by a human brain. This, of course, is a weak constraint, and one meant to be so: what is known about neuroanatomy sets some parameters, but they are as yet fairly broad ones.

As I've said, the diversity of the phenomena makes a unified theory unlikely. It's better to be content with rough themes: confabulatory patients often present with deficient self-awareness and impaired control, while their confabulations often reflect motivational components and deficits in sociality. Rough as they are, these themes will illuminate related phenomena in non-clinical populations.

Health

Clinical confabulators are typically victims of neurological insults or psychiatric disorders that may be associated with delirium, dementia, psychosis, thought disorder, and detachment from reality; while eliciting provoked confabulations from healthy populations often requires leading probes, eliciting provoked confabulations in clinical populations need not require such artifice, and the distortions may be more severe (Schnider 2008: 200–1, 231–2). Nevertheless, there's something intriguingly like provoked confabulation present in the everyday lives of healthy people. The provocations are not the experimenter's or clinician's prods, but the often unintended prompts with which human beings incessantly bombard one another: our life together is lousy with suggestion. These suggestions are not always made with malice aforethought, but they are hardly random, and well serve the ubiquitous human need for coordinating and controlling behavior. Turns out, confabulatory phenomena are ordinary stuff, although the differences between the hospital and the rest of life counsel proposing, as I shall eventually do, a term other than "confabulation" for the everyday fabrications.

I've a two-stage strategy for establishing the prevalence of confabulatory phenomena in healthy people. First, I'll survey direct evidence. The experimental literature is remarkable, but not as extensive as one might expect, given the vast literature on clinical confabulation. I will therefore augment the direct evidence with indirect argument, asserting that important processes underlying clinical confabulation are pervasively implicated in normal functioning. If facilitators of confabulation in clinical populations are also present in healthy populations, we've some reason to expect confabulatory phenomena in healthy populations, the very considerable differences between the groups notwithstanding.

The customary motivation for positing confabulation in experimental settings goes like this (e.g. Nisbett and Wilson 1977): first, identify a stimulus that can plausibly be assumed to have influenced a certain performance. Then, in debriefing, ask the participant why she performed as she did. If her answer does not reference the stimulus, it may be supposed that she is confabulating.

Hypnosis makes an amusing illustration. Hypnotists ("operators") can induce incomprehensible behavior in their subjects, yet "the subject always finds an excuse to justify his conduct" (Estabrooks 1957: 86–7):

> The operator hypnotized a subject and told him that when the cuckoo clock struck he was to walk up to Mr. White, put a lamp shade on his head, kneel on the floor in front of him and "cuckoo" three times.

After the poor fellow did as required, he was asked to explain himself:

> Well, I'll tell you. It sounds queer but it's just a little experiment in psychology. I've been reading on the psychology of humor and I thought I'd see how you reacted to a joke in very bad taste. Please pardon me, Mr. White, no offense intended whatsoever.

An explanation failing to reference the hypnotic suggestion is grossly deficient. But this is precisely what was given: something vaguely plausible, tinted with grandiosity, and (crucially) as socially acceptable as the outlandish circumstances allow.

Confabulatory performances can also be induced by less exotic manipulations. In his classic study, Maier (1931: 182) asked that participants tie together two cords hanging from the ceiling, when the distance separating them was such that if a participant "held either cord in his hand he could not hold the other." Various aids were available, such as a pole that could be used to pull the cords together, but there was one especially inobvious solution: tying a weight to one cord and swinging it like a pendulum, thus bringing it close enough to the other cord so that both could be grasped simultaneously. Participants who had difficulty finding this solution were given a "hint": the experimenter bumping into one cord and setting it into motion. Apparently, the hint helped, yet people did not typically credit it for their success (Maier 1931: 186). Instead, they said things like it just "dawned" on them, or was suggested by a course in physics; a psychology professor claimed inspiration from a vision:

Having exhausted everything else, the next thing was to swing it…. I had imagery of monkeys swinging from trees. This imagery appeared simultaneously with the solution. The idea appeared complete. (Maier 1931: 188–9)

Here, the intimations of grandiosity may say less about the nature of confabulation than the nature of the professor. But there's a sense in which one needn't doubt him; perhaps he really did have a simian vision as he found the solution. What one should doubt is that this monkey business represents a complete causal account of the cognitive processes implicated in the problem solving, since it omits mention of the hint. And this omission misleads, in a way not unlike the way plagiarism misleads: the professor failed to credit the source of his insight (a common occupational failing).

Not only do people fabricate with leaping imaginations, they maintain their fictions with plodding tenacity. Consider Latané and Darley's canonical demonstrations of the Group Effect, a well-documented tendency for increasing numbers of bystanders to depress the likelihood of individual helping (Doris 2002: 32–3; Latané and Nida 1981). In debriefing participants who had been subject to this influence, Latané and Darley (1970: 124) wondered why they failed to help:

We asked this question every way we knew how: subtly, directly, tactfully, bluntly. Always we got the same answer. Subjects persistently claimed that their behavior was not influenced by the other people present. This denial occurred in the face of results showing that the presence of others did inhibit helping.

It's possible that the Group Effect caused the perception of non-emergency, which in turn caused the omission; in this case, the participants would be possessed of an accurate, but incomplete, causal history. Another possibility is that participants identified a correct and complete causal explanation for their behavior, but chose to report something presenting them in a more favorable light. It's likely that people favored self-serving explanations—such as saying they didn't believe there was a "real" emergency (Latané and Darley 1970: 65)—but I doubt their spinning was conscious prevarication.

To see why, consider the growing body of evidence suggesting that folk psychology is heavily infused with folk morality (Knobe 2003, 2010; Malle 2004); when people interpret and explain their own and others' behavior, normative considerations may be at least as important as are descriptive ones. Accordingly, questions like "Why didn't you help?" may be heard as demands for justification rather than demands for causal explanation. When the query is understood this way, "it wasn't a real emergency," looks a better answer than "I was influenced by other bystanders," even though it does not fully report the psychological facts. Supposing so, it is quite unsurprising that self-reports on the origins of behavior are inaccurate or incomplete; the purposes of such reports are as much (or more) normative or practical as they are scientific or epistemic. As we'll now see, volumes of evidence indicate that self-awareness is pervasively influenced by extra-epistemological factors.

Motivation

While 66 percent of Americans in a 1997 poll thought television personality Oprah Winfrey likely to reach heaven, 87 percent rated themselves as likely to do so (Staglin 1997). If that's not hubris enough, only 79 percent of Americans thought Mother Teresa was likely to make the cut: you're more sainted than a talk show superstar, maybe, but more sainted than a *candidate for sainthood*? Mother Teresa got some bad press (Hitchens 1995), but still.

Self-admiration isn't limited to heavenly matters. In 1987, John Jacob Cannell (1988), a West Virginia physician, discovered that none of the 50 American states reported their students were below average on standardized test performance. He dubbed this circumstance the Lake Wobegon Effect, after Garrison Keillor's pastoral fantasy, where "all the children are above average."

Subsequently, psychologists appropriated Cannell's label to mark a tendency for most people think they are better than most people (Gilovich 1991: 77–8; Kruger 1999; Myers 1998). In one study, 88 percent of American drivers and 77 percent of Swedish drivers rated themselves safer than the median driver, while 93 percent of Americans and 69 percent of Swedes rated themselves more skilled than the median driver (Svenson 1981: 146). These assessments may be untroubled by fact: in a study comparing drivers who had been hospitalized due to a serious traffic accident with controls who had never been in a serious accident, mean self-ratings for driving performance were "almost identical" between the two groups, and much closer to the "expert" than the "very poor" pole of a scale (Preston and Harris 1965: 286). It's possible the injured drivers really were expert, and just unlucky, as they themselves may have thought. Not so much: police reports indicated that 34 of 50 hospitalized drivers were responsible for their accident (Preston and Harris 1965: 287).

Lake Wobegon would be a great place to live. Unfortunately, it's not only fictional, but also impossible: more than half of a population cannot exceed the population median in a given respect. (Of course, comparisons must be specified: nothing odd about saying that more than half of Cornell students are above the *national* median for parent income, but more than half of Cornell students can't be above the *Cornell* median.) Yet findings in the vicinity of the Lake Wobegon

Effect have been reported for a wide variety of valued attributes and behaviors, including popularity (Zuckerman and Jost 2001), fairness (Messick *et al.* 1985), cooperativeness, honesty, and politeness (Alicke *et al.* 2001: 13–17).

Enhancement is not an "undergraduate effect" confined to students who sleepwalk through experiments for course credit. Indeed, their teachers may be equally self-impressed: 94 percent of respondents to a faculty survey at the University of Nebraska (Cross 1977: 10) rated themselves as above average teachers, and 68 percent placed themselves in the top quarter. (I can't say for sure whether the Nebraska faculty is representative in this regard, but I'd be surprised to discover greater modesty among professors on the coasts.) Nor is self-congratulation confined to the ivory tower: in a study of engineers, more than 30 percent rated their performance in the top 5 percent relative to their peers, while only one of 714 respondents felt their performance was below average (Zenger 1992: 202).

Rosy self-assessment may be especially pronounced among the inept. When participants in a trap and skeet competition were tested on gun usage and safety, the worst performers estimated their ranking as in the 65th percentile, while their actual performance placed them around the 11th percentile (Ehrlinger *et al.* 2008; Study 3, and 105). Incompetence not only results in poor performance, it can also prevent the incompetent from competently assessing that performance.

There's some evidence that people don't actually understand questions about percentile rankings in terms of statistical comparisons (Klar and Giladi 1999: 592–3; Wood 1996: 524–5). People may intend "above average," as something like "pretty good," rather than as "above the median." If so, self-assessments would not necessarily exhibit the sort of statistical peculiarity intimated by the Lake Wobegon Effect, since most people might be pretty good at many things— water boiling, say, or elevator riding. I don't know how, or if, this interpretation could be made to work across all the relevant studies, but, fortunately, we needn't endure the labor. For even if above-average phenomena are an artifact of how participants interpret questions, people self-enhance, whether or not they understand their enhancements in terms of statistical comparisons. This summary of the evidence still seems to me a fair one: "most people possess inflated self-views: they overestimate their strengths and underestimate or are unaware of their weaknesses" (Dufner *et al.* 2012: 538; cf. Alicke *et al.* 2001: 9; Dunning 2006).

Why should a tendency exist? Why *shouldn't* it? Pretty good reasons for folks to view themselves favorably: if I'm convinced I'm stupid and ugly, I'll be afraid to ask, and how many dates will that get me? But if I think well enough of myself to toss the dice, I may get lucky sometimes, even if I *am* stupid and ugly. Additionally, thinking well of myself might actually make me more attractive than I might otherwise be (an important kind of self-formation we'll discuss later.) In fact, narcissists, who are notorious self-enhancers, may have higher "mate appeal," at least for the short term: one study found women more receptive to the advances of males higher in narcissism (Dufner *et al.* 2013: Study 3). In general, it is sensibly assumed that self-enhancement has considerable advantages, given that self-esteem is associated with well-being (Baumeister *et al.* 2003; Diener and Diener 1995) and self-enhancement may contribute to self-esteem.

I don't want to oversimplify: the extent to which self-enhancement occurs, or fails to occur, varies across individuals, behaviors, attributes, circumstances, and assessment criteria, and it's very probable that nobody self-enhances about everything all the time (Gosling *et al.* 1998; John and Robins 1994).[2] Accuracy in self-awareness is highly variable; people may be quite accurate about some things, and much less so about others (Vazire 2010).

Self-enhancement—where it exists—is a form of "motivated cognition," a fancy name for an old saw: folks tend to believe what they want to believe. In considering a disagreeable proposition, people in effect ask, "*Must* I believe this?", but when evaluating an agreeable proposition, people ask, "*Can* I believe this?" (Gilovich 1991: 84; cf. Dawson *et al.* 2002: 1379–41; Ditto and Lopez 1992). Thus, for disagreeable propositions, people focus on disconfirming evidence (considerations that support doubting what they want to doubt), while for agreeable propositions, they focus on confirming evidence (considerations that support believing what they want to believe).

For example, motivational manipulations may affect performance on the Wason (1966: 146) card-selection task, which is designed to investigate rule-testing strategies. Folks tend not to do especially well at this assignment, apparently because they often succumb to "confirmation bias," a propensity to seek confirming instances of a rule rather than disconfirming exceptions to the rule (Wason and Johnson-Laird 1972: 174–5). In one Wason task study, however, people were about four times as likely (46 percent vs 10 percent) to find the right testing strategy for threatening hypotheses (e.g. one intimating their early death) as they were when testing hypotheses that were unthreatening (Dawson *et al.* 2002: 1382–4). Along with motivational influences on the search for evidence, there may be motivational influences on the assessment of evidence: participants told they performed more poorly than they expected on an intelligence test

---

[2] In addition to self-enhancement—the tendency to attribute positive qualities and attributes to oneself, there's self-protection—the tendency to resist negative attributions to oneself, and self-maintenance or self-verification—the tendency to preserve an existing self-impression, whether positive or negative (Dunning 1999: 7–8; Swann and Schroeder 1995: 1311–12).

judged such tests to be less accurate than participants told they performed better than they expected (Wyer and Frey 1983: 550).

The existence of motivated cognition does not mean that intellection is completely undisciplined by fact. Although increasing a thinker's incentives for accuracy does not always improve performance, it's clear that "accuracy goals" are important in reasoning (Kunda 1990: 481–3). Not surprising: if one wants to avoid becoming tiger chow, one's question concerns where the tigers are, not where one wishes them to be.

But when its child is the self, cognition is a permissive parent. Motivated cognition may effect both self-enhancing understandings of attributes, and self-enhancing evaluation of the performances associated with some desired attribute (Dunning 1999: 5–6); an unproductive professor might think publications irrelevant to professional competence, while the professor who produces boatloads of drivel might evaluate his excessive output with undue generosity. This tendency might not much impair self-awareness in the case of relatively "unambiguous" attributes such as *thrifty*, *mathematical*, and *neat*, where conceptions of the attribute are tolerably clear and behavioral criteria for attribution are relatively uncontroversial. For unambiguous attributes, Dunning (1999: 3–4; cf. Dunning *et al.* 1989; Hayes and Dunning 1997) found the average self-rating close enough to average, but in the case of "ambiguous" attributes, the average person saw themselves as above average in desirable qualities like *sensible*, *idealistic*, and *disciplined*, and below average for undesirable qualities like *neurotic*, *impractical*, and *submissive*. (Hayes and Dunning (1997: 668) report an inter-rater reliability of 0.77 for judgments of ambiguity, meaning that, at least in their sample, people manifest a respectable amount of agreement regarding which attributes are ambiguous and which not.) Moreover, many important attributes have a strong evaluative component, and people's self-awareness appears to be less accurate for more evaluative attributes like creativity and more accurate for less evaluative attributes like anxiety (Vazire 2010).

Once again, consider teaching effectiveness. While academics tend towards favorable opinions of their own teaching, their self-assessment may not be widely shared: for professors at one liberal arts college, self-perceptions of teaching effectiveness correlated rather modestly with the perceptions of colleagues (0.28), students (0.19), and administrators (0.10) (Blackburn and Clark 1975: 249). As an academic, I've occasionally been amused to hear professors intoning pieties about the importance of pedagogy, when by all accounts they couldn't teach a dog to bark. Aren't these righteous incompetents faced with realities, like classrooms full of bored and surly students, that should shame them into silence? Well, even if students know a stinker when they see one, in many academic subjects it's uncertain what pedagogic effectiveness consists in, and how effectiveness should be assessed (Arum and Roska 2011). Supposing standards were settled, one might simply avoid the evidence, as in one case of my acquaintance, where a famously fatuous instructor simply declined to provide students with course evaluation materials. (Even if the professor provides the materials, they aren't compelled to consider the results.) When evidence cannot be so easily evaded, it can be interpreted in self-protective ways: for the reviled pedant, student evaluations are "popularity contests" and better-received colleagues are "panderers." Self-enhancement, one guesses, can be impressively resilient.

Although the extent of motivated cognition is the subject of controversy, and the boundaries between motivational and cognitive processes are both theoretically and empirically indeterminate, there seems little doubt that motivational forces powerfully influence cognition (Dunning *et al.* 1999: 79; Gilovich 1991: 75–87; Kruglanski 1996; Kunda 1990: 493). If, as C. I. Lewis (1946: 3) said, knowing is for doing, it's not surprising that cognition is shot through with motivation. Indeed, if it weren't for doing, there'd be relatively little pay-off in knowing (ecstasies of philosophical contemplation notwithstanding). Cognition is structured by extra-epistemological considerations because the cognitive often serves the biological: an animal needs to cogitate because it needs to go get 'em—shelter, food, and mates. One should expect the development of cognitive tendencies that serve these aims, even where this does not facilitate epistemological goals like accuracy.

In sum: healthy people share two important characteristics with confabulatory patients: their self-awareness is limited, and strongly influenced by motivational factors. The literature suggests that healthy self-perception is routinely inaccurate, and also helps explain why this is so: the general tendency to motivated cognition, and the particular tendency to self-enhancement, promote inaccuracy. Confabulatory utterances by healthy people, while not conscious boasting or prevarication, seem designed to make the speaker look good: the bystander is realistic rather than apathetic, the professor is brilliant rather than befuddled, and the hypnotic subject is running the show rather than playing the fool.

If this is right, it's hard to see how the argument from experience can rebut skepticism about agency, because it's highly doubtful that people's self-awareness is as reliable as the experiential argument requires. For experience to have epistemic heft sufficient to block skepticism, its reliability must not be subject to substantial doubts, but the empirical literature indicates that it is so subject. Saying this is not to say that self-perception is never accurate, or that cognition is always motivated, or that all self-perception is self-enhancement. Rejecting the experiential argument does not entail these implausibly strong claims. It requires only that there be sufficient cause to doubt the general reliability of the relevant experiences, and given the extent of the evidence documenting inaccuracies in self-perception, it may fairly be concluded that there is sufficient cause. If this is right, the experience of agency is an inadequate bulwark against skepticism about agency.

Confidence

It might be argued that the problem isn't self-ignorance, but difficulty in reporting self-awareness. Maybe people's awareness of self is tolerably accurate, but somehow "ineffable"; maybe people know their minds perfectly well, but can't find the words to talk about it. As it stands, this is hard to credit, at least in many cases; what's ineffable about, "I got it when I saw the cord swinging", "I thought someone else would help"? Nice short sentences, made up of nice short words: no call for poetry here. People have little difficulty going on about swinging monkeys, or heroically insisting on the irrelevance of other bystanders; what's the difficulty about reporting the accurate story, supposing it is known?

A more promising maneuver proceeds by reference to memory decay. In typical experiments, time elapses between the behavior of interest and the debriefing, which leaves the possibility that occurrent self-awareness is accurate, but correct reporting is impeded by poor memory for what participants were once aware of (Ericsson and Simon 1980: 246). But even if memory errors are sometimes implicated in confabulatory phenomena, it remains the case that self-reports are often inaccurate, and the reporters themselves are unaware of this inaccuracy. If the contents of such reports may be assumed to figure in practical reasoning—the reason for which I remember doing something may affect my propensity towards doing it again—uncertainty about agency remains.

It's not that folks are always wrong about themselves; people may provide accurate explanations of their cognition and behavior when the actual causal explanation corresponds to an intuitively accessible causal schema (Nisbett and Wilson 1977: 253; cf. Davies 2009: 146–57).

Q: "Why were you late picking me up at the airport?"
A: "I was stuck in traffic."

Assuming there's not call to suspect dissembling, there's little concern about accuracy here. But notice: this report does not report an agent experience. The speaker is heavily constrained, and that's a large part of why it is so plausible to think that report and the reality match up; there's little else she could do. I might correctly explain my behavior using an intuitively accessible causal schema—just as I might correctly explain *your* behavior using an intuitively accessible causal schema—with very little insight into the psychological antecedents of my behavior.

But where there are more degrees of freedom, things get muddy quickly. And it's these cases, unlike cases of being stuck in traffic, where issues about self-awareness are likely to arise:

Q: "Why were you late picking me up at the airport?"
A: "I needed to finish folding the laundry."

Really? Why not, "I'm a little angry with you"?

As the material, psychological, and social complexity of circumstances increase—just the sort of circumstances where worries about agency press hardest—self-awareness is increasingly imperiled. In many situations where ethically substantial questions of agency and responsibility emerge, there's likely to be any number of possible motivations in the air, and it may be hard to know which are doing the work. And many of these scenes are likely to be emotionally fraught: is my grasping for the family heirlooms sentiment or avarice? In such instances, one has powerful motives to be wrong about one's motives; tenderness is more appealing than covetousness. Matters appear even shakier when one reflects that motives are frequently mixed—no doubt I'm both sappy and greedy—and ascertaining the admixture may be difficult indeed.

I might here be accused of cooking the books: families are notoriously incomprehensible, and any sensible person will allow considerable opacity regards the psychological ingredients of family feuds. (Except in heat of battle, when one's motives present themselves as luminously pure). But surely, it will be argued, many cases are not so uncertain. One possibility for distinguishing the inaccurate from the accurate references the reporter's confidence (Fiala and Nichols 2009); perhaps the self-ignorant stammer where the self-aware speak assuredly. Not always. One study noted an "inverse correlation" between confabulation and response latency during recovery from a head trauma; as the patient's condition improved, latencies increased as responses received greater scrutiny (Mercer *et al.* 1977: 431–3). Here, confidence and confabulation may be *positively* associated. Nor is unfounded confidence confined to the unwell (cf. Carruthers 2009a: 169); for example, the group effect participants stuck bravely to their guns.

Then I'm not confident we should be confident about confidence. A large literature indicates that people are routinely and substantially overconfident about even relatively simple judgments (e.g. Dunning *et al.* 1990; Einhorn and Hogarth 1978; Gill *et al.* 1998); for the particular case of memory, the nature of the relationship between confidence and accuracy has been characterized as "it depends" (Roediger and DeSoto 2014: 89), which doesn't incline one to employ confidence as a bulwark against skepticism. The skeptical difficulty persists.

Signpost

I've argued that the confabulation literature undermines the experiential response to skepticism. In my discussion of clinical confabulation, four factors emerged as especially prominent: deficient self-awareness, deficient self-control, motivation, and deficient sociality. We've seen that deficient self-awareness is likewise common in healthy populations, and normal self-awareness is also strongly influenced by motivational factors. But there are also two important dissimilarities: healthy people do not suffer the deficiencies in control and sociality that characterize clinical confabulation. Exploring these dissimilarities will help locate the sort of agency healthy people enjoy.

Reprise

In the first four chapters, I articulated a skepticism about morally responsible agency. I identified a philosophically standard account, reflectivism, which char-acterizes agency in terms of deliberation informed by accurate self-awareness, and argued that this approach falls prey to skepticism. The skeptical difficulty is empirical in origin, drawing on dual process theories in psychology, which posit the existence of incongruent parallel processing, where different cognitive systems contemporaneously deliver divergent outputs regarding the same objects.

I used the term *defeaters* for cases of incongruence where the actor would not count the causes of her behavior and cognition as reasons. I contended that where the existence of defeaters cannot be confidently ruled out, the attribution of agency is unwarranted. Since reflectivism is not possessed of adequate resources for ruling out the existence of defeaters, I argued, it is afflicted by skepticism. Finally, I claimed that the prevalence of confabulatory phenomena means that the most obvious material the reflectivist might use for ruling out, the experience of agency, is untenable in that capacity.

My exposition was not entirely negative, however. I outlined a positive approach to morally responsible agency, the valuational approach, which locates the exercise of agency in the expression of an actor's values. In the second half of the book, I attempt to develop a valuational account in a way that withstands skeptical threat, while taking appropriate stock of the psychological findings. Instead of attempting to explain away the unnerving evidence, I commend a different approach: *praise it*. I'll argue that for healthy people, certain forms of confabulatory exchange *promote* agency. If we want to know how human beings suffering substantial self-ignorance can exercise morally responsible agency, we must look to the social nature of confabulatory phenomena. My positive account of agency, then, will begin with an account of sociality.

II

II

5

Collaboration

Human beings are profoundly social organisms who do everything together, from making love to making war. It may seem like philosophers fully appreciate this obvious observation: that humans are, in Aristotle's words, *zoa politika*, is a staple of introductory philosophy classes. Yet much Western philosophy bears the imprint of *individualism*, the supposition that people reason best asocially, doors closed and curtains drawn, as in the gripping fiction of Descartes' *Meditations*.[1] I contend individualism is mistaken, and will now defend *collaborativism*, which holds that optimal human reasoning is facilitated by social interaction.[2] Subsequently, I'll extend collaborativism about reasoning to collaborativism about agency: when one properly attends to the sociality of human organisms, one realizes that the exercise of individual agency is a substantially interpersonal phenomenon (cf. Oshana 2006; Vargas 2013b: 226 n33). This realization, in turn, will help illuminate the path away from skepticism.

Sociality

"Reasoning" covers a multitude of sins, and not all of them public; the magic moment when one is clobbered by the validity of a deductive inference, for example, seems a pretty internal affair. But this should not obscure the fact that much human reasoning is a social process. On the precise nature of sociality, I don't have—or need—anything very fancy to say. The social, on my view, is simply a circumstance where two or more people interact. While this often involves physical proximity, it needn't: distal interaction with technologies like cell phones or email certainly counts. Many of the most prominent instances of human sociality involve language use, and the centrality of language in thought

---

[1] Here, "individualism" about reasoning doesn't carry quite the same sense as does the "individualism" contrasted with "collectivism" in cultural psychology (see Ch. 3, p. 53; Ch. 8, p. 194), although there are likely affinities.

[2] Much of this chapter derives from Doris and Nichols (2012); I'm grateful to Nichols for indulging my appropriations. Thanks to Mark Timmons for the term "collaborativism."

and behavior is one motivation for collaborativism about reasoning. But much sociality doesn't involve speech: the companionable silence of friends, or the unspoken passion of lovers.

There's also virtual sociality, where a solitary person can be said to function socially. The disapproving gaze of the "imagined other" characterizing shame is familiar in moral philosophy, but examples abound, such as the private, but socially engaged, activity of journal writing (time was, *Dear Diary* received a lot of letters). Virtual sociality might facilitate reasoning, as when "debating" an imaginary interlocutor, but there are limits; too much time talking to yourself and not enough to other selves, you might go off the rails.

Anywhere there's culture—and that's anywhere with people—there's quite a lot of virtual sociality about, since even solitary behavior is often governed by cultural norms. Indeed, human organisms are so sensitive to their social surroundings that there is, as well see later on, quite a bit of difficulty in determining where the individual ends and the social begins (cf. Wilson 2004). For present purposes, however, I don't require delicacies; there exist more than enough clear-cut examples of sociality in reasoning to motivate collaborativism.

Rationality

Notoriously, theorizing about rationality risks interminable morass. Hopefully, I won't tarry long enough to get stuck, but a few clarifications are in order.

In the first instance, collaborativism is a descriptive thesis about how people actually reason, but as "optimal" cautions, it also has normative entailments about how people ought reason. One might aspire to "purely" normative inquiry, and articulate idealized standards for reasoning without attending to how people actually reason. On the other hand, it wouldn't be crazy to develop norms of reasoning with attention to how people—as opposed to, say, Rufous Spiny Bandicoots—actually think things through. In asking questions about optimal reasoning, I'm asking about the circumstances where actual human organisms are in fact able to reason best; optimal reasoning is here a more empirically constrained notion than ideal reasoning, as ideals needn't be beholden to the limitations of flesh, blood, and brain.

Where there's normativity, there's controversy. For instance, multiple standards of rational assessment exist, and which apply where is disputable. Consider proposals for a "flat tax," where everyone is taxed at the same rate, regardless of income. Suppose that a flat tax favors the wealthy. If so, the question of whether it is rational to support the flat tax might depend on one's financial circumstances: on economic conceptions of rationality, the rich should favor a flat tax, and the poor shouldn't. On the other hand, suppose that a flat tax would exacerbate the socio-economic polarization of American culture. If so, moral conceptions of rationality might counsel prosperous Americans opposing a flat tax, no matter the extent to which it would help them amass more wealth. What one thinks should count as good reasoning seems to depend, in each case, on what one thinks that reasoning should be about.

Nevertheless, philosophers have not despaired of a general account. Humean instrumentalism is refreshingly straightforward: given those beliefs and those desires, the rational thing for the agent to do is simply to act so as to satisfy the desires in light of the beliefs. But this, as has been noted many times, feels a bit slight (Korsgaard 1996; Velleman 2006: 17–19, 349): what if a person, like too many people, has blockheaded beliefs, or deplorable desires? Satisfying one's desires, plainly, is not always desirable. On the other hand, notions of reasons that do not somehow connect with a person's desires are a little mysterious (Williams 1981: 111): if the Queen doesn't care whether the unwashed masses eat bread or cake, what does it mean to say *she* has reason to feed the hungry?

Instrumentalism might be fattened up with "informed desire" riders (Brandt 1979; Railton 2003; Smith 1994), where what's rational is not what the agent desires, full stop, but what she *would* desire, were she fully and vividly informed of the relevant facts, and free of cognitive abnormalities: if the King really understood the risks of smoking, he'd want to quit, and if the Queen really understood the societal costs of florid inequity, she'd want to spread the bread around. The hope is for a notion of reason that both connects to, and allows, a robust critical perspective on, the reasoner's desires, which narrows the gap between the desired and the desirable (cf. Railton 2003: 11). This approach has its critics (Loeb 1995; Rosati 1995; Sobel 1994), but it represents one way to substantiate the thought that there are better and worse ways of reasoning.

Less ambitiously, one might simply note that very often, what counts as successful reasoning isn't especially controversial. While there will be disagreements, there will also be many cases where there's a pretty untroubled notion of what a *mistake* would be, and what it would be to avoid making one. These are the cases with which I'll illustrate collaborativism. Raising doubts in these instances, it seems to me, would trend in the direction of a general skepticism—a skepticism insisting that there's no sense to be given the thought that some reasonings are better, and others worse. If you're tempted to that kind of scorched earth skepticism, I don't know how to dissuade you, and our discussions are unlikely to be mutually satisfying. (Radical skeptics get that a lot, I reckon.)

This said, the relationship between assessments of rationality and attributions of agency is uncertain. In formulating the skeptical problem, I assumed a subjective notion of reasons: there, a reason was simply a consideration that a person would take as commending or justifying her judgment or behavior. This formulation has limited normative bite: it doesn't say anything about whether the considerations in question are admirable or despicable. The discretion may be welcome, however, for it's not clear that that the exercise of agency has much to do with the goodness or badness of the agent's reasons: one might reason in ways far short of optimal, yet still be acting as a responsible agent.

Picture a father courting ruin for himself and his family by embezzling money for his collection of rare books. This might be thought variously irrational: ruin sucks, so the joys of bibliophilia, no matter how sublime, don't justify courting it, and needlessly risking the welfare of one's family is, to put it mildly, morally suspect. At the same time, it's quite conceivable that our fanatical collector is exercising agency in pursuit of his misguided aims; barring evidence of a clinical condition like bibliomania (Basbanes 1996), it's appropriate to hold him responsible for his misdeeds. The contrary circumstance is also possible. One might act rationally in instances where it is not obvious one is acting as an agent; I might be coerced or manipulated into acting so as to secure the best outcome for myself.

Not infrequently, the associations between rationality and agency are closer. For instance, a plausible minimal requirement for rationality is a consistency or coherence constraint, and inability to abide by this constraint may impair agency. A gynecologist friend of mine reports that a surprising number of her patients avow the following constellation of inclination and disinclination: *I want to have intercourse—I do not want to use contraception—I do not want to have a baby.* These parents-to-be have mutually frustrating inclinations, and failure to appreciate the tension here may impair expression of their values, when their lives are disrupted by an unwanted pregnancy.

Like good reasoning, agency is plausibly thought to require "cognitive feats" (Doris and Murphy 2007). Inability to recognize which circumstances are conducive to the expression of one's values would presumably impair one's ability to act in ways expressing one's values; such a cognitive disability could be a disability afflicting the exercise of agency. Which suggests at least this much: conditions that support or disrupt reasoning may also support or disrupt agency. Here, I'll articulate a collaborativism about reasoning, and then extend it to agency—the thought being that some conditions conducive to optimal reasoning may have analogs in the conditions that are most conducive to the exercise of agency.

Canon

Collaborativism maintains that optimal human reasoning is substantially social, and therefore intimates that sociality facilitates problem solving, while individualism maintains that optimal human reasoning is asocial, and therefore intimates that sociality does not facilitate, and may impede, problem solving. An early appearance of "individualism" prefiguring my usage was Tocqueville's *Democracy in America*; his followers have employed it to describe an "American character," which "values independence and self reliance above all else" (Bellah *et al.* 1996: viii, 35–9). Certainly, these sentiments are readily identified in an America where the rugged individualist is celebrated, the conformist is castigated, and the child is admonished about succumbing to "peer pressure." But for my purposes, more relevant are assertions of individualist flavor found across the Western philosophical canon, over a variety of contexts.

So, Descartes (1641/1901: Meditations III, sec. 1):

I will now close my eyes, I will stop my ears, I will turn away my senses from their objects, I will even efface from my consciousness all the images of corporeal things;...holding converse only with myself, and closely examining my nature, I will endeavor to obtain by degrees a more intimate and familiar knowledge of myself.

The *Meditations*' problem is obtaining knowledge of the external world. The solution, it turns out, is not discussion with friends, or setting up a lab, but quite the opposite: the isolated enquirer is the one who achieves knowledge. Of course, Descartes in the *Meditations* is spinning an illustrative yarn. His method there, it might be said, is an ideal method; at most, a "once in life" epistemic ground-clearing for subsequent inquiry (Garber 1986). In either case, it is not meant to exclude sociality from inquiry. But whatever reading one adopts, this celebrated passage hardly looks an incitement to the social, and if one seeks inspirations for individualism, Descartes' masterpiece is not an iconoclastic place to look.

Still, the *Meditations* look to be a work of theoretical reason (concerning what to believe) and their relation to the questions of practical reason (concerning what to do) that preoccupy moral philosophers is tenuous. I don't suppose the distinction between the theoretical and practical is any sturdier than the distinction between the descriptive and normative, but no matter.[3] For strains of individualism also appear in venerable conceptions of practical reason, such as Kant's (1784/1963: 3), where "enlightenment is the release of human beings from

---

[3] I do suppose that reasoning in the vicinity of the theoretical (like that going into this book) is less prey than practical deliberation (like that going into career choice) to the skepticism under consideration, because I don't think the former sort of reasoning is much troubled by self-ignorance.

their self-incurred tutelage," and "[t]utelage is the inability to use one's own reason without direction from someone else."

Individualism is also evident in prominent conceptions of human excellence, including conceptions at substantial distance from Kant. Nietzsche (e.g. 1886/1966: 212) repeatedly warns of the danger "the herd" presents to his "higher type" of man, and insists that greatness requires "wanting to be by oneself, being able to be different, standing alone and having to live independently" (cf. Leiter 2002: 116–17). Individualism also appears in the writings of Mill (1863/2002: 65), when he insists that it is "only the cultivation of individuality which produces, or can produce, well-developed human beings." While the differences between Mill and Nietzsche are at least as conspicuous as those between Mill and Kant, Mill appears to share with Nietzsche an attachment to an individualist perfectionism, where the possibility of human excellence increases as the susceptibility to social influence decreases.

It doesn't take an overactive imagination to see individualism in Western philosophy, but as every graduate student knows, history is a dangerous thing, and Hell hath few Furies to rival scholars who fear their favorite thinker scorned. There's often good evidence for quite contrary interpretations within a particular text; perhaps the individualist passages I've selected are counterbalanced, or negated, by collaborativist passages. For instance, we'd not want to exaggerate the individualism of Mill, who defends free speech on the grounds that it facilitates public scrutiny of ideas (Mill 1863/2002: Ch. 2; cf. Appiah 2005: 4, 20–1). And Descartes, when not closing his eyes and stopping his ears, was an energetic philosophical correspondent, who accompanied his *Meditations* with "Objections and Replies," where he engages his critics (Ariew and Greene 1995; Cottingham *et al.* 1991).

Given the difficulty of deciding interpretative questions, it's lucky I don't have to decide them. Suppose my proffered individualist reading of the history is *right*, and canonical philosophers neglect the importance of sociality. Then we've the prospect of showing some of the greatest philosophers in the Western tradition to be guilty of serious error. This would be a largish result. Now suppose that I'm *wrong* about the history, and my intended targets, when read with proper care, give due weight to sociality. Then we have the prospect of showing some of greatest philosophers in the Western tradition to be vindicated by cognitive science produced ages after their deaths. This, too, would be a largish result.

Thus, collaborativism might be either a revision of canonical ideas in Western philosophy or a vindication of canonical ideas in Western philosophy. What matters to me is that if I'm right about collaborativism, intimations of individualism such as those appearing in the work of canonical philosophers are—whether or not such intimations reflect their comprehensive positions—to be studiously avoided. My dabbling in canon serves purposes heuristic rather than historical; it articulates collaborativism by highlighting familiar sentiments of the sort collaborativism rejects.

Furthermore, the tradition also contains inspirations for collaborativism. Whatever his considered view, Aristotle has moments that should endear him to collaborativists; as already remarked, he called human beings political animals, and he went so far as to liken humans to hiving organisms like bees (1984: *Pol.* 1253a19–39; 1298b20; *EN* 1155a15–16; *HA* 487b33–488a10; *Pol.* 1253a7–18; cf. Brown 2013; Cooper 1999: 362–3). In this, he prefigured contemporary evolutionary theorists, who have compared the social character of human reproduction and child-rearing to the reproductive biology of eusocial insects (Foster and Ratnieks 2005). It is the profoundly social character of human life, I'm contending, that has received inadequate stress in theorizing about reasoning and agency; even if the sociality of humanity is oft remarked upon, it is not sufficiently emphasized, in these contexts, *just how social* human organisms are.

Science

Whatever way one assigns credit and blame across the philosophical corpus, contemporary social science—the *social* in "social science" notwithstanding—often has an individualist cast, with much empirical work investigating personal (and sub-personal) processes at the expense of group dynamics.

Think of the social psychology vignette studies that have, in part because they are relatively inexpensive and uncomplicated, been the paradigm most often pursued by experimental philosophers studying moral cognition (Knobe and Nichols 2008): sneak into the department office under cover of darkness, Xerox the needed copies of your surveys, and you're good to go (given IRB approval), near enough for free. Now look, for a moment, as the dutiful participants quietly—though shockingly quickly—fill out their questionnaires: they're hunched over their desks, looking neither left nor right, as they work through the intricacies of some moral problematic.

If the silence isn't deafening, it should be. Instead of this monastic setting, go down to your neighborhood bar, where you might find the regulars discussing some moral conundrum: steroids in sports, maybe, or the finer points of marital infidelity. Voices are raised; fingers are pointed. And that's the point. In the wild, folks don't do this stuff quietly: they cajole, they argue, they abuse—in groups. It's hard to imagine something more unlike experimental participants mutely circling numbers on a Likert scale.

The same concern applies to another place where scientists study morality: scanner studies of neural activity in moral judgment (Cushman *et al.* 2010; Greene 2007; Greene *et al.* 2001, 2004; Moll *et al.* 2002a, b, 2008). Once again, things are pretty quiet (save the clang and clatter of the fMRI machine); the participants think alone (cf. Schilbach *et al.* 2013). In both vignette and scanner studies, moral cognition is treated as the activity of solitary individuals. Indeed, for scanners, the variables of interest often involve only *parts* of persons. The best of this work has had a transformative impact on moral psychology, but it can't take us all the way there.

Scientists probably don't appreciate uncharitable readings any more than historians of philosophy, so I should hasten to add that some psychology is properly social, and attends to the role of interpersonal dynamics in behavior (e.g. Kurzban *et al.* 2007; Kurzban and DeScioli 2008; Latané and Darley 1970; Milgram 1974). But to go further, we need more. This makes a noisy undertaking, because fully engaging the social introduces a great mess of factors inimical to the controlled observation that distinguishes experimental inquiry. But the racket is worth it, if what's wanted is an approach to moral psychology that's as garrulously social as the lived human life. I can't do as much as I'd like, because I consider phenomena taken in bits and pieces from a diversity of literatures, and these fragments make an unruly pastiche. But with luck, I'll do enough to motivate collaborativism.

Orientation

At this juncture, the plot has thickened. I've been opposing reflectivism, but I've now identified a new adversary, individualism. Reflectivism and individualism needn't be conjoined: you could hold one without holding the other, and there exist no obvious entailments between them. At the same time, they're united in sorrow: if reflectivism engenders skeptical difficulty, individualism obscures the best avenue of escape. Ameliorating skepticism about agency will require rejecting *both* reflectivism and individualism.

Isolation

In the 1950s and 1960s, Harlow conducted an infamous series of experiments documenting the effects of isolation on rhesus monkeys (Harlow 1986; Harlow *et al.* 1965). Within hours of their birth, infant monkeys were imprisoned in a stainless steel chamber and afforded no contact with any animal, human or non-human, for three to twelve months. The consequences were grievous. When removed from isolation, two of six monkeys in the three-month group stopped eating entirely, one of these died, and the other was force fed to keep it alive. Monkeys in all isolation groups developed florid psychopathologies, including aggression and withdrawal; in some instances females were unable to breed, or properly care for their young.

It was extremely difficult to restore the isolates to approximations of normalcy, but significantly, the only effective treatment was social. When debilitated monkeys that had been reared in isolation from birth to six months were paired with three-month-old normal monkeys (labeled "therapists"), within half a year isolates were almost indistinguishable from monkeys that had been raised in a social environment (Harlow and Suomi 1971: 1537–8).

Studies of this kind using human populations are, thankfully, prohibited on ethical grounds. (Indeed, many of Harlow's experiments with *monkeys* are ethically objectionable.) Yet history is scattered with "forbidden experiments" involving feral children, who have been found living in the wild or among animals, and confined children, who are the victims of egregious abuse and neglect. Although I'm inclined to believe some reports of feral children, it's safer to consider the somewhat better documented material on confined children.

Among the most notorious cases dates from the 1970s, when "Genie" was discovered by authorities in Los Angeles, having spent most of her thirteen years imprisoned alone in a single room (Newton 2002: 208–29). Unsurprisingly, Genie was tragically impaired: such formative social deprivation causes severe cognitive and social disability, such as deficiencies in language acquisition. Of course, this is not solely due isolation: confined children are typically subject to additional abuse and neglect, and impairment is also attributable to these factors. As I've said, the phenomena are noisy, and the causal factors at issue are not readily disentangled. But there is little reason to doubt that social isolation is a major pathogen in these cases, just as the Harlow studies would lead one to expect.

Although the etiology is incompletely understood, and there is no reason to think it a sequela of abuse and neglect, autism is another developmental condition with implications for thinking about sociality. Autistic children present with a broad range of deficits in social reasoning, including difficulty in attributing mental states to others (Baron-Cohen 1995; Nichols and Stich 2003). At the same time, they present similarly to normally developing (neurotypical) children on familiar moral judgment tasks, such as those designed to test facility in distinguishing moral and conventional rule violations (Blair 1996; Turiel 1983).

But some observers report that autistic children present atypically when asked to report their moral reasoning. In one study (cited in Doris and Nichols 2012: 432–3), neurotypical and autistic children (ages 5–9 years) were asked:

"Why was it wrong for Johnny to hit Billy?"

Neurotypical children gave the expected sorts of answers, exhibiting culturally appropriate instances of moral reasoning:

"Because it hurt Billy."

Autistic children, however, often produced quite inappropriate responses:

"I was on an escalator once."

This phenomenon is well known from clinical studies in the area: autistic children often produce conversational non-sequiturs, and present other evidence of social disconnection, such as presentation of strangely inappropriate gifts (cf. Dawson and Fernald 1987: 496–7). Evidently, impairments in sociality are associated with impairments in moral reasoning.

Adult populations are also suggestive. Consider Narcissistic Personality Disorder, where afflicted individuals present with self-importance and feelings of entitlement (American Psychiatric Association 2000: 715).[4] Unfortunately, the narcissist's affliction is an affliction on those around him: individuals with Narcissistic Personality Disorder may believe they are exempt from social norms, such as waiting their turn in line. One patient, "Brian," was compelled into therapy after a series of legal problems resulting "from his belief that rules and laws for other people didn't apply to him" (Schwartzberg 2000: 106–88). Matters came to a head when Brian arrived at the airport for a trip minutes before his scheduled departure and discovered that his seat had been reassigned. Outraged, he claimed that his luggage was aboard the plane with a bomb in it, which did not endear him to authorities. Apparently, Brian was unable to grasp the fact that his flight was not literally *his* flight; the narcissist behaves, as Mom used to say, like the world revolves around him.

While the exact relation is unclear, narcissism may be associated with psychopathy (Geberth and Turco 1997; Kernberg 1998), with some researchers placing narcissism and psychopathy on a continuum where "malignant narcissism"

---

[4] There was considerable controversy surrounding inclusion of Narcissistic Personality Disorder in the current (5th) edition of the *Diagnostic and Statistical Manual*, but narcissistic tendencies can certainly be clinically significant (Miller *et al.* 2010; Ronningstam 2011). It is also arguable that subclinical narcissism may involve difficulties in practical and moral reasoning (see Carlson *et al.* 2011; Vazire and Funder 2006; Vazire *et al.* 2008).

occupies an intermediate position (Kernberg 2004: 20). These waters are muddy: psychopathy is incompletely understood, and some have questioned whether (or to what extent) it should be typed as a mental disorder (Mealey 1995; cf. Maibom 2008). The best answer is probably affirmative, since considerable research demonstrates that psychopaths manifest a range of cognitive and neurological deficiencies sufficient for attribution of mental illness (Blair *et al.* 2006). All the same, a measure of cynicism is appealing: the line between a clinical psychopath and an egregious asshole looks a fine one. After a fashion, that's the lesson. Both clinical narcissists and psychopaths present abnormally with regard to sociality, and whether you think them ill, insufferable, or just plain nasty, both populations fail to reason and behave appropriately on moral matters. As sociality goes—or fails to go—so goes morality.

The evidence indicates that environmental and congenital impoverishments of sociality are implicated in the development of deficits in practical and moral reasoning. But this does not entail that optimal reasoning in adults is an ongoing social process. An individualist might allow that normal development requires sociality, while denying that optimal reasoning in mature individuals requires it. This isn't an untoward suggestion, but it won't work out. Practical and moral reasoning are not only socially *developed*, they are socially *sustained*; many times, optimal reasoning occurs in social context.

While the isolation to which confined children are subjected is considered criminal, such treatment of adults is socially sanctioned, in the form of solitary confinement and "security housing units." The terrors of solitary confinement are well known:

The air in your cell vanishes. You are smothering. Your eyes bulge out; you clutch at your throat; you scream like a banshee. Your arms flail the air in your cell...The walls press you from all directions...You become hollow and empty...You are dying. Dying a hard death. (Abbott 1991: 25)

If anyone thinks that such effects are limited to the faint of heart, note that this description was penned by Jack Henry Abbott, a murderer and hardened recidivist.

American penitentiary practice has, with the aid of technological innovations, refined the practice of solitary confinement into "supermax" institutions, where prisoners are held for extended periods with radically curtailed human interaction. At California's Pelican Bay supermax, the "pinky shake," which consists of touching fingers through nickel-sized holes in cell doors, can be the only physical contact prisoners have with other human beings for years at a time (Sullivan 2006). The effects of such deprivation now have a name, Security Housing Unit Syndrome (Grassian 1983). To put it mildly, sufferers are not feeling very well.

Interviews with prisoners at Pelican Bay indicated grossly inflated incidences of psychopathology (Haney 2003: 136; cf. Brodsky and Scogin 1988). Below are the percentages of inmates reporting various symptoms; the figure in parentheses indicates the factor by which this percentage exceeds estimates of base rates in non-incarcerated populations.

Chronic Depression 77 percent *(3x)*
Trouble Sleeping 84 percent *(5x)*
Perspiring Hands 68 percent *(4x)*
Heart Palpitations 68 percent *(18x)*
Dizziness 56 percent *(8x)*
Nightmares 55 percent *(7x)*
Irrational Anger 88 percent *(30x)*
Confused Thought Processes 84 percent *(8x)*
Hallucinations 41 percent *(24x)*

Afflictions that are rare in the population at large are common in victims of "secure" penal housing; these prisoners are eight times as likely to have confused thought processes, twenty-four times as likely to hallucinate, and thirty times as likely to experience irrational anger. It hardly needs remarking that these afflictions are not conducive to optimal reasoning.

The prison demographic exhibits considerable distress prior to incarceration—for example, criminal behavior is strongly associated with substance abuse (Sinha and Easton 1999)—which may obscure the pathogenic role of prison isolation. In this regard, a study of Danish prisoners is illuminating: after four weeks in solitary confinement the probability of being admitted to the prison hospital for psychiatric reasons was twenty times higher than for those prisoners held in the general prison population over a comparable period of time (Sestoft *et al.* 1998: 103). Whatever difficulties afflict people held in corrections systems, isolation looks to be an *added* pathogen. None of this is to say that human isolates never enjoy passable mental hygiene, particularly outside of prison—although anecdotal evidence, such as found in histories of polar exploration, gives cause for doubt (e.g. Bickel 1977: 166, 225–6).

If isolation is implicated in psychopathology, it may fairly be concluded that sociality is required to *sustain* normal adult reasoning, and is not merely a developmental prerequisite. But this might be taken in the following minimal sense: sociality is required for cognitive health, and isolation is causally implicated in pathologies that imperil cognitive health. Perhaps people can reason optimally on their own, so long as they enjoy such sociality as is required to keep madness at bay. Perhaps. But something stronger is defensible, and I'll be defending it: optimal reasoning is socially *embedded*. That is, human beings typically reason best when reasoning takes the form of an ongoing social process. Sociality is not merely a *precondition* of optimal reasoning, like adequate sleep and nutrition; optimal reasoning is *itself* characteristically social.

Embedding

Substantial cognitive achievement, such as scientific and technological discovery, is very often social achievement. In the first instance, knowledge is cumulative: the present generation learns from the previous generation, and the steam engine gives way to internal combustion, which in turn (one prays) gives way to some more sustainable technology. In the second instance, knowledge is specialized, especially in cases of large-scale industrial productions: it takes a lot of engineers, in a lot of fields, to make a skyscraper stand, or an airliner fly. Moreover, a diversity of researchers employing a range of methodologies facilitates scientific progress, because a larger percentage of the empirical and theoretical space is thereby investigated, increasing the likelihood of identifying undersubscribed, but high pay-off, research programs (Kitcher 1993: 70, 2001: Ch. 9; cf. Longino 1990).

While the advance of knowledge requires diversity, it equally requires conformity. As Boyd and Richerson (2006: 24) remark in their account of cultural evolution, to "get the benefits of social learning, humans have to be credulous, for the most part accepting the ways they observe in their society as sensible and proper." If each generation has to reinvent the wheel, or in Boyd and Richerson's example, the kayak, not a lot of wheels, or kayaks, will get built. Inevitably, in kayak builders we trust: innovation may modify the shape of the kayak—if not the wheel—from one generation to the next, but a lot has to be taken on the authority of those who previously worked the field. This contrasts starkly with a familiar Romantic picture of genius, where intellectual achievement is the province of rogue and rebel (Blanning 2010: Ch. 1; Brennan 2005). Sometimes, innovators refuse to see the wisdom in the old wisdom, but it is equally true that science (at least Kuhn's (1962) normal science) is driven by true believers—those able to absorb and exploit the insights of others.

Something similar can be said for morality. Skepticism seems to have more bite here than elsewhere (Railton 2003: 3), so notions of progress and expertise are more uncertain in moral inquiry than in technical and scientific enterprises. But even on broadly skeptical accounts of moral norms (e.g. Sripada and Stich 2007), it remains the case that basic moral competence requires a substantial measure of conformity. Surprisingly, reformers are no exception: maybe it was a moral innovation when abolitionists began to insist that African slaves be regarded as persons, but these same abolitionists were also drawing on a body of cultural norms governing how persons should be treated. The point sharpens when one thinks of spiritual leaders in moral dissent: King and Gandhi were not only innovators, but also conservatives, drawing on ancient religious traditions. Without a large measure of fealty to custom, it is unclear how people could function morally at all.

The fact that social interactions and institutions transmit information requisite for optimal reasoning does not entail that optimal reasoning itself is an ongoing social process. Maybe once the needed information is in hand, the reasoner can go her own lonely way with no ill effects. Well, if this were true, it would make the existence of institutions like universities rather mysterious, since the transfer of information can be accomplished—especially with modern information technology—without reasoners living and working together. Cyber-assisted "distance learning," may be the future of higher education, and I've substantial sympathy for the suspicion that a core function of American universities is the provision of socially acceptable couplings for the upper middle class, but it would seem a little odd, given the familiar and plausible views in science studies mentioned above, if collaborative learning and research were only a spandrel of cultural evolution. Indeed, if you've engaged in collaborative research, I'm guessing you've noticed that often more gets done in a few hours face to face than in a few months—or longer—of exchanges over the wire. Somehow, being there makes a difference.

There's further reason for thinking that the role of sociality in reasoning cannot be merely informational. Reasoning involves not simply passively *absorbing* information, but actively *determining* which information to accept. While there's evidence that people tend to believe propositions they entertain (Gilbert 1991; Gilbert *et al.* 1993); it's also true that people don't accept everything they consider. This filtering will often have a social component; for example, the reasoner may be influenced by the prestige or perceived reliability of someone giving testimony (McGinnies and Ward 1974; Pornpitakpan 2004). It's not that these processes always facilitate good reasoning: prestigious testimony is not always credible testimony, as even the most casual attendance to the bloviations of politicians and pundits makes painfully clear. The present point is that, even supposing the notion of "merely informational" is one of which we can make adequate sense, the role of the social is not merely informational, since sociality looks to have a central role in the filtering of information. One might argue that finally, after all the consultation and collaboration is done, it's a process of individual reflection that makes the call; in the end, it's the individual who determines what the individual believes (cf. Sosa 2004: 291). As should by now be expected, I'm not drawn to this characterization, but I'm not sure I need disagree with someone who is; if individuals finally sign bills into law, legislation remains a social process.

The impact of sociality on cognition may be for better or worse, and is everywhere sensitive to variations in task and process. In early studies of group reasoning, groups often outperformed individuals (e.g. Davis 1969; Laughlin 1965; Maier 1970). But that work compared the output of a group with the output of a single individual, meaning that the effect may simply have been the function of greater numbers rather than any positive effect of the group process itself (more people may output more ideas, increasing the odds of a good idea appearing). In work comparing the output of a group of n individuals with a matched "nominal" group of n individuals working alone, the results were mixed, with numerous findings favoring individuals (Hill 1982; Paulus et al. 1995). For example, in a study comparing the output of four people "brainstorming" in group discussion to the pooled output of four people working separately, it was found that those who worked individually produced more overall ideas, more unique ideas, and higher quality ideas than those who worked together (Taylor et al. 1958). Collective ineffectiveness may itself result from social processes: free riding, social anxiety, and "production blocking" (where each individual's effective work time is reduced by listening to others) can all contribute to lower, and lower quality, output (Camacho and Paulus 1995; Diehl and Stroebe 1987).

In other circumstances, groups do better. Part of the explanation may be the importance of error correction; individuals are frequently slower than groups to see the problems in their own work (Hill 1982: 524). Moreover, groups may be quicker to uncover an inobvious solution, as Schwartz (1995) demonstrated with "turning gear" problems. Eight problems were presented, varying only in how many gears were involved; for example, Schwartz asked people to imagine a row of five interlocked gears, and asked them in which direction the fifth gear would turn if the first gear turned to the right. There's a rule for these problems: if the number of gears is odd, then the last gear will turn in the same direction as the first. Schwartz found that only 14 percent of individuals discovered the rule, but 58 percent of pairs did. This large difference between individuals and groups cannot be accounted for by appealing to nominal groups, since the success rate in finding the rule for nominal pairs (28 percent) was less than half that of the actual pairs. Somehow, working together on these problems helped people to recognize the deeper principle; interaction, not just numbers, matters.

If the laboratory results are to be believed, it's not surprising that corporations have honed collaborative research into an extremely successful technique; companies like Gore-Tex, the "guaranteed to keep you dry" fabric manufacturer, use small group research to develop innovations effecting remarkable market gains (Sawyer 2007). The salutary effects of sociality also help explain why important analyses of research productivity and impact indicate that *quantity predicts quality*; researchers who produce more research are more likely to produce impactful research (Simonton 1997, 2004).

For academic philosophers, this result may seem untoward, since survivors of graduate work in philosophy frequently report that disciplinary culture celebrates being "careful" and not publishing "too much." I've long thought this professional strategy suspect, akin to supposing that the best way to improve at golf is playing less golf. By subjecting your work to public (as opposed to in-clique) examination in journals, you may get more, and more diverse, feedback that improves the quality of future research. And since it is difficult to anticipate which of your ideas will "have legs" and generate an influential or provocative research program—just as it may be difficult to predict which mutations will confer reproductive advantage—you're well advised to avail yourself of more, rather than fewer, opportunities for such impact. (Indeed, I've noticed that a scholar's best-known research is sometimes outside her area of expertise.)

Relatedly, people may reason better when a diverse set of views is represented across the population of intellectual contestants (Zamzow and Nichols 2009: 377–9). In addition to the aggregate benefits of such "checks and balances," the agonistic character of intellectual discourse in a diverse population of motivated reasoners may provoke individual contestants to reason more compellingly (if not more impartially) while they advocate for their views. As you strive for fame and fortune, you're motivated to maintain your own theory and repudiate opposing theories, so you're likely pretty good at producing support for your view and objections to your opponent's. At the same time, you may be substantially worse at recognizing weakness in your theory and strength in your opponent's. Thus, your reasoning may be lopsided in your favor. In the aggregate, this partiality may be a good thing, so long as there are people effectively expounding a range of competing views, and the bugs and features of the contending positions receive balanced exposure. Again, the point is not simply that people reason using socially acquired information; it's that the reasoning is itself a social process.

Morality

Specifically moral reasoning is also socially embedded. The idea is not that solitary individuals are somehow bereft of moral views; it's that people are most likely to reason about those views when justifying themselves to others

(Haidt 2001; cf. Haidt *et al.* 2000). Complex moral cognition will tend to appear in the context of social interaction, which suggests that moral reasoning is typically socially embedded reasoning.

While armchair observation indicates the sociality of morality—just read the paper, or browse the internet—systematic evidence is sparser than I'd like. Part of the problem is methodological: it is difficult to design well-controlled studies of group interaction, and even in the absence of methodological obstacles, doing so is resource intensive, requiring large numbers of participants (which may be in short supply at smaller colleges and universities). For the moment, anyway, we'll need to make do with what we have.

If collaborativism is true, one should expect not only that moral reasoning is socially embedded, but also that moral reasoning is *better* when socially embedded. The prima facie case for this is not promising, as consideration of mass movements like National Socialism indicates, and experimental study may seem to give the same impression. The moral dumbfounding paradigm induced moral reasoning, but not moral reasoning that was much good (Chapter 3, p. 59), and classic findings in social psychology are similarly dispiriting: in Latané and Darley's (1970: e.g. 101, 111) group effect paradigms the presence of bystanders depressed individual probability of helping in (simulated) emergencies, while Milgram's (1974) work on obedience associates sociality and destructive behavior.

We need to slow down. In Milgram's (1974: 55–7; version 5) iconic finding, two-thirds of subjects were willing to repeatedly shock a vehemently protesting victim in response to the experimenter's "not impolite" request. Less often noted is that obedience dropped to 10 percent in the "two peers rebel" condition (Milgram 1974: 119), where participants were asked to shock the victim in the presence of two experimental confederates who were not complying with the experimenter. Natural contexts also present both sides: while the Nazis exploited social dynamics to secure compliance in the commission of atrocities, such as peer "mentoring" of doctors involved in medicalized killing at Auschwitz (Lifton 1986: 193–217), sociality also facilitated resistance to the Nazis, as when the village of Le Chambon, joined by a Huguenot religious tradition under charismatic leadership, collectively sheltered Jews (Hallie 1979). In short, the *kind* of group matters: Latané and Darley (1970: 63) found that pairs of friends were faster to intervene in a group effect scenario than were pairs of strangers (although pairs did not help as quickly as individuals).

Good examples also make a difference. In one study of the Precedent Effect, participants were nearly twice as likely (46 percent vs 25 percent) to donate to the American Heart Association if they were first shown a list of eight students who had previously done so, and participants were ten times as likely to sign up for donating blood (30 percent vs 3 percent) after having been shown a list of previous signers (Reingen 1982). In another study, participants' estimates of how likely they were to take part in an unpaid survey varied dramatically with the number of classmates they had been told agreed to do so: the greater the number of potential co-participants, the greater their estimated likelihood of helping (Cialdini *et al.* 1999).

The role of social embedding in moral reasoning is especially clear for a paradigmatic instance of moral improvement (the existence of evaluative controversy duly noted), the development of more inclusive moral attitudes (i.e. less racist, sexist, xenophobic). Such attitudes are not engendered by solitary reflection, but neither are they born simply of being in the same building with a diversity of people. In the early days of American desegregation, it was hoped that putting African American and white children in the same place would effect increased racial harmony. After all, one of the staple results in social psychology is that familiarity facilitates attraction (e.g. Grush 1976; Matlin 1970; Zajonc 1968). What happened instead was the formation of ethnic in-groups, which eventuated in in-group/out-group conflict (see Oskamp and Schultz 1998; Rogers *et al.* 1984).

One factor that may have contributed to the divisiveness of desegregated classrooms is the competitive nature of many school environments, an interpretation supported by Sherif and colleagues' (1961) classic Robbers Cave experiment. The first part of the experiment generated group competition between two "teams" of children at a boys' camp, which led to significant intergroup antagonism. The researchers initially tried to reduce friction by bringing the groups together for pleasant activities like movies and picnics, but this failed miserably; these occasions merely served as opportunities for the boys to express hostility by such charming expedients as shouting and throwing food. However, when the experimenters introduced situations in which boys from each team had to work together in pursuit of a common goal, such as dislodging a vehicle trapped in the mud, conflict was significantly reduced. It was only when members of the different teams had to engage in cooperative activity that hostility was alleviated: the critical factor was not merely living together, but *working* together (cf. Aronson *et al.* 1978; Aronson and Bridgeman 1979).

Relatedly, advocates of "deliberative democracy" promote increased social interaction as a means to better functioning polities (Gutmann and Thompson 2004). Deliberative polling puts deliberative democracy to the empirical test: participants are surveyed before and after a weekend of moderated small group discussion and plenary discussion with expert panelists. According to Ackerman and Fishkin (2004: 52), "it is not unusual for deliberation to significantly change the balance of opinion on two-thirds of the policy questions," and more than half of participants change their positions on particular policy items. For instance, at a deliberative polling event held in Austin during 1996 (Ackerman and Fishkin 2004: 52), the proportion of participants:

agreeing that the "biggest problem facing the American family" is "breakdown of traditional values" decreased 10 percent;
favoring a "flat tax" decreased 14 percent;
agreeing that the "biggest problem facing the American family" is economic pressure increased 15 percent;
favoring "a tax reduction for savings" increased 17 percent;
agreeing that "divorce should be made harder to get" to strengthen families increased 21 percent.

This is a motley assortment of opinion, and we again face stubborn normative questions: why suppose that the changes induced by discussion are changes for the better?

Well, participants in these studies tend to become much better informed (Luskin *et al.* 2008: 23), and better-informed reasoning is not implausibly held, as it is by informed desire theories, to be better reasoning. Moreover, there is reason to believe that participants are, with the appropriate structure, able to reason cooperatively (once again, not just any group will do). People report being better able to respect one another's beliefs and circumstances (Luskin *et al.* 2008: 14); at the end of one weekend, a man was heard confessing to someone he had previously disparaged, "What are the three most important words in the English language? They are 'I was wrong'" (Ackerman and Fishkin 2004: 54). Sounds pretty good to me: deliberative polling events have the feel of reasoned discussion, and it is not unlikely that judgments so secured could better withstand critical scrutiny than unconsidered political opinions.

In deliberative polling, something like conscious reflection—socially provoked conscious reflection—may play a role. However, the ethical influence of sociality may also proceed more implicitly. For example, exposure to pictures of admired African Americans (e.g. Denzel Washington) and disliked whites (e.g. Jeffrey Dahmer) has been found to weaken implicit racism (Dasgupta and Greenwald 2001; Joy-Gaba and Nosek 2010) as has white participants interacting with an African American experimenter rather than a white experimenter (Lowery *et al.* 2001).

Frequently, the relevant pathways will be emotional. Group interactions are likely to be emotionally freighted, in ways both dramatic and mundane, and many familiar emotions like anger, guilt, and sympathy are characteristically triggered by social cues: it's the tone of your colleague debasing a peer that makes you angry, it's your friend's stunned look that makes you feel guilty for slighting him, and it's the tears running down a child's face that triggers your sympathy. While such processes may follow conscious pathways, they needn't. A celebrated example is "emotional contagion," where people unconsciously mirror the affective states of those around them (Hatfield *et al.* 1994): your good spirits may give me a lift without my realizing it, and my foul mood may have the opposite effect on you.

Guilt, anger, and sympathy are paradigmatically moral emotions (Prinz and Nichols 2010), yet from the perspective of one's short-term material interests, these emotions may seem counterproductive. As the serial killer Ted Bundy philosophized:

Guilt? ... It's a kind of social control mechanism – and it's very unhealthy. It does terrible things to our bodies.... I guess I am in the enviable position of not having to deal with guilt. There's just no reason for it. (reported in Michaud and Aynesworth 1989: 288)

In contrast to Bundy's psychopathic insouciance, many people appear liable to guilt when they mistreat others. Such emotional liabilities have salutary consequences: when people feel guilt over hurting someone, it may motivate them to avoid future transgressions (Baumeister *et al.* 1994), and when people feel empathy at the plight of a person in distress, it may motivate them to help that person (Batson 1991). Thus, there's another reason to think that sociality supports morality: moral emotions like sympathy and guilt tend to improve moral behavior, and the moral emotions are emotions that are especially likely to be triggered in a social context. (Although I've previously emphasized how emotions may function as defeaters, the present considerations indicate they need not.)

I now take myself to have secured the following generalizations: human problem solving is characteristically socially embedded, and this sociality facilitates optimal reasoning. With collaborativism about reasoning secured, I can extend the approach to a collaborativism about agency. But at this point, you might suspect I've wandered off the trail—and for a good many slow miles. What has sociality to do with the exercise of *individual* agency? Perhaps sociality actually impedes individual agency, an eventuality that may seem especially likely in light of concerns about how situational factors threaten skeptical trauma. But this impression is misleading: while sociality insinuates skeptical difficulty, it also intimates how to solve it. Given just how social human beings are, a viable solution to the problem of agency will reserve a central role for sociality.

Intervention

To begin collaborativism about agency, consider some familiar phenomena: seat belt laws have been found to increase seat belt use (Gantz and Henkle 2002; Shults *et al.* 2004), while public health interventions have been found to decrease rates of smoking (Fiore *et al.* 2000). It's likely that most smokers want to quit: 79 percent of those responding to a 2002 Gallup Poll said they did (Saad 2002). In the argot, most smokers are dissonant, rather than consonant (McKennell and Thomas 1967; cf. Kunze 2000). Quitting is notoriously hard, as witnessed by my favorite slogan in the smoking cessation business, "Don't quit trying to quit." Yet for some smokers, public health campaigns help them realize their goal.

Like quitting smoking, buckling up is strongly in one's interest, and this is something most Americans get: in 2007 seat belt use was 82 percent, with the lowest being 64 percent in New Hampshire, where people apparently prefer to live free *and* die (National Highway Traffic Safety Administration, May 2008). Unlike quitting smoking, wearing a seat belt is easy to do, but for some people, laziness or inattention intrudes, and they fail to buckle up. Seat belt laws, and their aggressive enforcement, work: in states with primary enforcement laws, where violators may be cited even if no other violation is noted, people apparently buckle up more frequently, and die in (and around) their vehicles less frequently, than in states with weaker laws (National Highway Traffic Safety Administration, February 2008). Perhaps seat belt laws are effective because the possibility of a ticket seems a more likely bad outcome of failing to wear one's seat belt than does a collision serious enough to result in significant injury; maybe the vivid and proximate presence of Officer Friendly packs more motivational punch than the dimly imagined possibility of a serious accident.

However exactly these interventions work, process matters. While there is little doubt that avoiding adverse consequences associated with failing to quit and neglecting to buckle up is (for most people) a rational outcome, one might wonder if realizing these outcomes as a result of public health intervention should count as an exercise of agency. Institutional techniques akin to smoking cessation programs and seat belt laws might work pretty well on *children*, and I'd not attribute this success to children being responsible agents. The intuition here resembles a familiar conviction in epistemology—a true belief that comes about any old way doesn't count as knowledge (e.g. Alston 1989). And similarly, one might think, for agency: value realized does not always entail agency exercised.

It might further be said that even if a value is expressed, and agency manifested, when people conform to public health initiatives, the operative value should be understood as that of avoiding punishment or censure, rather than promoting wellness. We'd now have found agency, but not quite in the place I was trying to find it. I incline to a different description: the external influences help people to better attend to the value they place on their life and health, and when they attend better, they're sometimes able to live better. After all, the public health interventions are not strongly coercive, and many people seem quite able to resist them. (I sheepishly admit to twice being ticketed for seat belt violations, though in one case I plead police harassment.) I'd contend that when the interventions work, they often work *via* the value people place on their health, and that's just the kind of story I want to tell.

If you're not persuaded, perhaps you'll find psychotherapy a more convincing illustration. Quite often, people *seek out* psychotherapy in hopes of making their lives go better, so this active process has a more agential appearance than the capitulations just described. Of course, people often enter therapy in response to something like duress: a stalled career, a strife-torn marriage, or stacks of unpaid bills. But these incentives are not obviously inimical to agency. On the contrary, people trying to change their lives for the better is an excellent place to look for agency. Psychotherapy can help effect this change. Numerous outcome studies, using both clinician assessment and client self-report, indicate that talk therapy works; it can ameliorate various adverse psychological conditions, such as depression and anxiety (Lambert and Ogles 2004; Luborsky *et al.* 1985: 609; Seligman 1993).

We've now an appealing example of collaborativism about agency. First, the "talking cure" is very much a social treatment, where client and therapist work things through together more effectively than the client could do on his own. There's the collaborativism. Second, decreasing psychological discomfort and increasing personal efficacy are very likely values many clients in therapy hold, so the clinical process is reasonably thought to facilitate the expression of these values. There's the agency.

To be sure, psychotherapy suffers an uneven reputation. Even sympathetic observers acknowledge that many psychological problems are recurring, so that the talking cure is rarely a permanent cure (Keller *et al.* 2000). This doesn't worry me much, any more than I'd be worried about the effectiveness of aspirin if a user someday got another headache. More serious, perhaps, is the assessment of outcomes: who's to say, for psychiatric conditions, whether there was improvement, and how much? Nosology, the categorization of psychiatric conditions, is a turbulent discipline (Murphy 2006), and observers—especially observers with money at stake—may disagree about whether a given adverse condition should be counted as a mental illness (Woolfolk and Doris 2002).

Some disputes may be more tractable than others. Consider somatization disorder, where sufferers exhibit unexplained physical symptoms, discomfort, disability, and may incur health care expenditures that are 6 to 14 times the US average (Smith, Rost and Kashner 1995). One clinical study evaluated a short course of cognitive therapy designed to help patients increase their awareness of emotions, modify dysfunctional beliefs, and enhance communication; twelve months after initiation of treatment, the severity of patients' symptoms, compared to controls, was rated as significantly reduced by independent evaluators and by the patients themselves, and average health care expenditures were reduced by more than a third (Allen *et al.* 2006; cf. Kroenke and Swindle 2000). It seems relatively uncontroversial to infer that the values at issue here—reducing pain, disability, and health care expenses—are values worth promoting, and are values held by the patients themselves; indeed, to assert the opposite would be controversial. Moreover, the patients *work* to realize their values. Is there good reason to deny them agency, even if they did not implement their values as completely independent individuals?

Uncertainties remain. Therapists' theoretical predilections have relatively little to do with client outcomes, and the means by which therapy works are imperfectly understood (Brown *et al.* 1999; Dawes 1994: 38–74; Luborsky *et al.* 1975; Wampold *et al.* 1997; Woolfolk 1998). However, there seems to be strong evidence for the following: a "positive alliance" between therapist and client is associated with positive outcomes (Horvath and Symonds 1991; Krupnick *et al.* 1996; Martin *et al.* 2000; Orlinsky *et al.* 2004). To the collaborativist, this is an unsurprising finding: sociality—*of the right sort*—does people good. If it's correct to say that the good in question is a good the people in question value, we've got a place to look for agency: sociality may facilitate agency in circumstances where people are unable to do so on their own.

Moreover, the theoretical indeterminacy of psychotherapy is congenial to the critic of reflectivism. If the explicit theoretical rubric under which therapy is conducted is not a critical determinant of therapeutic outcomes, it's tempting to say that accurate reflection is not required for clinical success: whether you think your troubles are due your relationship with your mother or your father may not matter much, so long as you've a good relationship with your therapist. If we also conclude, as I've just concluded, that therapy can facilitate agency, we've here a case where agency is achieved without accurate self-awareness. In this instance, collaborativism and anti-reflectivism may travel together.

Signpost

I've now advocated a collaborativism maintaining that optimal human reasoning, including moral reasoning, is socially embedded. I've also begun extending collaborativism about reasoning to collaborativism about agency, contending that the exercise of individual agency is socially embedded. It is my conviction that this expedient represents the best response to skepticism, but my conviction is as yet underdeveloped. What's needed is a more explicit account of *how* sociality facilitates agency. I'll now attempt to provide it.

6

Agency

As the confabulation literature suggests, people suffer impoverished self-awareness, and possess limited awareness of this fact; among the things people are ignorant of is the extent of their self-ignorance (Pronin 2008; Pronin *et al.* 2002). Thus, misapprehensions of self can go undetected, leaving folks quite fully in their grip. But misapprehensions needn't entail delusions. People are frequently wrong about themselves, but these wrongs help make a right: a self-understanding that enables agency.

Indirection

According to professional football standout Elvis Dumervil, the "only thing you can control is the thing you can control." Hard to deny, but also a little depressing: so many things I can't control, like my edgy digestion. And for thinking about agency, Dumervil's counsel threatens to mislead. It doesn't follow from the fact that one can't *directly* control something that one can't *indirectly* control it: if I take the right supplements and avoid irritating acquaintances, I'll subdue my edgy digestion, even though I can't simply will it better. In many cases, my determination to control something cannot effect an outcome by means of simple intentional action (*Gas and bloating, be gone!*) but it can help effect material and social circumstances that serve to realize the desired end. Turns out, much human agency is characterized by indirection: achieving outcomes that are not amenable to direct volitional control, but are manipulable *via* causal intermediaries. Securing the expression of one's values, and thereby exercising agency, frequently requires workarounds.

I don't have the patent on this thought. Reflectivists may allow that direct deliberative control is comparatively rare, but insist that reflection indirectly figures in self-direction, through inculcation of principles (Nahmias 2007) or formation of habits (Wigley 2007: 217–18) that structure cognition and behavior. This strategy finds worthy provenance in Aristotle's (1984: 1103a14–b26) account of habituation (whether Aristotle himself be judged a reflectivist or not): the good person, Aristotle insists, acts knowingly (1984: 1105a30–2; cf. Annas 1993: 67–8, 87), but virtue does not require conscious deliberation at the moment of behavior. While virtuous actions often get performed unreflectively, they are nevertheless intelligent, since virtuous habits are developed through education and study. If so, there's still a place where reflection matters: not so much in the moment of action, but in the practice of habituation.

Unfortunately, philosophical accounts of habituation frequently run light on psychological detail (e.g. Brett 1981, Pollard 2006, 2010), and gestures at "the proper upbringing" are of comparatively little help. Whatever the particulars, there's more than one question here. Habituating right behavior and habituating agency may pose different problems, and one might come without the other: an upstanding automaton, or a despicable agent. My problem is agency, and I'm trying to explain how agency gets indirectly exercised in the presence of self-ignorance.

One strategy exploits the large empirical literature on goals. Goals can be construed as desired actions or outcomes, and habits as "a form of goal directed automatic behavior" where the goal-relevant situation becomes, through repetition, associated with the goal-relevant activity (Aarts and Dijksterhuis 2000: 54). The obvious problem is how a desired habit becomes habit in the first place; "implementation intentions," which enable people to "pass the control of their behavior on to the environment," are supposed to help (Gollwitzer 1993: 173; cf. Gollwitzer 1999). If I form a vague intention to exercise more, I may never drag my lazy butt from the couch, but if I specify a concrete plan to run the Carolina North Trail, Tuesdays and Thursdays at 5pm, then quitting time on Tuesdays and Thursdays may stimulate thoughts of my lumbering along the trail, which may in turn facilitate the planned-on lumbering. Evidence suggests that this approach may be effective for exercise (Milne *et al.* 2002: 173) and a variety of other health interventions: in one study, people missed fewer doses of a vitamin if they committed to when and where they would take it each day (Sheeran and Orbell 1999: 359, 364), in another, women who committed to location and time were more than four times as likely to perform a breast self-examination in the following month (Orbell *et al.* 1997: 950). Here, reflection supports self-direction, not as deliberation proximate to action, but as prior strategizing about implementation: think about your plan, and you won't have to think about your performance (cf. Holton 2009: 7–9).

Sounds good, but it can't be the whole shebang. First, the prospect of fragility remains. Countervailing pressures may perturb the goal relevant situation (you invite me for drinkies at 5pm Tuesday, and there goes my run), while the salience of goal relevant cues may be imperfectly reliable (on Thursday, a deadline has me working frantically, and 5pm comes and goes unnoticed). However much planning and policy-making one does, there will be circumstances where even highly organized individuals will be pressed to on-the-spot reflection, with all its perils. Then pursuing reflection mainly in the context of habituation will not provide the necessary coverage; habits may structure behavior in ways supporting agency, but they won't be enough. The problem of self-ignorance also lingers, in the form of what might get called, a bit portentously, "inauthentic" habit. How exactly does one know if a habit is an expression of, and not a subversion of, one's values? What is it about habit-forming reflection, the skeptic will want to know, which escapes the difficulty self-ignorance poses for direct reflective control?

My approach identifies sources of "indirect agency" in phenomena we've already considered: sociality and confabulation. The social exchange of explanatory and justificatory narratives erects a scaffolding that supports behavior expressing the actor's values. These dialogs effect the exercise of agency in conditions of self-ignorance where direct reflective control may falter. In the right social milieu, agency obtains in spite of—or rather *because* of—self-ignorance. As it turns out, ignorance is the life-blood of agency.

Illusion

Human beings are prey to myriad perceptual inaccuracies. For instance, there are errors of omission, such as inattentional blindness (Simons and Chabris 1999): when focusing on a task, like playing ball, people may miss even shatteringly intrusive stimuli, like a PERSON IN A GORILLA SUIT strolling through the middle of their game. (The movie is better than the book; check out the video of "Gorillas in Our Midst.") Cognitive capacity is limited, so people can't focus on everything equally: attention to one thing may require inattention to another.

Thinking may be the most impressive thing humans do, but it's not the only thing humans do, and given finite biological resources, what's spent on the brain can't be spent on muscle, blood, and bone (Wrangham 2009: 105–27). Moreover, a cognitive system less prone to omissions might be, for many problems, an over-engineered system. Processing power is a mixed blessing, an observation underscored by Luria's (1987: 159) celebrated mnemonist, whose prodigious memory so saturated his mind with detail that he experienced life "as though through a haze." One might suspect something similar of self-awareness. Attending to what's within your head may prevent you from attending to what's without; lose yourself in your thoughts, get lost on the way to the store.

Other illusions are commissions; perception seems to contain more information than the sense organs provide. For example, vision "tracks" occluded surfaces: people quite effortlessly see someone viewed through Venetian blinds as possessed of a whole body, rather than a body sliced to ribbons (O'Callaghan 2008: 808–11). Famously, there's a philosophical argument to the effect that *all* perception involves illusions of commission. If a certain venerable picture is right, many of the properties objects appear to have, like colors and tastes, don't inhere in the objects themselves. Instead, such properties are, in Hume's (1978/1740: I.ii.14, 167) sticky expression, instances of the mind's tendency to "spread itself" on the world (cf. Boghossian and Velleman 1989).

Many people, former house painters like me among them, may think this a bit of philosophical chicanery ("That's not really green paint in your white carpet, ma'am, it just *seems* that way"). But so long as I can enjoy my pumpkin smoothies, I'm not much worried. Even if foods only seem to have tastes, there are systematic patterns of seemings that help animals get around in the world: bitter-seeming things are more likely to be poisonous, sweet-seeming things are more likely to be calorie rich, and so on (Glendinning 1994; Kreps 2009). The appearances are invaluable, though not infallible, signals.

While some perceptual illusions may be adaptive in the sense of helping the organisms that are prey to them (and prey to other organisms) muddle along, it doesn't follow that illusions of self are similarly felicitous. Take self-enhancement: it's not obviously advantageous for me to think I'm good at something I'm lousy at; in fact, it wastes a lot of time. One can't assume that because a tendency is "selected by evolution", or otherwise "natural," it's good for people, and still less that it's good (Doris 2009; Prinz 2007: 246). There are evolutionary explanations for the Cinderella Effect—elevated child mistreatment, including lethal mistreatment, by step-parents (Daly and Wilson 1996, 2007)—but these explanations are not recommendations. What recommends illusions of self?

It's probable that some illusions of self, namely, positive illusions of self, are implicated in well-being (Taylor and Brown 1988, 1994; cf. Lazarus 1983). For example, individuals with greater tendencies to self-enhancement may be more resilient in the face of traumatic events, as has been found with survivors of the 9/11 terrorist attacks (Bonanno *et al.* 2005). Nevertheless, the thesis that self-enhancement is generally advantageous has drawn heated criticism (Badhwar 2008; Block and Colvin 1994; Colvin and Block 1994; Kurt and Paulhus 2008). The connection between surplus positivity and happiness is hardly transparent: excessive optimism about one's finances might cause one to under-save, and excessive optimism about one's health might cause one to under-insure (Haybron 2008: 232–4).

To find positive illusions with more salutary effects, look to the fields of the heart. Evidence indicates that supportive social relationships promote well-being

(Baumeister and Leary 1995; Diener and Seligman 2004: 18–19), and in some cultures, marriage is a primary context for such relationships, so one may infer that marriage promotes well-being for members of these cultures. Numerous studies point to a "marriage protection" effect where marriage is causally implicated in lower mortality rates, perhaps especially for men (Johnson *et al.* 2000; Kolip 2005; Lynch 1979; Wilson and Oswald 2005). In America, the happily married may enjoy lower rates of unemployment (Forthofer *et al.* 1996) and better health (DeLongis *et al.* 1988; Kiecolt-Glaser and Newton 2001), while dissolution of marriage is associated with depression and loneliness, even when the union in question was an unhappy one (Price and McKenry 1988; Weiss 1976). In Germany, widows were found to be more depressed than non-widowed comparison groups (Stroebe *et al.* 1996), and German women's life satisfaction was observed to decline immediately before and after the death of a spouse (Lucas *et al.* 2003: 534). Contra Plato's *Phaedrus*, it's not love that's madness, but want of love: a review of mental hospital admissions found them highest in the separated and divorced, lowest in the married, with singletons in the middle (Bloom *et al.* 1978: 869; cf. Horwitz *et al.* 1996). Although the nature of the causal relationship is uncertain (and likely bidirectional), it seems safe to surmise that relationships like marriage support well-being (Diener and Seligman 2004: 19–20).

In turn, marriages are associated with illusion. According to one group of marital researchers, the presence of positive illusions is "nearly universal" among "satisfied spouses" (Fowers *et al.* 2001: 96). In an early study by Edmonds (1967: 684–6), it was found that married people tended to strongly agree with sentences such as "If my mate has any faults I am not aware of them." Why think this indicates positive illusions? Are you kidding? Thus, in an amusing example of *a priori* reasoning in science, was roughly how Edmonds reasoned. *Nobody's* mate is *that* splendid; if you agree with such superlatives, you're agreeing through rose-tinted glasses.

Subsequent research has explored more readily quantifiable indicators. Fowers and colleagues (2001: 97–9, 102) asked American couples to estimate their likelihood of divorce: the mean estimate was 10 percent, the modal estimate was 0 percent, and those on their second marriage were no less optimistic. Although divorce rates likely exhibit substantial demographic variation (Wilcox and Marquardt 2010), scientific estimates of the likelihood of divorce typically range from over 40 percent to over 60 percent (Fowers *et al.* 2001: 105), so these people appear to be overestimating their prospects. Moreover, unmarried people also substantially underestimated their probability of divorce (mean estimate 22.6 percent, modal estimate 0 percent), indicating that the tendency is not solely explained by whatever marital success people happen to enjoy (Fowers *et al.*

2001: 103–5). The Marriage Illusion is especially remarkable, given that hand wringing over "the fifty percent divorce rate" is, as any reader of *Divorce Magazine* could tell you, a prominent component of public discourse in the United States (*Divorce Magazine* 2004). Apparently, romantic illusions persist alongside a well-known body of undermining fact.

Maybe people are aware of the daunting odds, but suppose they'll occupy the lucky half. It's also possible that people clearly appreciate that the difficulty applies to them, but decide to go forward anyway; as the saying goes, it's better to have loved and lost than never to have loved (for some loves, anyway). If so, why doesn't everyone get prenuptial agreements? It's not easy to find records of how many do (perhaps because the practice is largely restricted to the wealthy), but given the state of the divorce courts, it's safe to say that lots don't. With the advantages prenups offer in the rather likely event that unhappy push comes to unhappy shove, forgoing one looks like irrational optimism, not so different from neglecting to save or insure. On the other hand, maybe people fear that prenups sour marriages with defeatism, and decide the advantages of planning for the worst are not worth the risk of relationship damage; as one divorce mediator put it, the "premises of prenuptial agreements are logically contradictory to the premises of modern marriage" (Margulies 2003: 426). But if this is what people believe, they take the point I want to make: relationships benefit from positivity exceeding a sober assessment of the probabilities.

After the initial leap of crazy faith, inflated optimism may help sustain a union. In the dark hours of domesticity, could one muster the gumption to tough it out while vividly aware that it's only a coin flip the bloody toil will pay off? Indeed, since prospects may be even worse for distressed couples (Karney and Bradbury 1995), clear awareness of one's (or rather two's) odds may be even more dispiriting in rocky patches. Whatever the exact percentages, I advise against chanting "we've got a 50/50 chance," as you once more return the toilet seat to its proper position, or yet again dislodge a hair-bomb from the bathtub drain.

Romantic optimism is widespread: in addition to heterosexual marriages, positive illusion appears in lesbian, gay, married homosexual, and cohabiting heterosexual couples (Conley *et al.* 2009: 1423–5). This is not to say that relationship positivity is everywhere, or that it is everywhere good. For instance, while positivity may help sustain a healthy relationship, unrealistic positivity in distressed relationships may hasten their decline (McNulty *et al.* 2008: 643–4). Moreover, mates may be positive about some things and not others (Neff and Karney 2005: 489–90), viewing their spouses' global qualities with unrealistic positivity ("Doris is a wonderful man"), but assessing specific qualities with reasonable accuracy ("Doris is not unfailingly polite").

The existence of accuracy in relationship awareness suggests that some measure of experimentally identified positivity reflects a "performance demand": people may recognize shortcomings in their relationships, but have internalized social norms that prohibit their reporting them. Thus, romantic partners may be aware that they're accentuating the positive in the interests of putting a good face on things (or trying to craft a better one). There's evidence that people simultaneously maintain inflated and accurate views of their romantic partner's attractiveness; they think their partners are more attractive than their partner's friends and their partners themselves do, but are aware of this discrepancy, and are able to fairly accurately report their partner's reputation for attractiveness (Solomon and Vazire 2014). Close relationships, like other human endeavors, are characterized by a mixture of awareness and ignorance. The present—and empirically well-supported—point is that ignorance makes a major ingredient in the mix.

Should you want to be happy, it's perhaps better to love well than wisely. Talk of happy runs a little sloppy; the "positive psychology" literature is rife with contention about what we should be talking about when we talk about happiness, and how best it might be measured (Alexandrova 2005, 2008; Bishop 2015; Haybron 2008; Tiberius 2008; Tiberius and Plakias 2010). These issues needn't detain us, for questions of agency decouple from questions of well-being. Even if agency is always good, agency is not always good for you. Sometimes, the automaton has the shinier coat and colder nose, as intimated by dystopian fantasies like *Brave New World*.

If it's easy to believe that convenient fictions can make life happier, it's harder to believe that convenient fictions can make for agency. Indeed, classic philosophical thought experiments, such as Nozick's (1974: 42–5) Experience Machine, seem to exploit the divergence of agency and happiness: if you're disinclined to plug into a device that induces delicious illusion as you pass your life comatose in bed, it may be the loss of agency you're worried about, and it may be you're thinking that being an unhappy agent is preferable to being a happy pig. Such intuitions are familiar: better to find out you've been a victim of egregious romantic betrayal, and make of your life what you can, than not find out, and go on as a contented cuckold (Badhwar 2008: 877–8). Personally, I've mixed feelings. Authenticity has its place, but that's not every place: I've always been mystified, for instance, by eulogies that fetishize honesty. (*Note to friends:* everyone will know I was a jerk. Accentuate the positive, embellishing as necessary.) But I digress. The point is that my road is a hard one, because while there may be good reason to welcome illusions, there's less reason to suppose they facilitate agency. How, then, to proceed?

Control

Consider a particular illusion of self, the illusion of control, and begin with an evocative observation: deviations from normal perceptions of control are a symptom of mental disorder. Most striking is schizophrenia, where afflicted individuals may experience atrophied perceptions of control. As one patient described it, "[m]y fingers pick up the pen, but I don't control them. What they do is nothing to do with me" (quoted in Mellor 1970; Blakemore *et al.* 2002). Where you or I would likely have an agent experience, the schizophrenic may not; at the extreme, patients feel like *puppets*: "when the strings are pulled my body moves and I cannot prevent it" (Mellor 1970: 18; Murphy 2006: 89–90). For these people, things that should be experienced as doings are experienced as happenings. Conversely, those in manic phases of bipolar disorder sometimes manifest hypertrophied perceptions of control; they may "view themselves as having unlimited current and future resources, [and] believe they have close to infallible prediction and control of outcomes" (Leahy 1999: 83; cf. Chandlera *et al.* 2009). While schizophrenics fail to have agent experiences when you and I would, those going through bipolar mania may have agent experiences when you and I wouldn't.

One might guess that healthy people fall, Goldilocks like, somewhere in the middle. Actually, while healthy experiences of control should not be likened to pathological grandiosity, regards either extremity or underlying process, the best conjecture is that they tend to hypertrophy. In Langer's (1975: 315–17) lottery experiment, office workers bought one-dollar tickets for a prize drawing: some participants were simply handed a ticket, while others were allowed to select their own. No ticket in a fair lottery is more likely to win than another, so one ticket is no better (or worse) than the next. But when the experimenter attempted a buy-back prior to the drawing, a mean expenditure of under two dollars was sufficient for participants who didn't choose their ticket, while a mean expenditure of nearly nine dollars was required for participants who did. Perhaps people were reluctant to sell their chosen ticket for fear of regret if it won, but I doubt this explains a four-fold difference in selling price, since the prospect of regret also obtains for unchosen tickets. Nor could the difference be fully explained by an Endowment Effect, where people exhibit a preference for what belongs to them (Kahneman *et al.* 1991), since both chosen and unchosen tickets belonged to the sellers. Apparently, people believed that chosen tickets were more likely to win than unchosen ones; they seemed to believe they could exercise some control over a manifestly uncontrollable outcome.

Gamblers commonly seem to believe they influence chance events. In one study, Reno craps players bet more on their own throws than on the throws of other players (Davis *et al.* 2000: 1236–7), while in a study of heavy gamblers, 84 percent reported strategies, such as using "lucky numbers," indicative of illusions of control (Toneatto *et al.* 1997: 262). Lottery players are likewise unwilling to leave chance to chance: around the world, quick pick options, where a computer picks random numbers, account for only 10–20 percent of tickets sold (Simon 1998: 247). As one player insisted, you shouldn't "trust the computer to pick your numbers. I trust myself more" (quoted in Cowley *et al.* 2006: 597).

Gamblers' illusions are expensive, but other illusions of control have more going for them. Unrealistic positivity has been repeatedly implicated in good health outcomes (Taylor *et al.* 2003), and it appears that this positivity extends to perceptions of control. In a study of cancer patients, perceptions of control were negatively associated with maladjustment; patients with higher perceptions of control were less likely to experience anxiety and depression (Thompson *et al.* 1993: 297–8). Moreover, there was a stronger negative relationship between perceptions of control and maladjustment for those rated lower in physical functionality (Thompson *et al.* 1993: 299–300); perceived control may have been doing more good for those who had less control of their circumstances. Given the abundant evidence implicating psychological well-being in physical well-being, and psychological distress in physical distress (Brenner 1979; Steptoe *et al.* 2005; Veenhoven 1988), it becomes very tempting to say that elevated perceptions of control, in so far as they're associated with better adjustment, are good for one's health. While resignation may be psychologically adaptive in truly uncontrollable circumstances (Affleck *et al.* 1987; Folkman 1984), defiance may often be healthier.

Our worry recurs: that illusions of control are good for *you* doesn't imply that they're good for *agency*. Lots of things make one better off, such as better weather or higher air quality, that don't have much to do with one's agency. Framing this point in a valuational theory, not every behavior that realizes an actor's values is an agential expression of her values: for the realization of value to count as an expression of value, it must be realized in the right way. Minimally, that the actor holds the value should be causally implicated in her undertaking a behavior suited to realize the value: if government intervention causes a beneficial increase in air quality where I live, the government action is not an exercise of my agency, even if I value the benefit. On the other hand, if I'm part of a grass-roots effort that forces elected officials out of their fatal complacency about environmental desecration, it becomes tempting to attribute to me a measure of agency, since the expression of my values in my behavior played a causal role, however small, in the outcome.

To quiet counter-examplers, we'd better stigmatize deviant causal chains. If your love of nature inspires the gods to clean our air and water, these salubrious circumstances aren't appropriately attributable to your exercising agency, even if your values, by way of inspiring godly environmentalism, form part of the causal history. I have to show that realization of values facilitated by self-ignorance needn't involve an objectionably deviant causal pathway, and I think I can show as much. For example, my valuing my health is presumably part of the reason I strive to maintain it. Perhaps my beliefs about the efficacy of these efforts are motivated cognitions. I may think my labors more effective than they are, in part because I want them to succeed. (However much you go running, you can't hide from your genes.) But these motivated cognitions may simultaneously be *motivating* cognitions; my believing my efforts will work inspires me to make efforts that in fact work, even if they don't work so well as I believe. Here, it seems appropriate to say that my holding the value of good health facilitates the value's expression in my intentional action, and this looks to be an exercise of agency, on the account of agency I favor.

For further illustration, let's return to romantic illusions. It is a truism, perhaps one of the true truisms, that "marriage takes work." Marital outcomes appear sensitive to effort: some couples work hard, and make a go of it, while others "take things for granted" and blow it. (Of course you won't make the mistakes your parents made.) But are the fortunate 50 percent really harder workers, or just more fortunate? Factors implicated in marital outcomes may be things beyond a couple's control, at least after they've pulled the trigger: socio-economic similarity is associated with marital success (Heaton 2002; Tzeng 1992), and premarital births are predictors of divorce (Martin and Bumpass 1989; Teachman 1983). Yet it doesn't follow that people do better when they leave everything to fate. There are things that can be done to better the odds, even for those with the wrong past: numerous studies indicate that couples counseling is effective (Bray and Jouriles 1995; Hahlweg and Richtera 2010; Sayers *et al.* 1988; Snyder *et al.* 2006).

In relationships, as with illness, people are often motivationally challenged: *I've had enough. I'm out of gas. I can't go on.* Here, I'm willing to speculate, sturdy perceptions of control have motivational utility: if you don't think marital outcomes are responsive to effort, how do you get yourself to undertake the effort? By supporting value-relevant motives, illusions of control may facilitate behavior that helps to realize values. If so, we've identified a pathway whereby self-ignorance supports, rather than impairs, agency. This pathway is indirect:

falsely believing I can directly influence something may effect efforts eventuating in behaviors or circumstances that influence the something in question. The fact is the child of the fiction.

There are also perverse cases, where illusory *lack* of control facilitates agency. Say you've really had it with a relationship: you're convinced rigor mortis has set in. As a result, you end up behaving as though things that are responsive to effort aren't. This might be bad faith; you're aware some things would help, but you convince yourself otherwise to justify your inaction. (One party refusing to enter couples' therapy may signal doom, whether or not therapy would have worked: the symbolism is potent.) I find sincere hopelessness more interesting: you really do think it's end times, so you wrongly think effort is futile, and you therefore don't make the effort. Suppose this results in a parting of ways. To my way of thinking, this sad tale might be a tale of agency. You value being done, which, via motivated cognition, engenders the despair that supports the behavior, or lack of behavior, which helps being done get done. Once more, it looks like your behavior expresses your values—by way of ignorance rather than awareness.

Questions about sincerity provoke delicate questions about the extent to which folks buy into their illusions. For instance, some evidence indicates that people believe happy relationships are characterized by positive biases, and also recognize that both themselves and their partners are positively biased towards the other (Boyes and Fletcher 2007). I've been supposing that for the illusions to do their good work, people must be fully in their grip, but it's not clear that the subjects of romantic illusion are actually so gripped.

Imagine that in an amorous moment, besotted Sidney tells the pleasant-enough-looking Jessie that Jessie is the sexiest person alive. In all probability, neither of them really believes *People* magazine has been making an egregious omission from their annual "sexiest" list, but Jessie probably won't be much cheered if Sidney's sweet nothings come across as *mere* flattery. On one way of thinking about it, Jessie adopts a sort of dual perspective: Jessie believes Sidney is sincere, even if it's unlikely that Jessie would, if asked, insist that Sidney's guilty of the lunatic enhancement taking the statement at face value would suggest. Sidney's perspective may be similarly bifurcated: the compliment isn't shameless flattery, but neither is Sidney's enhancement of Jessie completely unnoticed by Sidney.

Something similar looks to be going on for self-enhancement; in some contexts, "meta-awareness" concerning the accuracy of self-assessment may be reasonably good (Carlson *et al.* 2010). People are aware that they suffer positive and negative biases about themselves, and they can be pretty accurate about where these biases show up; the areas I think I self-enhance may very well be the areas in which I self-enhance (Bollich and Vazire forthcoming). Near as I can tell, much of life is lived in the vast grey expanse separating conviction and doubt, where behavior is governed by something less than full-throated belief. Probably, this often involves a sort of pretense (here aligning with Gendler (2007) on self-deception as pretense). It's not easy to say how people relate to their pretenses (Gendler 2010), yet one thing that can be said is that illusions of control and other positive illusions are part of a performance, where the actors may, as it were, buy into their parts. To see how this works, we must again attend to the social.

Rationalization

Let's continue with Johansson, Hall, and colleagues' jaw-dropping studies of "choice blindness." In one variant (Johansson *et al.* 2005), participants were shown pairs of photographs depicting a female face, and asked to choose the face they found more attractive. For twelve trials, nothing was amiss. But for three "manipulated" trials, the experimenter, using a magician's sleight of hand, contrived to treat the photo participants did *not* choose as though they *did* choose it. In no more than 26 percent of all trials did participants remark on the switch, regardless of whether the appearance of the paired face shots was high or low in similarity. When participants were asked to explain their choices for three of the non-manipulated trials and the three manipulated trials—for example, "she looks very hot," "I like earrings," "I thought she had more personality"—the investigators found no differences in length of explanations, the degree to which explanations were phrased in the past or present tense, the verbal content of explanations (rated along the dimensions of emotionality, specificity, and certainty), or the number of empty reports (where participants were unable to give a reason for their choice).

A follow-up used word frequency measures and latent semantic analysis in attempt to differentiate manipulated and non-manipulated explanations: frequency searches for linguistic markers of certainty, specificity, emotionality, complexity, and deceit yielded little in the way of differences between the two conditions, and there were no statistical differences in semantic content (Johansson *et al.* 2006). That is, next to nothing distinguished the explanations participants gave for the choices they *did* make from the explanations they gave for the choices they *didn't* make. It is fair to conclude that participants were generally unaware of their fabrications, even as they "explained" a choice exactly contrary to one they had made only moments before. This unlikely result isn't a fluke: consistent results were obtained for manipulated taste tests of teas and jams, even when the aromas were quite different (Hall *et al.* 2010).

You'd not expect this trick to affect consequential decisions: people aren't easily duped into misremembering which person they married, or what house they purchased. Yet choice-blindness isn't limited to the trivial. In Sweden, Hall and colleagues (2012; cf. Hall *et al.* 2013) obtained the effect for moral attitudes of the sort folks often hold quite vehemently. People strolling through a park were given a 12-item survey with statements concerning either general moral principles or current moral issues, and asked to report their attitudes on a 9-point scale anchored at "Completely Agree" and "Completely Disagree." After completing the survey, participants read aloud three of the statements they had responded to, and explained their positions. In manipulated trials, two of these statements were reversed: if someone originally agreed with "Even if an action might harm the innocent, *it can still be morally permissible* to perform it," it now appeared that they had agreed to "If an action might harm the innocent, then *it is not morally permissible* to perform it" (emphasis added). The reversal was noticed in only 47 percent of trails, and 69 percent of participants accepted at least one reversed statement. Although the politically active were more likely to correct reversals, people claiming to generally hold strong moral opinions weren't more likely to make corrections. Unsurprisingly, level of agreement was associated with correction; the more participants agreed or disagreed with a statement, the more likely they were to correct the reversal. But nearly a third (31.4 percent) of all manipulated trials rated at the endpoints of the scale (1 or 9) were not corrected. Incredibly, when it came to explaining manipulated choices, 53 percent of the participants argued unequivocally for the reversal of their original position.

What's going on? Why don't more subjects notice the subterfuge, and why don't they confront the experimenter? Psychological jargon like "debrief" may obscure this, but experimental conversations are conversations, and exhibit the same subtleties other conversations do (Schwarz 1996). And here's the thing about conversations: people want them to go well. There are few things more deflating than a sputtering discussion, be it a first date, a job interview, or a long-awaited reunion with an old friend. And talk goes better, all things being equal, when folks are nice. People can be remarkably averse to contradicting others, even when those others are flamingly wrong-headed, as in Asch's (1955) famous conformity demonstration, where participants deferred to the majority in blatantly erroneous perceptual judgments. The choice-blindness participants presumably were under pressure, as in so many social interactions, for things to go smoothly: their self-awareness may have been compromised, but their social awareness was working just fine.

While people sometimes hold their nose and knowingly "go along to get along," the social influence in the choice-blindness experiments must have proceeded subliminally. Otherwise it would be difficult to explain the fluidity with which participants explained their (non-)choices, as well as the apparently genuine surprise participants evinced in post-experimental debriefing (Hall *et al.* 2010). Pretty clearly, the pseudo-explanations weren't conscious social niceties.

This doesn't mean they weren't social. Recall a puzzling feature of romantic illusions: how are people able to offer, and accept, painfully obvious enhancements like "you're the sexiest person alive" as (relatively) sincere statements of conviction? I suggested taking them as a kind of performance, and the thing to stress now is that the requirements for a good performance vary contextually: what your lover says to your face and what he says to his best friend can be expected to differ. But this doesn't always involve conscious pretense, and still less, I think, duplicity; these are completely different conversations. In the 2nd person, *you* are especially salient, and the motivational pressures on your lover tend to enhancement. When you're off stage, you're figuring in the 3rd person, and the *friend* is more salient, and this attentional difference may result in very different motivational effects. (Poor form for your lover to brag on your sexiness to a friend stuck in a loveless marriage.)

There's a suggestive analogy with the malleability of speech (Giles and Ogay 2007). People fluidly shift their linguistic presentation (vocabulary, accent, etc.) according to social context and conversational goals: asking for a beer in a scruffy bar and asking for a raise in a stuffy firm ain't (*are not*) the same thing, and they sound different. As a kid, I remember being amazed how very Bronx-y my father, a university professor in upstate New York, sounded on family visits to Irish relatives in the Bronx. But I didn't suspect my dad, a man with no patience for affectation, of disingenuousness. This "style-shifting" must be something people do unconsciously, or it would be exhausting to do, and damn difficult to do convincingly (consciously affected accents can be pathetically easy to detect). Similarly for the variation of cognition and attitude with social milieu, which won't generally be conscious, effortful, pretense.

At the same time there's pressure to say something agreeable, there's pressure to say *something*. In many circumstances, standing mute or pleading ignorance simply won't do, and most any answer, or at least a wide range of answers, is better than not answering (Hirstein 2005: 4–5). Not so much for factual questions tapping semantic memory; fine to say that I don't remember the name of the 23rd US president, or the first person to summit Everest. But for queries of self, the situation is different, and particularly so for reports of reasons. I suspect that instances of "rational dumbfounding," where people are unable to produce an explanatory account of their behavior, especially their intentional behavior, are pretty unusual. Even if rational dumbfounding is more common than my speculations allow, admitting it may yet be noteworthy—noteworthy enough to stop the show. (My impression is that children more often suffer rational dumbfounding; if so, this sharpens the point about adults.)

I therefore doubt Carruthers' (2009b: 132) contention that "there are all sorts of circumstances in which people are perfectly content" to confess ignorance of their motives. I'm especially inclined to doubt it for occasions of practical significance, a suspicion undiminished by Carruthers' example of "absent-mindedly" moving a household object about: professions of ignorance may be fine for doodling, but not so much for marrying. While it may be that people are genuinely clueless about the causes of their romantic commitments, I don't think they often proclaim their ignorance. Coupled readers might try an informal experiment: go home and announce to your partner, "You know babe, I have no idea, I mean *no idea*, why I'm with you." I suspect the results, if your better half took this as sincere puzzlement, would be impressive—the notorious difficulty of *Why do you love me?* questions notwithstanding. ("Let me count the ways" is a poet's stall for time.)

The key point concerns the facility with which people produce serviceable explanations for their behavior, even when their information, including infor- mation about their own psychological states, is seriously inaccurate and/or incomplete. To put the point in philosophy-speak, people readily interact in the "space of reasons," even when this space fails to overlap with the "space of motives" where the causal and psychological origins of behavior are found.[1] I'll call these performances *rationalizations* rather than confabulations, to distin- guish them from the clinical phenomena, and I'll deploy "rationalization" in a non-pejorative sense, absent the connotations of bad faith it often seems to carry. Here, a rationalization is a (typically verbal) performance that presents judgment and behavior as rational. Or, slightly less circularly: rationalizations make judgment and behavior make sense (cf. Gibbard 1990: 37–8, 156–9). And this sense-making is as much, or more, for one's others as for oneself; a central function of explaining one's behavior is "managing social inter- action" (Malle 2004: 70). Again, rationalizations do not require accurate self-awareness; the requisite sense-making needn't be predicated on an accurate causal history.

---

[1] "Space of reasons" is apparently due to Sellars (1997: sec. 36, cf. sec. 5). Sellars, if I understand him, thought the space of reasons necessarily distinct from the empirical region I've gestured at with "space of motives." On my view, any divergence is contingent.

There's more than one way to make sense. Something might make clinical sense, as when a neurologist attributes confabulation to brain trauma. But in this case, the explanation presents the subject as fit for what Strawson (1962: 6–10; cf. Watson 1993) called the *objective* reactive attitudes, where individuals, such as children and the seriously deranged, are considered as objects of manipulation and control. In contrast, when someone is regarded with Strawson's *participant* reactive attitudes, that someone is regarded as an entity fit for reciprocal engagement (cf. Boxer 2013: 76–80). These attitudes may be negative, like resentment, or positive, like admiration, but either way, they seem to presuppose their subject is not an object, but an agent. Once again, it may help to note the grammar: objective attitudes take up their object in the 3rd person, as appropriate for a doing *to*, while participant attitudes take up their object in the 2nd person, as appropriate for a doing *with* (cf. Darwall 2006).

If I'm right, a central form of rationalization presents behavior as an exercise of agency: *I chose to do this. I meant to do that. I had my reasons.* By presenting behaviors as exercises of agency, rationalizations depict their bearer as appropriately subject to participant reactive attitudes, and a fit partner for reciprocal social exchange. The confabulatory patient can be understood as attempting to explain her behavior in a way that enables attributions of agency: "it's not that I'm damaged," the anosognosic is perhaps saying, "but that I've a perfectly good reason for not moving my arm." Tragically, these attempts are often unsuccessful; many clinical confabulations can be thought of as failed rationalizations. But this failure cannot be fully explained in terms of epistemic deficiency, by noting that confabulations lack "contact with reality," for the same is not infrequently true— if in less florid form—for altogether healthy people. The relevant standards are more conversational than epistemological, and rationalizations reporting illusions of agency readily meet them.

In experimental milieus, rationalizations can look ridiculous (recall the Good Professor's simian vision), but this context is atypical: the experimenter has access to information that real world interlocutors often do not. Barring such information, the rationalizations would work just fine; if one's audience didn't know about the Group Effect, omitting to mention social influence would be perfectly acceptable. Something like this may also obtain in clinical cases; sometimes, confabulations are only identified when clinicians "fact-check" with family, friends, and significant others, or with information the patient has provided on another occasion (Moscovitch 1995: 226–7). Once again, this opportunity is frequently unavailable in ordinary conversations; the inaccuracies go unnoticed, and discussion moves happily forward.

Then a principal requirement for successful rationalization concerns what you can get away with—or rather, what your audience will let you get away with. These are boundaries confabulatory patients fail to navigate. Remember, for example, their curious lack of discomfort when confronted with inaccuracies, which problematizes the idea of "confabulations of embarrassment." Conversely, healthy rationalizations *are*, after a fashion, confabulations of embarrassment. Where self-awareness fails, and "I don't know" won't do, rationalization ensues, disciplined not by some bedrock reality, but by acute sensitivity to social cues.

Biography

My account favors approaches that construe agency as structured by narrative: who people are, and what they do, is partly determined by the stories which they tell and figure in (Dennett 1991, 1992; Fischer 2006: 106–23, 2009: 145–77; Schechter forthcoming; Schechtman 1996, 2011; Velleman 2006).[2] Unfortunately, the notion of narrative is a bit of a hairball, cursed with competing associations drawn from dizzying variety of research programs, which seems to make abstinence the better part of valor (Velleman 2003: 22). "Autobiography" is a tempting replacement, but "auto" encourages slighting sociality (much as does the philosophically perilous "autonomy"), so I'll favor "biography."

I don't intend anything fancy here, certainly not anything that requires monumental tomes. The subject of biography may be short or long in duration, and trivial or profound in substance: a great woman's riveting memoirs are biography, but so are banalities like "the almond butter was yummy, so I decided to take another bite." What matters here is the prominent role such stories—be they great or small—play in both individual psychologies and social interactions. However overburdened the notion of narrative, there's abundant evidence that people routinely make stories to make sense of their lives (McAdams 2008). And this sense-making, I'm going to argue, helps fashion agency.

According to Velleman (2006: 211–12), "an autobiography and the behavior that it narrates are mutually determining": the author's behavior shapes her story, but her story also shapes her behavior, in part because people are motivated to maintain a correspondence between story and self. In support, Velleman (2006: 214–17; 227–35) notes people's tendency to reduce "dissonance" between attitudes

---

[2] My anti-skepticism aligns me with Velleman (2006: 211–12) against the more skeptical narrative account of Dennett (1991: 207; cf. 1992; but see Humphrey and Dennett 1998: 41, 47 for a less skeptical tone).

and behavior (Festinger and Carlsmith 1959), and research indicating that people who predict they will vote turn out in higher numbers than those who don't so predict (Greenwald *et al.* 1987: 315–18). I'm tempted again to remark that *whom* one votes for may be influenced by ballot order, but I'm now on the anti-skeptical part of my theory, and I'm waxing optimistic. The optimistic thought is that one's biography helps tie one to the mast, and secures behavior expressing one's values, even in the face of unfavorable circumstance or unstable inclination. That one understands one has *made* a promise, and further understands oneself to be a person who *honors* her promises, may help ensure that the promise is *kept*. One's understanding of one's biography, then, shapes what one does.

On my view, this process need not require conscious effort; biographies can be implicitly held. Neither need biography be accurate. Despite a spotty record of keeping promises, thinking of oneself as a dutiful promiser may be causally implicated in one keeping promises on those occasions that one does so. A biography containing prospective elements needn't be limited to probable events in order to be efficacious: my forming the intention to vote might make it more likely that I vote, even if the chances of my doing so, based on prior evidence, are rather low. The influence of biography has as much (or more) to do with subjective personal salience than objective historical accuracy, and an inaccurate biography may sometimes be more motivationally compelling than an accurate one. Professor Drudge might better be able to grind out long hours at his desk under the auspices of the "talented" biography than the "mediocre" biography, and given the contribution of perspiration to inspiration, the self-enhancing biography can help earn Drudge the title "talented"—his mediocrity notwithstanding.

This sounds like saying you become your bullshit. Yes—but your bullshit had better become you. Fictive biography may facilitate agency, but living by fantasy isn't the formula for agency; self-conceptions that are completely uncorrelated with ability may impede the expression of values. More so, where fantasy lapses into solipsism: *your* thinking I'm a leader may make it so, but *my* thinking it so does not (Neu 2000: 281). Nevertheless, it remains the case that accurate self-awareness is not necessary for the kind of biographical self-direction I'm considering, which leaves open the possibility that agency might be relatively commonplace in the presence of pervasive self-ignorance. In fact, I'm arguing something stronger. Self-ignorance often functions to effect self-direction, and its *absence* can be an impediment to agency: a complete and accurate understanding of your relationship, or your health, might prevent you from making them all you want them to be.

This, it might be said, is a curious way to build a beast. While one should hesitate to assume that natural selection is benign, and hesitate still more to engage in kindergarten evolutionary biology, one still wants to ask if it would have been easier for Mother Nature to design a more exacting animal, whose behavior is funded by accurate self-awareness, rather than one whose reflections are pervasively inaccurate, but who manages self-direction indirectly, by means of rationalization.

Easier for what? To the extent that self-ignorance allows getting on in the world, and getting on with each other, why spend on accurate awareness of psychological states? Notice that the accurate animal may suffer a certain disadvantage when compared with the rationalizing animal: the accurate animal is epistemically fragile. Given the vagaries of mind and world, she can be expected to often get it wrong, and if accuracy is requisite for behavioral control, behavioral control will, on these not-infrequent occasions, founder. In contrast, the rationalizing animal is an epistemically resilient beast: for her, behavioral control may persist when the exact contours of mind and world are—as they are so often—imperfectly accessible.

There's a range of evolutionary theory on offer here. On one view, self-deception is adaptive because it allows people to deceive others with less "cognitive load" than conscious deception; to put it roughly, pretense burns more energy than sincerity, so the self-deceived deceiver is the more efficient deceiver (von Hippel and Trivers 2011: 4). Then if Mother Nature's not a Kantian, she might think self-ignorance a fine thing, in a dog-eat-dog world. A somewhat less sinister story with room for the adaptive utility of self-ignorance maintains that reasoning capacities evolved not so much to discover the facts—probably lots of considerably less fancy ways to do that—but to persuade conspecifics (Mercier and Sperber 2009). On this account, failures of self-awareness are not themselves adaptive, but are by-products of a reasoning system that developed with other (namely, other-directed) priorities.

My main questions won't get decided by evolutionary theory, but I'd be concerned if the theory I'm developing looked incredible when viewed in that light. Fortunately, I see little reason for such concern. To be clear, I'm not arguing that either agency or perceptions of agency are adaptive products of natural selection. I'm only insisting that my understanding of agency is not disqualified when human capacities are understood as resulting from such processes.

To say that the kind of biographical self-direction I've identified meets standards of scientific plausibility is not to say it defuses skepticism about agency. For there remains an uncomfortable question: What makes one's biography one's own? Regrettably, *mine* is among the most difficult words in philosophy. I've already bitten the "currentist" bullet, and denied that responsibility is "essentially" historical (Chapter 2, pp. 30–2), but the question prompts lingering unease, if it leads to identifiable influences on biography that are alien to the agent—if our stories tell us, rather than us telling our stories. Sometimes, the role of the actor is less author than audience, and if I'm right about the science, there are disturbingly many such cases.[3]

Much biographical material, such as that associated with stereotypes, may be imposed on people without their knowledge or consent. Perhaps it's true (arbitrary influences like name letter effects here judiciously neglected) that I've somehow chosen the "professor biography" (for doubts, see Doris 2002: 89–91). But I didn't much choose central themes in the "male biography," or the "tall biography," and certainly these biographies also profoundly influence my behavior. (No, you mayn't ask me how tall I am.) And which stories are influencing my behavior without my awareness? (Surely you're not suggesting I did that because I'm a Missourian?) The difficulty worsens with derogatory categories: research on "stereotype threat" indicates that making a negative stereotype, such as the alleged inferiority of women's mathematical ability, salient to members of a stigmatized group decreases their performance on dimensions relevant to the derogatory stereotype (Steele and Aronson 1995; for cautions, see Sackitt *et al.* 2004). The skeptical worry has now recurred, this time fixing on the determinants of biographies. But once again, the problem will figure in the solution: the social formation of biography facilitates agency.

Negotiation

Biographies are often structured by norms governing social roles, and this climate of expectation facilitates, through channels both conscious and unconscious, role-appropriate behavior.[4] When someone presents herself as a gourmet she restricts her conduct; the professed gourmet risks censure by her acquaintances (or her self) if she exhibits behavior, like serving bargain wine at an important dinner, which confounds her self-appointed role. Some things fit the gourmet

---

[3] Velleman (1989: 17 n4; 2006: 244) is less troubled than I by the scientific evidence pressing skepticism. Like Humphrey and Dennett (1998: 39–40), I take the science to motivate skepticism about the notion of "unified" agency, a notion with which Velleman (2006: 208, 223) appears to have some sympathy, although he (2006: 222), seems less committed to agential unity than narrative theorists like Taylor (1989: 51–2) and MacIntyre (1984: 203–4).

[4] I owe much of my thinking at this juncture to the pleasure of supervising Jesse Slavens' Masters thesis at the University of California, Santa Cruz, which developed allied themes in the company of Goffman (1959, 1967) and Bourdieu (1984).

role and some don't, and these fits are not easily flouted. Moreover, this influence may obtain whether or not previous behaviors that the gourmet interprets as manifesting her gustatory values were in fact structured by those values: a grossly inaccurate causal history of behavior may serve to organize subsequent behavior in accordance with the values that history enshrines.

Biographies fund rationalizations; it's often apt to say one did something because one's experienced a certain thing, like a divorce, or because one occupies a certain social position, like a teacher. Rationalization is not merely retrospective; when someone presents a rationalization, people—herself included—will expect her behavior to accord with it, so the rationalizing performance may facilitate future behavior appropriate to the rationalization. Think again of our happy lovers, with their enviable propensity for positive illusion. In my experience, many romantically involved couples indulge in telling and retelling the story of their beginnings. The point of these tellings and retellings, it seems to me, is not to *discover* an *accurate* history; it is to *create* a *shared* history. For American couples, there's research indicating that something like the famous "we knew right away" chronicle associated with "love at first sight" may be the dominant form (McCollum 2002). My informal impression is that, in addition to "we knew right away," there's a second major form, "we hated each other." Could either be accurate? The eventual outcome makes the "we hated" story a strain to embrace, and the thought that lust, a dark corner table, and two pints of skunked beer facilitate the extraordinary epistemic position posited by the "we knew" history is even more difficult to credit.

Yet again, fiction needn't be delusion. On the contrary. In the two archetypal forms, love stories seem to share a theme: they celebrate strong feelings, and therefore help create and sustain emotional connections. With the mutual formation and endorsement of romantic biographies, lovers become couples. In contrast, a story like, "I wasn't much drawn to your father, but I hadn't been on a date in 17 months," doesn't seem to have the requisite bounce. (*Note to reader*: keep stories like that to yourself, even if—*especially* if—true.) Moreover, sharing idealizations can help make them reality: studies of dating couples suggest that positive illusions can be "self-fulfilling prophecies," where idealized partners internalize their partners' idealizations, and may thereby act in ways more closely approximating the ideal (Murray *et al.* 1996: 1170; 2003; cf. Drigotas *et al.* 1999). The endearment "you make me a better person," sounds cheesy, but there you are.

Human beings order their lives together by jointly developing rationalizations, and the central requirement for these rationalizations is not accuracy, but accord: friends may jointly recall a big night on the town as bigger than their bar tabs report, neighbors may jointly recall a harsh winter as harsher than the meteorological record shows, and colleagues may jointly recall a dull perform- ance by a professional rival as duller than unbiased assessment suggests. We've laughed and cried *together*, such stories say, and this commonality helps provide the foundation for together going forward.

Once again, I don't mean to suggest that "contact with reality" is irrelevant; gross violations of epistemic parameters may make rationalizations unsharable, as they do in clinical confabulation. (Joint delusions like *folie à deux, folie à trois, folie à quatre, folie à famille*, and *folie à plusieurs* notwithstanding.) But harmony with one's interlocutor is often more important than epistemic parameters: having a good conversation is typically more important—far more important—than conversing in facts. Then the functional importance of purported introspections—*I'm happy to see you, You're making me angry*— is less "inward-looking" and epistemic than "outward-looking" and pragmatic. The romantic collaborations I've recounted are especially telling in this regard, but I see little cause to doubt that the processes at work there appear elsewhere.

This commerce can transpire quietly, on a personal level, as when the bound- aries of a relationship are adjusted and readjusted: a friend becomes a lover, a colleague becomes a friend, a student becomes a colleague. It can also go on noisily, at the societal level, as in mass movements like suffrage and civil rights, where people demand, in effect, a change of identity—an identity that better expresses their values. In none of these cases does the individual act alone; here agency supposes not *in*dependence, but *dependence*: on family, friends, or comrades in arms. Human beings living in groups shape their lives, not as isolated reflectors, but as participants in an ongoing negotiation—a negotiation that simultaneously constrains and expresses who they are. In a slogan, agents are negotiations. If you like, call this notion of agency *dialogic*.

For agency, the key word is *participant*. While it's true that people are subject to social influences that constrain their self-understandings, they are not passive entities in these negotiations, the outcome of which is influenced by whatever values each party brings to the table. This is not to deny that inequalities of power may impede the exercise of agency; that's one thing that makes inequalities of power bad. But in other instances, the opposite is true: relationships help people express their values in their lives, as they do in the right sort of friendships, romantic involvements, and institutions. Agency requires not *freedom* from influence, but *mutual* influence.

Apology

The regulative function of negotiation is particularly evident in the practice of apology. Many times, those from whom an apology is demanded—those who "owe" an apology—are believed morally responsible for what they've done (Radzik 2009: 92–3). Save exceptions like government apologies for historical wrongs, and apologies extracted from children as part of their education, the practice of apology appears to concern the conduct of those perceived to have exercised agency for the conduct in question. Where there's an exercise of agency, reactive attitudes are apt, and these attitudes track whether or not people's behaviors "reflect attitudes towards us of good will, affection, or esteem" (Strawson 1962: 5). Apologies are in order when someone has behaved—and behaved as an agent—in a manner reflecting an absence of good will. If the offending party wants her relationship with the offended party to go on as before—if good will is to be restored in the relationship—she must offer apology.

Of course, these offerings frequently fail their restorative function; recall the latest televised mortification featuring the latest philandering politician. Apologies are frequently buttressed by explanation, and one cause of failure is omitting an appropriate account of the transgression (Radzik 2009: 97). Suppose I've done something rude, and you ask me what the hell I thought I was doing. Suppose further that there's no weaseling possible: I was undeniably a jackass. If I respond by saying, "Who knows?" or "I've no idea," you are, I submit, unlikely to find this very satisfying—even if, since you've been reading this book, you think it might well be true. Nor is it likely to mollify if I simply say, "I apologize," full stop. You want to know I'm contrite, but you also want my contrition contextualized in a way that allows the relationship to go on. At these junctures, I maintain, professions of ignorance will often fail badly.

Such performances might manifest lack of effort: I simply don't feel like explaining myself to the likes of you. In this case, it looks as though I don't care enough to continue with you in a relationship of mutual regard. If I routinely give such responses, I suspect we are rather unlikely to have much of a relationship: our conversation is over. On the other hand, suppose that I'm sincerely baffled about what I did. I've already contended that folks don't regularly report rational dumfounding, whatever the state of their reflective access. Some clinical populations exhibit such perplexity: patients in advanced stages of schizophrenia are sometimes unable to explain their behavior (Firth 1992). But again, it's objective reactive attitudes that are appropriate for those individuals: they are subjects of treatment rather than participants in reciprocal relationships. When I sincerely tell you, "I've no idea why I did that," I exhibit important affinities with such individuals. And now you've a problem: with what manner of organism are you dealing?

Conversely, the usual explanations can do the needed work, however hackneyed they be: "I'm sorry, I had a bad day at work," or "I apologize, my back is killing me." One thing these explanations do is indicate that the problematic behavior is compatible with "good will, affection, or esteem," and they provide assurance of future conduct manifesting this regard. "I don't know" accomplishes neither of these things. The explanation in question must not unduly strain credulity, but neither must it be historically accurate. Indeed, an accurate rationalization may not do the needed social work. If I say, "I'm sorry, it's just that I was finding you incredibly tiresome," the addition will undermine, not augment, my apology. This doesn't mean that effective apologies must be exercises in bad faith. Indeed, an automatically produced rationalization may be superior to a consciously fabricated explanation, since rationalizations may be sincerely offered, enabling both speaker and listener to be fully gripped.

Once more, we have the materials of dialogic agency. By offering apology for, and rationalization of, a behavior in a way that situates the transgression in a context of ongoing good will, the apologizer helps foster a relationship of mutual regard. An apology being offered and accepted may serve as a kind of commitment device: both parties agree to holds themselves, and one another, to standards befitting their relationship. Here again, the rationalization needn't be historically accurate; it can do its work even if the transgression really was a case of indifference, spite, or what have you. What matters is that apology and rationalization signal—in ways convincing to both speaker and audience—a return to good will. In cases where the apologizer values this return, the practice of apology and rationalization facilitates the expression of his values, and thereby facilitates agency.

The reflectivist may happily allow some of this. Indeed, one might endorse both dialogism and reflectivism (Westlund 2003: esp. 500); as I've said, reflectivism does not entail individualism. But on my view, this admixture would be only half right. I don't think dialog, even justificatory dialog, need be reflective dialog. The fluidity that many conversations exhibit—conversations among non-philosophers, anyway—indicates that much conversation is supported by automatic processing. A good thing, or conversation would be a painfully halting affair. Moreover, even where conversation appears reflective, and conversants are together thinking aloud, this reflection needn't require accurate self-awareness. So even if the exchange of rationalizations sometimes involves reflection, the dialogist should, at a minimum, want to jettison the accuracy corollary of reflectivism. I'm guessing this isn't a concession reflectivists will be eager to make.

Normativity

Granting the sort of dialogic self-direction I'm celebrating is a significant feature of human life, one might wonder if it displays sufficient normative substance. The exercise of agency is an achievement, it might be said, an achievement worth wanting, and it's not obvious that the social self-manipulations of delusional chatterboxes approximate this standard. Not the most tactful way to put the point, but a point well taken: a viable theory must accommodate the normative significance of agency.

Here's opportunity for the reflectivist to re-enter the fray: although reflective agency is not empirically dominant, she might argue, it is normatively dominant. Even if reflective agency is relatively infrequent, it might be agency par excellence, with other forms of agency, such as dialogic agency, being departures from the reflectivist benchmark of "ideal agency." The issue is not easily resolved; it will be hard to produce uncontestable considerations establishing that one form of agency is "better" than another. Allowing this is a contest where a champion may be crowned, I'm not sure it's a competition someone defending a pluralism like the one I'm going to defend should want to enter. This said, the kind of socially embedded agency I'm depicting may have normative appeal that alternatives lack.

Consider someone who—quite unlike ordinary human organisms—doesn't do rationalization; someone who takes "never apologize, never explain" completely to heart. This advice is attributed to, among others, the laconic Hollywood icon John Wayne, so let's call our creation Duke. A strong silent type, Duke never participates in the dialog I associate with agency; if he's in the space of reasons, he doesn't have much to say about it. Duke, then, is a sort of agential mute, and he definitely isn't a negotiation; not only does he refuse to negotiate with terrorists, he refuses to negotiate with anyone else.

Duke may nevertheless exercise agency. One possibility is that while Duke doesn't go in for dialogic agency, he does go in for reflectivist agency: he occasionally deliberates about what to do, based on accurate self-awareness, and occasionally acts in accordance with his deliberations. Another possibility is that Duke goes in for libertarian agency, and somehow produces, at least some of the time, the undetermined events, or "flickers of freedom" that are implicated in libertarian free actions (cf. Fischer 1994: Ch. 7).[5] A third possibility is that

---

[5] I'll use "flicker" to refer to whatever event the libertarian takes to be necessary for freedom, and ignore the more particular connotations sometimes found in the literature (e.g. Della Rocca 1998). For more on flickers, see Chapter 7, pp. 166–8.

Duke goes in for a sort of "instinctive" agency; his impulses express his values without the aid of reflection or social facilitators. So there may be room for a strong and silent sort of agency—in our fiction.

Whatever of these sorts Duke is, he's missing out. If in other regards like an actual person, Duke will less often be an agent than more garrulous types, on the hypothesis that for actual persons, the exercise of agency is facilitated by dialog. One might contend that less is more: Duke exercises agency on fewer occasions than those who are dialogically engaged, but these occasions, as occasions of agency par excellence, are of higher worth. I have the contrary intuition: Duke would be less richly an agent than chattier sorts, because many exercises of agency that make life worth living emerge in dialog, as we negotiate our selves with our intimates. To put it another way, Duke exhibits a certain lack of texture: he'd not be a full participant in many of the shared processes and projects distinctive of (and good about) actual human agency.

Successful negotiation makes hard work, and it's an admirable achievement if anything is. If so, it's quite arguable that the dialogic conception has normative appeal that less social conceptions lack. Doubtless, the contrary is also arguable. If one inclines to individualism (not to say rugged individualism) one may find Duke's asociality more appealing than dialogic alternatives. But that's just the thing: normative appeal is arguable. And if it's arguable, it's not a standard which one side can be untendentiously said to fail, which means it's not a standard that can be readily used to decide among competitors.

In the end, the pluralism I'll defend allows eschewing contention, at least to a considerable extent. I'm not saying dialogic control is the only source of human agency; in Chapter 7 I'll develop an account that has room for multiple sources. Different individuals may present with different admixtures of agency-support- ing processes, and some agents may look more like Duke, while others are more outgoing. A reflectivist might join me here, and attempt to take pluralism aboard, by saying that agency based on accurate self-awareness is the dominant form of agency, with agency supported by rationalization taking over in epistemic *extremis*, as a sort of back-up system. The empirical evidence compels the contrary: rationalization with impoverished self-awareness is the typical case, with paradigmatic instances of reflectivist agency being atypical. So there's going to be rather more instances of agency about, on my way of fixing the frame. For anyone who shares my conservative sensibilities about the frequency of agency, that's welcome news.

Signpost

This chapter's problem was to explain how agency might obtain in the face of pervasive self-ignorance. I observed that illusions are ubiquitous and often beneficial, and then argued that illusions of self, such as the illusion of control, may facilitate agency. I suggested that this facilitation is effected by the exchange of rationalizations, the sense-making explanations of judgment and behavior that are the healthy analog of provoked clinical confabulation. In their turn, rationalizations figure in the biographies by which people interpret and structure their own, and each other's, behavior. By negotiating the contours of their biographies in interaction with others, people are able to shape their lives in ways that express their values. That's agency, on the theory I'm developing here.

7

Responsibility

I've assumed that answering questions about agency helps answer questions about moral responsibility: to find responsibility, look for agency. This assumption is assailable, because there are candidates for responsible behavior that aren't exercises of agency. Consider an inadvertent oversight: distracted by his child's misadventure at school on a warm spring afternoon, a father leaves the family dog in the car when he goes to extricate his offspring from the principal's office, and poor doggers succumbs to hyperthermia. Arguably, dad is appropriately attributed responsibility for this mishap (Sher 2009: 24–5). But there doesn't look to be an exercise of agency, especially if agency involves the expression of value. Probably, dad likes doggers just fine, and he more probably doesn't wish her dead; had he noticed his potentially lethal mistake, he'd have rescued doggers *post haste*.

Pets aren't the only victims of hyperthermia accidents; across the USA, some thirty children die in hot cars each summer (McLaren *et al.* 2005). Details vary, but maybe it happens like this: a harried father neglects to drop a youngster at day care and instead drives straight to work, leaving his child quietly sleeping in the back seat when he goes on the job. Such catastrophes are nearly incomprehensible, but they're relatives of familiar and trivial "slips," like neglecting to drop off the dry-cleaning, or hopping in the shower with one's socks on, that occur everyday (Amaya 2013). Unless things are tense at home, there's not much trouble over the dry-cleaning, but when slips are sufficiently consequential, perpetrators may be blamed and punished, as they sometimes are in hyperthermia accidents.

These cases might be thought of as imposing strict liability, where someone is subject to punishment for a misdeed despite being in excusing conditions during its commission. As I've already said (Chapter 2, p. 24), certain atrocities of warfare may appropriately be treated this way; heinous transgressions mandate penalty, even though the chaos of war often impairs judgment enough that perpetrators occupy excusing conditions, in that they cannot reasonably be expected to appreciate the wrongfulness of their conduct. On this understanding, strict liability is liability to punishment *sans* moral responsibility: there are rationales for punishing perpetrators of atrocity, such as signaling moral outrage and enforcing military discipline, that do not presuppose their moral responsibility (Doris and Murphy 2007: 51–5).

Catastrophic slips aren't likely targets for strict liability. The actors aren't usually in excusing conditions: a frenetic workday doesn't undo the expectation that one not abandon one's child in a dangerously hot vehicle. But if there's not much here that looks like an excuse, neither is there much here that looks like agency. Manifestly, the outcome isn't an expression of the parents' values, and it seems preposterous to say they valued something else, like getting to work on time, more than they valued the life of their child. Nor is a relevant exercise of agency easily located at some previous juncture; it's not as though there were reasonable precautions the parents declined to take. Most every time, precautions are quite unnecessary—which may help explain why car alarm systems designed to prevent such tragedies have so far been slow to catch on (Stenquist 2010). All this inclines me to eschew attributions of moral responsibility for slips. Although my lenience may be an artifact of thinking they've "suffered enough," I don't find myself directing anger (or other condemnatory reactive attitudes) at the unfortunate parents, and neither am I sure they should be punished; in fact, people are prosecuted in only around half of such cases (Collins 2006: 807 n2, 825).

If, unlike me, you're convinced that the parents should be subject to disapprobation and punishment, you may want to deny that agency is necessary for responsibility. Another option would be to introduce a different notion for cases where disapprobation or punishment is appropriate, the actor is not in excusing conditions, and the conduct in question is not an exercise of agency. To motivate the introduction of a *tertium quid*, contrast a case where someone deliberately abandons his child in a hot car, attempting a return to his carefree younger days, and disguises the murder as a tragic accident. This looks like a case of "full-on" moral responsibility, and it's worth employing another notion—accountability, perhaps—for the very different case of a truly inadvertent slip (Amaya 2013; Amaya and Doris, forthcoming). Not easy to say exactly what the wanted notion of accountability comes to, and I'm not going to try, so long as I can maintain my insistence that responsibility is typically associated with agency. This insistence encounters adversity, for as we'll now see, a dissociation of agency and responsibility might be motivated not by appeal to phenomena like slips, but by general theoretical considerations.

Revisions

On Korsgaard's (2009: xii–xiii) Kantian theory of agency, "you can't maintain the integrity you need in order to be an agent with your own identity on any terms short of morality itself." This seems to bear an untoward implication. If one is only an agent when self-governed on morality's terms, conduct departing these terms is not the conduct of an agent (or perhaps, it's the conduct of a lapsed agent). On the supposition that the exercise of agency is a standard condition for responsibility attribution, it looks as though no one is ever responsible for wrongdoing—as Korsgaard (2009: 159-60) registers the concern, "nothing exactly counts as a bad action."

One might respond, as one should, that agency comes in degrees. Then one says, on a picture like Korsgaard's, that intentional wrongdoers act as agents, but less so than the intentional right-doers. If responsibility is associated with agency and also comes in degrees, the bad, while less responsible than the good, are nevertheless responsible, and we seem to have blocked the untoward implication. But Korsgaard (2009: 174) disavows this; she insists that on her (and every other) moral theory, "[t]here is no general principle saying that you are responsible to the extent that you acted" as an agent.

Conversely, I've been assuming that the following proposition is impressively plausible: generally, to the extent that an actor's exercise of agency is impaired or prohibited, their moral responsibility is reduced or eliminated. Motivating the proposition is fairly straightforward. The disruption of agency (say, by accidental ingestion of a highly potent psychoactive substance) is a prototypical feature of excusing conditions, and identifying excusing conditions is a prototypical means of blocking responsibility attribution; together, these observations indicate that agency is a condition of responsibility. From here, it takes little work to recognize a sort of continuum from mitigation to excuse, and say that agency and responsibility are typically coextensive.

Korsgaard (2009: 174) rejects this linkage, because she contends that "every sensible moral theory, like every sensible friend, lover, colleague, family member, and fellow citizen, holds people just as responsible for *omissions* as they do for actions." The appearance is notable: could a Kantian be joining consequentialists in rejecting the act/omission distinction? But brand integrity is not the only issue. If we say people are equally responsible for actions and omissions, we apparently lose the thought that people are especially responsible for what they *do*, which threatens, as Williams (1973: 109–10) warned, a yoke of "boundless obligation."

Korsgaard (2009: 174–5) identifies a boundary: you are legitimately held responsible for an omission when "the thing you omitted was in some general sense your job." Maybe it's not your job to make me a birthday cake with lavender buttercream, but seeing your child safely to day care surely is; therefore, omitting to make me a birthday cake with lavender buttercream is a non-responsible omission, while omitting to ensure your child's safe arrival at day care is a responsible omission.

For Korsgaard (2009: 175), there's a job that everyone has, the job of "making yourself into an agent." Now, "responsibility in general is going to look a lot more like responsibility for omission" (Korsgaard 2009: 175), as responsibility accrues to a particular sort of omission, the failure to properly constitute oneself, on the terms of morality, as an agent. This allows Korsgaard to block the untoward implication: bad actors are responsible, not so much for what they did do, but for what they didn't: they didn't properly constitute themselves.

There's something to this: one might castigate Sloth not so much for the consequences of his slothfulness—a mope like that could hardly have done better—but for allowing himself to lapse into such a sorry state. Matters complicate, though, when intentional and unintentional omissions are distinguished. An intentional "act of omission" occurs when someone explicitly forbears or refrains from doing something (*I refuse to partake in such foolishness!*); here, responsibility attribution seems relatively unproblematic (Clarke 1994: 196). But many omissions are unintentional, and their association with responsibility is more tenuous. Certainly, failures of self-constitution often look this way. While some people explicitly refrain from treating themselves better—they're here for a good time, not for a long time—I reckon many of the world's Sloths slide unintentionally into slothdom: healthy lifestyles simply doesn't make their radar, or other priorities swamp their efforts in this direction.

I don't claim that responsibility never accrues to unintentional omissions; perhaps, when an action (like deciding not to use a day planner) results in an omission (like forgetting a meeting) responsibility for the omission is somehow derived from responsibility for the action (Clarke 1994: 198). Whether or not this proposal, or some other, can be worked out, the appeal of treating responsibility "in general" as responsibility for omission is questionable. Take Korsgaard's example of a serial killer, and imagine this killer is not a stark raving, "disorganized" offender, but among the "organized" offenders, sexual sadists who kill, as one former FBI profiler insists, because they enjoy it (Trimarco 2009; see also Ressler and Schactman 1992: 102–3). Now imagine, if you can, that this monster tortured and killed a family member. Would you be angry (to use an inadequate word) because the killer omitted to properly constitute himself on the terms of morality, or because he *tortured and killed your loved one?* It certainly seems as though people direct reactive attitudes at actions, or at actors in regard to their actions, as much—or considerably more—than at omissions of self-constitution.

Of course, the best philosophical theory of responsibility might be highly revisionary, since folk theories of responsibility might be badly wrong. My own approach appears revisionary in some regards and conservative in others. Conservative, in that I think many ordinary attributions of moral responsibility, together with the associated reactive attitudes, are passably felicitous: people are right to get angry at those who exploit children for profit, for example, and right to admire those who fight against the exploitation. At the same time, I believe there's endless room for improvement: for instance, the origins of criminality in mental illness are scandalously underappreciated (Slate *et al.* 2013), and I've my reservations about American attitudes towards criminal justice more generally. Even where I accept conventional attitudes and attributions, the rationale I propose for these judgments may be revisionary: I doubt that folk theories of responsibility are anti-reflectivist, anti-individualist, and dialogic, and I similarly doubt they maintain that self-ignorance facilitates agency. Thus, I'm a conservative in that I'm likely to accept many particular attributions and attitudes comprising everyday practices of responsibility, and a revisionist regards the theoretical backing of these attitudes and attributions (cf. Vargas 2013b: 1–5).

Of course, the outlines of folk practice and theory are less than crystalline, and I'm not confident that experimental philosophers and psychologists can provide so much clarity as might be wished for. The theoretical underpinnings of everyday responsibility attribution are likely underspecified, imprecise, and less than optimally coherent; and even if we possessed the experimental wherewithal to exhaustively articulate The Folk Theory of Responsibility, we likely wouldn't find constructions that are readily compared to one or another of the many intricate philosophical theories on offer (Nichols 2014: Chs 1, 4). I'm pretty sure my theory presents revisionary rationales for the attribution of responsibility; I've after all argued that the reflectivism I reject is widely endorsed and highly intuitive. But I'm not sure empirical research currently enables—or ever will enable—definitive verdicts of this kind.

This said, it's worth remarking on just how revisionary Korsgaard's theory looks; whatever the exact contents of folk theory and practice, her view contravenes observations that very arguably have the status of commonplaces. Korsgaard starts with the claim that agency requires conformity with the terms of morality, which contravenes the commonplace that bad people often exercise agency in doing bad deeds. Since she doesn't want to give the baddies a pass, she's moved to disassociate agency and responsibility. This too contravenes the commonplace: it's apparently at odds with a natural understanding of excuses as destabilizations of agency. Finally, to explain how bad people can be held responsible while failing to be agents, Korsgaard asserts that responsibility accrues to people not through their actions, but through their omissions of constitution. Here again, she contravenes the commonplace, since people are routinely assigned responsibility for their actions.

Now, the contrary: bad people may exercise agency in their misdeeds, responsibility is closely associated with agency, and responsibility often accrues to people *via* their actions. This is a rather less interesting cluster of views, even a boringly conventional one. But it's also reassuringly plausible. I don't find the conviction that moral probity is required for agency—the conviction driving Korsgaard down the interesting road—compelling enough to depart the reassuring cluster. I'm willing to be concessive, and grant that agency is not necessary for responsibility; I don't see any shame in resigning the notoriously unwinnable necessary-and-sufficient-conditions game. However, neither do I see incentive to reject a generalization: typically, instances of morally responsible behavior involve exercises of agency.

Attribution

On the understanding just defended, the question of whether someone is morally responsible for their behavior usually concerns the question of whether the conduct in question involved an exercise of agency. According to the valuational approach explicated in Chapter 2, archetypal exercises of agency are expressions of the actor's values, so the question becomes one of determining whether the actor's values are expressed in their conduct. To view matters in the frame I've developed, when we are justified in asserting that a person's conduct expresses her values, we are justified in ruling out the presence of defeaters, and are therefore justified in attributing an exercise of agency. On these occasions we usually will, given the association of agency and responsibility, be justified in attributing responsibility.

Putting flesh on these bones ain't easy. Folks don't always know what their values are, or how to realize their values in their lives: *What really matters to me? What do I want out of life? How can I get it?* If my cautions about self-ignorance are heeded, the problem is even harder than it initially appears, for people may be no better acquainted with their values than with other furnishings of their minds. From the outside, things look still worse: if *you* have trouble identifying your values, why think *I* will be able to identify your values? Perhaps my arguments have succeeded too well, and skepticism plagues me no less than the reflectivist.

I take this difficulty seriously, but I won't succumb to skeptical panic. People are frequently ignorant of their psychological history, but it doesn't follow that people are ignorant of their values. Recall choice blindness, where people happily rationalize choosing things they didn't choose. That's a remarkable phenomenon, but there's another phenomenon worth remarking on: even if people were wrong about which choices they made, they apparently offered what they took to be good reasons for their ostensible selections. Remember their explanations: "she looks very hot," "I like earrings," "I thought she had more personality." Not, "she's anything but hot," "I hate earrings," "I thought she was dull as dry toast." People were defending choices they didn't make, but their rationalizations presumably referenced considerations they could respect. Why not say these rationalizations reflected their values?

This is on the right track, but it's not quite so simple. Like other behaviors, rationalizations may fail to express the actor's values. That rationalizations are commonly socially appropriate may actually increase suspicion that it's circumstance, rather than value, shaping them; perhaps rationalizations are structured less from the inside out than from the outside in.

Epistemological difficulty is exacerbated by the observation that behavior is often associated with fluctuating, multiple, and conflicting values. For illustration, consider Huck Finn cases, where someone does the right thing by acting other than he thinks best (Arpaly and Schroeder 1999; Bennett 1974). As Twain writes him, Huck appears to believe that he should report his friend Jim, a runaway slave, to the authorities. But when push comes to shove, Huck cannot, to his consternation, actually do so. In contrast to ordinary *akrasia*, the sadly familiar source of misdoings from boudoir to buffet table, Huck's weakness produces admirable behavior, earning it the appellation "inverse *akrasia*."

On one reading of the story, it's a tale of self-ignorance: while Huck thinks he holds values typical of ante-bellum white American southerners, he really values his friendship with Jim more than slave owners' "property rights." Since attitudes in the neighborhood of admiration seem a customary—and defensible—response to Huck's conduct, it would be convenient if my approach allowed that his behavior was an instance of agency. To allow it, I have to say that someone may exercise agency even where their ignorance extends to the values expressed in their behavior.

That's the thing to say, as comes clear in cases where valuational self-ignorance issues in deplorable behavior. If I speak out of cruelty while thinking I'm speaking out of honesty, you may well hold me responsible for hurting your feelings. And if pressed to defend your attribution, you might say something like, "Whatever he thought he was doing, he really *wanted* to be cruel." Hopefully, you'd have me wrong, but the point is that if you were right, you'd have a serviceable justification. Similarly for Huck; whatever (he thought) he thought was right, what mattered to him most was that he help his friend. Pretty good reason to attribute an exercise of agency, where someone acts on what matters to her. The less likely thing would be to say that someone did what mattered to her, because it mattered to her, but didn't do so as an agent. Like other forms of self-ignorance, valuational self-ignorance doesn't always impede the exercise of agency.

On another telling, Huck held values favoring *both* the conventional course of action and the course he actually followed: his values conflicted, and the better trumped the worse. Here, Huck suffered a kind of ambivalence. This isn't lukewarmness, where one doesn't much care one way or the other; someone like Huck can have strong feelings on each side of an issue. (While such ambivalence might be accompanied by an experience of conflict, it might not, if the individual in question is unaware of one or more of the values at play.) Not a bad way to describe Huck, and also more ordinary cases: at least occasionally, the *akratic* values *both* their health and a meditative smoke, their marriage and sexual novelty, and so on.

Other times, the actor is "all in," or "wholehearted" (cf. Frankfurt 1988: 165), and her values are unconflicted with regard to what she does: there's nothing I'd rather be doing right now, than writing these words. In still others, the actor is "all out," or wholeheartedly opposed to the behavior she performs, as with coercion or compulsion: I'd never in a million years have done that, if you hadn't twisted my arm. In between are many variants of half-heartedness, where *akrasia* makes a prime example: this is gonna feel great, but I'll pay for it later.

The pure types, perhaps, are easily treated on a valuational approach: "all in" behaviors look like samples of agency ripe for responsibility attribution, while "all out" behaviors look like performances where agency and responsibility don't obtain. Yet much human life occupies the wide middle ground, where all a person's values don't speak with one voice. Sometimes, I suppose, the most strongly held value wins out, and there's little cause to deny that such cases are exercises of agency: they're simply instances of people doing what matters to them most, in the face of contrary considerations. More puzzling are cases where the less strongly held value carries the day, as perhaps happens with *akrasia*.

I'd not want to lose the thought that *akratic* behaviors can be instances of responsible agency; millions of betrayed spouses can't be wrong. To vindicate their outrage, it helps to notice that there's more than one way to fail. Maybe some *akrasia* is a matter of pathological compulsion, like addiction, where the actor places no value on his *akratic* behavior. And maybe such unwilling *akratics* are not responsible for what they do. But as I've already remarked (Chapter 3, pp. 70–1), this probably isn't the typical case. Much *akratic* behavior looks like garden variety temptation, where the actor, if not wholehearted, is plenty willing enough. Correctly describing such cases is no easy matter (cf. Holton 2009: 97–111), but on one very plausible description, what the actor does is an expression of a value he holds (such as carnal pleasure), even if he also holds contrary values (such as sexual fidelity). The question of degrees may recur here, and it may be that that *akratic* behavior is less an exercise of agency, and the actor less responsible, than the wholehearted actor. But that doesn't mean the half-hearted bear no responsibility at all (cf. Buss 2012: 655–6).

People aren't all in all that much, it seems to me. That's life, not skepticism about responsibility.[1] While the disintegration of mind—in the particular form of incongruence—may destabilize agency, the present considerations make evident that the exercise of agency does not require "unity" understood as the absence of conflict (but see Ekstrom 2005, 2011: 372). No doubt, the multiplicity of values with which people live sometimes makes it difficult to say where their treasure lies, but that doesn't mean there's no hope of uncovering it, and still less that there's no treasure.

Excavation begins to look less daunting when one realizes that valuing has a temporal dimension: values are expressed over time, and can, oftentimes, only be identified over time. There are two issues here: how values come to be, and how they come to be identified. Values are developed, sustained, and revised during extended periods, as in lasting romantic relationships, when lust seasons to love and partners negotiate their mutual matterings. Additionally, it will often be difficult to determine whether someone holds a value, in the absence of a temporally extended pattern of cognition, rationalization, and behavior: distinguishing love from lust takes time. With extended observation, a pattern of symptoms may emerge: as cognitions, rationalizations, and behaviors appropriate to a value tend to recur in a person's life, we, and they, may begin to have confidence that this person holds that value (even if their behavior is less than consistent with respect to that value, as it very probably will be).

Conversely, if one focuses on isolated events, diagnosis may falter. (Come to think of it, the same is true of medical diagnosis; that's why your doctor takes your history, or holds you overnight for observation.) It will frequently be obscure whether some one doing some thing is an expression of her values; the evaluative signal may be quite weak, against the background of situational

---

[1] One might go further: in his defense of libertarianism, Kane (e.g. 2011a: 386–7) develops the intriguing suggestion that ambivalence, and its resolution in action, is not contrary to agency, but distinctive of it.

noise. There are dramatic exceptions, like sacrificing one's life for a political cause, where a single behavior seems grounds enough for attributing a value. But even here, it would be better to know more: How long were they with the movement? Under what circumstances did they get involved? And so on.

All this applies to the third personal perspective, but something similar is going on in the first. Frequently, one's values are only revealed to oneself over time: *Maybe I've been unhappy all these years at the brokerage because money is less important to me than I thought. I guess I'd not have spent so much time with someone so superficial and attractive if I didn't care about appearances.* First personal inquiry will frequently be augmented by second personal, collaborative, inquiry: a friend observes that I'm often downcast after work, or an old lover observes that I seem happier with a new one. Collaboration also occurs in institutional contexts: therapeutic and educational endeavors can help people figure out what matters to them. Sometimes, others have better access—or at least instructively different access—to a person's values than does the person herself. The extent of self-ignorance is considerable, but people are collectively possessed of epistemic assets fit to ameliorate it, assets deployed in the continuing social negotiation by which people order and make sense of their lives.

Given the diachronic character of value, agency also has a diachronic character: the exercise of agency emerges not only in discrete, synchronic, actions, but also in temporally extended processes. In many endeavors—a relationship, career, or cause—the exercise of agency is temporally developed, which means that attributions of responsibility may attach to processes as much as actions. This realization is not especially evident in philosophical writing on agency and responsibility, which characteristically focuses on more or less discrete behavioral units (e.g. Davidson 2001: 4, 10, 30, 31, 43, 45, 49)—*Why did he drink the paint thinner?*—rather than complex, temporally extended processes—*Why did they stay together, during all those lean years?* (Bratman's (2007) "temporally extended agency" excepted). The second query wants explication in terms of values—*They were committed to their marriage vows* or *They really loved each other*—while the first sort of question may often be answered without direct reference to values— *He thought it was gin, and the hour was five.* Of course, extended performances don't always require valuational explanations; they might have stayed together because they were the last two people on Earth. But the answer you get depends on the question you ask, and by asking about ongoing processes rather than discrete actions, you may end up with different sorts of answers. Thinking about agency and responsibility as temporally extended processes should move us in the direction I've been moving: towards an understanding of agency as structured by ongoing negotiation—a dialog where people discover and develop their values.

Attribution of agency and responsibility may be warranted when a pattern of cognition, rationalization, and behavior emerges, and that pattern is best explained as involving the expression of some value. Whether a particular action expresses a value may be uncertain, but the emergence of trends across iterated cognitions and behaviors can underwrite confidence that the trend is to be accounted for by reference to a person's values, rather than a massively coincidental run of defeaters. In such cases, the presence of defeaters need not be treated as a live possibility, which means that in such cases, the skeptical challenge is defanged. These welcome conditions are less likely to obtain, I contend, for isolated cases of reflective deliberation. There, the possibility of defeaters—given all that is known about the potential for rationally arbitrary influences on judgment and decision—cannot usually be ruled out with confidence sufficient to warrant attribution of responsibility.

The reflectivist may insist they can accommodate my advice to depart emphasis on atomistic behaviors in favor of extended behavioral processes. Fair enough. But there's not only the problem of how agency is identified, but also the problem of how agency is facilitated. A compelling response to the skeptic will provide standards for attribution of agency, *and* an account of how agency may be realized in human lives—lives afflicted with surprisingly high levels of practically relevant self-ignorance. Articulating standards will be cold comfort, without an account of how people may live up to those standards. (Erecting unreachable benchmarks is the blueprint for skepticism.) A dialogic understanding of agency offers one such account—an explanation of how agency may emerge as part of the continuing negotiation by which people living together organize their lives.

The reflectivist may again join in; what prevents her from emphasizing sociality, self-ignorance, and rationalization in her account of agency? Perhaps nothing—nothing besides fealty to the traditional picture of agency as typified by autonomous individuals engaging in reflective deliberation funded by accurate self-awareness. If the reflectivist repudiates this picture, and makes a very explicit emphasis on sociality, self-ignorance, and rationalization, we needn't disagree. I'll make my conciliatory dispositions more explicit later on, in the course of asserting pluralism about agency and responsibility; for now, I'll note, in a less irenic spirit, that the reflectivist who makes peace in this fashion has ceded territory characteristic of their view.

Matterings

If I've now a decent answer to the epistemological problem, another problem remains: just as with my account of agency, one might wonder whether my approach to responsibility has sufficient normative bite. In a sense, this problem is readily solved: if I established the association of agency and responsibility in this chapter, and established the normative substance of dialogic agency in the last, it seems I've found some normativity in the vicinity of responsibility. Still, one could ask for more to be said. If the volumes devoted to normativity in philosophical ethics (where it was arguably the twentieth century's dominant preoccupation) are any indication, one could ask for a lot more to be said.

All the same, I'm hoping it's possible to say something that is both reasonably useful and relatively concise. It's widely accepted that normativity has something to do with the guidance of thought and behavior: as opposed to descriptive questions about how the world is, normative questions are prescriptive questions concerning what ought be done about it. Normative discourse, then, is oughty discourse. If one accepts this widely accepted thought, accounts of responsibility such as mine, centered on reactive attitudes, capture something of normativity rather easily. The various reactive attitudes may make a motley assortment, but whatever else they are, they often involve emotions, such as guilt and anger. Emotions are standardly thought to involve "action tendencies" (Nichols 2007: 412–14), and even where they don't immediately move people to action, they prepare people for action: emotions structure the range of behavioral options (Prinz 2004: 191–6). To suffer an emotion is to be told what to do, or not do.

But emotional imperatives don't carry all the normativity that might be desired. For people can, and do, ask whether their emotions are appropriate, justified, or fitting (D'Arms and Jacobson 2000a, 2006). In so doing, they're asking about what is helpfully called normative *authority* (Railton 2003: 344): why should a command issued by an emotion command my assent?

One way to establish normative authority is by reference to theory. Regards the present problem, an attribution of responsibility has normative authority when it can be seen to have a rationale sufficiently compelling to serve as a justifiable guide to thought and action. When responsibility is understood as I understand it, *via* the reactive attitudes, the challenge is to identify compelling theoretical grounds for when and what reactive attitudes are appropriate. On my theory, responsibility is associated with the exercise of agency, and the exercise of agency with expressions of values, so the question becomes whether these expressions are appropriate targets for the reactive attitudes.

I think this question is readily answered: when someone's deed manifests their values, it makes good sense to direct anger or admiration their way. I'm angry at the Wall Street Oligarch who orders a million-dollar renovation for his office (1400-dollar wastebasket included) as his company fails and the economy falters, because I think he values status too much and humanity too little.

I admire the man who donates 10 percent of his 1,000-dollar monthly disability check to charity, because I think he's moved by the opposite complex of values. And were I pressed to justify my reactions, I could make a convincing case on the grounds of what matters, and fails to matter, to each man. While I'll decline to linger on yet another philosophically contested notion, the point might be put in the language of desert (Vargas 2013b: 234–66): reference to each man's values explains why they deserve the attitudes I subject them to.

Others may find this less satisfying than do I. They might think reactive attitudes are most appropriate when what we do is *up-to-us*, where "up-to-us" designates some metaphysically robust notion of freedom of the sort I said, early on, that I didn't intend to provide. It's this, the unsatisfied might say, that makes someone genuinely responsible for her deeds, and truly deserving of the associated responses. The views that make up-to-us most conspicuous are libertarianisms suggesting that in responsible actions, the actor herself is the ultimate cause of behavior. In contrast, I've been operating as a kind of compatibilist, insisting that causal determinism is not necessarily in tension with responsibility. I've thereby made a navigational decision at one of the most contentious crossroads in philosophy, where compatibilists and incompatibilists part ways.

This parting, one fears, leaves neither side the richer; rather than talking, there seems to be talking past. Incompatibilists think compatibilists are, as Kant (1956/1788: 189–90) put it, engaged in "wretched subterfuge," for compatibilists seem to evade, rather than engage, the problem of determinism. For their part, compatibilists claim to find incompatibilist solutions, in classic libertarian forms, altogether mystifying: how could human beings be detached from the causal fabric of the world, and is it credible that this detachment, supposing it obtained, would entail responsible agency, rather than randomness? (The other classic strain of incompatibilism, "hard determinism," is not mysterious, but starkly skeptical, and compatibilists and libertarians are united in disparaging that.)

Libertarians realize their position may seem a mouthful. As Chisholm (2002/1964: 55–6) confessed, if his libertarianism is true, people "have a prerogative which some would attribute only to God: each of us, when we act, is a prime mover unmoved. In doing what we do, we cause certain events to happen, and nothing—or no one—causes us to cause those events to happen." Part of why Chisholm finds himself in this predicament is that he starts with the conviction that for a man to be responsible for an action, that action must be "entirely up to the man himself" (2002/1964: 26; compare Campbell's (1957: 160) requirement that the self be the "*sole* author" of a responsible action).

If I'm right about the role of sociality in agency, Chisholm has doomed himself from the get go: if you think responsible agency in the ultra-social organisms that are human beings requires that behavior be entirely up to the actor, you're gonna need a miracle. But I'm not out to saddle libertarians with miracles; and indeed, libertarians after Chisholm have argued that their understandings of freedom can be situated, quite unmiraculously, in the world, and brain, as revealed by science (e.g. Kane 2011a: 367).

In fact, libertarianism may enjoy an advantage many alternatives lack: libertarianism isn't easy prey for anti-reflectivist arguments, for it needn't be a reflectivist theory (Kane 2005: 144). On libertarianism, what's necessary for freedom is what I've called, for convenience's sake, a flicker, and the libertarian needn't maintain that flickers require reflection. If so, we've got the amusing result that libertarianism is more psychologically plausible than many conventional views, including views of those who would charge libertarians with mysterianism; to put it more precisely, libertarianism is not *im*plausible in the way that many of its competitors are, in that it is not committed to reflectivism.

That said, there's a difficulty I suspect is unique to libertarianism, a difficulty epistemic in nature. Obviously, not all behavior involves responsible agency; people sometimes exercise agency, and sometimes not. The game that must be played, for purposes of both theory and life, is determining which cognitions and behaviors are which. The approach I've been following requires that one look to a combination of psychology and circumstance. On libertarianism, something more is required, a flicker. The problem for responsibility attribution, if libertarianism be right, is determining when a flicker has occurred.[2]

Perhaps there are physiological markers, like a type of brain state. But so far as I know, neuro-imaging has neither established nor excluded the existence of flickers, and conclusive results do not appear imminent (Haggard 2008; Haggard and Libet 2001; Mele 2009b, 2011). Given that neuroscience has failed to produce convincing positive evidence for the existence of flickers, those who are not already in the libertarian fold will wonder what should compel them to join it (Vargas 2007a: 205–6).

There might also be phenomenal markers: maybe flickers have a feeling. Personally, I don't seem to detect any such sensation in myself. More persuasively, it seems there could be two phenomenally indistinguishable behaviors performed by the same actor, one where a flicker obtains and one where it does not. I expect the experience of agency is associated with distinct phenomenal

---

[2] On Kane's (1996: 74–9) libertarianism, there needn't be the sort of freedom-making event I'm calling a flicker on the occasion of free action, so long as the action can be traced to a "self-formative" moment. I think this reasonable, but it is unlikely to make the epistemological problem easier, since one still has to identify a self-formative moment.

characteristics, like the perception of intentionality—the *meaning-to-do*—when one seems to be acting on a decision. That's the sort of thing psychologists call "perceptions of control." Yet one might have these perceptions in cases where agency is in doubt, as in cases of ignorance or manipulation, so they don't look like promising candidates for the flicker-experience. *Ex hypothesi libertariani*, where there's a flicker there's agency, but there's not always agency where there's a feeling of meaning-to-do. If it's some other feeling that's needed, one wants to know what it is. Things are worse in the second and third person, when there is only indirect access to the phenomenology: did you see a flicker when I did that?

There might, finally, be psychological markers; perhaps, when certain psychological conditions obtain, flickers also obtain. One could hope that some of these conditions are of a piece with those that are familiarly associated with responsible agency on a wide range of theories, be the libertarian or not; that way, the disputants would at least be agreeing about what signs to seek. But whatever the sought after psychological conditions are, one should require from the libertarian an account of how these conditions are identified, together with an account of why they should be taken as evidence for flickers. I don't say this can't be done. But I'm not sure that it needs be done. If we can confidently identify the psychological states associated with responsible agency, it looks like we have the materials needed for distinguishing those who are responsible from those who are not, without undertaking the search for additional events. The libertarian may remark that there's plenty of epistemological difficulty to go around, whatever approach is proposed; after all, I've allowed that making the determinations about psychology and circumstance required on my own view is no easy matter. But the libertarian, I think, has a harder challenge, if she requires something in addition to the psychology and circumstance.

Libertarians, to be sure, have noticed incredulity in the air. If her view seems a little crazy, the libertarian will contend, it's only as crazy as the philosophical exigencies require; desperate times require desperate measures. In addition to the "not insanity, but exigency" argument, there's the "less crazy than thou" argument; the libertarian sees little reason to abandon her own theory, given the maladies afflicting the alternatives (Kane 2007: 181; van Inwagen 1983: 150). And when the libertarian chooses to go negative, a tempting channel for censure is the thought that compatibilist approaches don't provide a notion of responsibility fit to underwrite normative practice. This charge is especially pointed for the dialogic conception: why think the kind of Rube Goldberg self-direction I celebrate counts as agency in a sense sturdy enough to ground attributions of responsibility?

I've admitted—if not freely admitted—that I can't deliver whatever normativity is predicated on freedom in the up-to-us sense. But I'm not persuaded I should be required to deliver it. In associating responsibility attribution with emotionally infused reactive attitudes, I've identified something of the oughtiness associated with normativity. And by locating agency in the expression of values, I've located a perspicuous rationale for these reactive attitudes: once more, there's pretty good reason for you to be angry with me for what I did, if what I did is a function of my mean-spirited matterings. This, it seems to me, is an account possessed of sufficient normative authority to support responsibility attribution.

Sharing

Not only have I failed to show human actions can be free, in the sense of being up-to-us, my failure is even more abject than familiar compatibilisms, since I identify *susceptibility* to external influence as crucial to agency. This, I'll allow, has certain peculiar implications. If the exercise of agency typically emerges as part of a group process, it seems that no one is ever *solely* responsible for what they do; "It's nobody's fault but mine" is almost never true, however good a song it might make. In saying this, I'm not proffering a theory of shared agency (Bratman 2014; Gilbert 2014: 23–128) or collective responsibility (Gilbert 2014: 58–80; Tollefsen 2003, 2006). Sometimes, I'm guessing, collectives exercise morally responsible agency (I'd applaud predatory corporations being imprisoned, if the logistics could be worked out), but my problem is how *individual* responsibility is to be understood, if it is socially embedded.

The problem is surmountable. Consider a topic dear to my heart, the apportioning of academic glory. Some people are compulsive acknowledgers, and thank everybody and their dog (or cat) in everything they write. As a collaborativist, this seems to me altogether appropriate. But who gets a byline? The shopworn "I couldn't have done it without my loving wife" invites an impertinent question: "If the pompous old goat couldn't have done it without his spouse, why isn't her name on the dust jacket?" No doubt, there are many instances where her name *should* be on the dust jacket. But this isn't a deep difficulty for a theory of responsibility; it's an all too familiar feature of gender inequity.

As to the question of why your name is not on my dust jacket, when it's absolutely true I couldn't have done it without you, the answer is not far to seek. I've put more hours in. A *lot* more hours, believe me: "couldn't have done it without you" doesn't entail "you did as much as I." Strictly speaking, gaggles of folks are probably entitled to a small share of whatever depressingly modest royalties this book earns, but implementing the distribution is impractical: the amount on the checks wouldn't justify the paper. If there were more cash to go around, questions of fairness might become more pressing: at the very least, I'd have to buy you a beer.

Economic considerations won't always serve fairness: I once proposed using the name of a research group for the editorial byline of the group's collected essays, and was told by the press that marketing considerations required using an individual's name. All the same, there are mechanisms, like joint authorship, for sharing credit, and while they don't always work as well as we'd like (what co-author hasn't been screwed a time or two?), practical difficulties don't necessarily engender theoretical difficulty.

Similarly for blame and punishment. If I'm right, doing bad is often as much a group effort as doing good. So why send just one guy to jail? It's not always just one—that's where categories like accomplice, accessory, and co-conspirator come in. But often enough a solitary individual takes the fall, and on my way of thinking about agency, this may frequently be an injustice. At the same time, we can recognize differing levels of involvement, and differing degrees of responsibility, just as we do for intellectual credit: however contemptible, the neglectful father didn't have as much to do with the murder as did the neglected son who committed it. (Dad didn't kill anyone, for a start.)

Criminal law has resources for recognizing the diffusion of responsibility: presently, many American states have some form of a "parental responsibility" statute (Brank and Weisz 2004; Geis and Binder 1990; Graham 2000), and under the Racketeer Influenced and Corrupt Organizations Act, individual members of criminal organizations may be held liable for illegal acts in which they did not directly participate (Spaulding 1989; Tarlow 1983). No doubt there's difficulty here—for example, parental responsibility laws have been pointedly criticized (e.g. Scarola 1997)—but such laws are not obviously indefensible. If I'm right about the sociality of agency, they enjoy considerable theoretical support.

Practical limitations remain. For example, American prisons are already scandalously overfull, which counsels against apportioning criminal liability too widely; I find it difficult to see the social benefit in a non-dangerous father being incarcerated along with his dangerous son, even if it's right to say the son wouldn't have done what he did without dad's abominable parenting. Reactive attitudes, however, are not subject to the same practical constraints: they seem to extend quite readily over the full range of implicated parties. Surely people become angry and disgusted with the negligent parents of delinquent children, or the willfully oblivious employees of rapacious corporations. I'd argue that they are often right to do so. In point of fact, very little a person does, be it good or bad, is entirely up to the person herself. That's what comes, and quite unsurprisingly so, with being intensely social organisms. Spreading the responsibility around, as dialogism counsels, is more virtue than vice.

All the same, I've no need of unseemly triumphalism. My aim is not to refute alternative views of responsibility, be they reflectivist, libertarian, or what-have-you. While I have concerns about these approaches, I won't say they cannot be addressed. I believe that they will be best addressed by adopting a pluralism that has a prominent role for dialogism and a diminished role for reflectivism and individualism. I'll now say something about how this goes.

Pluralism

I don't claim to have refuted competing theories of agency and responsibility. I do claim there is a large body of fact that sits awkwardly—very awkwardly—with familiar theories. For a theory to be credible it must do something—quite a lot of something—to reduce the awkwardness. I believe my approach makes better headway in this endeavor than can be made by holding fast to individualism and reflectivism, but I will not demand unconditional surrender.[3]

On my view, human psychology supports numerous and diverse forms of self-direction that are appropriately counted exercises of agency, so I won't assert that all such exercises are dialogic (cf. Bratman 2007: 196–9). Most conspicuously, some exercises of agency may conform to reflectivist paradigms, with conscious and self-conscious deliberation about what to do resulting in the doing express-ing the results of the deliberating. But the empirical evidence indicates that this may very well be a relatively unusual occurrence, and there's difficulty in deter-mining when these unusual occurrences occur, because there's difficulty ruling out the presence of defeaters that undermine reflective deliberation. I am there-fore forced, as someone who thinks that exercises of agency are both reasonably common and epistemically tractable, to depart the tradition that enshrines reflective activity as the dominant form of self-direction and the paradigmatic target for responsibility attribution. Nonetheless, I'm happy to allow that reflec-tivism captures part—if a relatively small part—of the story.

Philosophers are not always so ecumenical: they typically develop *invariantist* theories of responsibility, which posit *exceptionlessly relevant* attribution criteria (Doris *et al.* 2007; Nelkin 2007: 245–7; Sommers 2012: 113–14). Frequently, these criteria take the form of necessary conditions. For example, incompatibilists

---

[3] The material in this section draws on Doris *et al.* (2007) and Knobe and Doris (2010). My pluralism previously ran under the flag of "variantism"; I here favor "pluralism" for mostly stylistic reasons.

argue that responsibility requires either alternate possibilities, where the agent could have done otherwise, or ultimacy, where the agent is the ultimate source of her behavior, or both (Haji 2002: 202–3; Kane 2002a: 5). Compatibilists also offer invariantist proposals, such as reason requirements, where "the ability to do the right thing for the right reasons" is required for responsibility (Wolf 1990: 81) or Aristotelian conditions, where the absence of ignorance and force is required on "any plausible specification of the application of the concept of moral responsibility" (Fischer and Ravizza 1998: 12). When responsibility is associated with the reactive attitudes, as many compatibilisms do, invariantism maintains there are criteria applicable to every instance where determining the propriety of praise and blame, and the other reactive attitudes, is at issue.

While many renderings of incompatibilism and compatibilism are joined in invariantism, folk morality evinces *pluralism*: in ordinary practice, there may be no exceptionlessly applicable attribution criteria for moral responsibility, and the salience of different criteria may vary quite sharply with circumstance (Doris *et al.* 2007; Knobe and Doris 2010). Despite a formerly solid philosophical consensus to the effect that folk morality is incompatibilist,[4] the empirical evidence is mixed: people seem pretty content to attribute responsibility even when the actor is compelled, or inhabits a deterministic world. In one study, participants attributed responsibility to a man for a shooting performed under the coercive influence of a "mind control drug" (Wegner 2008: 238; Woolfolk *et al.* 2006); in another, participants blamed a bank robber despite it being made painfully obvious that his behavior was causally determined (Nahmias *et al.* 2007). At the same time, many philosophy teachers report that their students readily appreciate the incompatibilist intuition, and my own students are similarly appreciative; perhaps reports of folk incompatibilism reflect accurate polling of philosophy classrooms (Kane 1999: 219).

Systematic research has also identified incompatibilist strains in folk morality: Nichols and Knobe (2007) found that people were willing to attribute responsibility for a concrete case of wrongdoing in a universe stipulated to be deterministic, but also affirmed the abstract proposition that determinism is incompatible with responsibility. To loosely summarize, when the question is "Are people morally responsible in a deterministic universe?" the answer is "No," but when the question is "Is Jones, who lives in a deterministic universe, morally responsible

---

[4] Find the consensus assessment in Campbell (1951: 451); Ekstrom (2002: 310); Kane (1999: 218; cf. 1996: 83–5); Nagel (1986: 113, 125); Nahmias *et al.* (2007); O'Connor (2000: 4); Pereboom (2001: xvi); Pink (2004: 12); Smilansky (2003: 259); and Strawson (1986: 88) share my reading of the literature.

for murdering his wife and children so he can run off with his mistress?" the answer is "Yes." Then if the question is "Is folk morality compatibilist or incompatibilist?" the empirically responsible answer may be "both."

You might think this a bit of a mess: the folk notion of moral responsibility may be incompletely coherent. Another possibility is that there is a tolerably coherent notion out there somewhere, but people are guilty of "performance errors" when applying it. There's something to both suggestions: people's notions of responsibility may form an inconsistent collage, and people may make mistakes in applying whatever notions they have. A comprehensive assessment would be premature, since much of real world responsibility attribution remains unknown. As I've already said, while I expect well-developed philosophical theories will be revisionary theories, I'm not inclined to dismiss folk theory baby and bathwater; I also expect a defensible philosophical theory will support conservative verdicts on many judgments and attitudes associated with responsibility. In the end, however, vindicating (or repudiating) folk morality is not my concern: my question is not whether pluralism about agency and responsibility is evident in folk morality, but whether pluralism is required for a tenable philosophical theory.

Even a preliminary answer—which is all the answer I'm able to give—requires thinking a bit more about what pluralism involves. Variation in token attributions of responsibility and excuse surprises no one, the invariantist included: you're excused whether coerced by cudgel on Tuesday morning or cleaver on Friday evening. A substantive pluralism operates at a higher level of generality; to deny that coercion always functions as an excuse, for example, is to reject one of the Aristotelian conditions as a necessary condition for responsibility. Additionally, there are insubstantial renderings of invariantism: given sufficient ingenuity with such expedients as disjunctive rules, just about any group of considerations, no matter how arbitrarily related, may be fashioned into a "merely formal" invariantism. (Philosophers of science face allied problems in Goodman's (1955) "new riddle of induction.") But extant invariantisms about responsibility, such as those just noted, have more than merely formal substance, so the trickery needn't detain us.

One might be a pluralist about agency, responsibility, or both, and one might be a pluralist at some junctures in their account of agency and responsibility, but not others.[5] On my theory, agency has to do with the expression of values; were

---

[5] Like epistemological contextualists, I'm proposing that the attribution criteria for a philosophical notion may vary with circumstance (see DeRose 1995, 1999, 2005; Hawthorne 2004; Lewis 1996; Sosa 2004; Stanley 2005). Unlike some epistemological contextualists (e.g. DeRose 2005), I'm not

I an invariantist, I'd say that the expression of values is necessary for agency, and were I a pluralist, I'd say that there may be instances where such expression is not required. Application of the theory might also force a decision between pluralism and invariantism: what conditions are required for a behavior to be counted as an expression of values and exercise of agency? Were I an invariantist, I'd say that dialogic self-direction is necessary for the exercise of agency, and were I pluralist, I'd allow that other things, like reflective deliberation, sometimes do the trick.

Similarly for responsibility. I might have an invariantist theory of responsibility, and insist that agency is always required for responsibility, or I might go pluralist, and say it isn't. Once again, the division also arises in application: as an invariantist, I might say that the absence of certain conditions, such as force or ignorance, is always requisite for responsibility attribution, as a pluralist, I'd deny there are such exceptionlessly relevant attribution criteria (for a suggestive pluralism, see Shoemaker 2011).

My inclination is to go pluralist at *all* of these junctures, for agency and responsibility as well as theory and application. However, my pluralism is somewhat tentative; I'm fairly sympathetic to the thought that the expression of value is necessary for agency, and also to the thought that the exercise of agency is necessary for responsibility. So while I lean strongly towards pluralism here, I'd not be too insistent, and I'd not sneeze at invariantisms featuring these two claims. What I do insist on is pluralism regards application of theory: there are irreducibly diverse psychological processes fit to be called agency, and irreducibly diverse considerations relevant to the attribution of responsibility.

I've argued for one form of agency, the dialogic, and guardedly acknowledged another, the reflectivist. Two makes pluralism, albeit pluralism of rather limited sweep. But this duality is a rhetorical artifact. I started out by arguing that reflectivism was threatened by skepticism, and set out to develop a conception of agency better fit to withstand the threat. Since I'm eschewing unseemly contention, I've allowed that there may sometimes be warranted attributions of reflectivist agency. Hence the two forms. But as the scientific study of mind continues, it may well be that other forms of control are discovered, forms that philosophical inquiry determines to be forms of agency. For all I've said, future science will definitively establish the existence of libertarian flickers, or

pursuing "ordinary language philosophy," where the best grounds for accepting contextualism has to do with how sentences "are used in ordinary, non-philosophical talk," and neither will I address semantic questions like those prominent in discussions of epistemological contextualism (e.g. Stanley 2005: 35–73).

future philosophy will articulate decisive arguments for positing flickers, whatever the lab rats find.

The libertarian might herself go pluralist, allowing that a metaphysically modest compatibilism about responsibility, such as my own, is sufficient for the everyday practice of responsibility, while insisting that her metaphysically ambitious notion of responsibility has a philosophical significance modest compatibilisms lack (Kane 1996: 91–2). A compatibilist might try much the same thing, allowing that the libertarian captures a notion of philosophical significance, while insisting on the everyday utility of her more modest notion. This is unobjectionable enough, if discussants squelch triumphalist impulses; experience indicates that arguing about which responsibility is "real," or "deeper" is unlikely to get us very far (cf. Fischer and Tognazzini 2011: 414–15). So long as we can agree on a pluralism where dialogic agency is appropriately prominent, this sort of dispute is one I'll leave alone. Human beings are enormously variable and complex organisms, navigating enormously variable and complex environments by employing multiple forms of self-direction, and I see little reason to deny that more than one of these forms should be counted forms of morally responsible agency.

Pluralism can also be motivated by thinking not about the psychological underpinnings of agency, but about the practice of responsibility attribution. A large body of experimental work suggests that putatively factual judgments about notions such as causation and intentionality often depend on evaluative judgments as to whether the associated outcome is good or bad (Knobe 2003, 2010). For example, an anticipated but unsought consequence of someone's behavior (playing loud music) is more likely to be seen as intentional if the outcome is bad (waking the neighbors) than if it is good (causing the neighbors to dance joyously in the streets).

Something similar could be said of responsibility attribution. Instead of the normative status of a behavior or outcome determining the appropriateness of praise or blame *subsequent* to an attribution of responsibility based on evaluatively neutral causal and psychological attribution, responsibility attribution may be *from the outset* deeply infused with normative considerations: it is, one might say, normative "all the way down." Then judgments of moral responsibility may drive judgments of causal responsibility, rather than the other way round; if it's tempting to say that Hitler's invading Poland was more properly the cause of the Second World War than was Chamberlain's pledge to defend Poland, perhaps it's because Hitler's conduct was blameworthy while Chamberlain's was not (Dray 1957: 100; Feinberg 1970: 200–7; Mackie 1955: 145). In short, to be a folk scientist is to be a folk moralist.

If so, we might expect responsibility attribution to vary with context. For instance, the relationship in which an attribution is situated may affect that attribution. A study comparing attributions of distressed couples in relationship counseling to those of undistressed couples not seeking treatment found members of distressed couples assigned more credit to themselves and more blame to their spouses than to themselves, while members of undistressed couples assigned more credit to their partners than they did to themselves (Fincham *et al.* 1987; cf. Madden and Janoff-Bulman 1981). In the context of well-functioning romantic relationships, people may be attributional altruists, but this tendency may not emerge in other circumstances.

Evaluative standards may quite generally exhibit this sort of variation: one's critical standards might be lower for a friend's poetry than for a stranger's. The interesting suggestion is not that one be more tactful in expressing one's critical views about a friend's work, but that appropriate critical standards are actually less demanding (Keller 2007: 24–51). I think the interesting suggestion is also true; at least, I don't see why the burden of proof should be on the person defending variability, unless one assumes invariantism about critical standards.

In addition to relational variation, there's also institutional variation. To wit: it may be quite appropriate for civilians to treat a coercive illegal order as an excuse, while military personnel should not do so, because in military contexts it is paramount that soldiers resist unlawful orders, and not treating coercion as an excuse encourages this resistance. In fact, empirical work suggests that military personnel are less inclined to treat coercive orders as excuses than are their civilian counterparts (Woolfolk *et al.* forthcoming); one might say that the standards of "reasonable firmness" vary across contexts, and soldiers are expected to resist what ordinary people cannot (Doris and Murphy 2007: 35). This is not necessarily to say that the appropriate theoretical account of responsibility varies across civilian and military settings, although it might; it is to say that the application conditions for responsibility vary. The important point here is that the variation makes good ethical sense, given the different contexts.

So far, there're two good reasons to go pluralist about agency and responsibility: the diversity of control systems, and the diversity of attributional contexts. But there's also a third good reason: the responsibility literature remains locked in dialectical stalemate, an entrenchment that shows little sign of dissipating. Invariantism exacerbates this circumstance: if the only possible resolution is winner takes all, there's little motivation for the combatants to negotiate, and if the sides are evenly matched, the fight will be a death match. But if warring parties are willing to consider pluralism, there exists the possibility of concessions facilitating progress towards peace. Any peace is likely to be partial and untidy—that's pluralism for you—but it may be preferable to unending stalemate.

My case for pluralism is as yet underdeveloped. But this doesn't concern me much, because pluralism is here offered in a concessive spirit, with the aim of making peace with the reflectivist. If there were decisive grounds for rejecting pluralism, matters would be more contentious, because either reflectivism or dialogism would have to go. I like dialogism's chances, in such a clash, but I don't think winner takes all is compelled by the facts, which suggest a diversity of control processes and attributional contexts, or the philosophy, which suggests that at least two of these processes, the dialogic and reflective, are fit to be called agency. If that's right, some form of pluralism is right, however exactly the details eventually work out.

Signpost

I've now defended a claim I've assumed throughout: questions of moral responsibility may be addressed *via* a theory of agency. On my theory, agency characteristically involves the expression of values; to address skeptical concerns about responsibility, I identified resources, particularly social resources, for diagnosing and facilitating the expression of values. I then argued that my understanding of responsibility is normatively robust, by showing that it may be employed to justify the reactive attitudes associated with responsibility. Finally, I advocated pluralism about agency and responsibility, which enables a concessive stance towards competing theories.

8

Selves

In August 1911, an emaciated man was found at a stockyard near Oroville, California, apparently having walked out of the rugged canyon land fronting Mount Lassen and the Sierra Nevada. It was eventually determined that he was from a group anthropologists call Yahi, one of the native cultures decimated by European settlers in California. Ishi, as he came to be known, was the last of his people.[1]

Songs

Ishi's story became widely known through Theodora Kroeber's bestselling memoir, *Ishi in Two Worlds* (2002/1961). Theodora was the widow of Alfred Kroeber, a distinguished Berkeley anthropologist who arranged for Ishi to reside at the University's San Francisco anthropology museum, where he lived from shortly after his appearance in the stockyard until his death from tuberculosis some four and a half years later. Although Kroeber was a sympathetic biographer, her account was animated by concern for her late husband's reputation, and contains demonstrable inaccuracies (Starn 2004: 28–9, 99). Nonetheless, some facts are plain enough.

At first contact with Spanish explorers in 1542, there may have been around 300,000 Native Californians scattered in hundreds of groups across the region; while native peoples mounted some lethal resistance, the predations of Spanish colonization and the Gold Rush left perhaps 20,000 alive at the nineteenth century's end (Starn 2004: 24–5, 65; cf. Thornton 1987: 25–32, 162). Lest enormity be lost in numbers, understand that Native Californians were *literally* hunted; some California towns offered 5 dollars per Native scalp (Starn 2004: 29–30).

---

[1] Who should be counted Ishi's relatives was contested in the 1990s, when Native Californians successfully fought to repatriate his remains from the Smithsonian Institution (Starn 2004: 215). That Ishi was the sole survivor of his immediate group is not in dispute.

Thus Ishi, who was probably born around 1860, was born to a culture in crisis (Kroeber 2002/1961: 68). The Yahi likely never numbered more than a few hundred, and by 1908 only four remained, concealed by remote backcountry. When their last encampment, *Wowunupo Mu Tetna* (Grizzly Bear's Hiding Place), was plundered by surveyors and cowboys, death probably came quickly for everyone but Ishi (Starn 2004: 41). Of his desperately solitary existence between the destruction of *Wowunupo Mu Tetna* and his emergence at Oroville, little is known, but Ishi gracefully acclimated to life in the museum: he learned some English, worked as an assistant custodian, demonstrated traditional skills to museum patrons, and developed seemingly warm relationships with a number of people (Heizer and Kroeber 1979: 97–103; Kroeber 2002/1961: 141–2; Starn 2004: 42–3). This might be taken as a redeeming chapter in a chronicle of atrocity, and Kroeber (2002/1961: 125) is eager to take it so, quaintly concluding that Ishi "remained himself – a well-born Yahi."

I'm less cheerful. While living at the museum, Ishi performed more than 200 traditional songs. Most were Yahi, but two were doctoring songs of the Maidu people; when recordings were played for Maidu elders, one said, "[h]e shouldn't have sung those songs. They were given by the spirit to the medicine man" (Starn 2004: 298–303). On hearing that Ishi perished within two years of his singing, she suggested that Ishi had been "hunting for his own death," by performing the powerful songs for whites. Another wondered, "[m]aybe, he figured it didn't matter what he sang because everything was over, there wasn't anyone else left." Perhaps Ishi believed that the songs still had power, and had deliberately courted death. Or perhaps, with everything gone, Ishi thought the songs had lost their power, and there was no danger in singing them. We'll never know.

But whatever else they were, Ishi's singings were singings of loss. Not ordinary loss, or ordinary longing, like when memories of lost loves come nipping at your heart, or the ache I feel when I wish my mother were still here, to help me figure out what needs doing. For Ishi, *everything* was gone. The old songs could be sung, but could they sound the same? And what could it mean to be the singer?

With these questions, I return to the problems of self until now I've slighted: continuity and identity—what is required for personal survival, and what distinguishes one person from another. I'll approach them by my favored route, through consideration of sociality and valuing. In so doing, I'll cast my lot with accounts of personal survival where psychological continuity is "person preserving" (Shoemaker, S. 2011). Such accounts allow that a person can predecease their body (as with medical "brain death") and, possibly, that a body can predecease its person (as with immortal souls). Here's another notorious tangle that I'll do little to untangle: the philosophical literature on "personal identity" is both intricate and immense, and I'll make no attempt to do it justice. Instead, I'll consider a particular sort of case where a person may predecease their body, with an eye towards illuminating the understanding of self associated with my understanding of agency. The result is programmatic, but it will help to further articulate my overall theory—and, hopefully, what seems right about it.

Coups

Mass exterminations like the California genocide were perpetrated across North America, most notoriously in the "Indian Wars" of the High Plains. Plenty Coups, sometimes called the last great chief of the Absorokee (I'll henceforth use the English "Crow," and similarly for other Native peoples), described the calamity that befell his people to a white "Sign Taker," Frank Linderman, who was compiling an oral history: "I can think back and tell you much more of war and horse stealing. But when the Buffalo went away the hearts of my people fell to the ground, and they could not lift them up again. After this nothing happened" (Coups and Linderman 2002: 169).

Lear (2006) makes Plenty Coups' "nothing happened" the inspiration for an ethics of "radical hope" in response to cultural devastation. In response, one reviewer speculates that Linderman may have fabricated the remarks he attributes to Plenty Coups, or plagiarized them from the Crow warrior Two Leggings, or placed "a conventional narrative trope of the Crow" in the mouth of Plenty Coups (Kuper 2008: 427). The North American genocide is an uncommonly ugly episode in a human history where ugliness is commonplace, and the associated debate is itself sometimes ugly. Being an amateur, I hesitate to join the discussion, but like Lear, I'm convinced there's philosophical importance in the words attributed to Plenty Coups, and I'll now attempt figuring it out.

Speculations about attribution don't shake my conviction. If Two Leggings voiced what was ascribed Plenty Coups, there's something to talk about, and if that something is important, there's something important to talk about. If "nothing happened" was a conventional way for the Crow to describe their circumstances, all the more so; then the text proceeds in terms familiar to them (see Lear 2006: 56). Of course, if Linderman made it up out of whole cloth, and there's nothing remotely like it in the historical record, that would be awkward. But it seems there *are* things like it in the historical record—compare the Maidu elder saying of Ishi, "everything was over"—so it's not untoward to think about what those things might tell us.

At Plenty Coups' birth in the mid-nineteenth century, the Crow were a martial people, who celebrated feats of courage, or *coups* (Hoxie 1995: 78–85). Society was structured by "counting coups"; a warrior with coups to his credit enjoyed status unavailable to those without martial attainments (Lear 2006: 14–21; Lowie 1935: 215–36). The warring was not merely ritual: the Crow were under pressure from the neighboring Blackfeet and the Sioux's westward migration, and military defeat threatened annihilation (Lear 2006: 21–4). During 1882 and 1884, the Crow, with their resources severely depleted by US treaty violations, moved to a reservation in Montana. Although a third of the 2,461 Crow recorded in the 1887 census perished in the 1890s, the move probably prevented the people's complete disappearance (Hoxie 1995: 130–5).

Yet disaster of another sort ensued. The US government prohibited intertribal warfare, and prevented the Crow from pursuing a nomadic life, which, together with the decimation of buffalo and beaver populations, made hunting impossible. Now, there were few *coups* to count. Traditional practices by which the Crow made sense of their lives were no longer available; as the medicine woman Pretty Shield put it, "I am trying to live a life I do not understand" (Lear 2006: 56). Lear imagines this in the first person:

As it turns out, only in the context of vibrant tribal life can I have any of the mental states that are salient and important to me. The situation is even worse: these are the mental states that help to constitute me as a Crow subject. In so far as I am a Crow subject there is nothing left for me to do, and there is nothing left for me to deliberate about, intend, or plan for. Insofar as I am a Crow subject, I have ceased to be. All that's left is a ghostlike existence that stands witness to the death of a subject. Such a witness might well say something enigmatic like, "After this, nothing happened." (Lear 2006: 49–50)

For Lear (2009: 85–6) the Crow's loss was a loss of the concepts by which their lives where made intelligible, but I'm not sure this framing is mandatory. When E. A. Robinson's despondent miller said, "there are no millers any more," and hung himself from the rafters of his mill amid the mealy fragrance of the past, did the concept *miller*—supposing he was the last miller—pass away with him? I think I understand Robinson's darkly elegant poem, and my father could take me to the Old Mill picnic ground many years later, and explain what millers did. Nevertheless, Lear is right to think the loss of culture forces searching questions about survival: how—and as whom—are those so afflicted able to go on?

Continuity

Cultural devastation causes profound psychological disruption, but it's not immediately apparent that this perturbation should prompt philosophical questions about personal continuity. Evidently, Plenty Coups led not a ghostlike life after the Crow's move to the reservation, but an extraordinary one, helping the Crow endure as a more agricultural people and retain a share of their lands (Lear 2006: 148). It seems that Ishi, Plenty Coups, Pretty Shield, and the others survived cultural devastation, while those lost to violence and disease did not. The obvious, and not obviously wrong, thing to think is that although the survivors' circumstances changed horribly, they themselves continued on.

I'm going to suggest a way of thinking about continuity that departs the obvious thought. The suggestion is that *continuity is socially contingent*: personal continuity is predicated on psychological continuity, and psychological continuity is sustained by societal continuity, so if cultural devastation is substantial enough, personal continuity may be compromised, physical survival notwithstanding.

My proposal seemingly conflicts with a standard dictum in the philosophical literature on personal identity: *extrinsic factors don't count*. According to this dictum, whether a person at one time bears an "identity relationship" to a person at another depends only on facts about the two "person stages" and the relations between them (Noonan 1989: 152). Or, more impressively: "intuitive conceptions of the nature of the total process which secures a given person's survival will locate that process wholly within the space-time envelope or four-dimensional total position swept out by that person's body over his lifetime" (Johnston 1989: 381). Whether or not you're the sort to have intuitions regarding space-time envelopes and four-dimensional total positions, you may have the intuition that your survival has to do with *you*, and not your neighbors, friends, or family: a neighbor dying, or even a lot of neighbors dying, doesn't mean you've failed to survive.

Yet a moment's thought reveals that *lots* of stuff has to do with you, and your survival: health care reform instigated (or obstructed) in Washington may impact the survival of those in Wichita. As for the body, so for the soul: events without the mind, like nasty goings on in the woodshed, effect events within, like psychiatric collapse. Given that human beings are entwined in causal webs with strands trailing far beyond their skin, it's hard to say what counts as intrinsic and what as extrinsic. Wasserman (2005: 584–8) suggests that changes in the "local environment" can matter for survival, but insists that "wildly extrinsic" factors having to do with "completely disconnected" objects and events cannot: whether two stages of a person are identity related is "stable under variations in the non-local environment."

Consider a "closest continuant" view of personal identity, where the identity relation tracks the person stage possessing the highest degree of qualitative continuity with antecedent person stages (Nozick 1981: 33–7; Wasserman 2005: 584–8). Suppose the gods make an exactly similar Doris in Santa Cruz (where I used to live) as I go about my business in St. Louis (where I presently live); exact except that Santa Cruz Doris is endowed with a clutch of Santa Cruz memories—of interminably bickering colleagues, maybe, or hopelessly bungled administrative decisions—that have recently disappeared from the fogging mind of St. Louis Doris. Let's say that at the moment of his creation, Santa Cruz Doris has, by virtue of the extra memories, greater qualitative continuity with previous Doris stages, so that the most Dorish of the Dori lives in Santa Cruz rather than St. Louis. Now Santa Cruz Doris has taken the title of closest continuant from St. Louis Doris, so Santa Cruz Doris is awarded the identity relation with the previous Doris stages, and the current St. Louis Doris has somehow been deprived of his past.

Excluding the wildly extrinsic blocks this sort of incompletely appealing result. Santa Cruz Doris and St. Louis Doris don't share a local environment, and if it be stipulated that the gods accidentally came up with Santa Cruz Doris, rather than looking to St. Louis Doris as a template, the two Dori are causally unrelated. The peculiar goings on in Santa Cruz are therefore counted wildly extrinsic, and by dint of the proposed exclusion, St. Louis Doris retains his past.

I'm not sure what to make of such thought-experimental mischief. Neither do I know how to give a systematic account of the intrinsic/extrinsic divide in this (or any other) context. This needn't end the game, however, for it's clear that cultural devastation is not wildly extrinsic. Cultural conditions figure in one's local environment if anything does, and cultures are causally related—powerfully and pervasively so—with the psychology of those associated with them. One can therefore conclude that culture may affect continuity, and is not excluded by any plausible "no extrinsic factors" principle. This isn't yet to say that cultural devastation can disrupt continuity to the extent that a victim is no longer the same person, but on my way of thinking, it might.

As I've said, I think of continuity in terms of values. Roughly: *personal continuity varies with evaluative continuity.* When a person's values change, they become less like the person they were before; at the extreme, if a person's values are completely changed, they are no longer the same person. To better see this, reconsider a life we considered a ways back (Chapter 2, p. 25), that of the evaluatively indeterminate Milksop, who lacks the vibrant desiderative complexes associated with valuing. What if you, with all your firmly held values, were to become, like Milksop, value-less? Imagine that the proverbial mad scientist was to threaten you with injection of a "values bleach" that would transform you into a Milksop, who didn't care much at all about much of anything. If the threat were credible, you'd have reason to be terrified—a feeling,

I submit, not utterly distant from that of facing one's death. Call this terrifying prospect *evaluative collapse.*

Life doesn't often involve such disasters: values wane and wax, sometimes pretty dramatically, but there doesn't often seem to be *complete* evaluative collapse. Loss of a totalist religious faith might be a real life example, and the subject of such loss might be a different person in some pretty literal sense. And so for the contrary case: after being waylaid by the heavenly light, Saul just wasn't the same guy. Yet even for such historic conversion, we may doubt the transformation was sufficiently extensive to threaten survival. While Saul's animating project changed from persecuting Christians to being a servant of Christ, there may yet have been any number of continuities. For all I know, being short on Bible learning, his taste in food, music, and clothing remained quite unchanged.

Much remains after cultural devastation, and actual examples of complete evaluative collapse may be vanishingly rare. One might be tempted to reach for Turnbull's (1972) notoriously unflattering ethnography of Uganda's Ik, which depicted a culture in moral—or amoral—ruin. But anthropologists denounced Turnbull's account, and the Ik themselves discussed legal action against him (Haine 1985). Regards the Crow, I seriously doubt they suffered complete evaluative collapse; I don't suppose they stopped caring about their children, for example, however "ghostlike" their existence had become. The Crow's circumstances were crucially different from that of a solitary survivor like Ishi, however: they had other Crow to go on with, while Ishi was the last of the Yahi. It is therefore more likely that there was a breakdown of continuity in Ishi's case. But if Ishi's tragedy is a singularity at the theoretical limit, it nevertheless underscores the observation that motivates the social contingency thesis: continuity is facilitated by the relationships, practices, and institutions that make up a culture.

To make proper sense of this, distinguish between expressing a value and having a value: if a nomadic people like the Crow are forced into a sedentary life, they can no longer express their nomadic values, but it seems wrong to say they no longer have these values. In fact, part of their misfortune is that they can no longer express the values they have. Are the victims of such catastrophe no longer agents? Perhaps better to say that while external circumstances may impair *efficacy*, they need not impair *agency*. Efficacy, in the sense of making one's life and environment conform to one's values, is contingent on external circumstances, while agency, in the sense of making one's thought and behavior conform to one's values, seems less so. But efficacy and agency aren't readily disentangled, and loss of efficacy can impair agency.

Imagine cultural devastation radically curtails a person's efficacy, so it's no longer possible for her to live her values, or realistically hope to do so again. (In a world without beauty, what becomes of the aesthete's values?) When a value goes too long without being expressed, the holder may suffer a sort of evaluative atrophy: memories of a life are not the same thing as living it. The last miller might demonstrate his craft to schoolchildren—just as Ishi demonstrated his crafts to visitors at the museum—but this is not quite the same as living as a miller: the mill at the "Colonial Village" museum, one suspects, is not really a mill. Here, the craft has become a "nostalgic gesture" (Lear 2006: 37), and rehearsing a lost craft is not the same thing as leading the life of a craftsperson.

Typically, in cultural change, circumstances are mixed: some practices go on, and others falter; some values persist, and others fade away. But it remains the case that when sufficient evaluative atrophy occurs, even if it falls short of complete evaluative collapse, there may be disruptions of psychological continuity sufficient to press questions about survival. Answers to these questions will rarely be all or nothing; although change is a constant, significant evaluative continuity is likely the rule rather than the exception. Cultural devastation is relatively seldom absolute, at least over a human generation or two. In genocide, cultures do not typically disappear without a trace—as indeed the survival of the Crow and other threatened cultures indicates. Yet the point I was trying to earn seems secure: factors well beyond the skin matter for continuity.

By lights of an important philosophical tradition, I'm leaving something out. In addition to psychological states, this tradition maintains, there must be something that *has* these states; it is this further entity that is the self, and its survival is what secures continuity (Sorabji 2006: 265–77). Opposed to such *something further* views are the *nothing further* views associated with Locke and Hume. Here, the psychological states and their relations are all there is, and the self is nothing apart from these; the states and relations just are the self (Bratman 2007: 31; Velleman 1992: 475). I've been tacitly proceeding as a nothing furtherist, but something furtherism has considerable appeal: it seems more natural to say I *have* a quick temper and a melancholic mien than to say I *am* a quick temper and a melancholic mien.

Let's suppose the self is something further, and also suppose that people's psychological states stand in evidential relation to the something further, so that disruption of the states may fairly be taken as evidence for disruption of the something. In that case, the nothing furtherist and something furtherist have ambitions in common, since both will want to know when psychological continuity obtains; one because that's all there is, and the other because psychological continuity is an epistemic portal to the fate of what else there is. On the other hand, suppose there's no evidential relation between the psychological states and the something further, so the cessation of the psychological states tells us nothing about whether the something further continues to exist. Now, the nothing further project has no bearing on the something further project, and shared ambitions have seemingly expired.

Like other nothing furtherists, I don't think something further is needed, but even if it is, the psychological states of our companions in this life are of abiding interest, as is the continuity of these states. People care whether their spouses still love them, whether their parents still remember them, whether their co-religionists still revere the same god. (Presumably, the something furtherist is not indifferent when a loved one falls into a persistent vegetative state.) These cares concern psychological states, not something further. There may be legitimate questions targeting something further, but these are not the only legitimate questions. Questions of psychological continuity are rightly associated with personal identity and survival—most conspicuously, in the context of ongoing social relationships.

Once again, I favor ecumenical pluralism: a variety of psychological, bodily, and other factors, in various admixtures, may contribute to continuity, and different continuities may be of differential interest across differing contexts. Just as there's more than one viable understanding of agency, there's likely more than one viable understanding of continuity, and these different continuities will not always co-occur. Obviously, evaluative continuity may depart bodily continuity; evaluative collapse does not preclude physical survival. So too, evaluative continuity can depart other forms of psychological continuity, such as that adduced in the "memory criterion" (Shoemaker 2003). Victims of evaluative atrophy certainly may remember a better past, and the haunting of these memories contributes to the perception of their existence as somehow ghostlike.

Perhaps for some purposes, the relevant continuity isn't evaluative. If our interest in persons is, in Lockean terms, a "forensic" interest in assigning legal liability (Strawson 2011: 17–21), it may be better to stick to bodies, or memories; even where conversion is genuine, the balance of pragmatic and moral considerations may tell against pardoning the newly religious criminal. But if the evaluative conception of agency I've defended is right, a continuity of central interest, when it comes to agency, will be evaluative continuity. Remember that exercises of agency, at least consequential exercises of agency, are typically temporally extended processes; if evaluative continuity is sufficiently disrupted, so too may be the exercise of agency.

Identity

It might have been better to begin with identity, rather than continuity. Determining whether I've survived a change seems to require knowing something about who I was before the change, which makes it look as though answers to questions of continuity presuppose answers to questions of identity.

Explicit discussions of identity are less visible in mainstream philosophy than discussions of continuity, but we can make a start with Taylor (1994: 25), who describes identity as "something like a person's understanding of who they are, of their fundamental defining characteristics as a human being." Terms like "fundamental" and "defining" are not easily subdued, but an opening gambit proceeds in terms of *individuation*: one's defining characteristics are those by virtue of which one is different from other people (Appiah 2005: Ch. 1; Taylor 1994: 28).

To be sure, people are a great mess of characteristics, of a great mess of kinds. Some features of my identity might be rather idiosyncratic, such as my proclivity for eating organic maple yogurt from the tub while standing before the fridge, wearing boxer shorts decorated with likenesses of buffalos, and tunelessly humming obscure folk songs. Other features, like the attributes studied by personality psychologists, might be "generic" attributes I share, to some extent or another, with countless other people; I display a below normal degree of conscientiousness, say, or an above normal degree of neuroticism.

In contrast to these individual aspects of identity are the collective identities that accrue to me by virtue of being associated with some group (Appiah 2005: 22–3). Most prominent are the social taxonomies familiar from discussions of identity politics and multiculturalism: in my case, white, man, American, and so on. There are also "finer grained" collective identities, which may be highly variable with regard to their political and institutional significance: academic, bourgeois, martial artist. Finally, there are characteristics that can (with appropriate caution) be characterized as biological properties shared by all human beings, such as needs for nutrition and elimination. A single performance may simultaneously express these various features of my identity: my snarfing organic yogurt from the tub involves a biological attribute (nutrition), a political attribute (environmentalism), a generic personal attribute (low conscientiousness), and an idiosyncratic personal attribute (buffalo clad). Moreover, different aspects of identity may sit in tension: my affection for luxury consumer goods may contradict my support of progressive causes. (The ubiquity of such tension in ordinary lives counsels, once more, against adopting a strong "unity requirement" in one's account of the self.)

Where, in all this, are my "fundamental defining characteristics"? Once again, look to valuing. Identity may be a source of value: a ritual observance might be of value to me by virtue of my identity as a member of a certain religion, but valueless to those who do not share my faith. Identity may also be the object of value: someone might value her profession, ethnicity, or political affiliation. Most important here is that value may be a source of identity (the relation between identity and value is bi-directional). A person has the identity they do partly by virtue of having the values they do: who I am has much to do with what matters to me. But not all matterings matter the same: you value your daily respite at the coffee shop that's long brightened your mornings, but if that shop goes under, you wouldn't—I hope—be facing existential threat. On the other hand, if the company you've endlessly worked to build up from nothing fails, the threat is more severe. Some values are more central to one's identity than others: the values associated with your coffee shop may be peripheral to your identity, while the values associated with your company may be central. Major losses accompanying cultural devastation, as for the Crow and their *coups*, may be more central still.

Admittedly, when philosophers reach for spatial imagery, the issues at hand are often incompletely understood—or badly misunderstood. ("Higher" and "lower" levels of explanation are but one of many deployments). Still, we need some way of articulating the thought that some aspects of identity do more to "define" people than others, and dubbing some aspects "central" and others "peripheral" is one serviceable way to do so.

Centrality might be understood in terms of continuity: the more threatening a loss is to continuity, the more central it is to identity, the less threatening, the more peripheral. If your favorite coffee shop fails, you'll likely soldier on, if a bit less cheerfully, much as before. But if your company fails, and you're unable to practice your chosen profession, it's the kind of calamity that may engender evaluative atrophy sufficient to raise questions about continuity, questions registered in expressions like "she was never the same," and "he's a different person now." (Which, some evidence suggests, people take rather literally, as referencing a failure of numerical identity where the transition involves not one person, but two (Prinz and Nichols, forthcoming; Strohminger and Nichols 2013).) The threat to identity will be still more serious in cases of cultural devastation, since the victims lose much more than vocations. Viewed in this light, Lear's account of the Crow does not seem a reach.

But now, we look to have come a short circle. A minute ago, the thought was that continuity gets explicated in terms of identity, while the present thought is that identity gets explicated in terms of continuity. I'm disinclined to fret.

Continuity and identity are, as I said at the outset, mutually insinuated, and it's near impossible to explicate one without making some assumptions about the other. Questions of continuity inevitably involve questions of identity, and questions of identity—the "central" or "defining" aspects of identity anyway—inevitably involve questions about what a person can, and cannot, continue without. Both questions, on my understanding, are questions involving values.

This leaves the problem of how the defining gets done. There's evidence that people may differ with even close associates about how funny, intelligent, and likable they are (Carlson *et al.* 2011). My self-awareness might in this way diverge from publically individuating characteristics: I think of myself as *the funny guy*, while I'm known to everyone else as *the obnoxious guy*. Thus, central aspects of identity are beyond my influence. Most obviously, for collective features of identity associated with ethnicity, gender and the like; whether or not being a white man is central to my self-understanding, it's going to have a lot to do with how others think of me. I can sometimes influence these involuntary identities: I might minimize my masculine identity by eschewing activities like talking sports (Kimmel 2006: 246), or accentuate my white identity by attending yoga class and buying an expensive water bottle (http://stuffwhitepeoplelike.com). All the same, identity is not monological but dialogical (Taylor 1994: 32–6); as Appiah (2005: 19) observes, to "make a life is to make a life out of the materials that history has given you."

Such realizations inform the "politics of recognition" where public acknowledgment of collective identities is contested; a society's failure to provide this recognition can be damaging to both collectives and their individual members (Taylor 1994: 36–7). These contests can be enormously divisive, and I can't usefully engage them here. But it will pay to examine a phenomenon at a (putatively) greater distance from contemporary industrial democracies.

Social exclusion, while taking a multitude of forms, is historically ubiquitous: from the Greeks' ostracism, to the Romans' exile, to the meidung, or "shunning," of the Old Order Amish (which may still be practiced in the contemporary United States). It's likely that exclusion was a form of social control in early human hunter-gatherer bands, and there's evidence of related behaviors, such as avoidance of the ill or abnormal, in primates like chimpanzees (Goodall 1986). Whether shunning is official expulsion from the state, as in exile and the internal ostracism of prison, or is simply the "cold shoulder" practiced informally everywhere from middle school to marriage, the results may be devastating.

In exile, Cicero wrote to his brother: "I was unwilling to be seen by you! For you would not have seen your brother...Not even a trace of him – Not a shadow, but the image of a breathing corpse" (Forsyth 1867: 190). Cicero may be overwriting. He was, after all, a rhetorician. But neither were the terrors of exile lost on the unflappable Socrates; though he might have remained in Athens for his execution in the name of morals rather than prudence, it's nevertheless clear that he didn't judge the prospect of exile an enticing one (Plato 1997: *Ap.* 37c ff., *Cri.* 53b ff.). Exile meant that Cicero was not Roman, and Socrates would no longer be Athenian—for prominent members of statist cultural orders, a calamitous loss of identity.

Of course, the costs of exclusion may be rather more pedestrian: the shunned lose economic, reproductive, and other social advantage. In 1947, an Ohio farmer named Andy Yoder successfully sued the Old Order Amish Church for imposing meidung as punishment for his purchasing a car to transport a chronically ill child to the hospital; as Yoder said, meidung meant "slow death" for a farmer, given the need for reciprocal exchange of goods and services in rural farm life (Gruter 1986).

To see matters in wholly economic terms is to not see the whole matter. In the lab, Twenge and colleagues (2003: 416) used two methods to induce feelings of exclusion, either telling participants that no one in a group they had just met wanted to interact further with them, or reporting that a personality test indicated that "You're the type who will end up alone later in life." Compared to unexcluded controls, the victims of these unsavory (but IRB approved) manipulations had difficulty in thinking about the future, favored immediate over deferred gratification, displayed lethargy, avoided mirrors, and were more likely to judge life meaningless. While social exclusion has been found to be associated with sadness and anger (Williams 2009: 290), the Twenge group's excluded participants exhibited something more like apathy; they seemed to care less about things, including themselves and their future. Twenge and her associates (2003: 409) describe this as "cognitive deconstruction" which they liken to the state of pre-suicidal individuals, while Williams (2001: 159) says participants in his social exclusion studies appeared "as though they had been hit with a stun gun." If metaphor ain't your thing, you might be more impressed by work in brain science indicating that social pain and physical pain share overlapping neural circuitry and computational processes (Eisenberger and Lieberman 2004); exclusion may literally hurt. Perhaps Cicero's lament isn't so excessive as it appears.

The point, once again, is that identity is socially sustained, and may be socially undermined. But if identity is interactive, how is it related to individuality? Taylor (1994: 34) contends that if "some things I value most are accessible to me only in relation to the person I love, then she becomes part of my identity."

Pleasingly romantic, but also a little disconcerting: do we absorb our loved ones, like hungry amoebas?

We've now the question of where you end and I begin, to which Clark and Chalmers (1998: 8–9) give a provocative response. According to them, the mind is "extended," and its boundaries extend beyond "skin and skull" to environmental supports like notebooks and computers; as it's sometimes put, minds are partly "constituted" by entities outside the organism. This picture of mind, Clark and Chalmers (1998: 17–18) conclude, implies an extended self: we should "see agents themselves as spread into the world."

The famous basketball coach, John Wooden, and his wife of fifty-three years, Nell, were touchingly devoted. John was lousy with names, and Nell was excellent; at social functions, Nell would coach the Coach on the names of the many acquaintances and admirers he was supposed to know (Clark and Chalmers 2010: 41 n9). Evidently, John could only successfully execute certain operations of memory with support from his "better half." This is congenial to my collaborativism, as it's a case of thinking better by dint of group process. But should we go farther, and conclude that agents are somehow constituted by other agents—that they are "spread" onto one another?

Humans navigating informationally complex environments couldn't manage without "off-loading," to cognitive props, from scrap paper to supercomputers (Dennett 1996: 134). But this can be understood on the model of tool use, rather than on the model of constitution; just as my use of a hammer to drive a nail shouldn't tempt us to say my hammer is part of my hand, my use of a map to find the trailhead shouldn't tempt us to say my map is part of my mind (Adams and Aizawa 2001: 46). Similarly, it's natural to say that Nell *helped* John remember names, rather than saying Nell's memory for names was *part* of John's memory; John couldn't remember without Nell, but neither could I pound nails without my hammer.

Distinguish an *extended* cognition hypothesis, which says that "human cognitive states literally comprise—as wholes do their proper parts—elements in the environment," from an *embedded* cognition hypothesis, which says that cognitive processes "depend *very* heavily ... on organismically external props and devices and on the structure of the external environment" (Rupert 2004: 389). Critics argue that embedded cognition, not extended cognition, is the hypothesis that should structure research in cognitive science (Rupert 2004), and even Clark (2007: 192), the most ebullient defender of extension, is willing to be concessive: cognition is "organism-centered" even if it is not "organism bound," and the cognitive scientist should "practice the art of flipping between" more organismic and environmental perspectives on the mind. I kind of *want* selves to be extended; there's something sweet about saying that the members of a devoted couple are *literally* part of one other. But I needn't embark on such adventures. My collaborativism about cognition—and the associated approach to agency, continuity, and identity—doesn't entail extension, but only the causal entanglement characteristic of embedded cognition.

Variety

If we agree that continuity and identity are socially contingent, we'll likely want to ask whether the ways in which they are understood and realized (or not), vary across societies. If we also agree that continuity and identity are insinuated with agency, we'll want to ask something similar about agency as well. In so asking, we come to a reckoning I've long postponed, the issue of cultural diversity.

In my experience, there are two kinds of philosophers: those impressed by diversity, and those not. The impressed often float skeptical arguments. (The unimpressed, one guesses, feel free to carry on as before.) For example, evaluative diversity funds arguments against moral objectivity (Doris and Plakias 2007; Doris and Stich 2005: 129–37; Loeb 1998; Machery *et al.* 2005; Mackie 1977): over here, they favor one moral practice, and over there, quite a different one; given that neither culture appears more or less viable than the other, and their members neither more or less rational, it seems as though there's no "moral facts," but only competing cultural norms—none better, or worse, than the others.

Perhaps something similar goes for the self of English-language philosophy. Notions of agency like those that have preoccupied me lie close to the heart of Western tradition of philosophical ethics, and are similarly focal to the Millian tradition in liberal political theory—theory that informs real world political contention (Appiah 2005: 6–17). Moreover, agency costs, because designing institutions to promote it may come at the expense of other goods, like community (Haybron 2008: 258–60). Westerners, anyway, have a lot invested in Western notions of agency. If these notions turned out to be parochial artifacts, disquiet might be in order; maybe agency is a local fashion of no deeper consequence than hat brims and hemlines.

Sommers (2012: 108) argues from cultural diversity to "metaskepticism" about responsibility, "the view that there are no universally true conditions for moral responsibility." (Metaskepticism is not skepticism, since the skeptic may be seen as positing universally applicable conditions for responsibility, and arguing that they are nowhere met.) This argument is not directed at agency, but it strikes nearby, since a central piece of supporting evidence is the observation that in many cultures the practice of responsibility is little concerned with the sort of psychologizing featured in Western philosophical thinking on agency (Sommers 2012: 47–62).

Could be. Nisbett (2003: 50) concludes, in surveying cultural psychology, that "the Western-style self is virtually a figment of the imagination to the East Asian." It's not only the Western self that may be parochial; the tools psychologists and experimental philosophers use to study it may be so as well. As Henrich and colleagues (2010) observe, experimental participants in the psychology departments of North America and Europe—where most of the psychology I've leaned on gets done—are overwhelmingly W.E.I.R.D.: Western, Educated, Industrialized, Rich, and Democratic. But the world's population is overwhelmingly— perhaps 88 percent—not W.E.I.R.D.; there's apparently a sampling error of epic proportions. Moreover, English-language philosophers are even W.E.I.R.D.er, since they are predominantly white men (Digest of Education Statistics 2009; Paxton *et al.* 2012). Does the rest of the world care what these white guys care about?

Maybe not. But one cannot simply assume that cultural or demographic variation bears substantial practical or theoretical import; sometimes such variation is associated with interesting differences, and sometimes it isn't. For example, while people's lives differ wildly from place to place, what it takes for their lives to go well may be surprisingly (or, perhaps, unsurprisingly) similar. There's a fairly extensive psychological literature on culture and well-being, and it does not unequivocally support claims of radical diversity: having one's material needs met and enjoying strong social support have both been found to be associated with well-being in a wide variety of cultures, even as the ways in which these goods get realized are exceedingly various (Diener and Seligman 2004; Tiberius 2004; Tiberius and Plakias 2010).

Cultural psychology does not often explicitly address philosophically delicate notions of agency, but there is suggestive research on a construct in the vicinity, "locus of control" (Rotter 1966). A person with an external locus of control experiences her behavior as compelled by circumstance, while someone with an internal locus of control experiences her behavior as self-generated; so far as I understand it, to experience oneself as having an internal locus of control is to experience oneself as an agent, in something roughly like the sense that interests Western philosophers.

This experience is an important one, which has been found to influence well-being and mental health in a variety of populations (Hobbs and McLaren 2009, Klonowicz 2001; Roth and Armstrong 1991; Williams and Ricciardelli 2003); people who experience themselves more as agents with an internal locus of control may be better off than those who do so less. Yet this propensity exhibits cultural variation. Residents of "individualist" nations with a strong emphasis on personal autonomy, like the United States, exhibit a higher internal locus of control than inhabitants of "collectivist" countries with strong emphasis on community, like China (Spector *et al.* 2001), and people in Western individualist nations may experience loss of control more adversely than their Eastern, collectivist counterparts (Sastry and Ross 1998; Weisz *et al.* 1984). These differences may be associated with differences in thinking about responsibility: according to one analysis (Morris and Peng 1994), the *New York Times* was more likely to emphasize the individual's propensities in reporting mass murders ("had a short fuse"), while the Chinese *World Journal* was more likely to emphasize the role of circumstance ("influenced by example of a recent mass slaying in Texas").

Nonetheless, the desire for something like internal control has been identified in various locales (cf. Deci and Ryan 2000: 246–7); for example, across samples from 23 countries and Hong Kong, including both individualist and collectivist cultures, external locus of control was negatively associated with job satisfaction (Spector *et al.* 2002). Perhaps workplace autonomy—which is very plausibly associated with agency—is something that resonates with employees the world over. Still, if forced to render a verdict regards the literature on culture and locus of control, I'd not hazard anything more definitive than, "it's complicated" (cf. Smith, Trompenaars, and Dugan 1995), not least because there's likely important variation, most notably gender variation, in how control (and it's absence) is experienced by different groups *within* cultures (Sherman *et al.* 1997).

I'm likewise inclined to hedge on evidence that judgments about philosophical conundrums related to agency are cross-culturally uniform (Sarkissian *et al.* 2010: 352–3): for a sample of college students in the United States, India, Hong Kong, and Colombia, a majority of participants in all four groups responded that determinism is incompatible with moral responsibility. However suggestive, this lone study on culture and free will is inconclusive (Sommers 2015), and for cultural variation in understandings of agency more generally, I'm not sure that much can be concluded.

While what is currently known about cultural variability and the experience of agency does not compel skeptical or metaskeptical conclusions, I remain impressed by the evidence for strong cultural variability in human psychology in general, and notions of the self in particular (Doris 2002: 105–6; Doris 2005: 673–4). It seems to me likely that a great deal of philosophically interesting diversity in notions of mind—and the minds themselves—will be established, at such time as the jury returns a verdict. But however that verdict reads (if a verdict can be reached), I don't think it will much affect what I've been up to here. As a pluralist, I'm happy to let a thousand flowers bloom in the garden of agency, and I'm also happy to acknowledge that there may be places where the flowers don't grow.

One needn't visit faraway lands for this tolerance to seem prudent; the commerce of self may proceed very differently in different contexts *within* Western culture. Discussions related to agency arise in a range of settings, from the intimacy of the familial to the agony of the political, and the understanding of agency grounding political relationships may be rather different than that involved in personal relationships; a romance has likely gone rather harshly awry by the time human rights become an issue. Similarly, different cultures may attend differently to different aspects of agency, or attend to them not at all, and I don't see that this entails that one or the other way of thinking about such things is mistaken. It could have turned out otherwise around here, or over there, given diverging happenstances, and natural selection may have selected other creatures than it did.

Various cultures enshrine various norms, and because the "thick" discourse of agency is partly normative, it will reflect this variety. At the same time, some materials of agency may admit of rather less variation; for instance, the emotions that structure human moral propensities, including basic emotions like anger and fear, may be pan-cultural (Ekman 1992a, b; Griffiths 1997: 55–64). My thinking on agency is broadly "constructivist," since agency is wrought—where it is wrought—of culturally available materials. But I mean this constructivism to be consistent with many avowedly anti-constructivist treatments of human organisms in evolutionary ecology—accounts concerned with human tendencies supposed to obtain (more or less) independently of cultural variation (Mallon and Stich 2000; Wilson 2005).

This leaves the usual trouble: giving both the constructivist and objectivist devils their due. While it would be folly to ignore the role of the cultural in the ethical, it would be equally unwise to suppose that cultural variation is unconstrained by biological facts about the entities that are united in culture: groups of hat racks uniformly fail to generate cultures, while groups of human beings quite reliably do so. I'm not possessed of novel insights on the difficult, and sometimes snarky, debates about culture and construction; I optimistically assume that the range of phenomena gestured at with talk of agency can to some extent be united into a "social kind" structured by both culture and nature (following Mallon 2003, forthcoming; cf. Haslanger 2012).

It is perhaps worth noting that this sort of admixture is altogether expected, if *agent, self,* and cognates are indeed thick terms comingling the normative and descriptive. On the normative side are cultural, social, and institutional factors associated with the ethical, while on the descriptive side are the biological and psychological capacities required for self-direction—capacities that may be substantially independent of cultural, social, and institutional factors. Being suitably impressed by culture does not require being unimpressed by nature. And *vice versa*. Human beings subsist at the boundary of biology and artifice, and so do human agents.

Signpost

I've now extended my treatment of agency to continuity and identity. In each case, the treatment is emphatically social. Continuity, identity, and agency are all socially contingent: where human organisms achieve these, they do so as members of groups. If my approach is right, there ought be a lot more attention to the social in moral psychology and ethics. When rational animals are viewed as social animals, they may appear less rational, but they will appear more as they really are.

Reprise

The book's second half forwarded a solution to the skeptical problem articulated in the first half. I began with collaborativism about reasoning, which holds that optimal human reasoning is a socially embedded process, and extended this collaborativism to agency, arguing that the exercise of individual agency is a socially embedded process. I then explicated this process as a dialogic form of agency, where the social negotiation of rationalizations, by which people explain and justify their judgment and behavior, may facilitate the expression of values. Since these rationalizations need not be historically accurate, my account of agency is not threatened by self-ignorance. This result complements a valuational understanding of agency, where one need not be aware of their values in order for their conduct to express those values in a manner appropriate to agency.

I went on to argue that the proposed theory of agency grounds a normatively robust account of responsibility: the reactive attitudes associated with responsibility are warranted when they track the actor's values. This approach has resources to ameliorate skepticism, since values and their contribution to behavior can, by means of a temporally extended social dialog, be identified with the confidence required to rule out the presence of defeaters. Although I argued that dialogic agency is a prominent form of human agency, I adopted a pluralism about both agency and responsibility, allowing that multiple forms of self-direction may fairly be counted exercises of morally responsible agency. Finally, I extended the dialogic approach to continuity and identity, arguing that these also are secured by means of socially embedded processes, and may be disrupted by cultural perturbations.

Afterwards

In summer 2010, as I was struggling to finish this book, the giant energy corporation BP ("Beyond Petroleum") was struggling to contain a catastrophic oil spill in the Louisiana Gulf. We both failed miserably. I didn't complete the book. BP took three months to cap the spill. The poisoning of the Gulf, if not irreversible, will extend for generations. While BP sucks at protecting the environment—and workers, eleven of whom perished in the tragedy—they're right good at making money; last I checked, company profits exceeded their flabbergasting pre-accident elevations.

Viewed with sufficient perversity, the Gulf disaster leaves one nostalgic for a time when environmental crises were limited to particular bioregions (recall, fondly, the *Exxon Valdez*) rather than the planet-wide catastrophe of anthropogenic climate instability. I'm not a climate scientist, but my advice is to be very afraid. If you have children, be very, very afraid. Mass extinction is unlikely to treat future generations kindly.

Faced with such calamity, what's a theorist to do? A lot more than they are doing, that's for damn sure. There must be less frivolous ways for decent people to spend their time, with time growing short. But even theorists have to eat, and like many theorists, I've few marketable skills, and those I have are of comparatively little use.

I'm sometimes able to console myself with the thought that I've identified an enemy deserving of enmity. Ideology is the parent of atrocity, and the predations of the Oilmen are spawned from a conception of nature as treasure to be plundered by human beings. The conception is occasionally justified—on those occasions when anyone bothers to justify it—by rationalisms treating humans, by virtue of their superior cognitive capacities, as entitled to dominion over the natural world. ("Rationalism" in this sense is expansive, including many who would reject the label.) However subtle and sophisticated these rationalisms, they share the hubris fueling the extraction industries' desecrations: the hubris of elevating humanity above the rest of nature.

Here, perhaps, is decent work for a theorist: re-envisaging human beings, not as little gods with big brains, but as animals that, alongside other animals, have evolved with a curious assortment of endowments for muddling through the world. Human cognition—including the rarified sort called Reason—is but one of these endowments, not so different than feather, fur, and fang: by turns comical, wonderful, and tragical. I've been trying to make sense of the distinctively human endowments—the endowments of social animals that endlessly explain themselves to one another. If I've been lucky enough to make good sense, perhaps there's a little less reason for hubris.

Acknowledgments

Taking an indecently long time writing a book has very little to recommend it, save the innumerable occasions for gratitude. Silver linings, alas, come with gray clouds: so many people have been so generous in helping this project along that I can no longer recall more than a fraction. Many others have made important contributions to the published literatures. In the body of the work I've marked, very imperfectly, my debts to the literatures; these acknowledgments mark, even less perfectly, my debts to individuals and institutions.

For the period I worked on this project, Mark Rollins and Kit Wellman chaired the Philosophy Department, while José Bermúdez and Ron Mallon directed the Philosophy-Neuroscience-Psychology Program, at my institutional homes at Washington University in St. Louis. Mindy Danner, Kimberly Mount, and Tamara Casanova helped keep the Department, and myself, running as smoothly as could possibly be expected. Thanks to each for their work in facilitating this, and many other, endeavors.

In addition to Washington University in St. Louis, my work was funded by the American Council of Learned Societies, the National Endowment for the Humanities, and the Research Triangle Park Foundation of North Carolina. I am enormously appreciative of their support.

Over the years, I've given talks on this material from Armidale to Oslo, and been endlessly helped by indulgent and insightful audiences. Versions of the manuscript were discussed in a reading group and graduate seminar at Washington University in St. Louis, as well as in a Jesse Ball duPont Summer Seminar for College Teachers at the National Humanities Center, very ably administered by Richard Schramm. Participants in these groups provided quantities of valuable discussion, as did those in less formal settings; warm thanks to: Berit Brogaard, Susanna Siegel, Michael Gettings, Keith Stanovich, Brett Hyde, Charles Wallis, Anna Alexandrova, Brian Leiter, Richard Samuels, Jeff Dauer, Dan Haybron, Sarah Malanowski, William Lycan, Al Mele, Jim Bohman, Allan Loup, Lizzie Schechter, Chris Hom, Felipe Romero, Joseph Spino, Tony Jack, Julia Driver, Nazim Keven, Carl Craver, Thomas Sattig, Eddy Nahmias, Keith Payne, Clanton Dawson, Nomy Arpaly, Tamler Sommers, the late John Pollock, Carol Dyer, Tyler Paytas, Casey O'Callaghan, Paul Audi, David Winchell, Kelly Roe, John Heil, Bryan Stagner, Julia Annas, Holly Lawford-Smith, Ernest Sosa, Nich Baima, Judith Ferster, Jerry Neu, Roddy Roediger, Isaac Wiegman, Justin D'Arms, Steve Laurence, Dennis DesChene, Marta Halina, and the late Robert Solomon, who took kind interest in my career from its fitful beginnings.

Substantial work was done while I was a guest at Dave Chalmers' Centre for Consciousness at the Australian National University during the summer of 2007. I'm most grateful to Dave, and all the members of the remarkable philosophical community at ANU.

I completed a major portion of research and writing while an Autonomy-Singularity-Creativity fellow at the National Humanities Center in 2008–2009; profuse thanks to Director Geoffrey Harpham, and then Deputy Director Kent Mullikin, together with all the exemplary staff of the Center, for a wonderful year. I benefitted from much engaging discussion over my term there; extra cheers to Florence Dore, Mary Floyd-Wilson, Colin Bird, Trevor Bernard, Gary Comstock, Cassie Mansfield, and Parker Shipton.

Once again, I'm hugely grateful to my estimable editor, Peter Momtchiloff of Oxford University Press, for his good sense and good humor. Two anonymous referees for the Press offered incisive criticisms. Thérèse Saba did the copy-editing, Lynn Aitchison the proofreading, while Eleanor Collins and Gayathri Manoharan oversaw production. Chapter 5 is derived from a paper, "Broadminded," co-authored with Shaun Nichols, which appeared in *The Oxford Handbook of Philosophy of Cognitive Science*; thanks to the Press for permission to reuse this material.

Eli Temkin, Alex Baron, and Melissa Turkiel helped with the research. Eric Brown, Adam Shriver, Jake Beck, and Dan Haybron provided detailed written comments on earlier drafts; Eric offered astute criticisms on countless occasions. Lauren Olin, Mike Dacey, and Santiago Amaya, bless them, worked through more than one version. Santiago provided quantities of editorial, research, and philosophical assistance.

Bob Kane commented extensively on central material, and saved me from many infelicities in my remarks on free will. Ric Otte advised me on all matters epistemological, while Edouard Machery did the same for methodology in the social sciences.

I relied at every turn on my extraordinary colleagues in the Moral Psychology Research Group, who read an early version of the manuscript, and made it much better: Liane Young, Alexandra Plakias, Jesse Graham, Natalia Washington, Gilbert Harman, Walter Sinnott-Armstrong, Daniel Kelly, Nina Strohminger, Jesse Prinz, Valerie Tiberius, Edouard Machery, Fiery Cushman, Ron Mallon, Erica Roedder, Timothy Schroeder, Simine Vazire, Victor Kumar, Stephen Stich, Victoria McGeer, Shaun Nichols, Joshua Greene, Maria Meritt, Jonathan Phillips, Joshua Knobe, Adina Roskies, John Mikhail, Chandra Sripada, and Daryl Cameron.

A late version of the manuscript was workshopped with Dominic Murphy, Shaun Nichols, and Manuel Vargas. Dominic has been a staunch ally from the early days of my career. I pester Manuel incessantly about the intricacies of the agency literature; he inevitably responds with erudition and good cheer. Here, and everywhere else, Shaun has been my closest philosophical confidant; nearly all I write is vetted by him. Throughout, this book owes most to countless conversations with Simine Vazire.

I depend always on the dear friends who are also my family; I'm very fortunate to have their love and support. Sharon Parker helped me keep body and self together in a period of serious uncertainty, and I am much in her debt. Thanks to Doug and Andrea Peacock for years of friendship and inspiration.

I benefit continuously from the example of my teacher, Mr. Karl W. Scott Sensei, and the fellowship of all my teachers, colleagues, and students in the martial arts. The teachers most responsible for my graduate education, Stephen Darwall, Allan Gibbard, Jim Joyce, Richard Nisbett, Peter Railton, and Gideon Rosen, continue to inform my work. In turn, I discussed everything in this book with wonderful students at both the undergraduate and graduate level; collectively and individually, they made the book much better, and my life much more fulfilling.

To properly acknowledge the friendship and mentoring of Stephen Stich, I'd have to go on for a great many pages. It therefore seemed wisest to dedicate this book to him. So that is what I've done.

St Louis
Missouri, USA

References

Aarts, A. and Dijksterhuis, A. 2000. "Habit as Knowledge Structures: Automaticity in Goal-Directed Behavior." *Journal of Personality and Social Psychology* 78: 53–63.

Abbott, J. H. 1991. *In the Belly of the Beast: Letters From Prison*. London: Vintage.

Abramowitz, J. S. and Houts, A. C. 2002. "What is OCD and What is Not? Problems with the OCD Spectrum Concept." *The Scientific Review of Mental Health Practice* 2: 139–56.

Ackerman, B. and Fishkin, J. S. 2004. *Deliberation Day*. New Haven, CT: Yale University Press.

Adams, F. and Aizawa, K. 2001. "The Bounds of Cognition." *Philosophical Psychology* 14: 43–64.

Adams, R. M. 2006. *A Theory of Virtue: Excellence in Being For the Good*. Oxford: Oxford University Press.

Affleck, G., Tennen, H., Pfeiffer, C., and Fiefield, C. 1987. "Appraisals of Control and Predictability in Adapting to a Chronic Disease." *Journal of Personality and Social Psychology* 53: 273–9.

Ainslie, G. 2001. *Breakdown of Will*. Cambridge and New York: Cambridge University Press.

Albritton, R. 2003. "Freedom of Will and Freedom of Action." In G. Watson (ed.), *Free Will* (2nd edn). New York: Oxford University Press.

Alexander, M. P., Stuss, D. T., and Benson, D. F. 1979. "Capgras Syndrome: A Reduplicative Phenomenon." *Neurology* 29: 334–9.

Alexandrova, A. 2005. "Subjective Well-Being and Kahneman's 'Objective Happiness'." *Journal of Happiness Studies* 6: 301–24.

Alexandrova, A. 2008. "First-Person Reports and the Measurement of Happiness." *Philosophical Psychology* 21: 571–83.

Alfano, M. 2013. *Character as Moral Fiction*. Cambridge: Cambridge University Press.

Alicke, M. D. 1985. "Global Self-Evaluation as Determined By the Desirability and Controllability of Trait Adjectives." *Journal of Personality and Social Psychology* 49: 1621–30.

Alicke, M. D., Vredenburg, D. S., Hiatt, M., and Govorun, O. 2001. "The Better than Myself Effect." *Motivation and Emotion* 25: 7–22.

Allen, L., Woolfolk, R., Escobar, J., Gara, M., and Hamer, R. 2006. "Cognitive-Behavioral Therapy for Somatization Disorder: A Randomized Controlled Trial." *Archives of Internal Medicine* 166: 1512–18.

Alston, W. 1989. *Epistemic Justification: Essays in the Theory of Knowledge*. Ithaca, NY: Cornell University Press.

Alter, A. L. and Oppenheimer, D. M. 2006. "Predicting Short-term Stock Fluctuations By Using Processing Fluency." *Proceedings of the National Academy of Sciences* 103: 9369–72.

Altschule, M. 1977. *Origins of Concepts in Human Behavior*. New York: Wiley.

Amadio, D., Harmon-Jones, E., and Devine, P. G. 2003. "Individual Differences in the Activation and Control of Affective Race Bias as Assessed by Startle Eyeblink Response and Self-Report." *Journal of Personality and Social Psychology* 84: 738–53.

Amarenco, P., Cohen, P., Roullet, E., Dupuch, K., Kurtz, A., and Marteau, R. 1988. "Syndrome Amnésique lors d'un Infarctus du Territoire de l'Artère Choroïdienne Antérieure Gauche." *Revue Neurologique* (Paris) 144: 36–9.

Amaya, S. 2013. "Slips." *Noûs* 47: 559–76.

Amaya, S. and Doris, J. M. forthcoming. "No Excuses." In J. Clausen and N. Levy (eds), *Handbook of Neuroethics*. New York: Springer.

American Psychiatric Association. 2000. *Diagnostic and Statistical Manual of Mental Disorders* (Revised 4th edn). Washington DC.

Andreou, C. 2007. "Morality and Psychology." *Philosophy Compass* 2: 46–55.

Annas, J. 1993. *The Morality of Happiness*. New York and Oxford: Oxford University Press.

Annas, J. 2005. "Comments on John Doris' *Lack of Character*." *Philosophy and Phenomenological Research* 73: 636–47.

Appiah, K. A. 2005. *The Ethics of Identity*. Princeton, NJ: Princeton University Press.

Appiah, K. A. 2008. *Experiments in Ethics*. Cambridge, MA: Harvard University Press.

Arico, A., Fiala, B., Goldberg, R. F., and Nichols, S. 2011. "The Folk Psychology of Consciousness." *Mind and Language* 26: 327–52.

Ariew, R. and Greene, M. (eds). 1995. *Descartes and His Contemporaries: Meditations, Objections, and Replies*. Chicago, IL: University of Chicago Press.

Aristotle. 1984. *The Complete Works of Aristotle, Vol. 1 and 2: The Revised Oxford Translation*. J. Barnes (ed.). Princeton, NJ: Princeton University Press.

Armstrong, D. M. 1968. *A Materialist Theory of the Mind*. New York: Routledge & Kegan Paul.

Aronson, E. and Bridgeman, D. 1979. "Jigsaw Groups and the Desegregated Classroom: In Pursuit of Common Goals." *Personality and Social Psychology Bulletin* 5: 438–46.

Aronson, E., Stephan, C., Sikes, J., Blaney, N., and Snapps, M. 1978. *The Jigsaw Classroom*. Beverly Hills, CA: Sage.

Arpaly, N. 2002. *Unprincipled Virtue: An Inquiry into Human Agency*. Oxford and New York: Oxford University Press.

Arpaly, N. 2005. "Comments on *Lack of Character* by John Doris." *Philosophy and Phenomenological Research* 73: 643–7.

Arpaly, N. and Schroeder, T. 1999. "Praise, Blame and the Whole Self." *Philosophical Studies* 93: 161–88.

Arpaly, N. and Schroeder, T. 2014. *In Praise of Desire*. Oxford: Oxford University Press.

Arum, R and Roska, J. 2011. *Academically Adrift: Limited Learning on College Campuses*. Chicago, IL: University of Chicago Press.

Asch, S. E. 1955. "Opinions and Social Pressure." *Scientific American* 193: 31–5.

Ayer, A. J. 1980. "Free Will and Rationality." In Z. van Stratten (ed.), *Philosophical Subjects: Essays Presented to P.F. Strawson*. New York: Oxford University Press pp. 37–46.

Baddeley, A. D. 2002. "The Psychology of Memory." In A. D. Baddeley, M. D. Koppelman, and B. A. Wilson (eds), *The Handbook of Memory Disorders* (2nd edn). Hoboken, NJ: John Wiley & Sons, pp. 3–15.

Badhwar, N. K. 2008. "Is Realism Really Bad for You? A Realistic Response." *The Journal of Philosophy* 105: 85–107.

Badhwar, N. K. 2009. "The Milgram Experiments, Learned Helplessness, and Character Traits." *Journal of Ethics* 13: 257–89.

Baer, J., Kaufman, J. C., and Baumeister, R. F. (eds). 2008. *Are We Free?: Psychology and Free Will.* Oxford: Oxford University Press.

Baldwin, T. T. and Ford, J. K. 1988. "Transfer of Training: A Review and Directions for Future Research." *Personnel Psychology* 41: 63–105.

Banaji, M. R. 2001. "Implicit Attitudes Can Be Measured." In H. L. Roediger, III, J. S. Nairne, I. Neath, and A. Surprenant (eds), *The Nature of Remembering: Essays in Honor of Robert G. Crowder.* Washington, DC: American Psychological Association, pp. 117–50.

Banse, R., Seise, J., and Zerbes, N. 2001. "Implicit Attitudes Toward Homosexuality: Reliability, Validity, and Controllability of the IAT." *Zeitschrift für Experimentelle Psychologie* 48: 145–60.

Bargh, J. A. 2012. "Priming Effects Replicate Just Fine, Thanks." *Psychology Today* <http://www.psychologytoday.com/blog/the-natural-unconscious/201205/priming-effects-replicate-just-fine-thanks>.

Bargh, J. A., Chen, M., and Burrows, L. 1996. "Automaticity of Social Behavior: Direct Effects of Trait Construct and Stereotype Activation on Action," *Journal of Personality and Social Psychology* 71: 230–44.

Bargh, J. A. and Uleman, J. S. (eds). 1989. *Unintended Thought.* New York and London: The Guilford Press.

Baron, J. 1994. "Nonconsequentialist Decisions." *Behavioral and Brain Sciences* 17: 1–42.

Baron, J. 2001. *Thinking and Deciding* (3rd edn). Cambridge: Cambridge University Press.

Baron, R. A. 1997. "The Sweet Smell of . . . Helping: Effects of Pleasant Ambient Fragrance on Prosocial Behavior in Shopping Malls." *Personality and Social Psychology Bulletin* 23: 498–503.

Baron-Cohen, S. 1995. *Mindblindness: An Essay on Autism and Theory of Mind.* Cambridge, MA: MIT Press.

Bartlett, T. 2013. "Power of Suggestion." *The Chronicle of Higher Education*, January 30. Available at: <http://chronicle.com/article/Power-of-Suggestion/136907/>.

Basbanes, N. A. 1996. *A Gentle Madness: Bibliophiles, Bibliomanes, and the Eternal Passion for Books.* New York: Henry Holt.

Bateson, M., Nettle, D., and Roberts, G. 2006. "Cues of Being Watched Enhance Cooperation in a Real-World Setting." *Biology Letters* 2: 412–14.

Batson, C. D. 1991. *The Altruism Question: Toward a Social-Psychological Answer.* Hillsdale, NJ: Lawrence Erlbaum Associates.

Baumeister, R. F., Bratslavsky, E., Muraven, M., and Tice, D. M. 1998. "Ego Depletion: Is The Active Self a Limited Resource?" *Journal of Personality and Social Psychology* 74: 1252–65.

Baumeister, R. F., Campbell, J. D., Kruger, J. L., and Vohs, K. D. 2003. "Does High Self-Esteem Cause Better Performance, Interpersonal Success, Happiness, or Healthier Lifestyles?" *Psychological Science in the Public Interest* 4: 1–44.

Baumeister, R. F. and Leary, M. R. 1995. "The Need to Belong: Desire for Interpersonal Attachments as a Fundamental Human Motivation." *Psychological Bulletin* 117: 497–529.

Baumeister, R. F., Stillwell, A. M., and Heatherton, T. F. 1994. "Guilt: An Interpersonal Approach." *Psychological Bulletin* 115: 243–67.

Baumeister, R. F. and Tierney, J. 2011. *Willpower: Rediscovering the Greatest Human Strength*. New York: Penguin.

Becker, L. C. 1998. *A New Stoicism*. Princeton, NJ: Princeton University Press.

Beevers, C. G. 2005. "Cognitive Vulnerability to Depression: A Dual Process Model." *Clinical Psychology* 25: 975–1002.

Begley, C. G. and Ellis, L. M. 2012. "Improve Standards for Preclinical Cancer Research." *Nature* 483: 531–3.

Bellah, R. N., Madsen, R., Sullivan, W. M., Swidler, A., and Tipton, S. M. 1996. *Habits of the Heart: Individualism and Commitment in American Life*. Berkeley, CA: University of California Press.

Bennett, J. 1974. "The Conscience of Huckleberry Finn." *Philosophy* 49: 123–34.

Benon, R. and LeHuché, R. 1920. "Traumatism Crâniens et Psychose de Korsakoff." *Archive Suisses de Neurologie, Neurochirurgie et Psychiatrie* 7: 316–22.

Benson H., Dusek, J. A., Sherwood J. B., *et al.* 2006. "Study of the Therapeutic Effects of Intercessory Prayer (STEP) in Cardiac Bypass Patients: A Multicenter Randomized Trial of Uncertainty and Certainty of Receiving Intercessory Prayer." *American Heart Journal* 151: 934–42.

Berlyne, N. 1972. "Confabulation." *British Journal of Psychiatry* 120: 31–9.

Bernstein, M. H. 1998. *On Moral Considerability: An Essay on Who Morally Matters*. New York and Oxford: Oxford University Press.

Berrios, G. E. 1998. "Confabulations: A Conceptual History." *Journal of the History of the Neurosciences* 7: 225–41.

Berrios, G. E. 2000. "Confabulations." In G. E. Berrios and J. R. Hodges (eds), *Memory Disorders in Psychiatric Practice*. Cambridge: Cambridge University Press, pp. 348–68.

Bertrand, M. and Mullainathan, S. 2003. "Are Emily and Greg More Employable than Lakisha and Jamal? A Field Experiment on Labor Market Discrimination." (May 27, 2003). MIT Department of Economics Working Paper No. 03–22. Available at SSRN: http://ssrn.com/abstract=422902 or DOI: DOI: 10.2139/ssrn.422902

Besser-Jones, L. 2008. "Psychology, Moral Character, and Moral Fallibility." *Philosophy and Phenomenological Research* 76: 310–32.

Bickel, L. 1977. *Mawson's Will: The Greatest Survival Story Ever Written*. New York: Stein and Day.

Bird, A. 1998. "Dispositions and Antidotes." *Philosophical Quarterly* 48: 227–34.

Birnbaum, P. 2005. "Clutch Hitting and the Cramer Test." *By the Numbers: The Newsletter of the SABR Statistical Analysis Committee* 15 (1): 7–13.

Bishop, M. A. 2015. *The Good Life: Unifying the Philosophy and Psychology of Well-Being*. New York: Oxford University Press.

Bishop, R. C. 2011. "Chaos, Indeterminism, and Free Will." In R. Kane, *The Oxford Handbook of Free Will* (2nd edn). New York: Oxford University Press, 84–100.

Bishop, R. C. and Atmanspacher, H. 2011. "The Causal Closure of Physics and Free Will." In R. Kane (ed.), *The Oxford Handbook of Free Will* (2nd edn). New York: Oxford University Press, pp. 101–11.

Bisiach, E. and Geminiani, G. 1991. "Anosognosia Related to Hemiplegia and Hemianopia." In G. P. Prigatano and D. L. Schacter (eds), *Awareness of Deficit After Brain Injury: Clinical and Theoretical Issues*. New York and Oxford: Oxford University Press, pp. 17–39.

Blackburn, R.T. and Clark, M.J. 1975. "An Assessment of Faculty Performance: Some Correlates Between Administrator, Colleague, Student and Self-Ratings." *Sociology of Education* 48: 242–56.

Blair, R. J. R. 1996. "Brief Report: Morality in the Autistic Child." *Journal of Autism and Developmental Disorders* 26: 571–9.

Blair R. J. R., Mitchell, D., and Blair, K. 2006. *The Psychopath: Emotion and the Brain*. Oxford: Blackwell.

Blakemore, S., Wolpert, D. M., and Firth, C. D. 2002. "Abnormalities in the Awareness of Action." *Trends in Cognitive Sciences* 6: 237–42.

Blanning, T. 2010. *The Romantic Revolution: A History*. New York: Modern Library.

Bleuler, E. 1923. *Lehrbuch der Psychiatrie*. Berlin: Julius Springer Verlag.

Block, J. and Colvin, C. R. 1994. "Positive Illusions and Well-Being: Separating Fiction from Fact." *Psychological Bulletin* 116: 28.

Block, N. 1981. "Review of Julian Jaynes' *Origins of Consciousness in the Breakdown of the Bicameral Mind*." *Cognition and Brain Theory* 4: 81–3.

Bloom, B. L., Asher, S. J., and White, S. W. 1978. "Marital Disruption as a Stressor: A Review and Analysis." *Psychological Bulletin* 85: 867–94.

Boghossian, P. A. and Velleman, J. D. 1989. "Colour as a Secondary Quality." *Mind* 98: 81–103.

Bollich, K. L. and Vazire, S. 2014. "Knowing More than We Can Tell: People Are Aware of Their Biased Self-Perceptions." (*Manuscript under review*).

Bonanno, G. A., Rennicke, C., and Dekel, S. 2005. "Self-Enhancement among High-Exposure Survivors of the September 11th Terrorist Attack: Resilience or Social Maladjustment?" *Journal of Personality and Social Psychology* 88: 984–98.

Bonhoeffer, K. 1901. *Die Akuten Geisteskrankenheiten der Gewohnheitstrinker*. Jena: Gustav Fischer.

Bornstein, R. F. and Pittman, T. S. (eds). 1992. *Perception without Awareness: Cognitive, Clinical, and Social Perspectives*. New York and London: The Guilford Press.

Botvinick, M., Braver, T., Barch, D., Carter, C. S., and Cohen, J. D. 2001. "Cognitive Monitoring and Cognitive Control." *Psychological Review* 108: 624–52.

Bourdieu, P. 1984. *Distinction*. Trans. Richard Nice. Cambridge, MA: Harvard University Press.

Boxer, K. E. 2013. *Rethinking Responsibility*. Oxford: Oxford University Press.

Boyd, R. and Richerson, P. J. 2006. "Culture, Adaptation, and Innateness." In P. Carruthers, S. Stich, and S. Laurence (eds), *The Innate Mind: Culture and Cognition*. Oxford: Oxford University Press, pp. 23–38.

Boyes, A. D. and Fletcher, G. J. O. 2007. "Metaperceptions of Bias in Intimate Relationships." *Journal of Personality and Social Psychology* 92: 286–306.

Brandt, R. B. 1979. *A Theory of the Good and the Right.* Oxford: Clarendon Press.

Brank, E. M. and Weisz, V. 2004. "Paying for the Crimes of their Children: Public Support of Parental Responsibility." *Journal of Criminal Justice* 32: 465–75.

Bratman. M. E. 1996. "Identification, Decision, and Treating as a Reason." *Philosophical Topics* 24: 1–18.

Bratman, M. E. 2007. *Stuctures of Agency: Essays.* New York: Oxford University Press.

Bratman, M. E. 2014. *Shared Agency: A Planning Theory of Acting Together.* Oxford: Oxford University Press.

Bray, J. and Jouriles, E. 1995 "Treatment of Marital Conflict and Prevention of Divorce." *Journal of Marital and Family Therapy* 21: 461–73.

Breen, N. Caine, D., Coltheart, M., Hendy, J., and Roberts, C. 2000. "Towards an Understanding of Delusions of Misidentification: Four Case Studies." In M. Coltheart and M. Davies (eds), *Pathologies of Belief.* Oxford: Blackwell, pp. 75–110.

Brennan, J. 2005. "Choice and Excellence: A Defense of Millian Individualism." *Social Theory and Practice* 31: 483–98.

Brenner, B. 1979. "Depressed Affect as a Cause of Associated Somatic Problems." *Psychological Medicine* 9: 737–46.

Brett, N. 1981. "Human Habits." *Canadian Journal of Philosophy* 11: 357–76.

Brewer, M. B. and Gardner, W. L. 1996. "Who Is This 'We'? Levels of Collective Identity and Self Representations." *Journal of Personality and Social Psychology* 71: 83–93.

Brink, D. O. 1989. *Moral Realism and the Foundations of Ethics.* Cambridge: Cambridge University Press.

Brink, D. O. 1992. "Mill's Deliberative Utilitarianism." *Philosophy and Public Affairs* 21: 67–103.

Brodsky, S. L. and Scogin, F. R. 1988. "Offenders in Protective Custody: First Data on Emotional Effects." *Forensic Reports* 1: 267–80.

Brown, E. 2013. "Aristotle on the Choice of Lives: Two Concepts of Self-Sufficiency." In P. Destrée and M. Zingano (eds), *THEORIA: Studies on the Status and Meaning of Contemplation in Aristotle's Ethics.* Louvain: Peeters, pp. 135–57.

Brown, J., Dreis, S., and Nace, D. K. 1999. "What Really Makes a Difference in Psychotherapy Outcome? Why Does Managed Care Want to Know?" In M. A. Hubble, B. L. Duncan, and S. D. Miller (eds), *The Heart and Soul of Change: What Works in Therapy.* Washington, DC: American Psychological Association, pp. 389–406.

Bullock, A. 2004. *The Secret Sales Pitch: An Overview of Subliminal Advertising.* San Jose, CA: Norwich Publishers.

Burger, J. M., Messian, N., Patel, S., Prado, A., and Anderson, C. 2004. "What a Coincidence! The Effects of Incidental Similarity on Compliance." *Personality and Social Psychology Bulletin* 30: 35–43.

Burnham, T. C. and Hare, B. 2007. "Engineering Human Cooperation – Does Involuntary Neural Activation Increase Public Goods Cooperation?" *Human Nature* 18: 88–108.

Buss, S. 1997. "Justified Wrongdoing." *Noûs* 31: 337–69.

Buss, S. 2012. "Autonomous Action: Self-Determination in the Passive Mode." *Ethics* 122: 647–91.

Buss, S. 2013. "The Possibility of Action as the Impossibility of Certain Forms of Self-Alienation." *Oxford Studies in Agency and Responsibility* 1: 12–46.

Camacho, L. and Paulus, P. 1995. "The Role of Social Anxiousness in Group Brainstorming." *Journal of Personality and Social Psychology* 68: 1071–80.

Cameron, C. D., Brown-Iannuzzi, J. L., and Payne, B. K. 2012. "Sequential Priming
Measures of Implicit Social Cognition: A Meta-Analysis of Associations with Behavior
and Explicit Attitudes." *Personality and Social Psychology Review* 16: 330–50.

Cameron, C. D., Payne, B. K., and Doris, J. M. 2013. "Morality in High Definition:
Emotion Differentiation Calibrates the Influence of Incidental Disgust on Moral Judgments." *Journal of Experimental Social Psychology* 49: 719–25.

Campbell, C. A. 1951. "Is 'Free Will' a Pseudo-problem?" *Journal of Philosophy* 60:
441–65.

Campbell, C. A. 1957. *On Selfhood and Godhood*. London: George Allen & Unwin.

Cannell, J. J. 1988. *How Public Educators Cheat on Standardized Achievement Tests: The
"Lake Wobegon" Report*. Albuquerque, NM: Friends for Education.

Cappa, S. F., Sterzi, R., Vallar, G., and Bisiach, E. 1987. "Remission of Hemineglect and
Anosognosia after Vestibular Stimulation." *Neuropsychologia* 25: 775–82.

Carlson, E. N., Furr, R. M., and Vazire, S. 2010. "Meta-Insight: Do People Really
Know How Others See Them?" *Journal of Personality and Social Psychology* 101:
831–46.

Carlson, E. N., Vazire, S., and Oltmanns, T. F. 2011. "You Probably Think this Paper's
about You: Narcissists' Perceptions of Their Personality and Reputation." *Journal of
Personality and Social Psychology* 101: 185–201.

Carruthers, P. 1996. "Autism as Mind-blindness: An Elaboration and Partial Defense."
In P. Carruthers and P. Smith (eds), *Theories of Theories of Mind*. Cambridge:
Cambridge University Press.

Carruthers, P. 2008. "Cartesian Epistemology: Is the Theory of the Self-Transparent Mind
Innate?" *Journal of Consciousness Studies* 15: 28–53.

Carruthers, P. 2009a. "Author's Response." *Behavioral and Brain Sciences* 32: 164–76.

Carruthers, P. 2009b. "How We Know Our Own Minds: The Relationship Between
Mindreading and Metacognition." *Behavioral and Brain Sciences* 32: 121–38.

Ceci, S. J. 1996. *On Intelligence: A Bioecological Treatise on Intellectual Development,
Expanded Edition*. Cambridge, MA, and London: Harvard University Press.

Cesario, J., Plaks, J. E., and Higgins, E. T. 2006. "Automatic Social Behavior as Motivated
Preparation to Interact." *Journal of Personality and Social Psychology* 90: 893–910.

Chaiken, S. and Trope, Y. (eds). 1999. *Dual-Process Theories in Social Psychology*. New
York and London: The Guilford Press.

Chalmers, D. J. 1993. "Self-Ascription Without Qualia: A Case-Study." *Brain and Behavioral Sciences* 16: 35–6.

Chalmers, D. J. 2003. "The Matrix as Metaphysics." Available at: <http://consc.net/
papers/matrix.html>.

Chandlera, R., Wakeleya, J., Goodwina, G., and Rogers, R. 2009. "Altered Risk-Aversion
and Risk-Seeking Behavior in Bipolar Disorder." *Biological Psychiatry* 66: 840–6.

Chisholm, R. 2002 [Originally published 1964]. "Human Freedom and the Self." In
R. Kane (ed.), *Free Will*. Malden, MA: Blackwell.

Cialdini, R. B., Wosinska, W., Barrett, D. W., Butner, J., and Gornik-Durose, M. 1999.
"Compliance with a Request in Two Cultures: The Differential Influence of Social Proof

and Commitment/Consistency on Collectivists and Individualists." *Personality and Social Psychology Bulletin* 25: 1242–53.

Clark, A. 2007. "Curing Cognitive Hiccups: A Defense of the Extended Mind." *Journal of Philosophy* 104: 163–92.

Clark, A. and Chalmers, D. J. 1998. "The Extended Mind." *Analysis* 58: 10–23.

Clark, A. and Chalmers, D. J. 2010. "The Extended Mind" [extended version]. In R. Menary (ed.), *The Extended Mind*. Cambridge, MA: The MIT Press, pp. 27–42.

Clarke, R. 1994. "Ability and Responsibility for Omissions. *Philosophical Studies* 73: 195–208.

Cohen, J. 1988. *Statistical Power Analysis for the Behavioral Sciences* (2nd edn). Hillsdale, NJ: Erlbaum.

Collins, J. 2006. "Crime and Parenthood: The Uneasy Case of Prosecuting Negligent Parents." *Northwestern University Law Review* 100: 807–56.

Colvin, C. R. and Block, J. 1994. "Do Positive Illusions Foster Mental Health? An Examination of the Taylor and Brown Formulation." *Psychological Bulletin* 116: 3–20.

Conley, T. D., Roesch, S. C., Peplau, L. A., and Gold, M. S. 2009. "A Test of Positive Illusions Versus Shared Reality Models of Relationship Satisfaction among Gay, Lesbian, and Heterosexual Couples." *Journal of Applied Social Psychology* 39: 1417–31.

Conway, M. A. and Fthenaki, A. 2000. "Disruption and Loss of Autobiographical Memory." In L. S. Cermak (ed.), *Handbook of Neuropsychology* (2nd edn), *Volume 2: Memory and Its Disorders*. Amsterdam: Elsevier, pp. 281–312.

Conway, M. A. and Tacchi, P. C. 1996. "Motivated Confabulation." *Neurocase* 2: 325–39.

Cooper, J. M. 1999. "Political Animals and Civic Friendship." In J. M. Cooper, *Reason and Emotion*. Princeton, NJ: Princeton University Press, pp. 356–77.

Cottingham, J., Murdoch, D., Stoothoff, R., and Kenny, A. 1991. *The Philosophical Writings of Descartes, Volume 3: The Correspondence*. Cambridge: Cambridge University Press.

Coups, P. and Linderman, F. B. 2002. *Plenty-Coups: Chief of the Crows*. Lincoln, NE and London: University of Nebraska Press.

Cowley, E., Farrell, C., and Edwardson, M. 2006. "Strategies to Improve the Probability of Winning a Lottery: Gamblers and Their Illusions of Control." *European Advances in Consumer Research* 7: 597–601.

Craver, C. F. 2007. *Explaining the Brain: Mechanisms and the Mosaic Unity of Neuroscience*. Oxford: Oxford University Press.

Craver, C. F. 2012. "A Preliminary Case for Amnesic Selves: Toward a Clinical Moral Psychology." *Social Cognition* 30: 449–73.

Cross, P. 1977. "Not Can But Will College Teaching Be Improved?" *New Directions for Higher Education* 17: 1–15.

Cushman, F., Young, L., and Greene, J. D. 2010. "Multi-system Moral Psychology." In J. M. Doris and the Moral Psychology Research Group (eds), *The Moral Psychology Handbook*. Oxford: Oxford University Press, pp. 47–71.

D'Arms, J. and Jacobson, D. 2000a. "The Moralistic Fallacy: On the 'Appropriateness' of Emotions." *Philosophy and Phenomenological Research* 61: 65–90.

D'Arms, J. and Jacobson, D. 2000b. "Sentiment and Value." *Ethics* 110: 722–48.

D'Arms, J. and Jacobson, D. 2006. "Anthropocentric Constraints on Human Value." *Oxford Studies in Metaethics* 1: 99–126.

Dalla Barba, G. 1993. "Different Patterns of Confabulation." *Cortex* 29: 567–81.

Dalla Barba, G., Cappelletti, J. Y., Signorini, M., and Denes, G. 1997. "Confabulation: Remembering 'Another' Past, Planning 'Another' Future." *Neurocase* 3: 425–36.

Dalla Barba, G., Cipolotti, L., and Denes, G. 1990. "Autobiographical Memory Loss and Confabulation in Korsakoff's Syndrome: A Case Report." *Cortex* 26: 525–34.

Daly, M. and Wilson, M. I. 1996. "Violence Against Stepchildren." *Current Directions in Psychological Science* 5: 77–81.

Daly, M. and Wilson, M. I. 2007. "Is the 'Cinderella Effect' Controversial? A Case Study of Evolution-Minded Research and Critiques Thereof." In C. Crawford and D. Krebs (eds), *Foundations of Evolutionary Psychology*. Mahwah NJ: Erlbaum, pp. 383–400.

Damasio, A. R., Graff-Radford, N. R., Eslinger, P. J., Damasio, H., and Kassell, N. 1985. "Amnesia Following Basal Forebrain Lesions." *Archives of Neurology* 42: 263–71.

Darwall, S. L. 1983. *Impartial Reason*. Ithaca, NY and London: Cornell University Press.

Darwall, S. L. 2006. *The Second-Person Standpoint: Morality, Respect, and Accountability*. Cambridge, MA: Harvard University Press.

Dasgupta, N. and Greenwald, A. 2001. "On the Malleability of Automatic Attitudes: Combating Automatic Prejudice With Images of Admired and Disliked Individuals." *Journal of Personality and Social Psychology* 81: 800–14.

Davidson, D. 2001. *Essays on Actions and Events*. New York: Clarendon Press.

Davies, M. and Coltheart, M. 2000. "Introduction: Pathologies of Belief." In M. Coltheart and M. Davies (eds), *Pathologies of Belief*. Oxford: Blackwell, pp. 1–46.

Davies, P. S. 2009. *Subjects of the World: Darwin's Rhetoric and the Study of Agency in Nature*. Chicago, IL: The University of Chicago Press.

Davis, D., Sundahl, I., and Lesbo, M. 2000. "Illusory Personal Control as a Determinant of Bet Size and Type in Casino Craps Games." *Journal of Applied Social Psychology* 30: 1224–42.

Davis, J. H. 1969. *Group Performance*. Reading, MA: Addison-Wesley.

Dawes, R. M. 1994. "Psychotherapy: The Myth of Expertise." In R. M. Dawes, *House of Cards: Psychology and Psychotherapy Built on Myth*. New York: Free Press, pp. 38–74.

Dawson, E., Gilovich, T., and Regan, D. T. 2002. "Motivated Reasoning and Performance on the Wason Card Selection Task." *Personality and Social Psychology Bulletin* 28: 1379–87.

Dawson, G. and Fernald, M. 1987. "Perspective-Taking Ability and Its Relationship to the Social Behavior of Autistic Children." *Journal of Autism and Developmental Disorders* 17: 487–98.

Deci, E. L. and Ryan, R. M. 2000. "The 'What' and 'Why' of Goal Pursuits: Human Needs and the Self-Determination of Behavior." *Psychological Inquiry* 11: 227–68.

DeCoster, J. and Claypool, H. M. 2004. "A Meta-Analysis of Priming Effects on Impression Formation Supporting a General Model of Informational Biases." *Personality and Social Psychology Review* 8: 2–27.

Della Rocca, M. 1998. "Frankfurt, Fischer and Flickers." *Noûs* 32: 99–105.

DeLongis, A., Folkman, S., and Lazarus, R. S. 1988. "The Impact of Daily Stress on Health and Mood: Psychological and Social Resources as Mediators." *Journal of Personality and Social Psychology* 54: 486–95.

DeLuca, J. 2001. "A Cognitive Neuroscience Perspective on Confabulation." *Neuropsychoanalysis* 2: 119–32.

Dennett, D. C. 1984. *Elbow Room: The Varieties of Free Will Worth Wanting.* Cambridge, MA: MIT Press.

Dennett, D. C. 1991. "The Reality of Selves." In D. C. Dennett, *Consciousness Explained.* Boston, MA: Little, Brown, and Company, pp. 412–30.

Dennett, D. C. 1992. "The Self as a Center of Narrative Gravity." In F. S. Kessel, P. M. Cole, and D. L. Johnson (eds), *Self and Consciousness: Multiple Perspectives.* Hillsdale, NJ: Erlbaum Associates, pp. 103–15.

Dennett, D. C. 1996. *Kinds of Minds: Towards an Understanding of Consciousness.* New York: Basic Books.

DeRose, K. 1995. "Solving the Skeptical Problem." *Philosophical Review* 104: 1–52.

DeRose, K. 1999. "Contextualism: An Explanation and Defense." In J. Greco and E. Sosa (eds), *The Blackwell Guide to Epistemology.* Oxford: Blackwell Publishers, pp. 187–205.

DeRose, K. 2005. "The Ordinary Language Basis for Contextualism, and the New Invariantism." *Philosophical Quarterly* 55: 172–98.

Descartes, R. 1901 [Originally published in 1641]. *The Method, Meditations and Philosophy of Descartes, trans.* John Veitch. New York: Tudor Publishing Company.

Detterman, D. K. 1993. "The Case for the Prosecution: Transfer as Epiphenomenon." In D. K. Detterman and R. J. Sternberg (eds), *Transfer on Trial: Intelligence, Cognition, and Instruction.* Norwood, NJ: Ablex, pp. 1–24.

Devine, P. G. 1989. "Stereotypes and Prejudice: Their Automatic and Controlled Components." *Journal of Personality and Psychology* 56: 5–18.

Devine, P. G., Plant, E., Amodio, D., Harmon-Jones, E., and Vance, S. 2002. "The Regulation of Explicit and Implicit Race Bias: The Role of Motivations to Respond Without Prejudice." *Journal of Personality and Social Psychology* 82: 835–48.

Diehl, M. and Stroebe, W. 1987. "Productivity Loss in Brainstorming Groups: Toward the Solution of a Riddle." *Journal of Personality and Social Psychology* 53: 497–509.

Diener, E. and Diener M. 1995. "Cross-Cultural Correlates of Life Satisfaction and Self-Esteem." *Journal of Personality and Social Psychology* 68: 653–63.

Diener, E. and Seligman, M. E. P. 2004. "Beyond Money: Toward an Economy of Well-Being." *Psychological Science in the Public Interest* 5: 31.

Digest of Education Statistics: 2009. National Center for Education Statistics, Institute of Education Sciences, at: <http://nces.ed.gov/programs/digest/d09/tables/dt09_256.asp?referrer=list>.

Dijksterhuis, A., Aarts, H., Bargh, J. A., and van Knippenberg, A. 2000. "On the Relation Between Associative Strength and Automatic Behavior." *Journal of Experimental Social Psychology* 36: 531–44.

Dijksterhuis, A., Aarts, H., and Smith, P. K. 2005. "The Power of the Subliminal: On Subliminal Persuasion and Other Potential Applications." In R. R. Hassin, J. S. Uleman, and J. A. Bargh (eds), *The New Unconscious.* Oxford and New York: Oxford University Press, pp. 77–106.

Dijksterhuis, A., Spears, R., and Lépinasse, V. 2001. "Reflecting and Deflecting Stereotypes: Assimilation and Contrast in Impression Formation and Automatic Behavior." *Journal of Experimental Social Psychology* 37: 286–99.

Ditto, P. H. and Lopez, D. F. 1992. "Motivated Skepticism: Use of Differential Decision Criteria for Preferred and Nonpreferred Conclusions." *Journal of Personality and Social Psychology* 63: 568–84.

Divorce Magazine, 2004. "U.S. DIVORCE STATISTICS: Divorce and Marriage rates in the US for 2002." May 23, 2004, at: <http://www.divorcemag.com/articles/us-divorce-statistics>.

Donnellan, B., Lucas, R. E., and Fleeson, W. (eds). 2009. "Personality and Assessment at Age 40: Reflections on the Past Person–Situation Debate and Emerging Directions of Future Person-Situation Integration." *Journal of Research in Personality* 43 (special issue): 117–290.

Doody, R. S. and Jankovic, J. 1992. "The Alien Hand and Related Signs." *Journal of Neurology, Neurosurgery & Psychiatry* 55: 806–10.

Doris, J. M. 1998. "Persons, Situations, and Virtue Ethics." *Noûs* 32: 504–30.

Doris, J. M. 2002. *Lack of Character: Personality and Moral Behavior*. New York: Cambridge University Press.

Doris, J. M. 2005. "Précis" and "Replies: Evidence and Sensibility." *Philosophy and Phenomenological Research* 72: 632–5, 656–77.

Doris, J. M. 2006. "Out of Character: On the Psychology of Excuses in the Criminal Law." In Hugh La Follette (ed.), *Ethics in Practice*. Oxford: Blackwell Publishing, pp. 474–84.

Doris, J. M. 2009. "Skepticism about Persons." *Philosophical Issues* 19, *Metaethics*: 57–91.

Doris, J. M. 2010. "Heated Agreement: Lack of Character as Being for the Good." *Philosophical Studies* 148: 135–46.

Doris, J. M. forthcoming. *Character Trouble: Undisciplined Essays on Persons and Circumstance*. Oxford: Oxford University Press.

Doris, J. M., Knobe, J., and Woolfolk, R. L. 2007. "Variantism about Responsibility." *Philosophical Perspectives, Philosophy of Mind* 7: 337–48.

Doris, J. M. and the Moral Psychology Research Group (eds). 2010. *The Moral Psychology Handbook*. Oxford: Oxford University Press.

Doris, J. M. and Murphy, D. 2007. "From My Lai to Abu Ghraib: The Moral Psychology of Atrocity." *Midwest Studies in Philosophy* 31: 25–55.

Doris, J. M. and Nichols, S. 2012. "Broadminded: Sociality and the Cognitive Science of Morality." In E. Margolis, R. Samuels, and S. Stich (eds), *The Oxford Handbook of Philosophy and Cognitive Science*. Oxford: Oxford University Press, pp. 425–53.

Doris, J. M. and Plakias, A. 2007. "How to Argue about Disagreement: Evaluative Diversity and Moral Realism." In W. Sinnott-Armstrong (ed.), *Moral Psychology, Vol. 2: The Cognitive Science of Morality: Intuition and Diversity*. Oxford: Oxford University Press, pp. 303–32.

Doris, J. M. and Robins, S. 2007. "Review of Dominic Murphy, *Psychiatry in the Scientific Image*." *Notre Dame Philosophical Reviews* October 2, 2007. Available at: <https://ndpr.nd.edu/news/23162-psychiatry-in-the-scientific-image/>.

Doris, J. M. and Stich, S. P. 2005. "As a Matter of Fact: Empirical Perspectives on Ethics." In F. Jackson and M. Smith (eds), *The Oxford Handbook of Contemporary Philosophy*. Oxford: Oxford University Press, pp. 114–52.

Doris, J. M. and Stich, S. P. 2006. "Moral Psychology: Empirical Approaches." Edward N. Zalta (ed.), *The Stanford Encyclopedia of Philosophy* Winter 2003, <http://plato.stanford.edu/entries/moral-psych-emp/>.

Doyen, S., Klein, O., Pichon, C., and Cleeremans, A. 2012. "Behavioral Priming: It's All in the Mind, but Whose Mind?" *PLoS ONE* 7 (1): e29081. doi:10.1371/journal.pone.0029081

Dray, W. 1957. *Laws and Explanation in History*. London: Oxford University Press.

Drigotas, S. M., Rusbult, C. E., Wieselquist, J., and Whitton, S. W. 1999. "Close Partner as Sculptor of the Ideal Self: Behavioral Affirmation and the Michelangelo Phenomenon." *Journal of Personality and Social Psychology* 77: 293–323.

Dufner, M., Denissen, J. J., Zalk, M., Matthes, B., Meeus, W. H., van Aken, M. A., and Sedikides, C. 2012. "Positive Intelligence Illusions: On the Relation Between Intellectual Self-Enhancement and Psychological Adjustment." *Journal of Personality* 80: 537–72.

Dufner, M., Rauthmann, J. F., Czarna, A. Z., and Denissen, J. J. A. 2013. "Are Narcissists Sexy? Zeroing in on the Effect of Narcissism on Short-Term Mate Appeal." *Personality and Social Psychology Bulletin* 39: 870–82.

Dunning, D. 1999. "A Newer Look: Motivated Social Cognition and the Schematic Representation of Social Concepts." *Psychological Inquiry* 10: 1–11.

Dunning, D. 2006. *Self-Insight: Roadblocks and Detours on the Path to Knowing Thyself*. New York: Psychology Press.

Dunning, D., Griffin, D. W., Milojkovic, J. D., and Ross, L. 1990. "The Overconfidence Effect in Social Prediction." *Journal of Personality and Social Psychology* 58: 568–81.

Dunning, D., Kunda, Z., and Murray, S. L. 1999. "What the Commentators Motivated Us to Think About." *Psychological Inquiry* 10: 79–82.

Dunning, D., Meyerowitz, J. A., and Holzberg, A. D. 1989. "Ambiguity and Self-Evaluation: The Role of Idiosyncratic Trait Definitions in Self-Serving Assessments of Ability." *Journal of Personality and Social Psychology* 57: 1082–90.

Dutton, D. G. and Aron, A. P. 1974. "Some Evidence for Heightened Sexual Attraction Under Conditions of High Anxiety." *Journal of Personality and Social Psychology* 30: 510–17.

Dworkin, G. 1988. *The Theory and Practice of Autonomy*. Cambridge: Cambridge University Press.

Edmonds, V. H. 1967. "Marital Conventionalization: Definition and Measurement." *Journal of Marriage and the Family* 29: 681–8.

Ehrlinger, J., Johnson, K., Banner, M., Dunning, D., and Kruger, J. 2008. "Why the Unskilled Are Unaware: Further Explorations of (Absent) Self-Insight among the Incompetent." *Organizational Behavior and Human Decision Processes* 105: 98–121.

Eichenbaum, H. and Cohen, N. J. 2001. *From Conditioning to Conscious Recollection: Memory Systems of the Brain* Vol. X. Oxford Psychology Series; No. 35. New York: Oxford University Press.

Einhorn, H. J. and Hogarth, R. M. 1978. "Confidence in Judgment: Persistence of the Illusion of Validity." *Psychological Review* 85: 395–416.

Eisenberger, N. I. and Lieberman, M. D. 2004. "Why Rejection Hurts: A Common Neural Alarm System for Physical and Social Pain." *Trends in Cognitive Sciences* 8: 294–300.

Ekman, P. 1992a. "Are there Basic Emotions?" *Psychological Review* 99: 550–3.

Ekman, P. 1992b. "An Argument for Basic Emotions." *Cognition and Emotion* 6: 169–200.

Ekstrom, L. W. 2002. "Libertarianism and Frankfurt-style cases." In R. Kane (ed.), *The Oxford Handbook of Free Will*. New York: Oxford University Press, pp. 309–22.

Ekstrom, L. W. 2005. "Alienation, Autonomy, and the Self." *Midwest Studies in Philosophy* 29: 45–67.

Ekstrom, L. W. 2011. "Free Will is Not a Mystery." In R. Kane (ed.), *The Oxford Handbook of Free Will* (2nd edn). New York: Oxford University Press, pp. 366–80.

Ellenberger, H. 1970. *The Discovery of the Unconscious.* New York: Basic Books.

Ellis, A. W. and Young, A. W. 1988. *Human Cognitive Neuropsychology.* London: Lawrence Earlbaum.

Ellis, A. W. and Young, A. W. 1990. "Accounting for Delusional Misidentifications." *British Journal of Psychiatry* 157: 239–48.

Elster, J. 2000. *Strong Feelings: Emotion, Addiction, and Human Behavior.* Cambridge, MA: MIT Press.

Enoch, D. and Ball, H. 2001. "Folie à Deux (et Folie à Plusieurs)." In D. Enoch and H. Ball, *Uncommon Psychiatric Syndromes* (4th edn). London: Arnold.

Ericsson, K. and Simon, H. 1980. "Verbal Reports As Data." *Psychological Review* 87: 215–51.

Ernest-Jones, M., Nettle, D., and Bateson, M. 2011. "Effects of Eye Images on Everyday Cooperative Behavior: A Field Experiment." *Evolution and Human Behavior* 32: 172–8.

Eskine, K. J., Kacinik, N. A., and Prinz, J. J. 2011. "A Bad Taste in the Mouth: Gustatory Disgust Influences Moral Judgment." *Psychological Science* 22: 295–9.

Estabrooks. G. H. 1957. *Hypnotism* (revised edn). New York: E. P. Dutton.

Evans, J. St. B. T. and Frankish, K. 2009. *In Two Minds: Dual Processes and Beyond.* Oxford: Oxford University Press.

Evans, J. St. B. T. and Over, D. E. 1996. *Rationality and Reasoning.* Hove: Psychology Press.

Fazio, R. H., Jackson, J. R., Dunton, B. C., and Williams C. J. 1995. "Variability in Automatic Activation as an Unobtrusive Measure of Racial Attitudes: A Bona Fide Pipeline?" *Journal of Personality and Social Psychology* 69: 1013–27.

Feinberg, J. 1970. *Doing and Deserving: Essays in the Theory of Responsibility.* Princeton, NJ: Princeton University Press.

Feinberg, T. E. and Roane, D. M. 2003. "Anosognosia." In T. E. Feinberg and M. J. Farah (eds), *Behavioral Neurology and Neuropsychology* (2nd edn). New York: McGraw-Hill, pp. 345–81.

Festinger, L. and Carlsmith, J. M. 1959. "Cognitive Consequences of Forced Compliance." *The Journal of Abnormal and Social Psychology* 58: 203–11.

Fiala, B. and Nichols, S. 2009. "Confabulation, Confidence, and Introspection." *Behavioral and Brain Sciences* 32: 144–5.

Finch, J. F. and Cialdini, R. B. 1989. "Another Indirect Tactic of (Self-) Image Management: Boosting." *Personality and Social Psychology Bulletin* 15: 222–32.

Fincham, F., Beach, S., and Baucom, D. 1987. "Attribution Processes in Distressed and Nondistressed Couples: 4. Self-Partner Attribution Differences." *Journal of Personality and Social Psychology* 52: 739–48.

Fiore, M. C., Bailey, W. C., Cohen, S. J., Dorfman, S. F., Fox, B. J., Goldstein, M. G., *et al.* 2000. *Treating Tobacco Use and Dependence: A Clinical Practice Guideline.* Rockville, MD: US Department of Health and Human Services. Public Health Service. AHRQ Publication no. 00–0032.

Firth, C. D. 1992. *The Cognitive Neuropsychology of Schizophrenia.* Hove: Lawrence Erlbaum.

Fischer, J. M. 1994. *The Metaphysics of Free Will: An Essay on Control.* Oxford: Blackwell.

Fischer, J. M. 2000. "Chicken Soup for the Semi-compatibilist Soul: Replies to Haji and Kane." *The Journal of Ethics* 4: 404–7.

Fischer, J. M. 2005. "Introduction." in J. M. Fischer (ed.), *Free Will: Critical Concepts in Philosophy Vol. 1.* London: Routledge.

Fischer, J. M. 2006. *My Way: Essays on Moral Responsibility.* New York: Oxford University Press.

Fischer, J. M. 2009. *Our Stories: Essays on Life, Death, and Free Will.* New York: Oxford University Press.

Fischer, J. M. and Ravizza, M. 1998. *Responsibility and Control: A Theory of Moral Responsibility.* New York: Cambridge University Press.

Fischer, J. M. and Tognazzini, N. A. 2011. "The Physiognomy of Responsibility." *Philosophy and Phenomenological Research* 82: 381–417.

Fischer, R. S., Alexander, M. P., Esposito, M. D., and Otto, R. 1995. "Neuropsychological and Neuroanatomical Correlates of Confabulation." *Journal of Clinical and Experimental Neuropsychology* 17: 20–8.

Flament, J. 1957. "La Fabulation dans le Syndrome de Korsakoff d'Etiologie Traumatique." *Acta Neurologica Belgica* 57: 119–61.

Flanagan, O. 2009. "Moral Science? Still Metaphysical After All These Years." In D. Narvaez and D. K. Lapsley (eds), *Moral Personality, Identity and Character: Explorations in Moral Psychology.* Cambridge and New York: Cambridge University Press, pp. 52–78.

Flanagan, O. 2011. "What is it Like to Be an Addict?" In J. Polland and G. Graham (eds), *Addiction and Responsibility.* Cambridge, MA: MIT Press, pp. 269–92.

Folkman, S. 1984. "Personal Control and Stress and Coping Processes: A Theoretical Analysis." *Journal of Personality and Social Psychology* 46: 839–52.

Förstl, H., Almeida, O. P., Owen, A. M., Burns, A., and Howard, R. 1991. "Psychiatric, Neurological, and Medical Aspects of Misidentification Syndromes: A Review of 260 Cases." *Psychological Medicine* 21: 905–10.

Forsyth, W. 1867. *Life of Marcus Tullius Cicero.* London: J. Murray.

Forthofer, M. S., Markman, H. J., Cox, M., Stanley, S., and Kessler, R. C. 1996. "Associations Between Marital Distress and Work Loss in a National Sample." *Journal of Marriage and the Family* 58: 597–605.

Foster, C. A., Witcher, B. S., Campbell, W. K., and Green, J. D. 1998. "Arousal and Attraction: Evidence for Automatic and Controlled Processes." *Journal of Personality and Social Psychology* 74: 86–1021.

Foster, K. R. and Ratnieks, F. L. W. 2005. "A New Eusocial Vertebrate?" *Trends in Ecology and Evolution* 20: 363–4.

Fotopoulou, A., Solms, A., and Turnbull, O. 2004. "Wishful Reality Distortions in Confabulation: A Case Report." *Neuropsychologia* 47: 727–44.

Fowers, B. J., Lyons, E., Montel, K. H., and Shaked, N. 2001. "Positive Illusions about Marriage Among Married and Single Individuals." *Journal of Family Psychology* 15: 95–109.

Fraley, R. C. and Vazire, S. 2014. "The N-Pact Factor: Evaluating the Quality of Empirical Journals with Respect to Sample Size and Statistical Power." *PLoS ONE* 9(10): e109019. doi:10.1371/journal.pone.0109019

Frances, B. 2005. "When a Skeptical Hypothesis is Live." *Noûs* 39: 559–95.

Frankfurt, H. 1988. *The Importance of What We Care About.* Cambridge: Cambridge University Press.

Frankfurt, H. 1999. "The Faintest Passion." In H. Frankfurt, *Necessity, Volition and Love.* New York: Cambridge University Press, pp. 95–107.

Frankfurt, H. 2002. "Reply to John Martin Fischer." In S. Buss and L. Overton (eds), *Contours of Agency: Essays on Themes from Harry Frankfurt.* Cambridge, MA: MIT Press, pp. 27–31.

Frankish, K. and Evans, J. St. B. T. 2009. "The Duality of Mind: An Historical Perspective." In J. Evans and K. Frankish (eds), *In Two Minds: Dual Processes and Beyond.* Oxford: Oxford University Press, pp. 1–29.

Fulton, J. F. and Bailey, P. 1929. "Tumors in the Region of the Third Ventricle: Their Diagnosis and Relation to Pathological Sleep." *Journal of Nervous and Mental Disease* 69: 1–25, 145–65, 261–77.

Gainotti, G. 1975. "Confabulation of Denial in Senile Dementia: An Experimental Study." *Psychiatria Clinica* 8: 99–108.

Gantz, T. and Henkle, G. 2002. "Seatbelts: Current Issues." *Prevention Institute*: <http://www.preventioninstitute.org/traffic_seatbelt.html>.

Garber, D. 1986. "*Semel in vita*: The Scientific Background to Descartes' *Meditations.*" In A. O. Rorty (ed.), *Essays on Descartes' Meditations.* Berkeley, CA: University of California Press, pp. 81–116.

Gardner, W. L., Gabriel, S., and Hochschild, L. 2002. "When You and I Are 'We,' You Are No Longer Threatening: The Role of Self-expansion in Social Comparison Processes." *Journal of Personality and Social Psychology* 83: 239–51.

Gardner, W. L., Gabriel, S., and Lee, A. Y. 1999. "'I' Value Freedom But 'We' Value Relationships: Self-construal Priming Mirrors Cultural Differences in Judgment." *Psychological Science* 10: 321–6.

Gawronski, B., Hofmann, W., and Wilbur, C. J. 2006. "Are Implicit Attitudes Unconscious?" *Consciousness and Cognition* 15: 485–99.

Gazzaniga, M. S. 2000. "Cerebral Specialization and Interhemispheric Communication: Does the Corpus Callosum Enable the Human Condition?" *Brain* 123: 1293–326.

Geberth, V. J. and Turco, R. N. 1997. "Anti-social Personality Disorder, Sexual Sadism, Malignant Narcissism and Serial Murder." *Journal of Forensic Sciences* 42: 49–60.

Geis, G. and Binder, A. 1990. "Sins of their Children: Parental Responsibility for Juvenile Delinquency." *Notre Dame Journal of Law, Ethics and Public Policy* 5: 303–22.

Gendler, T. S. 2007. "Self-Deception as Pretense." *Philosophical Perspectives* 21: 231–58.

Gendler, T. S. 2010. "On the Relation between Pretense and Belief." In T. S. Gendler, *Intuition, Imagination, and Philosophical Methodology.* Oxford: Oxford University Press, pp. 135–54.

Gentilini, M., De Renzi, E., and Crisi, G. 1987. "Bilateral Paramedian Thalamic Artery Infarcts: Report of Eight Cases." *Journal of Neurology, Neurosurgery and Psychiatry* 50: 900–9.

Gertler, B. 2011. *Self-knowledge*. London and New York: Routledge.

Gibbard, A. 1990. *Wise Choices, Apt Feelings: A Theory of Normative Judgment*. Cambridge, MA: Harvard University Press.

Gigerenzer, G. 2000. *Adaptive Thinking: Rationality in the Real World*. Oxford: Oxford University Press.

Gigerenzer, G., Todd, P. M., and the ABC Research Group. 1999. *Simple Heuristics that Make Us Smart*. New York: Oxford University Press.

Gilbert, D. T. 1991. "How Mental Systems Believe." *American Psychologist* 46: 107–19.

Gilbert, D. T., Pelham, B. W., and Krull, D. S. 1988. "On Cognitive Busyness: When Person Perceivers Meet Persons Perceived." *Journal of Personality and Social Psychology* 54: 733–40.

Gilbert, D. T., Tafarodi, R. W., and Malone, P. S. 1993. "You Can't Not Believe Everything You Read." *Journal of Personality and Social Psychology* 65: 221–33.

Gilbert, M. 2014. *Joint Commitment: How We Make the Social World*. Oxford: Oxford University Press.

Gilboa, A., Alain, C., Suss, D. T., Melo, B., Miller, S., and Moscovitch, M. 2006. "Mechanisms of Spontaneous Confabulations: A Strategic Retrieval Account." *Brain* 129: 1399–414.

Giles, H. and Ogay, T. 2007. "Communication Accommodation Theory." In B. B. Whaley and W. Samter (eds), *Explaining Communication: Contemporary Theories and Exemplars*. Mahwah, NJ: Lawrence Erlbaum Associates, pp. 293–310.

Gill, M. J., Swann Jr, W. B., and Silvera, D. H. 1998. "On the Genesis of Confidence." *Journal of Personality and Social Psychology* 75: 1101–14.

Gilovich, T. 1991. *How We Know What Isn't So: The Fallibility of Human Reason in Everyday Life*. New York: The Free Press.

Gilovich, T., Griffin, T., and Kahneman, D. (eds). 2002. *Heuristics and Biases: The Psychology of Intuitive Judgment*. New York: Cambridge University Press.

Gist, M. E., Bavetta, A. G., and Stevens, C. K. 1990. "The Effectiveness of Self Management Versus Goal Setting in Facilitating Training Transfer." *Academy of Management Proceedings 1990* No. 1: 117–21.

Glendinning, J. 1994. "Is the Bitter Rejection Response Always Adaptive?" *Physiology & Behavior* 56: 1217–27.

Goffman, E. 1959. *The Presentation of Self in Everyday Life*. Garden City, NY: Doubleday.

Goffman, E. 1967. *Interaction Ritual: Essays in Face to Face Behavior*. Chicago, IL: Aldine Publishing.

Gollwitzer, P. M. 1993. "Goal A: The Role of Intentions." *European Review of Social Psychology* 4: 141–85.

Gollwitzer, P. M. 1999. "Implementation Intentions." *American Psychologist* 54: 493–503.

Goodall, J. 1986. "Social Rejection, Exclusion, and Shunning among the Gombe Chimpanzees." *Ethnology and Sociobiology* 7: 227–36.

Goodman, N. 1955. *Fact, Fiction, and Forecast*. Cambridge, MA: Harvard University Press.

Gopnik, A. 1993. "How We Know Our Own Minds: The Illusion of First-Person Knowledge of Intentionality." *Behavioral and Brain Sciences* 16: 1–14.

Gopnik, A. and Meltzoff, A. 1994. "Minds, Bodies, and Persons: Young Children's Understanding of the Self and Others as Reflected in Imitation and Theory of Mind

Research." In S. Parker, R. Mitchell, and M. Boccia (eds), *Self-awareness in Animals and Humans: Developmental Perspectives.* New York: Cambridge University Press, pp. 166–86.

Gosling, S. D., John, O. P., Craik, K. H., and Robins, R. W. 1998. "Do People Know How They Behave? Self-Reported Act Frequencies Compared with On-Line Codings by Observers." *Journal of Personality and Social Psychology* 74: 1337–49.

Gottfredson, L. S. 1998. "The General Intelligence Factor." *Scientific American Presents* 9: 24–29.

Graham, P. K. 2000. "Parental Responsibility Laws: Let the Punishment Fit the Crime." *Loyola of Los Angeles Law Review* 33: 1719–54.

Grassian, S. 1983. "Psychopathological Effects of Solitary Confinement." *American Journal of Psychiatry* 140: 1450–4.

Gray, K., Young, L., and Waytz, A. 2012. "Mind Perception is the Essence of Morality." *Psychological Inquiry* 23: 101–24.

Greene, J. D. 2007. "The Secret Joke of Kant's Soul." In W. Sinnott-Armstrong (ed.), *Moral Psychology, Volume 3: Emotions, Brain Disorders, and Development.* Cambridge, MA: MIT Press, pp. 35–80.

Greene, J. D. 2013. *Moral Tribes: Emotion, Reason, and the Gap between Us and Them.* New York: Atlantic Books.

Greene, J. D., Nystrom, L. E., Engell, A. D., Darley, J. M., and Cohen, J. D. 2004. "The Neural Bases of Cognitive Conflict and Control in Moral Judgment." *Neuron* 44: 389–400.

Greene, J. D., Sommerville, R., Nystrom, L., Darley, J., and Cohen, J. 2001. "An fMRI Investigation of Emotional Engagement in Moral Judgment." *Science* 293: 2105–108.

Greenwald, A. G. and Banaji, M. 1995. "Implicit Social Cognition: Attitudes, Self-Esteem, and Stereotypes." *Psychological Review* 102: 4–27.

Greenwald, A. G., Carnot, C. G., Beach, R., and Young, B. 1987. "Increasing Voting Behavior by Asking People if They Expect to Vote." *Journal of Applied Psychology* 72: 315–18.

Greenwald, A. G., McGhee, D., and Schwartz, J. 1998. "Measuring Individual Differences in Implicit Cognition: The Implicit Association Test." *Journal of Personality and Social Psychology* 74: 1464–80.

Griffiths, P. E. 1997. *What Emotions Really Are: The Problem of Psychological Categories.* Chicago, IL: University of Chicago Press.

Grush, J. 1976. "Attitude Formation and Mere Exposure Phenomena: A Nonartifactual Explanation of Empirical Findings." *Journal of Personality and Social Psychology* 33: 281–90.

Gruter, M. 1986. "Ostracism on Trial: The Limits of Individual Rights." *Ethology and Sociobiology* 7: 271–9.

Gutmann, A. and Thompson, D. 2004. *Why Deliberative Democracy?* Princeton, NJ: Princeton University Press.

Haggard, P. 2008. "Human Volition: Towards a Neuroscience of Will." *Nature Reviews Neuroscience* 9: 934–94.

Haggard, P. and Libet, B. 2001. "Conscious Intention and Brain Activity." *Journal of Consciousness Studies* 8: 47–63.

Hahlweg, K. and Richtera, D. 2010. "Prevention of Marital Instability and Distress. Results of an 11-year Longitudinal Follow-up Study." *Behavior Research and Therapy* 48: 377–83.

Haidt, J. 2001. "The Emotional Dog and Its Rational Tail: A Social Intuitionist Approach to Moral Judgment." *Psychological Review* 108: 814–34.

Haidt, J. 2006. *The Happiness Hypothesis: Finding Modern Truth in Ancient Wisdom*. New York: Basic Books.

Haidt, J., Bjorklund, F., and Murphy, S. 2000. *Moral Dumbfounding: When Intuition Finds No Reason*. Unpublished manuscript. University of Virginia.

Haine, B. 1985. "The Mountain People: Some Notes on the Ik of North-Eastern Uganda." *Africa: Journal of the International African Institute* 55: 3–16.

Haji, I. 2002. "Compatibilist Views of Freedom and Responsibility." In R. Kane (ed.), *The Oxford Handbook of Free Will*. New York: Oxford University Press, pp. 202–28.

Haley, K. and Fessler, D. M. T. 2005. "Nobody's Watching? Subtle Cues Affect Generosity in an Anonymous Economic Game." *Evolution and Human Behavior* 26: 245–56.

Hall, L., Johansson, P., and Strandberg, T. 2012. "Lifting the Veil of Morality: Choice Blindness and Attitude Reversals on a Self-Transforming Survey." *PLoS ONE* 7(9): e45457. doi:10.1371/journal.pone.0045457

Hall, L., Johansson, P., Tärning, B., Sikström, S., and Deutgen, T. 2010. "Magic at the Marketplace: Choice Blindness for the Taste of Jam and the Smell of Tea." *Cognition* 117: 54–61.

Hall, L., Strandberg, T., Pärnamets, P., Lind, A., Tärning, B., *et al.* 2013. "How the Polls Can Be Both Spot On and Dead Wrong: Using Choice Blindness to Shift Political Attitudes and Voter Intentions." *PLoS ONE* 8(4): e60554. doi:10.1371/journal.pone.0060554

Hallie, P. P. 1979. *Lest Innocent Blood Be Shed: The Story of the Village of Le Chambon and How Goodness Happened There*. New York: Harper and Row.

Haney, C. 2003. "Mental Health Issues in Long-Term Solitary and 'Supermax' Confinement." *Crime & Delinquency* 49: 124–56.

Harlow, H. F. 1986. *From Learning to Love: The Selected Papers of H. F. Harlow*, C. M. Harlow (ed.). New York: Praeger.

Harlow, H. F., Dodsworth, R., and Harlow, M. 1965. "Total Social Isolation in Monkeys." *Proceedings of the National Academy of Science USA* 54: 90–7.

Harlow, H. F. and Suomi, S. 1971. "Social Recovery by Isolation-Reared Monkeys." *Proceedings of the National Academy of Science USA* 68: 1534–8.

Harman, G. 1999. "Moral Philosophy Meets Social Psychology: Virtue Ethics and the Fundamental Attribution Error." *Proceedings of the Aristotelian Society* 99: 315–31.

Harman, G. 2000a. *Explaining Value and Other Essays in Moral Philosophy*. Oxford: Oxford University Press.

Harman, G. 2000b. "The Nonexistence of Character Traits." *Proceedings of the Aristotelian Society* 100: 223–6.

Harman, G. 2012. "Naturalism in Moral Philosophy." In S. Nuccetelli and G. Seay (eds), *Ethical Naturalism: Current Debates*. Cambridge: Cambridge University Press, pp. 8–23.

Haslanger, S. 2012. *Resisting Reality: Social Construction and Social Critique*. New York: Oxford University Press.

Hassin, R. R., Uleman, J. S., and Bargh, J. A. (eds). 2005. *The New Unconscious*. New York: Oxford University Press.

Hatfield, E., Cacioppo, J., and Rapson, R. L. 1994. *Emotional Contagion*. New York: Cambridge University Press.

Hawthorne, J. 2003. "Identity." In M. J. Loux and D. W. Zimmerman (eds), *The Oxford Handbook of Metaphysics*. Oxford: Oxford University Press, pp. 99–130.

Hawthorne, J. 2004. *Knowledge and Lotteries*. Oxford: Oxford University Press.

Haybron, D. M. 2008. *The Pursuit of Unhappiness: Well-Being and the Limits of Personal Authority*. Oxford: Oxford University Press.

Hayes, A. F. and Dunning, D. 1997. "Construal Processes and Trait Ambiguity: Implications for Self-Peer Agreement in Personality Judgment." *Journal of Personality and Social Psychology* 72: 664–77.

Heaton, T.B. 2002. "Factors Contributing to Increasing Marital Stability in the United States." *Journal of Family Issues* 23(3): 392–409.

Heizer, R. F. and Kroeber, T. (eds). 1979. *Ishi, the Last Yahi: A Documentary History*. Berkeley, CA: University of California Press.

Hemphill, J. F. 2003. "Interpreting the Magnitudes of Correlation Coefficients." *American Psychologist* 58: 78–80.

Henrich, J., Heine, S. J., and Norenzayan, A. 2010. "The Weirdest People in the World?" *Behavioral and Brain Sciences* 33: 61–135.

Herman, B. 2007. *Moral Literacy*. Cambridge, MA: Harvard University Press.

Hill, G. 1982. "Group Versus Individual Performance: Are N + 1 Heads Better Than One?" *Psychological Bulletin* 91: 517–39.

Hirstein, W. 2005. *Brain Fiction: Self-Deception and the Riddle of Confabulation*. Cambridge, MA and London: MIT Press.

Hirstein, W. and Ramachandran, V. S. 1997. "Capgras' Syndrome: A Novel Probe for Understanding the Neural Representation of the Identity and Familiarity of Persons." *Proceedings of the Royal Society of London, B* 264: 437–44.

Hitchens, C. 1995. *The Missionary Position: Mother Theresa in Theory and Practice*. London and New York: Verso.

Hobbs, M. and McLaren, S. 2009. "The Interrelations of Agency, Depression, and Suicidal Ideation among Older Adults." *Suicide and Life-Threatening Behaviour* 39: 161–71.

Hodgson, D. 2011. "Quantum Physics, Consciousness, and Free Will." In R. Kane (ed.), *The Oxford Handbook of Free Will* (2nd edn). New York: Oxford University Press, pp. 57–83.

Holton, R. 2009. *Willing, Wanting, Waiting*. Oxford: Oxford University Press.

Horowitz, T. 1998. "Philosophical Intuitions and Psychological Theory." In M. DePaul and W. Ramsey (eds), *Rethinking Intuition: The Psychology of Intuition and its Role in Philosophical Inquiry*. Lanham, MD: Rowman & Littlefield, pp. 143–60.

Horvath, A. O. and Symonds, B. D. 1991. "Relation Between Working Alliance and Outcome in Psychotherapy: A Meta-analysis." *Journal of Counseling Psychology* 38: 139–49.

Horwitz, A. V., White, H. R., and Howell-White, S. 1996. "Becoming Married and Mental Health: A Longitudinal Study of a Cohort of Young Adults." *Journal of Marriage and the Family* 58: 895–907.

Hoxie, F. E. 1995. *Parading through History: The Making of the Crow Nation in America 1805–1935*. Cambridge: Cambridge University Press.

Hull, J., Slone, L., Metayer, K., and Matthews, A. 2002. "The Nonconsciousness of Self-consciousness." *Journal of Personality and Social Psychology* 83: 406–24.

Hume, D. 1978 [Originally published 1740]. *A Treatise of Human Nature* (2nd edn), P. H. Nidditch (ed.). Oxford: Clarendon Press.

Humphrey, N. and Dennett, D. C. 1998. "Speaking for Our Selves." In D. C. Dennett, *Brainchildren: Essays on Designing Minds*. Cambridge, MA: MIT Press, pp. 31–58.

Hurlburt, R. and Schwitzgebel, E. 2007. *Describing Inner Experience*. Cambridge, MA: MIT Press.

Ioannidis, J. P. A. 2005. "Why Most Published Research Findings Are False." *PLoS Med*: e124. doi:10.1371/journal.pmed.0020124

Jack, A. I. and Robbins, P. 2004. "The Illusory Triumph of Machine over Mind: Wegner's Eliminativism and the Real Promise of Psychology." *Behavioral and Brain Sciences* 27: 665–6.

Jaynes, J. 1976. *The Origins of Consciousness in the Breakdown of the Bicameral Mind*. Boston, MA: Houghton Mifflin Company.

Jennings, D., Amabile, T. M., and Ross, L. 1982. "Informal Covariation Assessment: Data-based vs. Theory-based Judgments." In A. Tversky, D. Kahneman, and P. Slovic (eds), *Judgment Under Uncertainty: Heuristics and Biases*. New York: Cambridge University Press, pp. 211–30.

Johansson, P., Hall, L., Sikström, S., and Olsson, A. 2005. "Failure to Detect Mismatches Between Intention and Outcome in a Simple Decision Task." *Science* 310: 116–19.

Johansson, P., Hall, L., Sikström, S., Tärning, B., and Lind, A. 2006. "How Something Can Be Said About Telling More Than We Can Know." *Consciousness and Cognition* 15: 673–92.

John, L., Loewenstein, G., and Prelec, D. 2012. "Measuring the Prevalence of Questionable Research Practices with Incentives for Truth Telling." *Psychological Science* 23: 524–32.

John, O. P. and Robins, R. W. 1994. "Accuracy and Bias in Self-Perception: Individual Differences in Self-Enhancement and the Role of Narcissism." *Journal of Personality and Social Psychology* 66: 206–19.

Johnson, M. K., Hayes, S. M., D'Esposito, M., and Raye, C. L. 2000. "Confabulation." In F. Boller and J. Grafman (eds), *Handbook of Neuropsychology*, Vol. 2 (2nd edn). Amsterdam: Elsevier, pp. 383–407.

Johnson, M. K. and Raye, C. L. 1998. "False Memories and Confabulation." *Trends in Cognitive Science* 2: 137–45.

Johnson, S. 2005. "Reasoning about Intentionality in Preverbal Infants." In P. Carruthers, S. Laurence, and S. Stich (eds), *The Innate Mind: Structure and Content*. Oxford: Oxford University Press, pp. 254–71.

Johnston, M. 1987. "Human Beings." *The Journal of Philosophy* 84: 59–83.

Johnston, M. 1989. "Fission and the Facts." *Philosophical Perspectives 3: Philosophy of Mind and Action Theory* 3: 369–87.

Jollimore, T. 2008. "Impartiality." In E. N. Zalta (ed.), *The Stanford Encyclopedia of Philosophy* Fall 2008, Metaphysics Research Lab, CSLI, Stanford University, Stanford, CA, at: <http://plato.stanford.edu/archives/fall2008/entries/impartiality/>.

Joy-Gaba, J. A. and Nosek, B. A. 2010. "The Surprisingly Limited Malleability of Implicit Racial Evaluations." *Social Psychology* 41: 137–46.

Kahneman, D. 2011. *Thinking, Fast and Slow*. New York: Farrar, Straus, and Giroux.

Kahneman, D. and Frederick, S. 2002. "Representativeness Revisited: Attribute Substitution in Intuitive Judgment." In T. Gilovich, D. Griffin, and D. Kahneman (eds), *Heuristics and Biases*. New York: Cambridge University Press, pp. 49–81.

Kahneman, D., Knetsch, J. L., and Thaler, R. H. 1991. "Anomalies: The Endowment Effect, Loss Aversion, and Status Quo Bias." *The Journal of Economic Perspectives* 5: 193–206.

Kahneman, D., Slovic, P., and Tversky, A. 1982. *Judgment Under Uncertainty: Heuristics and Biases*. Cambridge: Cambridge University Press.

Kahneman, D. and Tversky, A. 1982. "The Simulation Heuristic." In D. Kahneman, P. Slovic, and A. Tversky (eds), *Judgment under Uncertainty: Heuristics and Biases*. Cambridge: Cambridge University Press, pp. 201–8.

Kamtekar, R. 2004. "Situationism and Virtue Ethics on the Content of Our Character." *Ethics* 114: 458–91.

Kane, R. 1996. *The Significance of Free Will*. Oxford: Oxford University Press.

Kane, R. 1999. "Responsibility, Luck, and Chance: Reflections on Free Will and Indeterminism." *Journal of Philosophy* 96: 217–40.

Kane, R. 2000. "Non-Constraining Control and the Threat of Social Conditioning (Comments on John Martin Fischer's Presentation)." *The Journal of Ethics* 4: 401–3.

Kane, R. 2002. "Introduction: The Contours of Contemporary Free Will Debates." In R. Kane (ed.), *The Oxford Handbook of Free Will*. New York: Oxford University Press.

Kane, R. 2005. *A Contemporary Introduction to Free Will*. New York: Oxford University Press.

Kane, R. 2007. "Response to Fischer, Pereboom, and Vargas." In J. M. Fisher, R. Kane, D. Pereboom, and M. Vargas (eds), *Four Views on Free Will*. Malden, MA: Blackwell, pp. 166–83.

Kane, R. 2011. "Rethinking Free Will: New Perspectives on an Ancient Problem." In R. Kane (ed.), *The Oxford Handbook of Free Will* (2nd edn). New York: Oxford University Press, pp. 381–405.

Kant, I. 1956 [Originally published 1788]. *The Critique of Practical Reason*. Trans. L. W. Beck. Indianapolis, IN: Bobbs-Merrill.

Kant, I. 1963 [Originally published 1784]. *Idea for a Universal History from a Cosmopolitan Point of View*. Trans. L. W. Beck. In L. W. Beck (ed.), *Kant: On History*. New York: Bobbs-Merrill.

Kaplan-Solms, K. and Solms, M. 2000. *Clinical Studies in Neuro-Psychoanalysis: Introduction to a Depth Psychology*. London: Karnac.

Kapur, N. and Coughlan, A. K. 1980. "Confabulation and Frontal Lobe Dysfunction." *Journal of Neurology, Neurosurgery and Psychiatry* 43: 461–3.

Karg K., Burmeister, M., Shedden K., and Sen, S. 2011. "The Serotonin Transporter Promoter Variant (5-HTTLPR), Stress, and Depression Meta-analysis Revisited: Evidence of Genetic Moderation." *Archives of General Psychiatry* 68: 444–54.

Karney, B. and Bradbury, T. 1995. "The Longitudinal Course of Marital Quality and Stability: A Review of Theory, Method, and Research." *Psychological Bulletin* 118: 3–34.

Kawakami, K., Young, H., and Dovidio, J. F. 2002. "Automatic Stereotyping; Category, Trait, and Behavioral Activations." *Personality and Social Psychology Bulletin* 28: 3–15.

Keller, M. B., McCullough, J. P., Klein, D. N., Arnow, B., Dunner, D. L., Gelenberg, A. J., Markowitz, J. C., *et al.* 2000. "A Comparison of Nefazodone, the Cognitive Behavior-Analysis System of Psychotherapy, and Their Combination for the Treatment of Chronic Depression." *New England Journal of Medicine* 342: 1462–70.

Keller, S. 2007. *The Limits of Loyalty*. Cambridge: Cambridge University Press.

Keller, S. 2013. *Partiality*. Princeton, NJ: Princeton University Press.

Kelly, D. 2011. *Yuck!: The Nature and Moral Significance of Disgust*. Cambridge, MA: MIT Press.

Kelly, D., Machery, E., and Mallon, R. 2010. "Race and Racial Cognition." In J. M. Doris and the Moral Psychology Research Group (eds), *The Moral Psychology Handbook*. Oxford: Oxford University Press, pp. 433–72.

Kennett, J. and Fine, C. 2009. "Will the Real Moral Judgment Please Stand Up? The Implications of Social Intuitionist Models of Cognition for Meta-ethics and Moral Psychology." *Ethical Theory and Moral Practice* 12: 77–96.

Kernberg, O. F. 1998. "The Psychotherapeutic Management of Psychopathic, Narcissistic, and Paranoid Transferences." In T. Millon, E. Simonsen, M. Birket-Smith, and R. D. Davis (eds), *Psychopathy: Antisocial, Criminal, and Violent Behavior*. New York: Guilford, pp. 372–82.

Kernberg, O. F. 2004. *Aggressivity, Narcissism, and Self-Destructiveness in the Psychotherapeutic Relationship*. New Haven, CT: Yale University Press.

Kiecolt-Glaser, J. K. and Newton, T. L. 2001. "Marriage and Health: His and Hers." *Psychological Bulletin* 127: 472–503.

Kihlstrom, J. F. 2008. "The Automaticity Juggernaut." In J. Baer, J. C. Kaufman, and R. F. Baumeister (eds), *Are We Free? Psychology and Free Will*. New York: Oxford University Press, pp. 155–80.

Kimmel, M. 2006. *Manhood in America: A Cultural History* (2nd edn). New York: Oxford University Press.

Kitayama, S. and Karasawa, M. 1997. "Implicit Self-esteem in Japan: Name Letters and Birthday Numbers." *Personality and Social Psychology Bulletin* 23: 736–42.

Kitcher, P. 1993. *The Advancement of Science*. Oxford: Oxford University Press.

Kitcher, P. 2001. *Science, Truth, and Democracy*. Oxford: Oxford University Press.

Klar, Y. and Giladi, E. E. 1999. "Are Most People Happier than Their Peers, or Are They Just Happy?" *Personality and Social Psychology Bulletin* 25: 586–95.

Klonowicz, T. 2001. "Discontented People: Reactivity and Locus of Control as Determinants of Subjective Well-Being." *European Journal of Personality* 15: 29–47.

Knobe, J. 2003. "Intentional Action in Folk Psychology: An Experimental Investigation." *Philosophical Psychology* 16: 309–24.

Knobe, J. 2010. "Person as Scientist, Person as Moralist." *Behavioral and Brain Sciences* 33: 315–29.

Knobe, J. and Doris, J. M. 2010. "Responsibility." In J. M. Doris and the Moral Psychology Research Group (eds), *The Moral Psychology Handbook*. Oxford: Oxford University Press, pp. 321–54.

Knobe, J. and Leiter, B. 2007. "The Case for Nietzschean Moral Psychology." In B. Leiter and N. Sinhababu (eds), *Nietzsche and Morality*. Oxford: Oxford University Press, pp. 83–109.

Knobe, J. and Nichols, S. 2008. *Experimental Philosophy*. Oxford: Oxford University Press.

Kolip, P. 2005. "The Association between Gender, Family Status and Mortality." *Journal of Public Health* 13: 309–12.

Kopelman, M. D. 1987. "Two Types of Confabulation." *Journal of Neurology, Neurosurgery and Psychiatry* 50: 1482–7.

Kor, A., Fogel, Y. A., Reid, R. C., and Potenza, M. N. 2013. "Should Hypersexual Disorder be Classified as an Addiction?" *Sexual Addiction & Compulsivity* 20: 27–47.

Kornblith, H. 2010. "What Reflective Endorsement Cannot Do." *Philosophy and Phenomenological Research* 80: 1–19.

Kornblith, H. 2012. *On Reflection*. Oxford: Oxford University Press.

Korsakoff, S. S. 1889. "Étude Médico-Psychologique sure une Forme des Maladies de la Mémoire." *Revue Philosophique* 20: 501–30.

Korsgaard, C. M. 1996. *The Sources of Normativity*. Cambridge: Cambridge University Press.

Korsgaard, C. M. 2003. "Christine M. Korsgaaard: Internalism and the Sources of Normativity." (*interview*) In H. Pauer Struder (ed.), *Constructions of Practical Reason*. Palo Alto, CA: Stanford University Press.

Korsgaard, C. M. 2009. *Self-Constitution: Agency, Identity, and Integrity*. New York: Oxford University Press.

Kozuch, B. and Nichols, S. 2011. "Awareness of Unawareness: Folk Psychology and Introspective Transparency." *Journal of Consciousness Studies* 18: 135–60.

Kreps, J. R. 2009. "The Gourmet Ape: Evolution and Human Food Preferences." *The American Journal of Clinical Nutrition* 90: 707–11.

Kroeber, T. 2002 [Originally published 1961]. *Ishi in Two Worlds: A Biography of the Last Wild Indian in North America*. Berkeley and Los Angeles, CA: University of California Press.

Kroenke, K. and Swindle, R. 2000. "Cognitive-Behavioral Therapy for Somatization and Symptom Syndromes: A Critical Review of Controlled Clinical Trials." *Psychotherapy and Psychosomatics* 69: 205–15.

Krosnick, J. A., Miller, J. M., and Tichy, M. P. 2004. "An Unrecognized Need for Ballot Reform: Effects of Candidate Name Order." In A. N. Crigler, M. R. Just, and E. J. McCaffery (eds), *Rethinking the Vote: The Politics and Prospects of American Election Reform*. New York: Oxford University Press, pp. 51–74.

Kruger, J. 1999. "Lake Wobegon Be Gone! The 'Below-average Effect' and the Egocentric Nature of Comparative Ability Judgments." *Journal of Personality and Social Psychology* 77: 221–32.

Kruger, J. and Dunning, D. 1999. "Unskilled and Unaware of It: How Difficulties in Recognizing One's Own Incompetence Lead to Inflated Self-Assessments." *Journal of Personality and Social Psychology* 77: 1121–34.

Kruglanski, A. W. 1996. "Motivated Social Cognition: Principles of the Interface." In E. T. Higgins and A. W. Kruglanski (eds), *Social Psychology: Handbook of Basic Principles*. New York and London: Guilford Press, pp. 493–520.

Krupnick, J. L., Sotsky, S. M., Simmens, S., Moyher, J., Elkin, I., Watkins, J., and Pilkonis, P. A. 1996. "The Role of the Therapeutic Alliance in Psychotherapy and Pharmacotherapy Outcome: Findings in the National Institute of Mental Health Treatment of Depression Collaborative Research Project." *Journal of Consulting and Clinical Psychology* 64: 532–9.

Kuhn, T. 1962. *The Structure of Scientific Revolutions*. Chicago, IL: University of Chicago Press.

Kühnen, U., Hannover, B., and Schubert, B. 2001. "The Semantic-Procedural Interface Model of the Self: The Role of Self-Knowledge for Context-Dependent Versus Context-Independent Modes of Thinking." *Journal of Personality and Social Psychology* 80: 397–409.

Kunda, Z. 1990. "The Case for Motivated Reasoning." *Psychological Bulletin* 108: 480–98.

Kunze, M. 2000. "Maximizing Help for Dissonant Smokers." *Addiction* 95: 13–17.

Kuper, A. 2008. "A Philosopher Among the Crow." *Journal of the Royal Anthropological Institute (N.S.)* 14: 426–30.

Kupperman, J. J. 2001. "The Indispensability of Character." *Philosophy* 76: 239–50.

Kurt, A. and Paulhus, D. L. 2008. "Moderators of the Adaptiveness of Self-enhancement: Operationalization, Outcome Domain, and Outcome Evaluator." *Journal of Research in Personality* 42: 839–52.

Kurzban, R. and DeScioli, P. 2008. "Reciprocal Cooperation in Groups: Information-Seeking in a Public Goods Game." *European Journal of Social Psychology* 38: 139–58.

Kurzban, R., DeScioli, P., and O'Brien, E. 2007. "Audience Effects on Moralistic Punishment." *Evolution and Human Behavior* 28: 75–84.

Lakhani, D. 2009. *Subliminal Persuasion: Influence and Marketing Secrets They Don't Want You to Know*. Hoboken, NJ: John Wiley and Sons.

Lambert, M. J. and Ogles, B. M. 2004. "The Efficacy and Effectiveness of Psychotherapy." In M.J. Lambert (ed.), *Bergin and Garfield's Handbook of Psychotherapy and Behavior Change*. New York: Wiley, pp. 139–93.

Lane, K. A., Banaji, M. R., Nosek, B. A., and Greenwald, A. G. 2007. "Understanding and Using the Explicit Association Test: IV." In B. Wittenbrink and N. Schwarz (eds), *Implicit Measures of Attitudes*. New York: The Guilford Press, pp. 59–102.

Langer, E. J. 1975. "The Illusion of Control." *Journal of Personality and Social Psychology* 32: 311–28.

Lappin, J. S., Shelton, A., and Reiser, J. 2006. "Environmental Context Influences Visually Perceived Distance." *Perception & Psychophysics* 68: 571–81.

Latané, B. and Darley, J. 1970. *The Unresponsive Bystander: Why Doesn't He Help?* New York: Appleton-Century-Crofts.

Latané, B. and Nida, S. 1981. "Ten Years of Research on Group Size and Helping." *Psychological Bulletin* 89: 308–24.

Laughlin, P. R. 1965. "Selection Strategies in Concept Attainment as a Function of Number of Persons and Stimulus Display." *Journal of Experimental Psychology* 70: 323–27.

Lazarus, R. S. 1983. "The Costs and Benefits of Denial." In S. Breznitz (ed.), *Denial of Stress*. New York: International Universities Press, pp. 1–30.

Leahy, R. L. 1999. "Decision-making and Mania." *Journal of Cognitive Psychotherapy* 13: 83–105.

Lear, J. 2006. *Radical Hope: Ethics in the Face of Cultural Devastation*. Cambridge, MA: Harvard University Press.

Lear, J. 2009. "Response to Hubert Dreyfus and Nancy Sherman." *Philosophical Studies* 144: 81–93.

Leiter, B. 2002. *Nietzsche on Morality*. London: Routledge.

Lemm, K. and Banaji, M. R. 1999. "Unconscious Attitudes and Beliefs about Women and Men." In U. Pasero and F. Braun (eds), *Wahrnehmung und Herstellung von Geschlecht* Opladen: Westdutscher Verlag, pp. 215–33.

Levy, B. 1996. "Improving Memory in Old Age Through Implicit Self-stereotyping." *Journal of Personality and Social Psychology* 71: 1092–107.

Levy, B. and Banaji, M. R. 2002. "Implicit Ageism." In T. Nelson (ed.), *Ageism: Stereotyping and Prejudice Against Older Persons*. Cambridge, MA: MIT Press, pp. 49–75.

Levy, N. 2011. *Hard Luck: How Luck Undermines Free Will and Moral Responsibility*. Oxford: Oxford University Press.

Levy, N. and Bayne, T. 2004. "Doing without Deliberation: Automatism, Automaticity, and Moral Accountability." *International Review of Psychiatry* 16: 209–15.

Lewis, C. I. 1946. *An Analysis of Knowledge and Valuation*. La Salle, Ill: Open Court.

Lewis, D. 1973. *Counterfactuals*. Oxford: Blackwell.

Lewis, D. 1996. "Elusive Knowledge." *Australasian Journal of Philosophy* 74: 549–67.

Lewis, D. 1997. "Finkish Dispositions." *Philosophical Quarterly* 47: 143–58.

Lifton, R. J. 1986. *The Nazi Doctors: Medical Killing and the Psychology of Genocide*. New York: Basic Books.

Lilenquist, K., Zhong, C., and Galinsky, A. D. 2010. "The Smell of Virtue: Clean Scents Promote Reciprocity and Charity." *Psychological Science* 21: 381–3.

Locke, J. 1975 [Originally published 1700]. *An Essay Concerning Human Understanding*. P. H. Nidditch (ed.). Oxford: Oxford University Press.

Loeb, D. 1995. "Full-Information Theories of Individual Good." *Social Theory and Practice* 21: 1–30.

Loeb, D. 1998. "Moral Realism and the Argument from Disagreement." *Philosophical Studies* 90: 281–303.

Loersch, C. and Payne, B. K. 2011. "The Situated Inference Model: An Integrative Account of the Effects of Primes on Perception, Behavior, and Motivation." *Perspectives on Psychological Science* 6: 234–52.

Loewer, B. 1996. "Freedom from Physics: Quantum Mechanics and Free Will." *Philosophical Topics* 24: 91–112.

Longino, H. 1990. *Science as Social Knowledge: Values and Objectivity in Scientific Inquiry*. Princeton, NJ: Princeton University Press.

Lowe, E. J. 2002. *A Survey of Metaphysics*. Oxford: Oxford University Press.

Lowery, B. S., Hardin, C. D., and Sinclair, S. 2001. "Social Influence Effects on Automatic Racial Prejudice." *Journal of Personality and Social Psychology* 81: 842–55.

Lowie, R. H. 1935. *The Crow Indians*. New York: Farrar and Reinhart.

Lu, L. H., Barrett, A. M, Schwartz, R. L., Cibula, J. E., Gilmore, R. L., Uthman, B., and K. M. Heilman. 1997. "Anosognosia and Confabulation during the WADA Test." *Neurology* 49: 1316–22.

Luborsky, L., McLellan, A. T., Woody, G. E., O'Brien, C. P., and Auerbach, A. 1985. "Therapist Success and its Determinants." *Archives of General Psychiatry* 42: 602–11.

Luborsky, L., Singer, B., and Luborsky, L. 1975. "Comparative Studies of Psychotherapies: Is it True that 'Everyone Has Won and All Must Have Prizes'?" *Archives of General Psychiatry* 32: 995–1008.

Lucas, R. E., Clark, A. E., Georgellis, Y., and Diener, E. 2003. "Reexamining Adaptation and the Set Point Model of Happiness: Reactions to Changes in Marital Status." *Journal of Personality and Social Psychology* 84: 527–39.

Luria, A. R. 1987. *The Mind of a Mnemonist: A Little Book about a Vast Memory* (2nd edn). Cambridge, MA: Harvard University Press.

Luskin, R. C., Crow, D. B., Fiskin, J. S., Guild, W., and Thomas, D. 2008. "Report on the Deliberative Poll on 'Vermont's Energy Future'." Austin, TX: Center for Deliberative Opinion Research, University of Texas at Austin.

Lutz, G. 2010. "First Come, First Served: The Effect of Ballot Position on Electoral Success in Open Ballot PR Elections." *Representation* 46: 167–81.

Lycan, W. G. 2009. "Giving Dualism its Due." *Australasian Journal of Philosophy* 87: 551–63.

Lynch, J. J. 1979. *The Broken Heart: The Medical Consequences of Loneliness*. New York: Basic Books.

Machery, E. 2010. "The Bleak Implications of Moral Psychology." *Neuroethics* 3: 223–31.

Machery, E., Kelly, D., and Stich, S. P. 2005. "Moral Realism and Cross-Cultural Normative Diversity." *Behavioral and Brain Sciences* 28: 830.

MacIntyre, A. 1984. *After Virtue* (2nd edn). Notre Dame, IN: Notre Dame University Press.

Mackie, J. L. 1955. "Responsibility and Language." *Australasian Journal of Philosophy* 33: 143–59.

Mackie, J. L. 1977. *Ethics: Inventing Right and Wrong*. New York: Penguin.

Madden, M. E. and Janoff-Bulman, R. 1981. "Blame, Control, and Marital Satisfaction: Wives' Attributions for Conflict in Marriage." *Journal of Marriage and the Family* 43: 663–74.

Maibom, H. 2005. "Moral Unreason: The Case of Psychopathy." *Mind & Language* 20: 237–57.

Maibom, H. L. 2008. "The Mad, the Bad, and the Psychopath." *Neuroethics* 1: 167–84.

Maibom, H. L. 2013. "Values, Sanity, and Responsibility." *Oxford Studies in Agency and Responsibility, Volume I*: 263–83.

Maier, N. R. F. 1931. "Reasoning in Humans II. The Solution of a Problem and its Appearance in Consciousness." *Journal of Comparative Psychology* 12: 181–94.

Maier, N. R. F. 1970. *Problem-Solving and Creativity in Individuals and Groups*. Belmont, CA: Brooks/Cole.

Malle, B. F. 2004. *How the Mind Explains Behavior: Folk Explanations, Meaning, and Social Interaction*. Cambridge, MA: MIT Press.

Mallon, R. 2003. "Social Construction, Social Roles, and Stability." In F. Schmitt (ed.), *Socializing Metaphysics*. New York: Rowman & Littlefield, pp. 327–53.

Mallon, R. forthcoming. *Making the World by Accident: Mind, Culture, and the Construction of Human Kinds*.

Mallon, R. and Stich, S. P. 2000. "The Odd Couple: The Compatibility of Social Construction and Evolutionary Psychology." *Philosophy of Science* 67: 133–54.

Marcinkiewicz, K. 2014. "Electoral Contexts that Assist Voter Coordination: Ballot Position Effects in Poland." *Electoral Studies* 33: 322–34.

Margulies, S. 2003. "The Psychology of Prenuptial Agreements." *Psychiatry & Law* 3: 415–32.

Martin, C. B. 1994. "Dispositions and Conditionals." *The Philosophical Quarterly* 44: 1–8.

Martin, D. J., Garske, J. P., and Davis, M. K. 2000. "Relation of the Therapeutic Alliance with Outcome and Other Variables: A Meta-analytic Review." *Journal of Consulting and Clinical Psychology* 68: 438–50.

Martin, T. C. and Bumpass, L. 1989. "Recent Trends in Marital Disruption." *Demography* 26: 37–52.

Matthews, K. E. and Canon, L. K. 1975. "Environmental Noise Level as a Determinant of Helping Behavior." *Journal of Personality and Social Psychology* 32: 571–7.

Matlin, M. W. 1970. "Response Competition as a Mediating Factor in the Frequency-Affect Relationship." *Journal of Personality and Social Psychology* 16: 536–52.

Mattioli, F., Miozzo, A., and Vignolo, L. A. 1999. "Confabulation and Delusional Misidentification: A Four-Year Follow-up Study." *Cortex* 35: 413–22.

McAdams, D. P. 2008. "Personal Narratives and the Life Story." In O. John, R. Robins, and L. Pervin (eds), *Handbook of Personality: Theory and Research* (3rd edn). New York: Guilford Press. pp. 241–61.

McCauley, R. N. and Henrich, J. 2006. "Susceptibility to the Müller-Lyer Illusion, Theory-neutral Observation, and the Diachronic Penetrability of the Visual Input System." *Philosophical Psychology* 19: 79–101.

McCollum, C. 2002. "Relatedness and Self-Definition: Two Dominant Themes in Middle-Class Americans' Life Stories." *Ethos* 30: 1–2, 113–39.

McDaniel, K. D. and McDaniel, L. D. 1991. "Anton's Syndrome in a Patient With Posttraumatic Optic Neuropathy and Bifrontal Contusions." *Archives of Neurology* 48: 101–05.

McDowell, J. 1994. *Mind and World*. Cambridge, MA: Harvard University Press.

McDowell, J. 1998. "Projection and Truth in Ethics." In J. McDowell, *Mind, Value, and Reality*. Cambridge, MA: Harvard University Press, pp. 151–66.

McDowell, J. 2002. "Responses." In N. S. Smith (ed.), *Reading McDowell on Mind and World*. London: Routledge, pp. 269–305.

McGeer, V. 1996. "Is 'Self-knowledge' an Empirical Problem? Renegotiating the Space of Philosophical Explanation." *The Journal of Philosophy* 93: 483–515.

McGinnies, E. and Ward, C. 1974. "Persuasibility as A Function of Source Credibility and Locus of Control – 5 Cross-Cultural Experiments." *Journal of Personality* 42: 360–71.

McKenna, M. 2004. "Responsibility and Globally Manipulated Agents." *Philosophical Topics* 32: 169–92.

McKenna, M. 2005. "Where Frankfurt and Strawson Meet." *Midwest Studies in Philosophy* 29: 163–80.

McKennell, A. C. and Thomas, R. K. 1967. *Adults' and Adolescents' Smoking Habits and Attitudes*. London: British Ministry of Health.

McLaren, C., Null, J., and Quinn, J. 2005. "Heat Stress from Enclosed Vehicles: Moderate Ambient Temperatures Cause Significant Temperature Rise in Enclosed Vehicles." *Pediatrics* 116: e109–12.

McNulty, J. K., O'Mara, E. M., and Karney, B. R. 2008. "Benevolent Cognitions as a Strategy of Relationship Maintenance: 'Don't Sweat the Small Stuff' . . . But It Is Not All Small Stuff." *Journal of Personality and Social Psychology* 94: 631–46.

Mealey, L. 1995. "The Sociobiology of Sociopathy: An Integrated Evolutionary Model." *Behavioral and Brain Sciences* 18: 523–99.

Mele, A. R. 1992. *The Springs of Action*. New York: Oxford University Press.

Mele, A. R. 2006. *Free Will and Luck*. Oxford: Oxford University Press.

Mele, A. R. 2009a. "Moral Responsibility and History Revisited." *Ethical Theory and Moral Practice* 12: 463–75.

Mele, A. R. 2009b. *Effective Intentions: The Power of Conscious Will*. Oxford: Oxford University Press.

Mele, A. 2011. "Libet on Free Will: Readiness Potentials, Decisions, and Awareness." In W. Sinnott-Armstrong and L. Nadel (eds), *Conscious Will and Responsibility: A Tribute to Benjamin Libet*. New York: Oxford University Press, pp. 23–33.

Mellor, C. S. 1970. "First-rank Symptoms of Schizophrenia." *British Journal of Psychiatry* 117: 15–23.

Mercer, B., Wapner, M., Gardner, H., and Benson, F. 1977. "A Study of Confabulation." *Archives of Neurology* 34: 429–33.

Mercier, H. and Sperber, D. 2009. "Intuitive and Reflective Inferences." J. St. B. T. Evans and K. Frankish (eds), *In Two Minds: Dual Processes and Beyond*. Oxford: Oxford University Press, pp. 149–70.

Meredith, M. and Salant, Y. 2013. "On the Causes and Consequences of Ballot Order Effects." *Political Behavior* 35: 175–97.

Merritt, M. 2000. "Virtue Ethics and Situationist Personality Psychology." *Ethical Theory and Moral Practice* 3: 365–83.

Merritt, M. 2009. "Aristotelean Virtue and the Interpersonal Aspect of Ethical Character." *Journal of Moral Philosophy* 6: 23–49.

Merritt, M., Doris, J. M., and Harman, G. 2010. "Character." In J. M. Doris and the Moral Psychology Research Group (eds), *The Moral Psychology Handbook*. Oxford: Oxford University Press, pp. 355–401.

Messick, D. M., Bloom, S., Boldizar, J. P., and Samuelson, C. D. 1985. "Why We Are Fairer Than Others." *Journal of Experimental Social Psychology* 21: 480–500.

Metcalfe, J. and Mischel, W. 1999. "A Hot/Cool-System Analysis of Delay of Gratification: Dynamics of Willpower." *Psychological Review* 106: 3–19.

Meyer, G. J., Finn, S. E., Eyde, L., Kay, G. G., Moreland, K. L., Dies, R. R., et al. 2001. "Psychological Testing and Psychological Assessment: A Review of Evidence and Issues." *American Psychologist* 56: 128–65.

Michaud, S. and Aynesworth, H. 1989. *Ted Bundy: Conversations with a Killer*. New York: New American Library.

Milgram, S. 1974. *Obedience to Authority*. New York: Harper and Row.

Mill, J. S. 2002 [Originally published 1863]. *On Liberty*. In *The Basic Writings of John Stuart Mill: On Liberty, The Subjection of Women, and Utilitarianism*, introduction by J. B. Schneewind, notes and commentary by D. E. Miller. New York: Modern Library.

Miller, C. B. 2003. "Social Psychology and Virtue Ethics." *The Journal of Ethics* 7: 365–92.

Miller, C. B. 2013a. *Moral Character: An Empirical Theory.* Oxford: Oxford University Press.

Miller, C. B. 2013b. *Character and Moral Psychology.* Oxford: Oxford University Press.

Miller, D. T., Downs, J. S., and Prentice, D. A. 1998. "Minimal Conditions for the Creation of a Unit Relationship: The Social Bond Between Birthdaymates." *European Journal of Social Psychology* 28: 475–81.

Miller, E. K. and Cohen, J. D. 2001. "An Integrative Theory of Prefrontal Cortex Function." *Annual Review of Neuroscience* 24: 167–202.

Miller, J. D., Widiger, T. A., and Campbell, W. K. 2010. "Narcissistic Personality Disorder and the DSM-V." *Journal of Abnormal Psychology* 119: 640–9.

Milne, S., Orbell, S., and Sheeran, P. 2002. "Combing Motivational and Volitional Interventions to Promote Exercise Participation: Protection Motivation Theory and Implementation Intentions." *British Journal of Health Psychology* 7: 163–84.

Mischel, M., Ebbesen, E. B., and Zeiss, A. R. 1972. "Cognitive and Attentional Mechanisms in Delay of Gratification." *Journal of Personality and Social Psychology* 21: 204–18.

Mischel, W. 1968. *Personality and Assessment.* New York: Wiley.

Mischel, W., Shoda, Y., and Peake, P. K. 1988. "The Nature of Adolescent Competencies Predicted by Preschool Delay of Gratification." *Journal of Personality and Social Psychology* 54: 687–96.

Mlodinow, L. 2013. *Subliminal: How Your Unconscious Mind Rules Your Behavior.* New York: Random House.

Moll, J., de Oliveira-Souza, R., Bramati, I. E., and Grafman, J. 2002a. "Functional Networks in Emotional, Moral, and Nonmoral Social Judgments." *Neuroimage* 16: 696–703.

Moll, J., de Oliveira-Souza, R., Eslinger, P. J., Bramati, I. E., Mourão-Miranda, J., Andreiuolo, P. A., and Pessoa, L. 2002b. "The Neural Correlates of Moral Sensitivity: A Functional Magnetic Resonance Imaging Investigation of Basic and Moral Emotions." *Journal of Neuroscience* 22: 2730–6.

Moll, J., de Oliveira-Souze, R., and Zahn, R. 2008. "The Neural Basis of Moral Cognition: Sentiments, Concepts, and Values." *The Year in Cognitive Neuroscience* 1124: 161–80.

Montero, B. 2010. "Does Bodily Awareness Interfere with Highly Skilled Movement?" *Inquiry* 53: 105–22.

Montmarquet, J. 2003. "Moral Character and Social Science Research." *Philosophy* 78: 355–68.

Moors, A. and De Houwer, J. 2006. "Automaticity: A Theoretical and Conceptual Analysis." *Psychological Bulletin* 132: 297–326.

Moran, R. 2001. *Authority and Estrangement: An Essay on Self-Knowledge.* Princeton, NJ: Princeton University Press.

Morris, M. and Peng, K. 1994. "Culture and Cause: American and Chinese Attributions for Social and Physical Events." *Journal of Personality and Social Psychology* 67: 949–71.

Moscovitch, M. 1995. "Confabulation." In D. L. Schacter (ed.), *Memory Distortion: How Minds, Brains, and Societies Reconstruct the Past.* Cambridge, MA: Harvard University Press, pp. 226–51.

Moscovitch, M. and Melo, B. 1997. "Strategic Retrieval and the Frontal Lobes: Evidence from Confabulation and Amnesia." *Neuropsychologia* 35: 1017–34.

Munafò, M. R., Durrant, C., Lewis, G., and Flint, J. 2009. "Gene × Environment Interactions at the Serotonin Transporter Locus." *Biological Psychiatry* 65: 211–19.

Murphy, D. 2006. *Psychiatry in the Scientific Image*. Cambridge, MA and London: MIT Press.

Murray, S., Holmes, J., and Griffin, D. 1996. "The Self-fulfilling Nature of Positive Illusions in Romantic Relationships: Love Is Not Blind, but Prescient." *Journal of Personality and Social Psychology* 71: 1155–80.

Murray, S., Holmes, J., and Griffin, D. 2003. "Reflections on the Self-fulfilling Effects of Positive Illusions." *Psychological Inquiry* 14: 289–95.

Myers, D. G. 1998. *Psychology* (5th edn). New York: Worth.

Nadelhoffer, T., Nahmias, E., and Nichols, S. (eds). 2010. *Moral Psychology: Historical and Contemporary Readings*. Hoboken, NJ: John Wiley & Sons.

Nagel, T. 1986. *The View From Nowhere*. New York: Oxford University Press.

Nahmias, E. 2007. "Autonomous Agency and Social Psychology." In M. Marraffa, M. De Caro, and F. Ferretti (eds), *Cartographies of Mind: Philosophy and Psychology in Intersection*. New York: Springer, pp. 169–87.

Nahmias, E. 2010. "Scientific Challenges to Free Will." In T. O'Connor and C. Sandis (eds), *A Companion to the Philosophy of Action*. Malden, MA: Wiley-Blackwell Publishing, pp. 345–56.

Nahmias, E. 2011. "Intuitions about Free Will, Determinism, and Bypassing." In R. Kane (ed.), *Oxford Handbook of Free Will* (2nd edn). New York: Oxford University Press, pp. 555–76.

Nahmias, E. A., Morris, S. G., Nadelhoffer, T., and Turner, J. 2007. "Is Incompatibilism Intuitive?" *Philosophy and Phenomenological Research* 73: 28–53.

National Highway Traffic Safety Administration, 2008. February, at: <http://www-nrd.nhtsa.dot.gov/Pubs/810921.pdf>.

National Highway Traffic Safety Administration, 2008. May, at: <http://www-nrd.nhtsa.dot.gov/Pubs/810949.pdf>.

Neff, L. A. and Karney, B. R. 2005. "To Know You Is to Love You: The Implications of Global Adoration and Specific Accuracy for Marital Relationships." *Journal of Personality and Social Psychology* 88: 480–97.

Nelkin, D. 2007. "Do We Have a Coherent Set of Intuitions about Moral Responsibility?" *Midwest Studies in Philosophy* 31: 243–59.

Nelkin, D. 2011. *Making Sense of Freedom and Responsibility*. Oxford: Oxford University Press.

Nettle, D., Harper, Z., Kidson, A., Stone, R., Penton-Voak, I. S., and Bateson, M. 2013. "The Watching Eyes Effect in the Dictator Game: It's Not How Much You Give, It's Being Seen to Give Something." *Evolution and Human Behavior* 34: 35–40.

Neu, J. 2012. *On Loving Our Enemies: Essays in Moral Psychology*. Oxford: Oxford University Press.

Newton, M. 2002. *Savage Boys and Wild Girls: A History of Feral Children*. London: Faber & Faber.

Nichols, S. 2004. *Sentimental Rules: On the Natural Foundations of Moral Judgment.* New York: Oxford University Press.

Nichols, S. 2007. "Sentiment, Intention, and Disagreement: Replies to Blair and D'Arms." In W. Sinnott-Armstrong (ed.), *Moral Psychology, Vol. 2: The Cognitive Science of Morality: Intuition and Diversity.* Cambridge, MA: MIT Press, pp. 291–301.

Nichols, S. 2008. "How Can Psychology Contribute to the Free Will Debate?" In J. Baer, J. Kaufman, and R. Baumeister (eds), *Are We Free? Psychology and Free Will.* New York: Oxford University Press, pp. 10–31.

Nichols, S. 2014. *Bound: Essays on Free Will and Responsibility.* Oxford: Oxford University Press.

Nichols, S. and Knobe, J. 2007. "Moral Responsibility and Determinism: The Cognitive Science of Folk Intuitions." *Noûs* 41: 663–85.

Nichols, S. and Stich, S. P. 2003. *Mindreading: An Integrated Account of Pretence, Self-awareness, and Understanding Other Minds.* Oxford: Oxford University Press.

Nietzsche, F. 1966 [Originally published 1886]. *Beyond Good and Evil.* Trans. Walter Kaufmann. New York: Vintage.

Nietzsche, F. 1974 [Originally published 1882, 1887]. *The Gay Science: With a Prelude in Rhymes and an Appendix of Songs.* Trans. Walter Kaufmann. New York: Vintage.

Nisbett, R. E. 2003. *The Geography of Thought: How Asians and Westerners Think Differently . . . And Why.* New York: The Free Press.

Nisbett, R. E. 2009. *Intelligence and How to Get It: Why Schools and Cultures Count.* New York and London: Norton.

Nisbett, R. E. and Borgida, E. 1975. "Attribution and the Psychology of Prediction." *Journal of Personality and Social Psychology* 32: 932–43.

Nisbett, R. E. and Ross, L. 1980. *Human Inference: Strategies and Shortcomings of Social Judgment.* Englewood Cliffs, NJ: Prentice-Hall.

Nisbett, R. E. and Wilson, T. D. 1977. "Telling More Than We Can Know: Verbal Reports on Mental Processes." *Psychological Review* 84: 231–59.

Noë, A. 2004. *Action in Perception.* Cambridge, MA: MIT Press.

Noonan, H. 1989. *Personal Identity.* London: Routledge.

Norman, J. 2002. "Two Visual Systems and Two Theories of Perception: An Attempt to Reconcile the Constructivist and Ecological Approaches." *Behavioral and Brain Sciences* 25: 73–96.

Northcott, R. 2005. "Pearson's Wrong Turning: Against Statistical Measures of Causal Efficacy." *Philosophy of Science* 72: 900–12.

Northcott, R. 2012. "Partial Explanations in Social Science." In H. Kinkaid and D. Ross (eds), *Oxford Handbook of Philosophy of Social Science.* Oxford: Oxford University Press, pp. 130–53.

Nozick, R. 1974. *Anarchy, State, and Utopia.* New York: Basic Books.

Nozick, R. 1981. *Philosophical Explanations.* Cambridge, MA: Harvard University Press.

Nuttin, J. M. 1985. "Narcissism Beyond Gestalt and Awareness: The Name Letter Effect." *European Journal of Social Psychology* 15: 353–61.

Nuttin, J. M. 1987. "Affective Consequences of Mere Ownership: The Name Letter Effect in Twelve European Languages." *European Journal of Social Psychology* 17: 381–402.

O'Callaghan, C. 2008. "Object Perception: Vision and Audition." *Philosophy Compass* 3: 803–29.

O'Connor, T. 1995. *Agents, Causes, and Events: Essays on Indeterminism and Free Will*. Oxford: Oxford University Press.

O'Connor, T. 2000. *Persons and Causes: The Metaphysics of Free Will*. New York: Oxford University Press.

O'Connor, T. 2008. "Free Will." In E. N. Zalta (ed.), *The Stanford Encyclopedia of Philosophy* (Fall 2008 edition), URL=<http://plato.stanford.edu/archives/fall2008/entries/freewill/>.

Olin, L. and Doris, J. M. 2014. "Vicious Minds: Virtue Epistemology, Cognition, and Skepticism." *Philosophical Studies* 168: 165–92.

Orbell, S., Hodgkins, S., and Sheeran, P. 1997. "Implementation Intentions and the Theory of Planned Behavior." *Personality and Social Psychology Bulletin* 23: 945–54.

Orlinsky, D. E., Rønnestad, M. H., and Willutzki, U. 2004. "Fifty Years of Process-Outcome Research: Continuity and Change." In M. J. Lambert (ed.), *Bergin and Garfield's Handbook of Psychotherapy and Behavior Change* (5th edn). New York: Wiley, pp. 307–90.

Oshana, M. 2006. *Personal Autonomy in Society*. Burlington, VT: Ashgate Publishing Ltd.

Oskamp, S. and Schultz, P. 1998. *Applied Social Psychology*. Englewood Cliffs, NJ: Prentice Hall.

Oyserman, D. and Lee, S. W. S. 2008. "Does Culture Influence What and How We Think? Effects of Priming Individualism and Collectivism." *Psychological Bulletin* 134: 311–42.

Pacherie, E. and Haggard, P. 2010. "What Are Intentions?" In W. Sinnott-Armstrong and L. Nadel (eds), *Conscious Will and Responsibility: A Tribute to Benjamin Libet*. Oxford: Oxford University Press, pp. 70–84.

Parfit, D. 1984. *Reasons and Persons*. Oxford: Oxford University Press.

Parfit, D. 1995. "The Unimportance of Identity." In H. Harris (ed.), *Identity: Essays Based on the Herbert Spencer Lectures Given in the University of Oxford*. Oxford: Oxford University Press, pp. 13–45.

Pashler, H. and Harris, C. R. 2012 "Is the Replicability Crisis Overblown? Three Arguments Examined." *Perspectives on Psychological Science* 7: 531–36.

Pashler, H., Harris, C., and Coburn, N. 2011. "Elderly-Related Words Prime Slow Walking." Accessed February 23, 2013 at: <http://www.PsychFileDrawer.org/replication.php?attempt=MTU%3D>.

Pashler, H., Rohrer, D., and Harris, C. R. 2013. "Can the Goal of Honesty be Primed?" *Journal of Experimental Social Psychology* 49: 959–64.

Paulus, P. B., Larey, T. S., and Ortega, A. H. 1995. "Performance and Perceptions of Brainstormers in an Organizational Setting." *Basic and Applied Social Psychology* 17: 249–65.

Paxton, M., Figdor, C., and Tiberius, V. 2012. "Quantifying the Gender Gap: An Empirical Study of the Underrepresentation of Women in Philosophy." *Hypatia* 27: 949–57.

Payne, B. K. 2001. "Prejudice and Perception: The Role of Automatic and Controlled Processes in Misperceiving a Weapon." *Journal of Personality and Social Psychology* 81: 181–92.

Peacock, D. 2013. *In the Shadow of the Sabertooth: A Renegade Naturalist Considers Global Warming, the First Americans, and the Terrible Beasts of the Pleistocene.* Oakland, CA: AK Press.

Pelham, B. W. and Carvallo, M. 2011. "The Surprising Potency of Implicit Egotism: A Reply to Simonsohn." *Journal of Personality and Social Psychology* 101: 25–30.

Pelham, B. W. and Carvallo, M. under review. "Why Tex and Tess Carpenter Build Houses in Texas: Moderators of Implicit Egotism in Three Major Life Decisions."

Pelham, B. W., Mirenberg, M. C., and Jones, J. K. 2002. "Why Susie Sells Seashells by the Seashore: Implicit Egotism and Major Life Decisions." *Journal of Personality and Social Psychology* 82: 469–87.

Pereboom, D. 2001. *Living Without Free Will.* Cambridge: Cambridge University Press.

Pereboom, D. 2002. "Living Without Free Will: The Case for Hard Incompatibilism." In R. Kane, (ed.), *The Oxford Handbook of Free Will.* New York: Oxford University Press, pp. 441–60.

Pereboom, D. 2011. "Free Will Skepticism and Meaning in Life." In R. Kane, (ed.), *The Oxford Handbook of Free Will* (2nd edn). New York: Oxford University Press, pp. 408–24.

Phelps, E., O'Connor, K., Cunningham, W., Funyama, S., Gatenby, C., Core, J., and Banaji, M. R. 2000. "Performance on Indirect Measures of Race Evaluation Predicts Amygdala Activation." *Journal of Cognitive Neuroscience* 12: 729–38.

Pink, T. 2004. *Free Will: A Very Short Introduction.* New York: Oxford University Press.

Pizarro, D. A. and Bloom, P. 2003. "The Intelligence of the Moral Intuitions: A Reply to Haidt (2001)." *Psychological Review* 110: 193–96.

Plato. 1997. *Complete Works.* Edited by J. Cooper. Cambridge: Hackett.

Pollard, B. 2006. "Explaining Actions with Habits." *American Philosophical Quarterly* 43: 57–68.

Pollard, B. 2010. "Habitual Actions." In T. O'Connor and C. Sandis (eds), *A Companion to the Philosophy of Action.* New York: Wiley Blackwell, pp. 74–81.

Pornpitakpan, C. 2004. "The Persuasiveness of Source Credibility: A Critical Review of Five Decades' Evidence." *Journal of Applied Social Psychology* 34: 243–81.

Pratkanis, A. R. and Greenwald, A. G. 1988. "Recent Perspectives on Unconscious Marketing: Still No Marketing Applications." *Psychology & Marketing* 5: 337–53.

Preston, C. E. and Harris, S. 1965. "Psychology of Drivers in Traffic Accidents." *Journal of Applied Psychology* 49: 284–88.

Price, S. J. and McKenry, P.C. 1988. *Divorce.* Beverly Hills, CA: Sage.

Prinz, J. J. 2004. *Gut Reactions: A Perceptual Theory of Emotion.* New York: Oxford University Press.

Prinz, J. J. 2007. *The Emotional Construction of Morals.* Oxford: Oxford University Press.

Prinz, J. J. 2009. "The Normativity Challenge: Cultural Psychology Provides the Real Threat to Virtue Ethics." *Journal of Ethics* 13: 117–44.

Prinz, J. J. and Nichols, S. 2010. "Moral Emotions." In J. M. Doris and The Moral Psychology Research Group (eds.), *The Moral Psychology Handbook.* Oxford: Oxford University Press, pp. 111–46.

Prinz, J. J. and Nichols, S. forthcoming. "Diachronic Identity and the Moral Self." In J. Kiverstein (ed.), *Handbook of the Social Mind.* London: Routledge.

Pronin, E. 2008. "How We See Ourselves and How We See Others." *Science* 320: 1177–80.

Pronin, E., Lin, D. Y., and Ross, L. 2002. "The Bias Blindspot: Perceptions of Bias in Self and Others." *Personality and Social Psychology Bulletin* 28: 369–81.

Pryor, J. 2000. "The Skeptic and the Dogmatist." *Noûs* 34: 517–49.

Radzik, L. 2009. *Making Amends: Atonement in Morality, Law, and Politics*. Oxford: Oxford University Press.

Railton, P. 1995. "Made in the Shade: Moral Compatibilism and the Aims of Moral Theory." *Canadian Journal of Philosophy Supplementary Volume 21*: 79–106.

Railton, P. 2003. *Facts, Values, and Norms: Essays Toward a Morality of Consequence*. Cambridge: Cambridge University Press.

Railton, P. 2009. "Practical Competence and Fluent Agency." In D. Sobel and S. Wall (eds), *Reasons for Action*. New York: Cambridge University Press, pp. 81–115.

Ramachandran, V. S. 1995. "Anosognosia in Parietal Lobe Syndrome." *Consciousness and Cognition* 4: 22–51.

Ramachandran, V. S. 1996. "What Neurological Syndromes Can Tell Us about Human Nature: Some Lessons from Phantom Limbs, Capgras' Syndrome and Anosognosia." *Cold Spring Harbor Symposia on Quantitative Biology* 65: 115–34.

Rawls, J. 1971. *A Theory of Justice*. Cambridge, MA: Harvard University Press.

Reber, A. S. 1993. *Implicit Learning and Tacit Knowledge*. Oxford: Oxford University Press.

Reingen, P. H. 1982. "Test of a List Procedure for Inducing Compliance with a Request to Donate Money." *Journal of Applied Psychology* 67: 110–18.

Ressler, R. K. and Schactman, T. 1992. *Whoever Fights Monsters*. New York: St. Martin's Press.

Rigdon, M., Ishii, K., Wantabe, M., and Kitayama, S. 2009. "Minimal Social Cues in the Dictator Game." *Journal of Economic Psychology* 30: 358–67.

Risch, N., Herrell, R., Lehner, T., *et al.* 2009. "Interaction Between the Serotonin Transporter Gene (5-HTTLPR), Stressful Life Events, and Risk of Depression: A Meta-analysis." *Journal of the American Medical Association* 301: 2462–71.

Robins, R. 2001. "Pharmaceutical Brand Name Development." In T. Blackett and R. Robins (eds), *Brand Medicine: The Role of Branding in the Pharmaceutical Industry*. New York: Palgrave, pp. 150–62.

Robbins, P. 2006. "The Ins and Outs of Introspection." *Philosophy Compass* 1.

Robinson, D. R. 1996. *Wild Beasts and Idle Humours: The Insanity Defense from Antiquity to the Present*. Cambridge, MA and London: Harvard University Press.

Roediger III, H. L. 1990. "Implicit Memory: Retention without Remembering." *American Psychologist* 45: 1043–56.

Roediger III, H. L. 2003. "Reconsidering Implicit Memory." In J. S. Bowers and C. J. Marsolek (eds), *Rethinking Implicit Memory*. New York: Oxford University Press, pp. 3–18.

Roediger III, H. L. and DeSoto, K. A. 2014. "Confidence and Memory: Assessing Positive and Negative Correlations." *Memory* 22: 76–91.

Rogers, M. and Smith, K. H. 1993. "Public Perceptions of Subliminal Advertising: Why Practitioners Shouldn't Ignore This Issue." *Journal of Advertising Research* 33: 10–18.

Rogers, M., Hennigan, K., Bowman, C., and Miller, N. 1984. "Inter-Group Acceptance in Classrooms and Playground Settings." In N. Miller and M. Brewer (eds), *Groups in Contact: The Psychology of Desegregation*. New York: Academic Press, pp. 213–27.

Rolls, E. T. and Grabenhorst, F. 1998. "The Orbitofrontal Cortex and Beyond: From Affect to Decision-Making." *Neurobiology* 86: 216–44.

Ronningstam, E. 2011. "Narcissistic Personality Disorder in DSM-V-In Support of Retaining a Significant Diagnosis." *Journal of Personality Disorders* 25: 248–59.

Rosati, C. S. 1995. "Persons, Perspectives, and Full Information Accounts of the Good." *Ethics* 105: 296–325.

Rosen G. 2004. "Skepticism about Moral Responsibility." *Philosophical Perspectives* 18 (Ethics): 295–313.

Roskies, A. 2003. "Are Ethical Judgments Intrinsically Motivational? Lessons from 'Acquired Sociopathy'." *Philosphical Psychology* 16: 51–66.

Ross, L. and Nisbett, R. E. 1991. *The Person and the Situation: Perspectives of Social Psychology*. Philadelphia, PA: Temple University Press.

Roth, D. M. and Armstrong, J. G. 1991. "Perceptions of Control over Eating Disorder and Social Behaviors." *International Journal of Eating Disorders* 10: 265–71.

Rotter, J. 1966. "Generalized Expectancies of Internal versus External Control of Reinforcements." *Psychological Monographs* 80: 1–28.

Rozin, P., Millman, L., and Nemeroff, C. 1986. "Operation of the Laws of Sympathetic Magic in Disgust and Other Domains." *Journal of Personality and Social Psychology* 50: 703–12.

Rupert, R. 2004. "Challenges to the Hypothesis of Extended Cognition." *Journal of Philosophy* 101: 389–428.

Russell, D. C. 2009. *Practical Intelligence and the Virtues*. Oxford: Oxford University Press.

Saad, L. "Tobacco and Smoking" *Gallop Poll*. August 15, 2002. <http://www.gallup.com/poll/9910/Tobacco-Smoking.aspx>.

Sackitt, P. R., Hardison, C. M., and Cullen, M. J. 2004. "On Interpreting Stereotype Threat as Accounting for African American–White Differences on Cognitive Tests." *American Psychologist* 59: 7–13.

Samuels, R. 2009. "The Magical Number Two, Plus or Minus: Dual Process Theory As a Theory of Cognitive Kinds." In J. Evans and K. Frankish (eds), *In Two Minds: Dual Processes and Beyond*. Oxford: Oxford University Press, pp. 129–46.

Samuels, R., Stich, S., and Bishop, M. 2002. "Ending the Rationality Wars: How to Make Disputes About Human Rationality Disappear." In R. Elio (ed.), *Common Sense, Reasoning, and Rationality*. Oxford: Oxford University Press, pp. 236–68.

Samuels, S. and Casebeer, W. D. 2005. "A Social Psychological View of Morality: Why Knowledge of Situational Influences on Behaviour Can Improve Character Development Practices." *Journal of Moral Education* 34: 73–87.

Sandifer, P. H. 1946. "Anosognosia and Disorders of Body Scheme." *Brain* 69: 122–37.

Sarkissian, H. 2010. "Minor Tweaks, Major Payoffs: The Problems and Promise of Situationism in Moral Philosophy." *Philosophers' Imprint* 10.

Sarkissian, H., Chatterjee, A., De Brigard, F., Knobe, J., Nichols, S., and Sirker, S. 2010. "Is Belief in Free Will a Cultural Universal?" *Mind & Language* 25: 346–58.

Sastry, J. and Ross, C. E. 1998. "Asian Ethnicity and the Sense of Personal Control." *Social Psychology Quarterly* 61: 101–20.

Sattig, T. 2012. "The Paradox of Fission and the Ontology of Ordinary Objects." *Philosophy and Phenomenological Research* 85: 594–623.

Sattig, T. 2015. *The Double Lives of Objects: An Essay in the Metaphysics of the Ordinary World*. Oxford: Oxford University Press.

Sawyer, R. K. 2007. *Group Genius: The Creative Power of Collaboration*. New York: Basic Books.

Sayers, S., Kohn, C., and Heavey, C. 1988. "Prevention of Marital Dysfunction: Behavioral Approaches and Beyond." *Clinical Psychology Review* 18: 713–44.

Scarola, T. 1997. "Creating Problems Rather than Solving Them: Why Criminal Parental Responsibility Laws Do Not Fit within Our Understanding of Justice." *Fordham Law Review* 66: 1029–74.

Schacter, D. L. 1987. "Implicit Memory: History and Current Status." *Journal of Experimental Psychology: Learning, Memory, and Cognition* 13: 501–18.

Schechter, E. forthcoming. *The Other Side: Stories, Bodies, and Split Brains*.

Schechtman, M. 1996. *The Constitution of Selves*. Ithaca, NY: Cornell University Press.

Schechtman, M. 2011. "The Narrative Self." In S. Gallagher (ed.), *The Oxford Handbook of the Self*. Oxford: Oxford University Press, pp. 394–416.

Schilbach, L., Timmermans, B, Reddy, V., Costall, A., Bente, G., Schlicht, T., and Vogeley, K. 2013. "Toward a Second-Person Neuroscience." *Behavioral and Brain Sciences* 36: 393–414.

Schneider, W. and Shiffrin, R. M. 1977. "Controlled and Automatic Human Information Processing I: Detection, Search, and Attention." *Psychological Review* 84: 1–66.

Schnider, A. 2008. *The Confabulating Mind: How the Brain Creates Reality*. Oxford: Oxford University Press.

Schwartz, D. 1995. "The Emergence of Abstract Representations in Dyad Problem Solving." *Journal of the Learning Sciences* 4: 321–54.

Schwartz, M. B., Vartanian, L. R., Nosek, B. A., and Brownell, K. D. 2006. "The Influence of One's Own Body Weight on Implicit and Explicit Anti-fat Bias." *Obesity* 14: 440–47.

Schwarz, N. 1996. *Cognition and Communication: Judgmental Biases, Research Methods, and the Logic of Conversation*. Mahwah, NJ: Lawrence Erlbaum Associates.

Sebanz, N. and Prinz, W. (eds). 2006. *Disorders of Volition*. Cambridge, MA: MIT Press.

Seligman, M. E. P. 1993. *What You Can Change and What You Can't: The Complete Guide to Successful Self-Improvement*. New York: Knopf.

Sellars, W. 1997. *Empiricism and the Philosophy of Mind*, R. B. Brandom (ed.). Cambridge, MA: Harvard University Press.

Sestoft, D., Andersen, H., Lillebaek, T., and Gabrielson, G. 1998. "Impact of Solitary Confinement on Hospitalization Among Danish Prisoners in Custody." *International Journal of Law and Psychiatry* 21: 99–108.

Shaffer, J. 2001. "Knowledge, Relevant Alternatives, and Missed Cues." *Analysis* 61: 202–8.

Shallice, T. 1988. *From Neuropsychology to Mental Structure*. Cambridge: Cambridge University Press.

Shapiro, B. E., Alexander, M. P., Gardner, H., and Mercer, B. 1981. "Mechanisms of Confabulation." *Neurology* 31: 1070–6.

Shariff, A. F., Schooler, J. W., and Vohs, K. D. 2008. "The Hazards of Claiming to Have Solved the Hard Problem of Free Will." In J. Baer, J. Kaufman, and R.F. Baumeister (eds), *Are We Free? Psychology and Free Will.* New York: Oxford University Press, pp. 181–204.

Sheeran, P. and Orbell, S. 1999. "Implementation Intentions and Repeated Behaviors: Augmenting the Predictive Validity of the Theory of Planned Behavior." *European Journal of Social Psychology* 29: 349–70.

Sher, G. 2009. *Who Knew? Responsibility without Awareness.* New York: Oxford University Press.

Sherif, M., Harvey, O., White, B., Hood, W., and Sherif, C. 1961. *Intergroup Conflict and Cooperation: The Robbers Cave Experiment.* Norman, OK: University of Oklahoma Institute of Intergroup Relations.

Sherman, A. C., Higgs, G. E., and Williams, R. L. 1997. "Gender Differences in the Locus of Control Construct." *Psychology and Health* 12: 239–48.

Shoda, Y., Mischel, W., and Peake, P. K. 1990. "Predicting Adolescent Cognitive and Self-Regulatory Competencies from Preschool Delay of Gratification: Identifying Diagnostic Conditions." *Developmental Psychology* 26: 978–86.

Shoemaker, D. 2011. "Attributability, Answerability, and Accountability: Toward a Wider Theory of Moral Responsibility." *Ethics* 121: 602–32.

Shoemaker, S. 1985. "Critical Notice of Reasons and Persons." *Mind* 94: 443–53.

Shoemaker, S. 1996. "On Knowing One's Own Mind." In S. Shoemaker, *The First Person Perspective and Other Essays.* Cambridge: Cambridge University Press, pp. 25–49.

Shoemaker, S. 2003. *Identity, Cause, and Mind: Philosophical Essays.* New York: Oxford University Press.

Shoemaker, S. 2011. "On What We Are." In S. Gallagher (ed.), *The Oxford Handbook of the Self.* Oxford: Oxford University Press, pp. 352–71.

Shults, R. A., Elder, R. W., Sleet, D. A., Thompson, R. S., and Nichols, J. L. 2004. "Primary Enforcement Seat Belt Laws are Effective Even in the Face of Rising Belt Use Rates." *Accident Analysis & Prevention* 36: 491–3.

Siegel, A. 2010. "The Captain of Crunch: Is Kobe Bryant Really the Best Clutch Player in the NBA?" *Slate*, June 8, 2010. <http://www.slate.com/id/2255932/pagenum/all/>.

Simon, J. 1998. "An Analysis of the Distribution of Combinations Chosen by UK National Lottery Players." *Journal of Risk and Uncertainty* 17: 243–77.

Simons, D. J. and Chabris, C. F. 1999. "Gorillas in Our Midst: Sustained Inattentional Blindness for Dynamic Events." *Perception* 28: 1059–74.

Simonsohn, U. 2011a. "Spurious? Name Similarity Effects (Implicit Egotism) in Marriage, Job, and Moving Decisions." *Journal of Personality and Social Psychology* 101: 1–24.

Simonsohn, U. 2011b. "In Defense of Diligence: A Rejoinder to Pelham and Carvallo." *Journal of Personality and Social Psychology* 101: 31–3.

Simonsohn, U. 2012. "It Does Not Follow: Evaluating the One-Off Publication Bias Critiques by Francis (2012a, 2012b, 2012c, 2012d, 2012e, in press)." *Perspectives on Psychological Science* 7: 597–9.

Simonton, D. 1997. "Creative Productivity: A Predictive and Explanatory Model of Career Trajectories and Landmarks." *Psychological Review* 104: 66–89.

Simonton, D. K. 2004. *Creativity in Science: Chance, Logic, Genius, and Zeitgeist.* Cambridge: Cambridge University Press.

Simpson, H. B., and Fallon, B. A. 2000. "Obsessive-Compulsive Disorder: An Overview." *Journal of Psychiatric Practice* 6: 3–17.

Singer, P. 2011. *Practical Ethics* (3rd edn). Cambridge: Cambridge University Press.

Sinha, R. and Easton, C. 1999. "Substance Abuse and Criminality." *Journal of the American Academy of Psychiatry and Law* 27: 513–26.

Sinnott-Armstrong, W. P. 2006. "Moral Intuitionism Meets Empirical Psychology." In T. Horgan and M. Timmons (eds), *Metaethics After Moore*. Oxford: Oxford University Press, pp. 339–66.

Sinnott-Armstrong, W. P. 2007a. *Moral Psychology, Vol. 1: The Evolution of Morality: Adaptation and Innateness*. Cambridge, MA: MIT Press.

Sinnott-Armstrong, W. P. 2007b. *Moral Psychology, Vol. 2: The Cognitive Science of Morality: Intuition and Diversity*. Cambridge, MA: MIT Press.

Sinnott-Armstrong, W. P. 2007c. *Moral Psychology, Vol. 3: The Neuroscience of Morality: Emotion, Brain Disorders, and Development*. Cambridge, MA: MIT Press.

Sinnott-Armstrong, W. P. 2007d. "Framing Moral Intuitions." In W. P. Sinnott-Armstrong (ed.), *Moral Psychology, Vol. 2: The Cognitive Science of Morality: Intuition and Diversity*, pp. 47–76. Cambridge, MA: MIT Press.

Slate, R. N., Buffington-Vollum, J. K., and Johnson, W. W. 2013. *The Criminalization of Mental Illness: Crisis and Opportunity for the Justice System*. Durham, NC: Carolina Academic Press.

Slater, L. 2005. *Opening Skinner's Box: Great Psychological Experiments of the Twentieth Century*. New York: W. W. Norton & Co.

Smart, J. J. C. 1961. "Free Will, Praise, and Blame." *Mind* 70: 291–306.

Smilansky, S. 2003. *Free Will and Illusion*. Oxford: Clarendon Press.

Smith, A. M. 2005. "Responsibility for Attitudes: Activity and Passivity in Mental Life." *Ethics* 115: 236–71.

Smith, G. R., Rost, K., and Kashner, M. A. 1995. "A Trial of the Effect of a Standardized Psychiatric Consultation on Health Outcomes and Costs in Somatizing Patients." *Archives of General Psychiatry* 52: 238–43.

Smith, M. 1994. *The Moral Problem*. Cambridge: Basil Blackwell.

Smith, P. B., Trompenaars, F., and Dugan, S. 1995. "The Rotter Locus of Control Scale in 43 Countries: A Test of Cultural Relativity." *International Journal of Psychology* 30: 377–400.

Snow, N. 2010. *Virtue as Social Intelligence: An Empirically Grounded Theory*. New York: Routledge.

Snyder, D., Castellani, A., and Whisman, M. 2006. "Current Status and Future Directions in Couple Therapy." *Annual Review of Psychology* 57: 317–44.

Sobel, D. 1994. "Full Information Accounts of Well-Being." *Ethics* 104: 784–810.

Solomon, B. C., and Vazire, S. 2014. "You Are So Beautiful . . . to Me: Seeing Beyond Biases and Achieving Accuracy in Romantic Relationships." *Journal of Personality and Social Psychology* 107: 516–28.

Solomon, R. 2003. "Victims of Circumstances? A Defense of Virtue Ethics in Business." *Business Ethics Quarterly* 13: 43–62.

Solomon, R. 2005. "What's Character Got to Do with It?" *Philosophy and Phenomenological Research* 73: 648–55.

Sommers, T. 2012. *Relative Justice: Cultural Diversity, Free Will, and Moral Responsibility.* Princeton, NJ and Oxford: Princeton University Press.

Sommers, T. 2015. "Free Will and Experimental Philosophy: An Intervention." In J. Clausens and N. Levy, (eds), *Springer Handbook of Neuroethics.* Berlin: Springer, pp. 273–86.

Song, H. and Schwarz, N. 2008. "Fluency and the Detection of Misleading Questions: Low Processing Fluency Attenuates the Moses Illusion." *Social Cognition* 26: 791–9.

Sorabji, R. 2006. *Self: Ancient and Modern Insights about Individuality, Life, and Death.* Chicago, IL: The University of Chicago Press.

Sosa, E. 1990. "Surviving Matters," *Noûs* 24: 305–30.

Sosa, E. 1991. "Knowledge and Intellectual Virtue." In E. Sosa, *Knowledge in Perspective: Essays in Epistemology.* Cambridge: Cambridge University Press, pp. 225–44.

Sosa, E. 2004. "Relevant Alternatives, Contextualism Included." *Philosophical Studies* 119: 35–65.

Spaulding, K. 1989. "'Hit Them Where It Hurts': RICO Criminal Forfeitures and White Collar Crime." *Journal of Criminal Law and Criminology* 80: 197–292.

Spearman, C. 1904. "'General Intelligence,' Objectively Determined and Measured." *American Journal of Psychology* 15: 201–93.

Spearman, C. 1927. *The Abilities of Man.* New York: Macmillan.

Spector, P. E., Cooper, C. L., Sanchez, J. I., O'Driscoll, M., Sparks, K., Bernin, P., Büssing, A., et al. 2001. "Do National Levels of Individualism and Internal Locus of Control Relate to Well-Being: An Ecological Level International Study." *Journal of Organizational Behavior* 22: 815–32.

Spector, P. E., Cooper, C. L., Sanchez, J., O'Driscoll, M., Sparks, K., Bernin, P., Büssing, A., et al. 2002. "Locus of Control and Well-Being at Work: How Generalizable Are Western Findings?" *Academy of Management Journal* 45: 453–66.

Sreenivasan, G. 2002. "Errors about Errors: Virtue Theory and Trait Attribution." *Mind* 111: 47–68.

Sripada, C. in preparation a. "Frankfurt's Willing and Unwilling Addicts."

Sripada, C. in preparation b. "Self-Expression: A Deep Self Theory of Moral Responsibility."

Sripada, C. and Stich, S. P. 2007. "A Framework for the Psychology of Norms," In P. Carruthers, S. Laurence, and S. Stich (eds), *The Innate Mind: Culture and Cognition.* Oxford: Oxford University Press, pp. 280–301.

Staglin, D. 1997. "Oprah: A Heavenly Body?" *U.S. News and World Report.* Posted March 23, 1997.

Stanley, J. 2005. *Knowledge and Practical Interests.* Oxford: Oxford University Press.

Stanley, J. 2008. "Knowledge and Certainty." *Philosophical Issues* 18: 35–57.

Stanovich, K. E. 2004. *The Robot's Rebellion: Finding Meaning in the Age of Darwin.* Chicago, IL: University of Chicago Press.

Stanovich, K. E. 2011. *Rationality and the Reflective Mind.* Oxford: Oxford University Press.

Starn, O. 2004. *Ishi's Brain: In Search of America's Last "Wild" Indian*. New York: W. W. Norton & Co.

Steele, C. M. and Aronson, J. 1995. "Stereotype Threat and the Intellectual Test Performance of African Americans." *Journal of Personality and Social Psychology* 69: 797–811.

Stenquist, P. 2010. "How to Remind a Parent of the Baby in the Car," *The New York Times*, May 28, 2010, at: <http://www.nytimes.com/2010/05/30/automobiles/30HEAT. html?pagewanted=all&_r=0All>.

Steptoe, A., Wardie, J., and Marmot, M. 2005. "Positive Affect and Health-related Neuroendocrine, Cardiovascular, and Inflammatory Processes." *Proceedings of the National Academy of Sciences* 102: 6508–12.

Stich, S. P. 1990. *The Fragmentation of Reason: Preface to a Pragmatic Theory of Cognitive Evaluation*. Cambridge, MA: MIT Press.

Stich, S. P., Doris, J. M., and Roedder, E. 2010. "Altruism." In J. M. Doris and the Moral Psychology Research Group (eds), *The Moral Psychology Handbook*. Oxford: Oxford University Press, pp. 147–205.

Strawson, G. 1986. *Freedom and Belief*. Oxford: Oxford University Press.

Strawson, G. 1994. "The Impossibility of Moral Responsibility." *Philosophical Studies* 75: 5–24.

Strawson, G. 2002. "The Bounds of Freedom." In R. Kane, (ed.), *The Oxford Handbook of Free Will*. New York: Oxford University Press, pp. 441–60.

Strawson, G. 2009. *Selves: An Essay in Revisionary Metaphysics*. Oxford: Oxford University Press.

Strawson, G. 2011. *Locke on Personal Identity: Consciousness and Concernment*. Princeton, NJ: Princeton University Press.

Strawson, P. F. 1962. "Freedom and Resentment." *Proceedings of the British Academy* 48: 1–25.

Stroebe, W., Stroebe, M., Abakoumkin, G., and Schut, H. 1996. "The Role of Loneliness and Social Support in Adjustment to Loss: A Test of Attachment Versus Stress Theory." *Journal of Personality and Social Psychology* 70: 1241–9.

Strohminger, N. and Nichols, S. 2013. "The Essential Moral Self." *Cognition* 131: 159–71.

Sturgeon, N. L. 1988. "Moral Explanations." In G. Sayre-McCord (ed.), *Essays on Moral Realism*. Ithaca, NY and London: Cornell University Press, pp. 229–55.

Stuss, D. T. and D. F. Benson. 1986. *The Frontal Lobes*. New York: Raven Press.

Suhler, C. L. and Churchland, P. S. 2009. "Control: Conscious and Otherwise." *Trends in Cognitive Science* 13: 341–7.

Sullivan, L. 2006. "At Pelican Bay Prison, a Life in Solitary" National Public Radio. <http://www.npr.org/templates/story/story.php?storyId=5584254>.

Sunstein, C. 2005. "Moral Heuristics." *Behavioral and Brain Sciences* 28: 531–42.

Svenson, O. 1981. "Are We All Less Risky and More Skillful than Our Fellow Drivers?" *Acta Psychologica* 47: 143–8.

Swann, W. B., Jr. and Schroeder, D. G. 1995. "The Search for Beauty and Truth: A Framework for Understanding Reactions to Evaluations." *Personality and Social Psychology Bulletin* 21: 1307–18.

Swanton, C. 2003. *Virtue Ethics: A Pluralistic View*. Oxford: Oxford University Press.

Talland, G. A. 1961. "Confabulation in the Wernicke-Korsakoff Syndrome." *Journal of Nervous and Mental Disease* 132: 361–81.

Talland, G. A. 1965. *Deranged Memory: A Psychonomic Study of the Amnesiac Syndrome.* New York and London: Academic Press.

Talland, G. A., Sweet, W. H., and Ballantine, H. T. 1967. "Amnesic Syndrome with Anterior Communicating Artery Aneurysm." *Journal of Nervous and Mental Disease* 145: 179–92.

Tane, K. and Takezawa, M. 2011. "Perception of Human Face Does Not Induce Cooperation in Darkness." *Letters on Evolutionary Behavioral Science* 2: 24–7.

Tarlow, B. 1983. "RICO Revisited." *Georgia Law Review* 17: 291–424.

Taylor, C. 1989. *Sources of the Self: The Making of the Modern Identity.* Cambridge, MA: Harvard University Press.

Taylor, C. 1994. "The Politics of Recognition." In A. Gutmann (ed.), *Multiculturalism: Examining the Politics of Recognition.* Princeton, NJ: Princeton University Press, pp. 25–73.

Taylor, D. W., Berry, P. C., and Block, C. H. 1958. "Does Group Participation when Using Brainstorming Facilitate or Inhibit Creative Thinking?" *Administrative Science Quarterly* 3: 23–47.

Taylor, S. E. and Brown, J. D. 1988. "Positive Illusion and Well-Being: A Social Psychological Perspective on Mental Health." *Psychological Bulletin* 103: 193–210.

Taylor, S. E., and Brown, J. D. 1994. "Illusions and Well-Being Revisited: Separating Fact from Fiction." *Psychological Bulletin* 116: 21–7.

Taylor, S. E., Lerner, J. S., Sherman, D. K., Sage, R. M., and McDowell, N. K. 2003. "Are Self-Enhancing Cognitions Associated with Healthy or Unhealthy Biological Profiles?" *Journal of Personality and Social Psychology* 85: 605–15.

Teachman, J. 1983. "Early Marriage, Premarital Fertility, and Marital Dissolution: Results for Blacks and Whites." *Journal of Family Issues* 4: 105–26.

Thompson, S. C., Sobolew-Shubin, A., Galbraith, M. E., Schwankovsky, L., and Cruzen, D. 1993. "Maintaining Perceptions of Control: Finding Perceived Control in Low-Control Circumstances." *Journal of Personality and Social Psychology* 64: 293–304.

Thorndike, E. L. 1906. *Principles of Teaching.* New York: Seiler.

Thornton, R. 1987. *American Indian Holocaust and Survival: A Population History Since 1492* (Vol. 186). Norman, OK: University of Oklahoma Press.

Tiberius, V. 2002. "Virtue and Practical Deliberation." *Philosophical Studies* 111: 147–72.

Tiberius, V. 2004. "Cultural Differences and Philosophical Accounts of Well-Being." *The Journal of Happiness Studies* 5: 293–314.

Tiberius, V. 2008. *The Reflective Life: Living Wisely with Our Limits.* Oxford: Oxford University Press.

Tiberius, V. 2014. *Moral Psychology: A Contemporary Introduction.* London and New York: Routledge.

Tiberius, V. and Plakias, A. 2010. "Well-Being." In J. M. Doris and the Moral Psychology Research Group (eds), *The Moral Psychology Handbook.* Oxford: Oxford University Press, pp. 402–32.

Tollefsen, D. 2003. "Participant Reactive Attitudes and Collective Responsibility." *Philosophical Explorations* 6: 218–34.

Tollefsen, D. 2006. "The Rationality of Collective Guilt." *Midwest Studies in Philosophy* 30: 222–39.

Toneatto, T., Blitz-Miller, T., Calderwood, K., Dragonetti, R., and Tsanos, A. 1997. "Cognitive Distortions in Heavy Gambling." *Journal of Gambling Studies* 13: 253–66.

Trimarco, J. 2009. *Dr. Phil*, February 17, 2009 at: <http://www.drphil.com/slideshows/slideshow/4987/?id=4987&slide=1&showID=&preview=&versionID=>.

Tulving, E. 2007. "Are There 256 Different Kinds of Memory?" In J. S. Nairne (ed.), *The Foundations of Remembering: Essays in Honor of Henry L. Roediger*. New York: Psychology Press, pp. 39–52.

Turiel, E. 1983. *The Development of Social Knowledge: Morality and Convention*. Cambridge: Cambridge University Press.

Turnbull, C. M. 1972. *The Mountain People*. New York: Simon & Schuster.

Turnbull, O. H., Berry, H., and Evans C. E. 2004a. "A Positive Emotional Bias in Confabulatory False Beliefs about Place." *Brain and Cognition* 55: 490–4.

Turnbull, O. H., Jenkins, S., and Rowley, M. L. 2004b. "The Pleasantness of False Beliefs: An Emotion-Based Account of Confabulation." *Neuropsychoanalysis* 6: 5–16.

Tversky, A. and Kahneman, D. 1981. "The Framing of Decisions and the Psychology of Choice." *Science* 211: 453–8.

Twenge, J. M., Catanese, K. R., and Baumeister, R. F. 2003. "Social Exclusion and the Deconstructed State: Time Perception, Meaninglessness, Lethargy, Lack of Emotion, and Self-awareness." *Journal of Personality and Social Psychology* 85: 409–23.

Tzeng, M. 1992. "The Effects of Socioeconomic Heterogamy and Changes on Marital Dissolution for First Marriages." *Journal of Marriage and the Family* 54: 609–19.

Upton, C. 2009. *Situational Traits of Character: Dispositional Foundations and Implications for Moral Psychology and Friendship*. Lanham, MD: Rowman & Littlefield.

van Inwagen, P. 1983. *An Essay on Free Will*. Oxford: Clarendon Press.

Vanman, E. J., Paul, B. Y., Ito, T. A., and Miller, N. 1997. "The Modern Face of Prejudice and Structural Features that Moderate the Effect of Cooperation on Affect." *Journal of Personality and Social Psychology* 71: 941–59.

Vargas, M. 2004. "Responsibility and the Aims of Theory: Strawson and Revisionism." *Pacific Philosophical Quarterly* 85: 218–41.

Vargas, M. 2006. "On the Importance of History for Responsible Agency." *Philosophical Studies* 127: 351–82.

Vargas, M. 2007a. "Response to Kane, Fischer, and Pereboom." In J. M. Fisher, R. Kane, D. Pereboom, and M. Vargas (eds), *Four Views on Free Will*. Malden, MA: Blackwell, pp. 204–19.

Vargas, M. 2007b. "Revisionism." In J. M. Fisher, R. Kane, D. Pereboom, and M. Vargas, M., *Four Views on Free Will*. Malden, MA: Blackwell, pp. 126–65.

Vargas, M. 2008. "Moral Influence, Moral Responsibility." In N. Trakakis and D. Cohen (eds), *Essays on Free Will and Moral Responsibility*. Cambridge: Cambridge Scholars Press, pp. 90–122.

Vargas, M. 2013a. "Situationism and Moral Responsibility: Free Will in Fragments." In A. Clark, J. Kiversein, and T. Vierkant (eds), *Decomposing the Will*. Oxford: Oxford University Press, pp. 325–49.

Vargas, M. 2013b. *Building Better Beings: A Theory of Moral Responsibility*. Oxford: Oxford University Press.

Vazire, S. 2010. "Who Knows What About a Person? The Self-Other Knowledge Asymmetry (SOKA) Model." *Journal of Personality and Social Psychology* 98: 281–300.

Vazire, S. and Funder, D. C. 2006. "Impulsivity and the Self-Defeating Behavior of Narcissists." *Personality and Social Psychology Review* 10: 154–65.

Vazire, S., Naumann, L. P., Rentfrow, P. J., and Gosling, S. D. 2008. "Portrait of a Narcissist: Manifestations of Narcissism in Physical Appearance." *Journal of Research in Personality* 42: 1439–47.

Vazire, S. and Wilson, T. D. 2012. *Handbook of Self-Knowledge*. New York: Guilford Press.

Velleman, J. D. 1989. *Practical Reflection*. Princeton, NJ: Princeton University Press.

Velleman, J. D. 1992. "What Happens when Someone Acts?" *Mind* 101: 461–81.

Velleman, J. D. 2000. *The Possibility of Practical Reason*. Oxford: Oxford University Press.

Velleman, J. D. 2003. "Narrative Explanation." *The Philosophical Review* 112: 1–25.

Velleman, J. D. 2006. *Self to Self: Selected Essays*. New York: Cambridge University Press.

Veenhoven, R. 1988. "The Utility of Happiness." *Social Indicators Research* 20: 333–54.

Victor, M., Adams, R. D., and Collins, G. H. 1989. *The Wernicke-Korsakoff Syndrome and Related Neurologic Disorders Due to Alcoholism and Malnutrition* (2nd edn). Philadelphia, PA: F.A. Davis Company.

Victor, M. and Yakovlev, P. I. 1955. "S.S. Korsakoff's Psychic Disorder in Conjunction with Peripheral Neuritis: A Translation of Korsakoff's Original Article with Brief Comments on the Author and his Contribution to Clinical Medicine." *Neurology* 5: 244–63.

von Hippel, W. and Trivers, R. 2011. "The Evolution and Psychology of Self-Deception." *Behavioral and Brain Sciences* 34: 1–16.

Vranas, P. B. M. 2005. "The Indeterminacy Paradox: Character Evaluations and Human Psychology." *Noûs* 39: 1–42.

Wallace, R. J. 2003. "Addiction as Defect of the Will: Some Philosophical Reflections." In Gary Watson (ed.), *Free Will* (2nd edn). Oxford: Oxford University Press, pp. 424–52.

Wallace, R. J. 2006. *Normativity and the Will*. New York: Oxford University Press.

Wampold, B. E., Mondin, G. W., Moody, M., Stich, F., Benson, K., and Ahn, H. 1997. "A Meta-Analysis of Outcome Studies Comparing Bona Fide Psychotherapies: Empirically, 'All Must Have Prizes.'" *Psychological Bulletin* 122: 203–15.

Warner, G. 2011. "What's in a Drug Name?" *Marketplace*, Thursday May 12, 2011, at: <http://www.marketplace.org/topics/life/whats-drug-name>.

Warrington, E. K. and Weiskrantz, L. 1970. "Amnesic Syndrome: Consolidation or Retrieval?" *Nature* 228: 629–30.

Wason, P. C. 1966. "Reasoning." In B. Foss (ed.), *New Horizons in Psychology*. London: Penguin, pp. 133–51.

Wason, P. C. and Johnson-Laird, P. 1972. *Psychology of Reasoning: Structure and Content*. Cambridge, MA: Harvard University Press.

Wasserman, R. 2005. "Humean Supervenience and Personal Identity." *The Philosophical Quarterly* 55: 582–93.

Wasserstrom, R. 1974. "The Responsibility of the Individual for War Crimes." In V. Held, S. Morgenbesser, and T. Nagel (eds), *Philosophy, Morality, and International Affairs:*

Essays Edited for the Society for Philosophy and Public Affairs. New York: Oxford University Press, pp. 47–70.

Watson, G. 1975. "Free Agency." *Journal of Philosophy* 72: 205–20.

Watson, G. 1993. "Responsibility and the Limits of Evil: Variations on a Strawsonian Theme." In J. M. Fischer and M. Ravizza (eds), *Perspectives on Moral Responsibility*. Ithaca, NY and London: Cornell University Press, pp. 119–50.

Watson, G. 1996. "Two Faces of Responsibility." *Philosophical Topics* 24: 227–24.

Watson, G. 2004. *Agency and Answerability: Selected Essays*. Oxford: Oxford University Press.

Webber, J. 2006a. "Virtue, Character and Situation." *Journal of Moral Philosophy* 3: 193–213.

Webber, J. 2006b. "Character, Consistency, and Classification." *Mind* 115: 651–8.

Webber, J. 2007a. "Character, Common-sense, and Expertise." *Ethical Theory and Moral Practice* 10: 89–104.

Webber, J. 2007b. "Character, Global and Local." *Utilitas* 19: 430–4.

Webber, R., Rallings, C., Borisyuk, G., and Thrasher, M. 2014. "Ballot Order Positional Effects in British Local Elections, 1973–2011." *Parliamentary Affairs* 67: 119–36.

Wegner, D. M. 2002. *The Illusion of Conscious Will*. Cambridge, MA: MIT Press.

Wegner, D. M. 2008. "Self is Magic." In J. Baer, J. C. Kaufman, and R. F. Baumeister (eds), *Are We Free? Psychology and Free Will*. Oxford: Oxford University Press, pp. 226–47.

Weinstein, E.A. 1971. "Linguistic Aspects of Amnesia and Confabulation." *Journal of Psychiatric Research* 8: 439–44.

Weinstein, E. A. 1996. "Symbolic Aspects of Confabulation Following Brain Injury." *Bulletin of the Menninger Clinic* 60: 331–50.

Weinstein, E. A. and Kahn, R. L. 1955. *Denial of Illness: Symbolic and Physological Aspects*. Springfield, IL: Charles C. Thomas.

Weiss, R. 1976. "The Emotional Impact of Marital Separation." *Journal of Social Issues* 32: 135–45.

Weisz, J. R., Rothbaum, F. M., and Blackburn, T. C. 1984. "Standing Out and Standing In: The Psychology of Control in America and Japan." *American Psychologist* 39: 955–69.

Westlund, A. C. 2003. "Selflessness and Responsibility for Self: Is Deference Compatible with Autonomy?" *The Philosophical Review* 112: 483–523.

Whitlock, F. A. 1981. "Some Observations on the Meaning of Confabulation." *British Journal of Medical Psychology* 54: 213–18.

Wigley, S. 2007. "Automaticity, Consciousness, and Moral Responsibility." *Philosophical Psychology* 20: 209–25.

Wilcox, B. W. and Marquardt, E. 2010. *State of Our Unions 2010: When Marriage Disappears: The New Middle America*. New York: Broadway Publications.

Williams, B. 1973. "A Critique of Utilitarianism." In J. J. C. Smart and B. Williams, *Utilitarianism: For and Against*. Cambridge: Cambridge University Press, pp. 77–155.

Williams, B. 1976. *Problems of the Self: Philosophical Papers 1956-1972*. Cambridge: Cambridge University Press.

Williams, B. 1981. *Moral Luck: Philosophical Papers 1973-1980*. Cambridge: Cambridge University Press.

Williams, B. 1985. *Ethics and the Limits of Philosophy*. Cambridge, MA: Harvard University Press.

Williams, K. D. 2001. *Ostracism: The Power of Silence*. New York: Guilford Press.

Williams, K. D. 2009. "Ostracism: A Temporal Need-threat Model." In M. Zanna (ed.), *Advances in Experimental Social Psychology* 41. New York: Academic Press, pp. 279–314.

Williams, R. J. and Ricciardelli, L. A. 2003. "Negative Perceptions about Self-control and Identification with Gender-role Stereotypes Related to Binge Eating, Problem Drinking, and to Co-morbidity Among Adolescents." *Journal of Adolescent Health* 32: 66–72.

Williamson, T. 2007. *The Philosophy of Philosophy*. London: Blackwell.

Wilson, C. and Oswald, A. J. 2005. "How Does Marriage Affect Physical and Psychological Health? A Survey of the Longitudinal Evidence." *IZA Discussion Paper No. 1619*.

Wilson, D. S. 2005. "Evolutionary Social Constructivism." In J. Gottshcall and D. S. Wilson (eds), The *Literary Animal: Evolution and the Nature of Narrative*. Evanston, IL: Northwestern University Press, pp. 20–37.

Wilson, R. A. 2004. *Boundaries of the Mind: The Individual in the Fragile Sciences*. Cambridge: Cambridge University Press.

Wilson, T. D. 2002. *Strangers to Ourselves: Discovering the Adaptive Unconscious*. New York: Belknap.

Wilson, T. D., Lisle. D., Schooler, J., Hodges, S. D., Klaaren, K. J., and LaFleur, S. J. 1993. "Introspecting about Reasons Can Reduce Post-choice Satisfaction." *Personality and Social Psychology Bulletin* 19: 331–9.

Winkielman, P. and Berridge, K. C. 2004. "Unconscious Emotion." *Current Directions in Psychological Science* 13: 120–3.

Wolf, S. 1990. *Freedom within Reason*. New York: Oxford University Press.

Wolf, S. 2003. "Sanity and the Metaphysics of Responsibility." In G. Watson (ed.), *Free Will* (2nd edn). Oxford: Oxford University Press, pp. 272–87.

Wood, J. V. 1996. "What Is Social Cognition and How Should We Study It?" *Personality and Social Psychology Bulletin* 22: 520–37.

Woolfolk, R. L. 1998. *The Cure of Souls: Science, Values, and Psychotherapy*. San Francisco, CA: Jossey Bass.

Woolfolk, R. L. and Doris, J. M. 2002. "Rationing Mental Health Care: Parity, Disparity, and Justice." *Bioethics* 16: 469–85.

Woolfolk, R. L., Doris, J. M., and Darley, J. M. 2006. "Identification, Situational Constraint, and Social Cognition: Studies in the Attribution of Moral Responsibility." *Cognition* 100: 283–301.

Woolfolk, R. L., Wasserman, R. H., Hannah, S. T., Doris, J. M., and Darley, J. M. *in preparation*. "Factors Affecting Attribution of Responsibility for Misconduct in a Military Context: An Examination of Constraint, Identification, and Severity."

Wrangham, R. 2009. *Catching Fire: How Cooking Made Us Human*. New York: Basic Books.

Wu, W. 2013. "Mental Action and the Threat of Automaticity." In A. Clark, J. Kiversein, and T. Vierkant (eds), *Decomposing the Will*. Oxford: Oxford University Press, pp. 244–6.

Wyer, R. S. (ed.) 1997. *The Automaticity of Everyday Life (Advances in Social Cognition, Volume X)*. Mahwah, NJ: Lawrence Erlbaum Associates.

Wyer, R. S., and Frey, D. 1983. "The Effects of Feedback about Self and Others on the Recall and Judgments of Feedback-Relevant Information." *Journal of Experimental Social Psychology* 19: 540–59.

Yong, E. 2012. "Replication Studies: Bad Copy." *Nature* 485: 298–300.

Young, A. W. 2000. "Wondrous Strange: The Neuropsychology of Abnormal Beliefs." In M. Coltheart and M. Davies (eds), *Pathologies of Belief*. Oxford: Blackwell, pp. 47–73.

Young, L. and Tsoi, L. 2013. "When Mental States Matter, when They Don't, and What that Means for Morality." *Social and Personality Psychology Compass* 7: 585–604.

Zajonc, R. 1968. "Attitudinal Effects of Mere Exposure." *Journal of Personality and Social Psychology Monograph Supplement* 9: 1–28.

Zald, D. H. and S. W. Kim. 2001. "The Orbitofrontal Cortex." In S. P. Salloway, P. F. Malloy and J. D. Duffy (eds), *The Frontal Lobes and Neuropsychiatric Illness*. Washington DC: American Psychiatric Publishing, pp. 33–70.

Zamzow, J. L. and Nichols, S. 2009. "Variations in Ethical Intuitions." *Philosophical Issues* 19: 368–88.

Zangwill, O. L. 1953. "Disorientation for Age." *Journal of Mental Science* 99: 698–701.

Zenger, T. R. 1992. "Why Do Employers Only Reward Extreme Performance? Examining the Relationships Among Performance, Pay, and Turnover." *Administrative Science Quarterly* 37: 198–219.

Zuckerman, E .W. and Jost, J. T. 2001. "What Makes You Think You Are So Popular? Self-Evaluation Maintenance and the Subjective Side of the 'Friendship Paradox'." *Social Psychology Quarterly* 64: 207–23.

Author Index

Subject Index